SCHOPENHAUER

SELECTIONS

SCHOPENHAUER
SELECTIONS

EDITED BY
DeWITT H. PARKER

CHARLES SCRIBNER'S SONS
New York

CONTENTS

ARTHUR SCHOPENHAUER

In the history of European philosophy Schopenhauer occupies a place apart. Born in the golden age of German literature and philosophy, and acknowledging Kant as his intellectual father, he nevertheless remained outside of the straight line of development that had its starting-point in Kant, and although a product of his age, he was not of his age. While his great contemporaries, Schleiermacher, Fichte, Schelling, Hegel, found immediate recognition, Schopenhauer had to wait almost a generation before achieving fame or exerting influence. They were professors with an official standing in the community; Schopenhauer was a private scholar, a mere gentleman philosopher. In this last respect he was more like the philosophers of England and France of the eighteenth century. Again, like them, he wrote a clear and literary as opposed to the highly technical and serious style of the contemporary German philosophers, and was not averse to invective, satire, and talking down to his readers. Viewed in relation to the larger spirit and trend of European thought, which is dominantly rationalistic, optimistic, genteel, and pious, Schopenhauer's position is even more eccentric; for Schopenhauer was an antirationalist, pessimist, atheist; 'tough' as opposed to 'tender' minded, a wild ass of the desert in philosophy. Hence his great value to the student: he ventured to question the validity of fundamental assumptions grown conventional, and called attention to aspects of experience unseen by averted eyes. That his own vision was partly perverse cannot be denied; yet every philosopher since must reckon with it.

Arthur Schopenhauer was born February 22, 1788. His father, Heinrich Floris, was a wealthy and honored merchant, doing business in Danzig, then a free city under the nominal suzerainty of Poland. His mother, Johanna Henrietta, was daughter of the senator Trosiener. The families of both parents were proud and aristocratic, and from them Schopenhauer believed he inherited his own independence of mind and high spirits. More specifically, he claimed that to his father he owed his 'will'; that is, his temperament and character; to his mother, the quality of his intelligence. However this be, Heinrich Floris was a man of intense passions and iron resolution, of sombre cast of mind, with a pathologic streak that showed up in other members of the family. Johanna, on the other hand, was gay and pleasure-loving, gifted and witty, destined to win fame as a novelist and essayist. Heinrich desired that his son should be born in England, a country which he greatly loved, so a journey thither was undertaken to this end; but the health of the mother demanded a return to Danzig, where the child was born. Later, there was another child, Adele.

It was planned that the boy should follow the career of the father, so he was carefully educated in what Heinrich Floris called 'the book of the world.' In order that he might learn the French language, young Arthur was placed at the age of ten in the home of a business correspondent at Havre. Two years later he began attendance at a private school in Hamburg, where, at great financial sacrifice, his family had taken up residence, too proud to live longer in Danzig after it had been robbed of its freedom by Prussia in 1793. A three months' journey through Germany with his travel-loving parents provided a pleasant interruption to the four

years of his schooling here. Meanwhile, enamoured of
his studies, Schopenhauer began to rebel at the thought
of a business career and longed to be a scholar. Shocked
and disappointed, his father offered him a grand tour
through Europe if he would relinquish his new ambitions. The bribe was effective, and the impressionable
boy, eager to see the world, gave in. Two busy and
many-colored years of travel were his, spent in Holland,
France, Switzerland, Austria, and Germany. Then on
his return to Hamburg, true to his promise, he took up
his post in the business house of his father. But he was
not happy in his work, and at every opportunity read
the books which he kept hidden under the counter.

His father's untimely death, in 1805, probably by
suicide, freed him. With the consent of his mother, he
withdrew from business and embraced the career of the
scholar. Undaunted by his late beginning, he made careful preparation. In June, 1807, he attended the gym-
nasium at Gotha, paying especial attention to the study
of Latin. In Weimar, next, where his mother had settled
and become a member of Goethe's admiring circle of
litterateurs, he studied Greek under Franz Passow.
From Passow he derived his lifelong devotion to classical learning. On attaining his majority, master of a
comfortable fortune inherited from his father, he entered the University of Göttingen, applying himself to
the study of philosophy and the natural sciences, and
continuing the while his reading of the Greek and Latin
classics. G. E. Schulze was his professor, but Kant and
Plato, whom he read on the advice of Schulze, were his
real teachers. He also made acquaintance with the work
of Schelling, to whom his own thought owed more than
he would ever admit. In 1811 he went to Berlin, where
he heard Fichte and Schleiermacher. Following Napoleon's disaster in Russia came the German battle for

independence. Unlike Fichte, whose discourses stirred his people to patriotic fervor, Schopenhauer took little interest and no active part in the conflict. He sought refuge in the little town of Rudolstadt and gave himself up to meditation. Here he composed his first work, originally intended as a dissertation for the doctor's degree at the University of Berlin, but actually presented at Jena.

This little book, *On the Fourfold Root of the Principle of Sufficient Reason,* published at the author's expense in 1813, was regarded by Schopenhauer as the introduction to his entire system, and later revised in order to bring it into harmony with his more mature thought. Its thesis is that reason, or cause in the sense of reason, is not a simple, single thing, but multiple. There are, in fact, four different ways, according to Schopenhauer, of asking the question Why, and four types of reason, often confused, which may be given in answer: reason of knowing or logical reason; reason of becoming, or causality; reason of being, arithmetical and geometrical reasoning; and, finally, reason for action or motivation. The doctrine is obviously reminiscent of the well-known four causes of Aristotle: the formal, efficient, material, and final. The greatest novelty appears in the development of the conception of reason of being, although Schopenhauer leaned on Kant. Mathematical reasoning, Schopenhauer argued, is fundamentally different from ordinary logical or syllogistic reasoning in being based on intuition or construction, not on deduction from premises to conclusion; and accordingly Schopenhauer advocated the revision of Euclid, who, he believed, mixes the genuinely geometrical with the spurious logical proof. Schopenhauer even offered specimens of the right kind of proof. While the .idea was interesting, Schopenhauer was unaware of the complexity of the problem he was raising, and his work on the logical foundations of mathematics has little value to-day. The book found few readers, yet won the praise of Goethe for its views on geometry.

Soon after the publication of this book, Schopenhauer lived for some time at Weimar with his mother. But it was not long before the incompatibility between the joyous, light-hearted mother and her bitter, misanthropic son made itself felt. An open break finally occurred, and Frau Schopenhauer frankly denied her home to her own son. So the young philosopher left Weimar, never to see his mother again, and with one more reason for distrusting life—and woman. The next stage in his wandering was spent in Dresden. In Weimar he had become acquainted with Goethe, for whom he felt an admiration almost religious in its intensity, and had studied the theory of colors which the poet was passionately advocating against the generally accepted theory of Newton. The result was a new work, *On Vision and Colors*. Schopenhauer followed in the footsteps of Goethe, attacking Newton unsparingly, but introduced certain speculations of his own not wholly in agreement with the poet's. While Newton studied color from the physical standpoint, Goethe and Schopenhauer viewed it from the physiological and psychological aspects. The two points of view were not utterly unreconcilable, but beyond calling attention to some interesting facts not always rightly interpreted, neither Goethe nor Schopenhauer worked out a satisfactory theory. Adding another drop of bitterness to the philosopher's already brimming cup, the poet received the latter's brochure with indifference.

It was in Dresden also that Schopenhauer's chief work, *The World as Will and Idea,* published in 1818, was composed. Certain parts of his philosophy, like the theory of morals and human freedom, were more systematically or brilliantly treated later, but, as Schopenhauer himself recognised, his essential thought is contained in this work. His whole philosophy is there, completed at the early age of thirty years. And, as is the case with most philosophers—there are, of course, the notable exceptions—Schopenhauer succeeded in expressing his thought more clearly and persuasively than any of his commentators have been able to re-express it. His style is so informal and good that he who runs may not only read but understand. It will be of interest, however, to indicate some of the historical affiliations of Schopenhauer's leading conceptions and their affinity with contemporary ideas. Despite his great originality, Schopenhauer was a product of his age, an age destined to be the fertile source of practically all speculative philosophy for a hundred years.

From Kant, Schopenhauer inherited the 'standpoint of idealism,' for which "this our world which is so real, with all its suns and milky ways, is nevertheless nothing but idea." Kant believed he had proved the validity of this standpoint by showing that not only the particular items of our world—as Berkeley had already asserted—are subjective elements of mind but that the space and time forms of objects, and larger conceptions (categories) under which we think objects, are also subjective. This result, which seems at first sight so sceptical, was thought by Kant to provide the indispensable foundation for certainty in the exact sciences. For if things are what the mind makes them, they are as the mind makes them, and must conform to its underlying pattern. We can therefore anticipate experience with reference to its form, and know certain truths about objects in advance of perceiving them. The sciences which are concerned with the form of objects—

mathematics and mechanics—are therefore *a priori*. Such was Kant's 'transcendental' idealism, offered in rebuttal of the scepticism which seemed to be the inevitable result of the train of thought initiated by the great English empiricists, Locke, Berkeley, and, above all, Hume.

The main outlines of Kant's transcendental idealism were accepted by Schopenhauer, but with certain modifications. Kant's elaborate table of categories was discarded, and the whole system of 'transcendental forms' reduced to three—space, time, and causality. This was an immense and able simplification. But, besides, there is a strain of irrationalism, a distrust of the concept, in Schopenhauer's theory of knowledge that goes beyond anything in Kant. Kant, to be sure, had made the famous statement "concepts without intuition are empty," but he never condemned, as Schopenhauer did, the whole apparatus of conception and reasoning as derivative and secondary; had he not, indeed, completed the statement quoted by adding "intuitions without concepts are blind"? The roots of Schopenhauer's irrationalism are to be found rather in Herder, the parent of romanticism, many of whose statements regarding the inferiority of the concept read like a page of Bergson. It must not be lost sight of, however, that for Schopenhauer the intuitions which are the source of all knowledge are rich with the work of the mind, being everywhere shot through with the forms of space, time, and causality. But Schopenhauer believed, as we shall see, that in a single case, at least, intuition can penetrate even these forms to a reality hidden beneath.

For to Schopenhauer, as to Kant, the world revealed in our ordinary intuitions, even when these intuitions are refined and systematized by science, is only, after all, a mere phenomenon, a moving-picture show cast on the screen of consciousness. Yet the show is not all there is, Kant taught; for behind it lies the 'thing-in-itself,' the thing as it is for itself in contradistinction to the thing as it appears to the mind in perception. We can never know what the thing-in-itself is like, because we cannot help perceiving it under the purely subjective forms of our own consciousness; but we can know that it exists. Kant's attitude was cautious, agnostic; there are limitations to knowledge which no man, however learned, can transcend. Indeed, the very basis of our certainty in matters of science—namely, the subjectivity of the forms of knowledge—is the basis also of our inescapable ignorance of reality. Nevertheless, while insisting that no one could ever prove it so, Kant believed that the thing-in-itself was somehow brought close to us in our practical, especially our moral, experience. And Fichte, under whom be it remembered Schopenhauer studied in Berlin, proclaimed as the principle of all true philosophy 'the primacy of the practical reason.' In that little classic of philosophy *Facts of Consciousness* he sought to show that only through action can we escape from the 'egocentric predicament' in which, like a fly in a spider's web, we must remain caught if we continue to occupy the standpoint of idealism alone; only through action do we know even ourselves to be real, and only through moral action do other persons become for us more than mere phantoms, real as we ourselves are real.

When, therefore, Schopenhauer made his famous announcement that the 'will' and the thing-in-itself are the same, he was not so far apart from his teachers as he supposed. By 'will' Schopenhauer means striving, impulse, instinct, interest, desire, emotion. In such experiences, he asserted, subject and object are not separate, as in other kinds, for the self that knows is also

the thing that it knows. Here is a veritable miracle in the
realm of knowledge. It is true—as Schopenhauer explains in the important Chapter XVIII of the supplements to Book Two of his chief work—that even the
knowledge that we get of reality through the experience of striving is still obscured through our incapacity
to dispense entirely with the forms of intuition; we are
exempt from space and causality, but not from time.
Not even in striving, therefore, can we get at the naked
reality of ourselves; yet here there are fewer veils between knowledge and reality than anywhere else. There
are two ways, in fact, by which what I call myself can
be known. By the one way, from the outside, I am
known as one object among other objects in the phenomenal world, the world as idea. As such an object,
I am my body. By the other way of knowing, from
the inside, I know myself immediately and as I really
am in my experience of striving. Putting the two ways
of knowing together, I may say that the body is 'the
objectification' of the will; that is, the way the will
appears to an outside observer (who may, of course, be
myself). Hunger, for example, is 'objectified' in teeth
and claws, the sexual instinct in the organs of reproduction. My fellow men and the lower animals are
known in the same two ways. In the first place, they
are known as certain bodies, phenomena of the minds of
whoever may perceive them. But even a transcendental
idealist whose head is in the jaws of a lion believes that
the lion is something more than his idea. His 'animal
faith' assures him that there is a very hungry will there
besides. And not only the bodies of the lower animals,
but the phenomena of inorganic nature as well, should
be interpreted after the analogy of our own wills; what
the physicist calls force is really will. Again Schopenhauer proves his spiritual kinship with the German ro-

manticists: "No one will understand nature," said No-
valis, "who does not in the most manifold relationships
with all bodies through the medium of feeling mix himself with all things, feeling himself as it were into
them."

Schopenhauer, however, parts company with both
Kant and Fichte in his interpretation of the will; for
whereas for them the will is reasonable, for him it is
blind and radically opposed to intelligence. Intelligence
is secondary to the will, and cannot formulate or prescribe its ends. It is the servant of the 'will to live,'
like the claw or teeth of the animal. Its function is practical, not metaphysical. In such views as these Schopenhauer anticipated much of contemporary pragmatism
and psychoanalysis, as well as one aspect of the philosophy of Bergson. The *Élan Vital* of Bergson, operating in ways impenetrable to intelligence, is an obvious
transcription of the 'will to live' of Schopenhauer. Yet
for Schopenhauer, as for Bergson, the will is blind only
in the sense of being independent of intelligence and
incapable of formulation on its terms; for it has its
own cunning in the realization of its obscure desires.
And Schopenhauer uses the very same type of illustration that Bergson employed later to show how accurately instinct, or 'the will,' works.

In all these respects Schopenhauer carried the philosophy of romanticism further than it had been carried
before, and broke sharply with the classical tradition.
But the break was not complete. Parallel with the development of romanticism in Germany there arose a
new enthusiasm for classical antiquity, and a fresh study
of its literature and history. The foundations of modern
classical scholarship were laid in the Germany of the
early nineteenth century. And in the case of the greatest of the thinkers and artists of the period, the inspi-

ration of Greek beauty and Greek reasonableness acted as a balancing and restraining force against the extravagances of the romantic movement. This was true, for example, of Herder, Goethe, Schiller, Schelling, and Hegel. In this enthusiasm and inspiration Schopenhauer shared. He believed that a knowledge of the classics is the basis of all sound education; and in his view of woman and his taste in art he thought he was following the Greek example. Man, he believed, is superior to and more beautiful than woman; classic architecture more beautiful than Gothic. And for his theory of art he leaned on Plato and modified his own irrationalism through a new and fruitful interpretation of the Platonic Idea.

The will—so Schopenhauer teaches—exists at various levels of development such as the inorganic, the vital, the human, and objectifies itself in various determinate forms, or species in the Aristotelian sense. These forms are the Platonic Ideas. They are not abstractions, least of all mere concepts, but what Goethe called Type—*Ur*—Phenomena, eternal patterns which exist only as embodied in individual instances. Being universal, they are the same in every individual that manifests them, and at all times and places. Every concrete thing and every event is an illustration of one or another of these eternal forms. There is, therefore, nothing essentially new under the sun, and all that Nature ever does is to vary endlessly, through what seems to be a wasteful bounty of fresh individuals, old themes laid down 'before the beginning of years.' History, therefore, never brings forth anything new; and he who has read Herodotus has read it all.

This Platonic supplement to Schopenhauer's metaphysics is seemingly opposed to modern historical and evolutionary modes of thought. Schopenhauer died one

year after the publication of *The Origin of Species* in
1859. Yet he did not deny the doctrine of descent, already much debated through the work of Lamarck and
others; he believed only that new forms of existence
are discontinuous with old forms, and, in some way
difficult to understand, predetermined in the nature of
things. Although descended from lower forms, the
higher cannot be reduced to or explained through the
lower. Life, for example, cannot be reduced to mechanism. His doctrine of levels of being and causality was
a remarkable anticipation of the notion of 'emergence'
introduced by Lloyd Morgan, Sellars, and Alexander,
and of the notion of the contingency of the laws of nature advocated by Boutroux. But, believing as he did
that time is an illusion, he could not have accepted the
notion of 'creative' evolution. Nor, making drafts on
the supposedly infinite possibilities of the future, did he
believe piously in 'progress,' or hope for a superman or
for the emergence of a form of life that should conquer
death, 'the last enemy.'

The classical and romantic elements in the metaphysics of Schopenhauer mingled with a new strain
brought from the East. Schopenhauer was the first important European philosopher to be influenced by Hindu
thought. In Dresden, while busy with the reflections
that issued in the *World as Will and Idea,* he had studied the Latin translation of the Persian version of the
Upanishads made by Anquetil Duperron, and found
there views congenial with his own. One was a conviction of the underlying unity of all things, and the
illusory character of individuality, even of one's own
individuality. 'That art thou' is written on the face of
everything we meet. Kant's doctrine of transcendental
idealism seemed to Schopenhauer to confirm this
thought; for, since space and time are the principles

of individuation, if they are subjective creations of the intellect, so is individuality. Space and time are the many-colored glass that stains the white radiance of eternity. Once this glass is broken, once the veil of Maya (illusion) is rent, there is seen to be no difference between a thing that exists here and now and another thing that exists at some remote place in space and time. All reality is a single striving.

Schopenhauer put his doctrine of the unity of being to use in explaining teleology and adaptation in the organic world, and, in so doing, employed arguments that make it difficult to believe that there is a merely chance resemblance between his thought and that of *Creative Evolution*. Teleology, he argued, as Bergson argued later, is not the result of the accumulation of small selected adaptations, neither is it the result of intelligent foresight, as supposed by the rationalist and theist, but the inevitable showing forth of the underlying unity of the 'will to live.' So are explained the similarities in structure and function in widely different species and the seeming prescience of instinct. It is through the underlying unity of the will, which ignores the distinctions between to-day and to-morrow and between one individual and another, that we can understand such facts as the parent animal's action in laying its eggs where the offspring will find the food that they need when they hatch out; or, to put the matter the other way round, it is owing to our own false vision which breaks the single reality into illusory differences of space and time and individuality that there is a problem here at all. To provide for another creature is, metaphysically, the same as to provide for oneself; and to take thought for to-morrow is the same as to take thought for to-day; for self and not-self, to-day and to-morrow, are one.

Another instance of the effect of Hindu thought on

the philosopher was his pessimism. I do not mean that he derived his pessimism from the Upanishads; for it had its primary source in his own temperament and character. Already as a youth he was impressed, as most young people are not, with the suffering and vanity of existence. We usually assume that a man is normally cheerful and optimistic, and when he is not, we scent pathology. And, in Schopenhauer's case, there is little doubt that he inherited from his father a psychopathic disposition; but only a complete psychoanalytic study of his personality, now for obvious reasons impossible, would reveal the causes of his sombre outlook upon life. One source was probably the antipathy between him and his mother; a genial attitude toward the larger environment can hardly exist unless there have been happy relations within the home. Schopenhauer seems never to have felt genuine love toward any one, except perhaps his dog—love which alone reconciles us to sorrow and death. Moreover, Schopenhauer's young manhood was passed during the period of misery, war, and disillusionment of the postrevolutionary and Napoleonic years. He was not the only great pessimist of his age—witness Byron, Leopardi, Pushkin, Chopin. The theoretical basis which Schopenhauer gave to his pessimism makes evil no accidental or incidental fact in the world, but inescapable, essential. It is our central illusion, he tells us, to suppose that we are destined to be happy. Evil is primary, good secondary. Following Hobbes, Schopenhauer defines the good as the objective of desire; but desire itself is painful; hence the underlying motive in desire is to get rid of desire itself. The good is therefore negative, not positive; it is the easing of a burden. Desire starts with an original frustration. If not unhappy, man is—what is perhaps worse—bored, when, having desires, he yet has no objects for them. (To supply such objects, men have invented cards or similar entertainments.) It is easy enough to criticise this theory of value for overlooking the positive element of good that springs from the satisfaction of desire, or, more vividly sometimes, from the imaginative anticipation of satisfaction. On the other hand, Schopenhauer called attention to the fact that every desire, in so far as its appeasement is postponed or incomplete—and of how few of our desires is this not true?—is partly frustrated, and so contains an element of evil. There is a soul of evil in things good. And in many a vivid page, long before the doctrine of the 'struggle for existence' became a commonplace of thought, Schopenhauer described the conflict, not now within the will, but between the will of one individual or species and another. Here again, in neglecting the facts of mutual aid and co-operation, Schopenhauer's vision was myopic, yet what he did observe is there in the world, to be reckoned with by any philosopher who aims to see life whole.

Upon the metaphysical foundation which we have been considering, Schopenhauer erected his æsthetics and his ethics. His observations on literature and art both in his chief work, including the appendices to it, and in his essays have been justly praised. Despite much absurdity in details, his theory of music as the image of emotion and desire as such, independent of all occasions or objects of desire—music expresses, for example, joy, but cannot express what joy may be about, or longing, but does not tell us what we long for—is essentially sound, and won for him the sympathy and discipleship of musicians; and his theory of architecture, while incomplete, anticipated the 'æsthetic mechanics' of Lipps.[1] The general purpose of art he declared to be the revelation of the Platonic Ideas under-

---

[1] See Geoffrey Scott's *The Architecture of Humanism.*

lying the various stages and forms of objectification of will; music alone among the arts reveals the will itself, bare of objectification. Art is a new way of knowing (notice how many there are for Schopenhauer, never quite clearly and satisfactorily distinguished by him). Ordinary knowledge is under the control of the principle of sufficient reason and seeks, in the service of the will, the space, time, cause, relationships of objects. Art, on the other hand, freed from the uses of desire, is pure contemplation, envisaging the timeless universals embodied in its creations. Art has, therefore, a double value: first, as a pure joy in knowledge; and, second, as a release from the pain of desire. In æsthetic contemplation the observer identifies himself with what he beholds, and in losing his individuality escapes from suffering. He becomes a will-less 'world-eye.' Nature seems beautiful to us when it induces this mood of contemplation without effort, and meets us half-way in our endeavor to decipher its eternal designs. An artist or man of genius is one who divines the intentions of Nature more readily than other men do, and lives not as they for the appeasement of desire but for the sake of the intuition of the eternal, which liberates from desire.

While Schopenhauer gave to this conception of art the stamp of his own unique personality, the conception was not entirely new. The theory that the object of art is the universal, not in the sense of the abstract concept, but of the typical individual, in which universality and individuality are fused, was the common property of the great thinkers of his age. To name just two examples: it is to be found in Goethe's little essay entitled *Imitation of Nature, Manner, and Style,* written in 1788; it is found again in Schelling's essay called *The Relation of the Plastic Arts to Nature,* written in 1807. The most original element of Schopenhauer's general theory of art was his reinterpretation of Kant's notion of the 'disinterestedness' of the æsthetic experience to mean will-lessness. Schopenhauer saw more clearly than any one before him the intimate connection between art and pain, and art's liberating function. But Schopenhauer was wrong in thinking that art liberates by ridding us of desire; for it is rather by giving a new, imaginative form to desire that art frees us, not from desire itself, but from its burdensomeness. And it is inconsistent with Schopenhauer's own presuppositions to assert that art rids us of desire; for if through art we become one with the reality of things, and that reality is desire, how can we escape desire? But here we touch upon one of the chief paradoxes of Schopenhauer's philosophy. Finally, if the world permits us the pure good of beauty, how is it nothing but evil? Is existence not thereby justified?

Schopenhauer's ethics bears the mark of his study of oriental philosophy and is, on the whole, consistent with the rest of his system. Owing to the fact that man knows only himself directly, and other people merely in idea, he is by original nature egoistic, selfish, ruthlessly seeking his own advantage against the good of his fellows. Yet reflection must convince that individuality is an illusion, and that it is absurd to oppose one's own will to the will of another, with whom one is, as a matter of fact, identical. Pity, which is the psychological spring of morality, is the phenomenal appearance of the underlying oneness of self and fellow man; to relieve the distress of another is to give assuagement to one's own. Schopenhauer believed that the state, with its system of justice, is not founded on morality, but—and here he borrowed from Hobbes and Rousseau—on enlightened selfishness; the citizens, by implicit contract, agreeing among themselves to refrain from injuring, or encroaching on the property of, each other. But morality enjoins more than merely refraining from injuring another; it bids us help him, so far as we can, and even, in the person of the saint as exemplar, to renounce individuality entirely, with the hope that others will do the same; so ending the sorry scheme of existence altogether. Yet, while praising sainthood, as renunciation of the will to live, Schopenhauer condemned suicide, on the ground that it expressed rather a surrender to the forces of the will than a mastery over them, and was useless because the will cannot be annihilated by the destruction of a single individual, when there are countless others in which it still lives on.

Such, in brief outline, is the philosophy expounded in *The World as Will and Idea*. Schopenhauer was convinced of its truth as few men are convinced of the truth of their speculations. For him it was true all through; he had no doubts of a single portion of it. He confidently expected to be hailed as a prophet. Yet his book created hardly a ripple on the sea of opinion and remained practically ignored for a generation. This indifference Schopenhauer attributed to a conspiracy of silence on the part of the professors of philosophy, called by him philosophers by trade, men who live by rather than for philosophy. This accusation was, of course, absurd, almost insanely absurd; the plain fact was that Schopenhauer's work was born out of season. There were other luminaries in the sky, and an uncongenial intellectual atmosphere, and so long as their light shone his was bound to be in the shadow.

His great work in the hands of the printer, Schopenhauer set off for Italy. And then began a lonely, obscure, homeless life, embittered by lack of recognition, yet tireless in its devotion to learning and philosophy, and never faltering in the belief in its own significance. One is reminded of Cézanne, who also had to wait a generation for recognition, and his proud assertion: "You know there is but one painter in Europe, myself." Once or twice he thought of marrying, but fearing to lose the independence he so highly prized, abandoned the idea and remained a bachelor to the end of his days. Yet, while professing to despise women, he was far from being insensible to their charms, and was often tortured by his passions; there were several love adventures, some sordid, some more poetic, yet he seems never to have had any very deep attachments to men or to women. His dogs, of which there were a succession, were his most devoted companions. He twice sought to enter upon a university career. In 1830 he matriculated at Berlin and announced lectures, at the same hour as Hegel's, then at the height of his popularity, but discontinued them, owing to lack of students, after a single semester. His second attempt at teaching was at Heidelberg, but he failed again. These facts explain some of his bitterness against the professors.

In June, 1833, Schopenhauer took up residence in Frankfurt, where he remained until his death. For a decade more he lived in retirement unknown to his contemporaries, yet confident of ultimate triumph. "Nature does nothing in vain," he asked; "then why does she give me so many deep thoughts which find no sympathy among men?" And he answered: "My generation is not my proper field of activity, but only the ground upon which my physical person stands, which is, however, only an insignificant part of my whole person." While waiting for the recognition that was eventually to be his, he was not idle. He read deeply, and in the original tongues, the literature of France, Spain, Italy, England, and Germany, including the moralists and essayists, Montaigne, La Rochefoucauld, Le Bruyère, Chamfort,

Shenstone, Shaftesbury, Vauvenargues, Lichtenberg. He continued his studies in the classics, and nursed the mystical strain in his nature with the works of Eckhart, the author of *German Theology*, Böhme, and Angelus Silesius. He attended theatres and concerts, and followed closely the development of scientific thought, looking everywhere for confirmations of his own system. In 1836 he brought out a new book, *On the Will in Nature*, an exposition of the confirmations which he believed he found in astronomy, physics, biology, and, be it added, in so-called 'spiritistic' phenomena. In 1839 he contended successfully with a prize essay written in answer to the question propounded by the Royal Norwegian Society of Sciences at Drontheim: Can the Freedom of the Human Will be proved from the evidence of Self-consciousness? The essay is one of the most brilliant discussions of this problem in philosophical literature, ranking with those of Edwards, James, and Bergson. This success brought him the keenest joy. But the following year he suffered a disappointment to balance it. For the essay which he wrote on the *Source and Foundation of Morality*, a problem propounded by the Royal Danish Society at Copenhagen, was not crowned. The failure was largely due to the fact that, not content to restate and amplify the theory of morality contained in Book Four of his chief work, he indulged in scurrilous attacks on his old, supposed enemies, the philosophy professors, particularly Fichte. The two essays were published together in 1841 under the title *The Two Main Problems in Ethics*. In 1844, despite the financial failure of the First Edition, his publishers were persuaded to bring out a revised edition of the *World as Will and Idea*, without cost, yet without profit to the writer. It contained fifty new chapters of supplementary material which Schopenhauer described, I think rightly, as the best he had written, the ripest fruit of his reflections, throwing light on many an obscure point in his system. Finally, in 1851, there appeared two volumes of essays on topics of general interest, embodying the wisdom garnered from his long life. Despite the forbidding Greek title, *Parerga and Paralipomena*, these essays were largely instrumental in bringing him the recognition for which he had so long waited.

But even before this his day had come at last. The fame of his great early rivals, Schleiermacher, Fichte, and Hegel, had waned, and he was to have his turn now. He began to make disciples, of whom the chief was Julius Frauenstädt, his able publicity agent, whom he called his arch-evangelist. At first his fame was among non-academic folk, merchants, musicians, men of letters, soldiers, lawyers; but finally even the professors recognized the importance of his philosophy, for in 1853 J. E. Erdmann gave him an extended notice in his *German Speculation Since Kant*. The last ten years of his life were the happiest. In his apartment on the Schöne Aussicht, unpretentious yet comfortable, where he lived in the company of his dog, surrounded by the likenesses of his favorite philosophers, including a bronze Buddha, and at the Englische Hof where he dined, he received many distinguished, admiring visitors. "Jupiter Tonans" was pointed out, no longer as a mere eccentric, but as a great man. And no item of attention was lost; he drank it all in with a naïve, childish delight. In the best of health almost to the very end, the turbulence of passion gone, the dream of his young manhood attained, his personality vibrated a mellower, quieter tone. After a brief illness, he died peacefully and alone, September 21, 1860.

Admirable as philosopher and writer, Schopenhauer was not lovable as a man. The great defect of his per-

sonality was his incapacity to love; and he who does not
love is rarely himself beloved. He was egotistical, childish, suspicious, morbidly timorous, passionate—no 'milk
and water' nature, as he said of himself. Just in his
dealings with other men, he was not generous or mag-
nanimous. A cosmopolitan by temper and training, he
was lacking in all patriotic and civic feeling. He felt
keenly the misery of humankind, but took no interest
in any efforts to alleviate it. Yet there were things in
him to like: of little things, his love for animals and his
appreciation of their significance for the spirit of man;
of great things, a steadfastness of purpose and a love
of truth such as few men have matched. And because he
possessed these, all his faults may well be forgiven him.
His appearance and personality in later life have been
vividly portrayed as follows by Foucher de Careil: "His
blue, lively eyes, his thin lips, about which played a fine,
sarcastic smile, his broad brow framed by two white
locks of hair, put the stamp of distinction and nobility
upon his physiognomy, which sparkled with wit and
mischief. His clothes, his lace ruffle, and white cravat,
reminded one of an old gentleman of the time of Louis
XV; his manners were those of a man of good society.
Of a retiring disposition often bordering on the suspicious, he consorted with only his most intimate friends
or with the strangers who came to visit Frankfurt. In
conversation his movements were often of extraordinary
liveliness. While he hated mere word-battles, he felt all
the more the charm of a spirited and earnest debate.
His conversation bubbled over with witticisms, citations,
and interesting details, making the hours pass unnoticed.
Many times his intimate friends listened to him until
midnight without feeling fatigue, the brightness of his
eye continuing undimmed. His conversation was distinguished above all for its peculiar clarity. Happy they

who were so fortunate as to hear this last of the conversationalists of a vanished century. In this respect he was the contemporary of Voltaire, Diderot, Helvetius, and Chamfort." [1]

The philosophy of Schopenhauer is notable rather for the richness, variety, and brilliance of its insights than for consistency and totality of vision. He lacked the broad intellectual justice of a Hegel or an Aristotle, and the logical rigor of a Descartes or a Leibniz. Even when one is compelled to accept the essential theses of his philosophy, one has to reject a great deal as sheer nonsense, mere personal fancy or perversity. While such a philosopher has something for every type of thinker, he cannot found a school. Moreover, some of his doctrines are so violently opposed to the fundamental 'vital axioms' of our civilization that he could not exert the widest influence. Yet many exceptional minds have found inspired guidance in his writings, especially those spirits who, for one cause or another, have been impressed with the suffering and evil in existence, or have become sceptical of reason. Among artists, the greatest who felt his influence were Wagner, Grillparzer, and Tolstoy. Among important philosophers—to omit all lesser names—the man who came nearest to being a disciple, while disagreeing in significant matters, was Eduard von Hartmann, whose *Philosophy of the Unconscious* sought a reconciliation between Schopenhauer and his rival, Hegel; Friedrich Nietzsche, starting from a pessimistic basis derived from Schopenhauer, yet rose to the strenuous optimism of the doctrine of the Superman; Hans Vaihinger, in his *Philosophy of the As-If*, leaned on both Schopenhauer and Nietzsche for his theory of the biological function and fictitious character of the

---

[1] Freely translated from the citation in *Schopenhauer*, by Heinrich Hasse, p. 54.

intellect; and, finally, Henri Bergson, if he did not actually borrow his theories of *Élan Vital,* of intuition, of the practical nature of the intellect, of teleology, directly from Schopenhauer, most certainly felt his influence. But more than this, one may rightly claim, as has already been observed, that the entire voluntaristic and antirationalistic movement of last century, and much of pragmàtism, while springing from many sources, had Schopenhauer as one of its originators.

DeWitt H. Parker.

DATED LIST OF SCHOPENHAUER'S WORKS

THE WORLD AS WILL AND IDEA
SELECTIONS

FIRST BOOK
THE WORLD AS IDEA
———
FIRST ASPECT

THE IDEA SUBORDINATED TO THE PRINCIPLE OF SUF-
FICIENT REASON: THE OBJECT OF EXPERIENCE
AND SCIENCE

I

§ 1. "THE world is my idea:"—this is a truth which
holds good for everything that lives and knows, though
man alone can bring it into reflective and abstract consciousness. If he really does this, he has attained to
philosophical wisdom. It then becomes clear and certain
to him that what he knows is not a sun and an earth,
but only an eye that sees a sun, a hand that feels an
earth; that the world which surrounds him is there only
as idea, *i. e.*, only in relation to something else, the consciousness, which is himself. If any truth can be asserted
a priori, it is this: for it is the expression of the most
general form of all possible and thinkable experience:
a form which is more general than time, or space, or
causality, for they all presuppose it; and each of these,
which we have seen to be just so many modes of the
principle of sufficient reason, is valid only for a particular class of ideas; whereas the antithesis of object and
subject is the common form of all these classes, is that
form under which alone any idea of whatever kind it
may be, abstract or intuitive, pure or empirical, is possible and thinkable. No truth therefore is more certain,
more independent of all others, and less in need of proof

3

than this, that all that exists for knowledge, and therefore this whole world, is only object in relation to subject, perception of a perceiver, in a word, idea. This is
obviously true of the past and the future, as well as of
the present, of what is farthest off, as of what is near;
for it is true of time and space themselves, in which
alone these distinctions arise. All that in any way belongs or can belong to the world is inevitably thus conditioned through the subject, and exists only for the
subject. The world is idea.

This truth is by no means new. It was implicitly involved in the sceptical reflections from which Descartes
started. Berkeley, however, was the first who distinctly
enunciated it, and by this he has rendered a permanent
service to philosophy, even though the rest of his teaching should not endure. Kant's primary mistake was the
neglect of this principle. How early again this truth
was recognised by the wise men of India, appearing
indeed as the fundamental tenet of the Vedânta philosophy ascribed to Vyasa, is pointed out by Sir William
Jones in the last of his essays: "On the philosophy of
the Asiatics" (Asiatic Researches, vol. iv. p. 164),
where he says, "The fundamental tenet of the Vedânta
school consisted not in denying the existence of matter,
that is, of solidity, impenetrability, and extended figure
(to deny which would be lunacy), but in correcting the
popular notion of it, and in contending that it has no
essence independent of mental perception; that existence and perceptibility are convertible terms." These
words adequately express the compatibility of empirical
reality and transcendental ideality.

In this first book, then, we consider the world only
from this side, only so far as it is idea. The inward
reluctance with which any one accepts the world as
merely his idea, warns him that this view of it, however

true it may be, is nevertheless one-sided, adopted in consequence of some arbitrary abstraction. And yet it is a conception from which he can never free himself. The defectiveness of this view will be corrected in the next book by means of a truth which is not so immediately certain as that from which we start here; a truth at which we can arrive only by deeper research and more severe abstraction, by the separation of what is different and the union of what is identical. This truth, which must be very serious and impressive if not awful to every one, is that a man can also say and must say, "the world is my will."

§ 6. For the present, however, in this first book we consider everything merely as idea, as object for the subject. And our own body, which is the starting-point for each of us in our perception of the world, we consider, like all other real objects, from the side of its knowableness, and in this regard it is simply an idea. Now the consciousness of every one is in general opposed to the explanation of objects as mere ideas, and more especially to the explanation of our bodies as such; for the thing in itself is known to each of us immediately in so far as it appears as our own body; but in so far as it objectifies itself in the other objects of perception, it is known only indirectly. But this abstraction, this one-sided treatment, this forcible separation of what is essentially and necessarily united, is only adopted to meet the demands of our argument; and therefore the disinclination to it must, in the meantime, be suppressed and silenced by the expectation that the subsequent treatment will correct the one-sidedness of the present one, and complete our knowledge of the nature of the world.

At present therefore the body is for us immediate object; that is to say, that idea which forms the starting-point of the subject's knowledge; because the body, with its immediately known changes, precedes the application of the law of causality, and thus supplies it with its first data. The whole nature of matter consists, as we have seen, in its causal action. But cause and effect exist only for the understanding, which is nothing but their subjective correlative. The understanding, however, could never come into operation if there were not something else from which it starts. This is simple sensation—the immediate consciousness of the changes of the body, by virtue of which it is immediate object. Thus the possibility of knowing the world of perception depends upon two conditions; the first, *objectively expressed*, is the power of material things to act upon each other, to produce changes in each other, without which common quality of all bodies no perception would be possible, even by means of the sensibility of the animal body. And if we wish to express this condition *subjectively* we say: The understanding first makes perception possible; for the law of causality, the possibility of effect and cause, springs only from the understanding, and is valid only for it, and therefore the world of perception exists only through and for it. The second condition is the sensibility of animal bodies, or the quality of being immediate objects of the subject which certain bodies possess. The mere modification which the organs of sense sustain from without through their specific affections, may here be called ideas, so far as these affections produce neither pain nor pleasure, that is, have no immediate significance for the will, and are yet perceived, exist therefore only for *knowledge*. Thus far, then, I say that the body is immediately *known*, is *immediate object*. But the conception of object is not to be taken here in its fullest sense, for through this immediate knowledge of the body, which precedes the operation of the understanding, and is mere sensation, our own body does not exist specifically as *object,* but first the material things which affect it: for all knowledge of an object proper, of an idea perceived in space, exists only through and for the understanding; therefore not before, but only subsequently to its operation. Therefore the body as object proper, that is, as an idea perceived in space, is first known indirectly, like all other objects, through the application of the law of causality to the action of one of its parts upon another, as, for example, when the eye sees the body or the hand touches it. Consequently the form of our body does not become known to us through mere feeling, but only through knowledge, only in idea; that is to say, only in the brain does our own body first come to appear as extended, articulate, organic. A man born blind receives this idea only little by little from the data afforded by touch. A blind man without hands could never come to know his own form; or at the most could infer and construct it little by little from the effects of other bodies upon him. If, then, we call the body an immediate object, we are to be understood with these reservations.

In other respects, then, according to what has been said, all animal bodies are immediate objects; that is, starting-points for the subject which always knows and therefore is never known in its perception of the world. Thus the distinctive characteristic of animal life is knowledge, with movement following on motives, which are determined by knowledge, just as movement following on stimuli is the distinctive characteristic of plant-life. Unorganised matter, however, has no movement except such as is produced by causes properly so called, using the term in its narrowest sense.

It follows from what has been said, that all animals, even the least developed, have understanding; for they all know objects, and this knowledge determines their movements as motive. Understanding is the same in all animals and in all men; it has everywhere the same simple form; knowledge of causality, transition from effect to cause, and from cause to effect, nothing more; but the degree of its acuteness, and the extension of the sphere of its knowledge varies enormously, with innumerable gradations from the lowest form, which is only conscious of the causal connection between the immediate object and objects affecting it—that is to say, perceives a cause as an object in space by passing to it from the affection which the body feels, to the higher grades of knowledge of the causal connection among objects known indirectly, which extends to the understanding of the most complicated system of cause and effect in nature. For even this high degree of knowledge is still the work of the understanding, not of the reason. The abstract concepts of the reason can only serve to take up the objective connections which are immediately known by the understanding, to make them permanent for thought, and to relate them to each other; but reason never gives us immediate knowledge. Every force and law of nature, every example of such forces and laws, must first be immediately known by the understanding, must be apprehended through perception before it can pass into abstract consciousness for reason. Hooke's discovery of the law of gravitation, and the reference of so many important phenomena to this one law, was the work of immediate apprehension by the understanding; and such also was the proof of Newton's calculations, and Lavoisier's discovery of acids and their important function in nature, and also Goethe's discovery of the origin of physical colours. All these discoveries are nothing more than a correct immediate passage from the effect to the cause, which is at once

followed by the recognition of the ideality of the force
of nature which expresses itself in all causes of the
same kind; and this complete insight is just an example
of that single function of the understanding, by which
an animal perceives as an object in space the cause
which affects its body, and differs from such a perception only in degree. Every one of these great discoveries
is therefore, just like perception, an operation of the
understanding, an immediate intuition, and as such the
work of an instant, an *apperçu,* a flash of insight. They
are not the result of a process of abstract reasoning,
which only serves to make the immediate knowledge of
the understanding permanent for thought by bringing
it under abstract concepts, *i. e.,* it makes knowledge
distinct, it puts us in a position to impart it and explain
it to others. The keenness of the understanding in
apprehending the causal relations of objects which are
known indirectly, does not find its only application in
the sphere of natural science (though all the discoveries
in that sphere are due to it), but it also appears in
practical life. It is then called good sense or prudence,
as in its other application it is better called acuteness,
penetration, sagacity. More exactly, good sense or prudence signifies exclusively understanding at the command of the will. But the limits of these conceptions
must not be too sharply defined, for it is always that
one function of the understanding by means of which
all animals perceive objects in space, which, in its keenest form, appears now in the phenomena of nature,
correctly inferring the unknown causes from the given
effects, and providing the material from which the reason frames general rules as laws of nature; now in-
venting complicated and ingenious machines by adapting
known causes to desired effects; now in the sphere of
motives, seeing through and frustrating intrigues and

machinations, or fitly disposing the motives and the men who are susceptible to them, setting them in motion, as machines are moved by levers and wheels, and directing them at will to the accomplishment of its ends. Deficiency of understanding is called *stupidity*. It is just *dulness in applying the law of causality*, incapacity for the immediate apprehension of the concatenations of causes and effects, motives and actions. A stupid person has no insight into the connection of natural phenomena, either when they follow their own course, or when they are intentionally combined, *i. e.*, are applied to machinery. Such a man readily believes in magic and miracles. A stupid man does not observe that persons, who apparently act independently of each other, are really in collusion; he is therefore easily mystified, and outwitted; he does not discern the hidden motives of proffered advice or expressions of opinion, &c. But it is always just one thing that he lacks—keenness, rapidity, ease in applying the law of causality, *i. e.*, power of understanding. The greatest, and, in this reference, the most instructive example of stupidity I ever met with, was the case of a totally imbecile boy of about eleven years of age, in an asylum. He had reason, because he spoke and comprehended, but in respect of understanding he was inferior to many of the lower animals. Whenever I visited him he noticed an eye-glass which I wore round my neck, and in which the window of the room and the tops of the trees beyond were reflected: on every occasion he was greatly surprised and delighted with this, and was never tired of looking at it with astonishment, because he did not understand the immediate causation of reflection.

While the difference in degree of the acuteness of the understanding is very great between man and man, it is even greater between one species of animal and another. In all species of animals, even those which are nearest to plants, there is at least as much understanding as suffices for the inference from the effect on the immediate object, to the indirectly known object as its cause, *i. e.,* sufficient for perception, for the apprehension of an object. For it is this that constitutes them animals, as it gives them the power of movement following on motives, and thereby the power of seeking for food, or at least of seizing it; whereas plants have only movement following on stimuli, whose direct influence they must await, or else decay, for they cannot seek after them nor appropriate them. We marvel at the great sagacity of the most developed species of animals, such as the dog, the elephant, the monkey or the fox, whose cleverness has been so admirably sketched by Buffon. From these most sagacious animals, we can pretty accurately determine how far understanding can go without reason, *i. e.,* abstract knowledge embodied in concepts. We could not find this out from ourselves, for in us understanding and reason always reciprocally support each other. We find that the manifestation of understanding in animals is sometimes above our expectation, and sometimes below it. On the one hand, we are surprised at the sagacity of the elephant, who, after crossing many bridges during his journey in Europe, once refused to go upon one, because he thought it was not strong enough to bear his weight, though he saw the rest of the party, consisting of men and horses, go upon it as usual. On the other hand, we wonder that the intelligent Orang-outangs, who warm themselves at a fire they have found, do not keep it alight by throwing wood on it; a proof that this requires a deliberation which is not possible without abstract concepts. It is clear that the knowledge of cause and effect, as the universal form of understanding, belongs to all animals

SCHOPENHAUER

a priori, because to them as to us it is the prior condition of all perception of the outer world. If any one desires additional proof of this, let him observe, for example, how a young dog is afraid to jump down from a table, however much he may wish to do so, because he foresees the effect of the weight of his body, though he has not been taught this by experience. In judging of the understanding of animals, we must guard against ascribing to it the manifestations of instinct, a faculty which is quite distinct both from understanding and reason, but the action of which is often very analogous to the combined action of the two.

Deficiency of *understanding* we call *stupidity:* deficiency in the application of *reason* to practice we shall recognise later as *foolishness:* deficiency of judgment as *silliness,* and lastly, partial or entire deficiency of *memory* as *madness.* But each of these will be considered in its own place. That which is correctly known by *reason* is *truth,* that is, an abstract judgment on sufficient grounds; that which is correctly known by *understanding* is *reality,* that is correct inference from effect on the immediate object to its cause. *Error* is opposed to *truth,* as deception of the *reason: illusion* is opposed to *reality,* as deception of the *understanding.* The full discussion of all this will be found in the first chapter of my essay on Light and Colour. Illusion takes place when the same effect may be attributed to two causes, of which one occurs very frequently, the other very seldom; the understanding having no data to decide which of these two causes operates in any particular case,—for their effects are exactly alike,—always assumes the presence of the commoner cause, and as the activity of the understanding is not reflective and discursive, but direct and immediate, this false cause appears before us as a perceived object, whereas it is

merely illusion. I have explained in the essay referred
to, how in this way double sight and double feeling take
place if the organs of sense are brought into an unusual
position; and have thus given an incontrovertible proof
that perception exists only through and for the understanding. As additional examples of such illusions or
deceptions of the understanding, we may mention the
broken appearance of a stick dipped in water; the reflections in spherical mirrors, which, when the surface
is convex appear somewhat behind it, and when the
surface is concave appear a long way in front of it. To
this class also belongs the apparently greater extension
of the moon at the horizon than at the zenith. This
appearance is not optical, for as the micrometre proves,
the eye receives the image of the moon at the zenith,
at an even greater angle of vision than at the horizon.
The mistake is due to the understanding, which assumes
that the cause of the feebler light of the moon and of
all stars at the horizon is that they are further off, thus
treating them as earthly objects, according to the laws
of atmospheric perspective, and therefore it takes the
moon to be much larger at the horizon than at the
zenith, and also regards the vault of heaven as more
extended or flattened out at the horizon. The same false
application of the laws of atmospheric perspective leads
us to suppose that very high mountains, whose summits
alone are visible in pure transparent air, are much
nearer than they really are, and therefore not so high
as they are; for example, Mont Blanc seen from Sa-
lenche. All such illusions are immediately present to us
as perceptions, and cannot be dispelled by any arguments of the reason. Reason can only prevent error,
that is, a judgment on insufficient grounds, by opposing
to it a truth; as for example, the abstract knowledge
that the cause of the weaker light of the moon and the

stars at the horizon is not greater distance, but the
denser atmosphere; but in all the cases we have referred
to, the illusion remains in spite of every abstract explanation. For the understanding is in itself, even in the
case of man, irrational, and is completely and sharply
distinguished from the reason, which is a faculty of
knowledge that belongs to man alone. The reason can
only *know;* perception remains free from its influence
and belongs to the understanding alone.

§ 8. As from the direct light of the sun to the borrowed
light of the moon, we pass from the immediate idea of
perception, which stands by itself and is its own warrant, to reflection, to the abstract, discursive concepts
of the reason, which obtain their whole content from
knowledge of perception, and in relation to it. As long
as we continue simply to perceive, all is clear, firm, and
certain. There are neither questions nor doubts nor
errors; we desire to go no further, can go no further;
we find rest in perceiving, and satisfaction in the present. Perception suffices for itself, and therefore what
springs purely from it, and remains true to it, for example, a genuine work of art, can never be false, nor
can it be discredited through the lapse of time, for it
does not present an opinion but the thing itself. But
with abstract knowledge, with reason, doubt and error
appear in the theoretical, care and sorrow in the practical. In the idea of perception, illusion may at moments take the place of the real; but in the sphere of
abstract thought, error may reign for a thousand years,
impose its yoke upon whole nations, extend to the
noblest impulses of humanity, and, by the help of its
slaves and its dupes, may chain and fetter those whom
it cannot deceive. It is the enemy against which the
wisest men of all times have waged unequal war, and
only what they have won from it has become the pos-

session of mankind. Therefore it is well to draw attention to it at once, as we already tread the ground to which its province belongs. It has often been said that we ought to follow truth even although no utility can be seen in it, because it may have indirect utility which may appear when it is least expected; and I would add to this, that we ought to be just as anxious to discover and to root out all error even when no harm is anticipated from it, because its mischief may be very indirect, and may suddenly appear when we do not expect it, for all error has poison at its heart. If it is mind, if it is knowledge, that makes man the lord of creation, there can be no such thing as harmless error, still less venerable and holy error. And for the consolation of those who in any way and at any time may have devoted strength and life to the noble and hard battle against error, I cannot refrain from adding that, so long as truth is absent, error will have free play, as owls and bats in the night; but sooner would we expect to see the owls and the bats drive back the sun in the eastern heavens, than that any truth which has once been known and distinctly and fully expressed, can ever again be so utterly vanquished and overcome that the old error shall once more reign undisturbed over its wide kingdom. This is the power of truth; its conquest is slow and laborious, but if once the victory be gained it can never be wrested back again.

Besides the ideas we have as yet considered, which, according to their construction, could be referred to time, space, and matter, if we consider them with reference to the object, or to pure sensibility and understanding (*i. e.*, knowledge of causality), if we consider them with reference to the subject, another faculty of knowledge has appeared in man alone of all earthly creatures, an entirely new consciousness, which, with very appro-

priate and significant exactness, is called *reflection*. For
it is in fact derived from the knowledge of perception,
and is a reflected appearance of it. But it has assumed
a nature fundamentally different. The forms of perception do not affect it, and even the principle of sufficient
reason which reigns over all objects has an entirely
different aspect with regard to it. It is just this new,
more highly endowed, consciousness, this abstract reflex of all that belongs to perception in that conception
of the reason which has nothing to do with perception,
that gives to man that thoughtfulness which distinguishes his consciousness so entirely from that of the
lower animals, and through which his whole behaviour
upon earth is so different from that of his irrational
fellow-creatures. He far surpasses them in power and
also in suffering. They live in the present alone, he lives
also in the future and the past. They satisfy the needs
of the moment, he provides by the most ingenious preparations for the future, yea for days that he shall never
see. They are entirely dependent on the impression of
the moment, on the effect of the perceptible motive; he
is determined by abstract conceptions independent of
the present. Therefore he follows predetermined plans,
he acts from maxims, without reference to his surroundings or the accidental impression of the moment. Thus,
for example, he can make with composure deliberate
preparations for his own death, he can dissemble past
finding out, and can carry his secret with him to the
grave; lastly, he has an actual choice between several
motives; for only in the abstract can such motives, present together in consciousness, afford the knowledge with
regard to themselves, that the one excludes the other,
and can thus measure themselves against each other
with reference to their power over the will. The motive
that overcomes, in that it decides the question at issue,

is the deliberate determinant of the will, and is a sure indication of its character. The brute, on the other hand,
is determined by the present impression; only the fear
of present compulsion can constrain its desires, until at
last this fear has become custom, and as such continues
to determine it; this is called training. The brute feels
and perceives; man, in addition to this, *thinks* and
knows: both *will.* The brute expresses its feelings and
dispositions by gestures and sounds; man communicates
his thought to others, or, if he wishes, he conceals it,
by means of speech. Speech is the first production, and
also the necessary organ of his reason. Therefore in
Greek and Italian, speech and reason are expressed by
the same word; *logos, il discorso. Vernunft* is derived
from *vernehmen,* which is not a synonym for the verb
to hear, but signifies the consciousness of the meaning of thoughts communicated in words. It is by the
help of language alone that reason accomplishes its
most important achievements,—the united action of several individuals, the planned co-operation of many thousands, civilisation, the state; also science, the storing
up of experience, the uniting of common properties in
one concept, the communication of truth, the spread of
error, thoughts and poems, dogmas and superstitions.
The brute first knows death when it dies, but man draws
consciously nearer to it every hour that he lives; and
this makes life at times a questionable good even to him
who has not recognised this character of constant annihilation in the whole of life. Principally on this account man has philosophies and religions, though it is
uncertain whether the qualities we admire most in his
conduct, voluntary rectitude and nobility of feeling,
were ever the fruit of either of them. As results which
certainly belong only to them, and as productions of
reason in this sphere, we may refer to the marvellous

and monstrous opinions of philosophers of various schools, and the extraordinary and sometimes cruel customs of the priests of different religions.

§ 10. Through all this, the question presses ever more upon us, how *certainty* is to be attained, how *judgments are to be established,* what constitutes *rational knowledge,* and *science,* which we rank with language and deliberate action as the third great benefit conferred by reason.

Reason is feminine in nature; it can only give after it has received. Of itself it has nothing but the empty forms of its operation. There is no absolutely pure rational knowledge except the four principles to which I have attributed metalogical truth; the principles of identity, contradiction, excluded middle, and sufficient reason of knowledge. For even the rest of logic is not absolutely pure rational knowledge. It presupposes the relations and the combinations of the spheres of concepts. But concepts in general only exist after experience of ideas of perception, and as their whole nature consists in their relation to these, it is clear that they presuppose them. No special content, however, is presupposed, but merely the existence of a content generally, and so logic as a whole may fairly pass for pure rational science. In all other sciences reason has received its content from ideas of perception; in mathematics from the relations of space and time, presented in intuition or perception prior to all experience; in pure natural science, that is, in what we know of the course of nature prior to any experience, the content of the science proceeds from the pure understanding, *i. e.,* from the *a priori* knowledge of the law of causality and its connection with those pure intuitions or perceptions of space and time. In all other sciences everything that is not derived from the sources we have just referred to belongs to experience. Speaking generally, *to know rationally* (*wissen*) means to have in the power of the mind, and capable of being reproduced at will, such judgments as have their sufficient ground of knowledge in something outside themselves, *i. e.*, are true. Thus only abstract cognition is *rational knowledge* (*wissen*), which is therefore the result of reason, so that we cannot accurately say of the lower animals that they *rationally know* anything, although they have apprehension of what is presented in perception, and memory of this, and consequently imagination, which is further proved by the circumstance that they dream. We attribute consciousness to them, and therefore although the word is derived from the verb to know rationally, the conception of consciousness corresponds generally with that of idea of whatever kind it may be. Thus we attribute life to plants, but not consciousness.

§ 12. *Rational knowledge* is then all abstract knowledge,—that is, the knowledge which is peculiar to the reason as distinguished from the understanding. Now, as reason only reproduces, for knowledge, what has been received in another way, it does not actually extend our knowledge, but only gives it another form. It enables us to know in the abstract and generally, what first became known in sense-perception, in the concrete. But this is much more important than it appears at first sight when so expressed. For it depends entirely upon the fact that knowledge has become rational or abstract knowledge (*wissen*), that it can be safely preserved, that it is communicable and susceptible of certain and wide-reaching application to practice. Knowledge in the form of sense-perception is valid only of the particular case, extends only to what is nearest, and ends with it, for sensibility and understanding can only comprehend one object at a time. Every enduring, arranged, and planned activity must therefore proceed from principles,—that is, from abstract knowledge, and it must be conducted in accordance with them. Thus, for example, the knowledge of the relation of cause and effect arrived at by the understanding, is in itself far completer, deeper and more exhaustive than anything that can be thought about it in the abstract; the understanding alone knows in perception directly and completely the nature of the effect of a lever, of a pulley, or a cog-wheel, the stability of an arch, and so forth. But on account of the peculiarity of the knowledge of perception just referred to, that it only extends to what is immediately present, the mere understanding can never enable us to construct machines and buildings. Here reason must come in; it must substitute abstract concepts for ideas of perception, and take them as the guide of action; and if they are right, the anticipated result will happen. In the same way we have perfect knowledge in pure perception of the nature and constitution of the parabola, hyperbola, and spiral; but if we are to make trustworthy application of this knowledge to the real, it must first become abstract knowledge, and by this it certainly loses its character of intuition or perception, but on the other hand it gains the certainty and preciseness of abstract knowledge. The differential calculus does not really extend our knowledge of the curve, it contains nothing that was not already in the mere pure perception of the curve; but it alters the kind of knowledge, it changes the intuitive into an abstract knowledge, which is so valuable for application. But here we must refer to another peculiarity of our faculty of knowledge, which could not be observed until the distinction between the knowledge of the senses and understanding and abstract knowledge had been made quite clear. It is this, that relations of space cannot as

such be directly translated into abstract knowledge, but
only temporal quantities,—that is, numbers, are suitable
for this. Numbers alone can be expressed in abstract
concepts which accurately correspond to them, not
spacial quantities. The concept "thousand" is just as
different from the concept "ten," as both these temporal quantities are in perception. We think of a thousand as a distinct multiple of ten, into which we can
resolve it at pleasure for perception in time,—that is to
say, we can count it. But between the abstract concept
of a mile and that of a foot, apart from any concrete
perception of either, and without the help of number,
there is no accurate distinction corresponding to the
quantities themselves. In both we only think of a spacial
quantity in general, and if they must be completely distinguished we are compelled either to call in the assistance of intuition or perception in space, which would
be a departure from abstract knowledge, or we must
think the difference in *numbers*. If then we wish to have
abstract knowledge of space-relations we must first
translate them into time-relations,—that is, into numbers; therefore only arithmetic, and not geometry, is the
universal science of quantity, and geometry must be
translated into arithmetic if it is to be communicable,
accurately precise and applicable in practice. It is true
that a space-relation as such may also be thought in
the abstract; for example, "the sine increases as the
angle," but if the quantity of this relation is to be given,
it requires number for its expression. This necessity,
that if we wish to have abstract knowledge of space-
relations (*i. e.*, rational knowledge, not mere intuition
or perception), space with its three dimensions must be
translated into time which has only one dimension, this
necessity it is, which makes mathematics so difficult.
This becomes very clear if we compare the perception of

curves with their analytical calculation, or the table of logarithms of the trigonometrical functions with the perception of the changing relations of the parts of a triangle, which are expressed by them. What vast mazes of figures, what laborious calculations it would require to express in the abstract what perception here apprehends at a glance completely and with perfect accuracy, namely, how the co-sine diminishes as the sine increases, how the co-sine of one angle is the sine of another, the inverse relation of the increase and decrease of the two angles, and so forth. How time, we might say, must complain, that with its one dimension it should be compelled to express the three dimensions of space! Yet this is necessary if we wish to possess, for application, an expression, in abstract concepts, of space-relations. They could not be translated directly into abstract concepts, but only through the medium of the pure temporal quantity, number, which alone is directly related to abstract knowledge. Yet it is worthy of remark, that as space adapts itself so well to perception, and by means of its three dimensions, even its complicated relations are easily apprehended, while it eludes the grasp of abstract knowledge; time, on the contrary, passes easily into abstract knowledge, but gives very little to perception. Our perceptions of numbers in their proper element, mere time, without the help of space, scarcely extends as far as ten, and beyond that we have only abstract concepts of numbers, no knowledge of them which can be presented in perception. On the other hand, we connect with every numeral, and with all algebraical symbols, accurately defined abstract concepts.

We may further remark here that some minds only find full satisfaction in what is known through perception. What they seek is the reason and consequent of being in space, sensuously expressed; a demonstration after the manner of Euclid, or an arithmetical solution of spacial problems, does not please them. Other minds, on the contrary, seek merely the abstract concepts which are needful for applying and communicating knowledge. They have patience and memory for abstract principles, formulas, demonstrations in long trains of reasoning, and calculations, in which the symbols represent the most complicated abstractions. The latter seek preciseness, the former sensible perceptions. The difference is characteristic.

The greatest value of rational or abstract knowledge is that it can be communicated and permanently retained. It is principally on this account that it is so inestimably important for practice. Any one may have a direct perceptive knowledge through the understanding alone, of the causal connection, of the changes and motions of natural bodies, and he may find entire satisfaction in it; but he cannot communicate this knowledge to others until it has been made permanent for thought in concepts. Knowledge of the first kind is even sufficient for practice, if a man puts his knowledge into practice himself, in an action which can be accomplished while the perception is still vivid; but it is not sufficient if the help of others is required, or even if the action is his own but must be carried out at different times, and therefore requires a pre-conceived plan. Thus, for example, a practised billiard-player may have a perfect knowledge of the laws of the impact of elastic bodies upon each other, merely in the understanding, merely for direct perception; and for him it is quite sufficient; but on the other hand it is only the man who has studied the science of mechanics, who has, properly speaking, a rational knowledge of these laws, that is, a knowledge of them in the abstract. Such knowledge of the understanding in perception is sufficient even for the construction of machines, when the inventor of the machine executes the work himself; as we often see in the case of talented workmen, who have no scientific knowledge. But whenever a number of men, and their united action taking place at different times, is required for the completion of a mechanical work, of a machine, or a building, then he who conducts it must have thought out the plan in the abstract, and such co-operative activity is only possible through the assistance of reason. It is, however, remarkable that in the first kind of activity, in which we have supposed that one man alone, in an uninterrupted course of action, accomplishes something, abstract knowledge, the application of reason or reflection, may often be a hindrance to him; for example, in the case of billiard-playing, of fighting, of tuning an instrument, or in the case of singing. Here perceptive knowledge must directly guide action; its passage through reflection makes it uncertain, for it divides the attention and confuses the man. Thus savages and untaught men, who are little accustomed to think, perform certain physical exercises, fight with beasts, shoot with bows and arrows and the like, with a certainty and rapidity which the reflecting European never attains to, just because his deliberation makes him hesitate and delay. For he tries, for example, to hit the right position or the right point of time, by finding out the mean between two false extremes; while the savage hits it directly without thinking of the false courses open to him. In the same way it is of no use to me to know in the abstract the exact angle, in degrees and minutes, at which I must apply a razor, if I do not know it intuitively, that is, if I have not got it in my touch. The knowledge of physiognomy also, is interfered with by the application of reason. This knowledge must be gained directly through the understanding. We say that the expression, the meaning of the features, can only be *felt,* that is, it cannot be put into abstract concepts. Every man has his direct intuitive method of physiognomy and pathognomy, yet one man understands more clearly than another these *signatura rerum.* But an abstract science of physiognomy to be taught and learned is not possible; for the distinctions of difference are here so fine that concepts cannot reach them; therefore abstract knowledge is related to them as a mosaic is to a painting by a Van der Werft or a Denner. In mosaics, however fine they may be, the limits of the stones are always there, and therefore no continuous passage from one colour to another is possible, and this is also the case with regard to concepts, with their rigidity and sharp delineation; however finely we may divide them by exact definition, they are still incapable of reaching the finer modifications of the perceptible, and this is just what happens in the example we have taken, knowledge of physiognomy.

This quality of concepts by which they resemble the stones of a mosaic, and on account of which perception always remains their asymptote, is also the reason why nothing good is produced in art by their means. If the singer or the virtuoso attempts to guide his execution by reflection he remains silent. And this is equally true of the composer, the painter, and the poet. The concept always remains unfruitful in art; it can only direct the technical part of it, its sphere is science. We shall consider more fully in the third book, why all true art proceeds from sensuous knowledge, never from the concept. Indeed, with regard to behaviour also, and personal agreeableness in society, the concept has only a negative value in restraining the grosser manifestations of egotism and brutality; so that a polished manner is its commendable production. But all that is attractive, gracious, charming in behaviour, all affectionateness and friendliness, must not proceed from the concepts, for if it does, "we feel intention, and are put out of tune." All dissimulation is the work of reflection; but it cannot be maintained constantly and without interruption; and so it is generally found out and loses its effect. Reason is needed in the full stress of life, where quick conclusions, bold action, rapid and sure comprehension are required, but it may easily spoil all if it gains the upper hand, and by perplexing hinders the intuitive, direct discovery, and grasp of the right by simple understanding, and thus induces irresolution.

Lastly, virtue and holiness do not proceed from reflection, but from the inner depths of the will, and its relation to knowledge. The exposition of this belongs to another part of our work; this, however, I may remark here, that the dogmas relating to ethics may be the same in the reason of whole nations, but the action of every individual different; and the converse also holds good; action, we say, is guided by *feelings*,—that is, simply not by concepts, but as a matter of fact by the ethical character. Dogmas occupy the idle reason; but action in the end pursues its own course independently of them, generally not according to abstract rules, but according to unspoken maxims, the expression of which is the whole man himself. Therefore, however different the religious dogmas of nations may be, yet in the case of all of them, a good action is accompanied by unspeakable satisfaction, and a bad action by endless remorse. No mockery can shake the former; no priest's absolution can deliver from the latter. Notwithstanding this, we must allow, that for the pursuit of a virtuous life, the application of reason is needful; only it is not its source, but has the subordinate function of preserving resolutions which have been made, of providing maxims to withstand the weakness of the moment, and give consistency to action. It plays the same part ultimately in art also, where it has just as little to do with the essential matter, but assists in carrying it out, for genius is not always at call, and yet the work must be completed in all its parts and rounded off to a whole.

§ 14. By means of these various discussions it is hoped that both the difference and the relation between the process of knowledge that belongs to the reason, rational knowledge, the concept on the one hand, and the direct knowledge in purely sensuous, mathematical intuition or perception, and apprehension by the understanding on the other hand, has been clearly brought out. This remarkable relation of our kinds of knowledge led us almost inevitably to give, in passing, explanations of feeling and of laughter, but from all this we now turn back to the further consideration of science as the third great benefit which reason confers on man, the other two being speech and deliberate action. The general discussion of science which now devolves upon us, will be concerned partly with its form, partly with the foundation of its judgments, and lastly with its content.

We have seen that, with the exception of the basis of pure logic, rational knowledge in general has not its source in the reason itself; but having been otherwise obtained as knowledge of perception, it is stored up in the reason, for through reason it has entirely changed its character, and has became abstract knowledge. All rational knowledge, that is, knowledge that has been raised to consciousness in the abstract, is related to *science* strictly so called, as a fragment to the whole. Every one has gained a rational knowledge of many different things through experience, through consideration of the individual objects presented to him, but only he who sets himself the task of acquiring a complete knowledge in the abstract of a particular class of objects, strives after science. This class can only be marked off by means of a concept; therefore, at the beginning of every science there stands a concept, and by means of it the class of objects concerning which this science promises a complete knowledge in the abstract, is separated in thought from the whole world of things. For example, the concept of space-relations, or of the action of unorganised bodies upon each other, or of the nature of plants, or of animals, or of the successive changes of the surface of the globe, or of the changes of the human race as a whole, or of the construction of a language, and so forth. If science sought to obtain the knowledge of its object, by investigating each individual thing that is thought through the concept, till by degrees it had learned the whole, no human memory would be equal to the task, and no certainty of completeness would be obtainable. Therefore, it makes use of that property of concept-spheres explained above, that they include each other, and it concerns itself mainly with the wider spheres which lie within the concept of its object in general. When the relations of these spheres to each other have been determined, all that is thought in them is also generally determined, and can now be more and more accurately determined by the separation of smaller and smaller concept-spheres. In this way it is possible for a science to comprehend its object completely. This path which it follows to knowledge, the path from the general to the particular, distinguishes it from ordinary rational knowledge; therefore, systematic form is an essential and characteristic feature of science. The combination of the most general concept-spheres of every science, that is, the knowledge of its first principles, is the indispensable condition of mastering it; how far we

advance from these to the more special propositions is a
matter of choice, and does not increase the thoroughness
but only the extent of our knowledge of the science.
The number of the first principles to which all the rest
are subordinated, varies greatly in the different sciences,
so that in some there is more subordination, in others
more co-ordination; and in this respect, the former make
greater claims upon the judgment, the latter upon the
memory. It was known to the schoolmen, that, as the
syllogism requires two premises, no science can proceed
from a single first principle which cannot be the subject
of further deduction, but must have several, at least
two. The specially classifying sciences: Zoology, Botany,
and also Physics and Chemistry, inasmuch as they refer
all inorganic action to a few fundamental forces, have
most subordination; history, on the other hand, has
really none at all; for the general in it consists merely
in the survey of the principal periods, from which, however, the particular events cannot be deduced, and are
only subordinated to them according to time, but according to the concept are co-ordinate with them. Therefore,
history, strictly speaking, is certainly rational knowledge, but is not science. In mathematics, according to
Euclid's treatment, the axioms alone are indemonstrable
first principles, and all demonstrations are in gradation
strictly subordinated to them. But this method of treatment is not essential to mathematics, and in fact each
proposition introduces quite a new space construction,
which in itself is independent of those which precede
it, and indeed can be completely comprehended from
itself, quite independently of them, in the pure intuition
or perception of space, in which the most complicated
construction is just as directly evident as the axiom;
but of this more fully hereafter. Meanwhile every mathematical proposition remains always a universal truth,

which is valid for innumerable particular cases; and a graduated process from the simple to the complicated propositions which are to be deduced from them, is also essential to mathematics; therefore in every respect mathematics is a science. The completeness of a science as such, that is, in respect of form, consists in there being as much subordination and as little co-ordination of the principles as possible. Scientific talent in general is, therefore, the faculty of subordinating the concept-spheres according to their different determinations, so that, as Plato repeatedly counsels, a science shall not be constituted by a general concept and an indefinite multiplicity immediately under it, but that knowledge shall descend by degrees from the general to the particular, through intermediate concepts and divisions, according to closer and closer definitions. In Kantian language this is called satisfying equally the law of homogeneity and that of specification. It arises from this peculiar nature of scientific completeness, that the aim of science is not greater certainty—for certainty may be possessed in just as high a degree by the most disconnected particular knowledge—but its aim is rather the facilitating of rational knowledge by means of its form, and the possibility of the completeness of rational knowledge which this form affords. It is therefore a very prevalent but perverted opinion that the scientific character of knowledge consists in its greater certainty, and just as false is the conclusion following from this, that, strictly speaking, the only sciences are mathematics and logic, because only in them, on account of their purely *a priori* character, is there unassailable certainty of knowledge. This advantage cannot be denied them, but it gives them no special claim to be regarded as sciences; for the special characteristic of science does not lie in certainty but in the systematic form of knowledge, based on the gradual descent from the general to the particular. The process of knowledge from the general to the particular, which is peculiar to the sciences, involves the necessity that in the sciences much should be established by deduction from preceding propositions, that is to say, by demonstration; and this has given rise to the old mistake that only what has been demonstrated is absolutely true, and that every truth requires a demonstration; whereas, on the contrary, every demonstration requires an undemonstrated truth, which ultimately supports it, or it may be, its own demonstration. Therefore a directly established truth is as much to be preferred to a truth established by demonstration as water from the spring is to water from the aqueduct. Perception, partly pure *a priori,* as it forms the basis of mathematics, partly empirical *a posteriori,* as it forms the basis of all the other sciences, is the source of all truth and the foundation of all science. (Logic alone is to be excepted, which is not founded upon perception but yet upon *direct* knowledge by the reason of its own laws.) Not the demonstrated judgments nor their demonstrations, but judgments which are created directly out of perception, and founded upon it rather than on any demonstrations, are to science what the sun is to the world; for all light proceeds from them, and lighted by their light the others give light also. To establish the truth of such primary judgments directly from perception, to raise such strongholds of science from the innumerable multitude of real objects, that is the work of the *faculty of judgment,* which consists in the power of rightly and accurately carrying over into abstract consciousness what is known in perception, and judgment is consequently the mediator between understanding and reason. Only extraordinary and exceptional strength of judgment in the individual can actually advance science; but every one who is possessed of a healthy reason is able to deduce propositions from propositions, to demonstrate, to draw conclusions. To lay down and make permanent for reflection, in suitable concepts, what is known through perception, so that, on the one hand, what is common to many real objects is thought through *one* concept, and, on the other hand, their points of difference are each thought through one concept, so that the different shall be known and thought as different in spite of a partial agreement, and the identical shall be known and thought as identical in spite of a partial difference, all in accordance with the end and intention which in each case is in view; all this is done by the *faculty of judgment.* Deficiency in judgment is *silliness.* The silly man fails to grasp, now the partial or relative difference of concepts which in one aspect are identical, now the identity of concepts which are relatively or partially different. To this explanation of the faculty of judgment, moreover, Kant's division of it into reflecting and subsuming judgment may be applied, according as it passes from the perceived objects to the concepts, or from the latter to the former; in both cases always mediating between empirical knowledge of the understanding and the reflective knowledge of the reason. There can be no truth which could be brought out by means of syllogisms alone; and the necessity of establishing truth by means of syllogisms is merely relative, indeed subjective. Since all demonstration is syllogistic, in the case of a new truth we must first seek, not for a demonstration, but for direct evidence, and only in the absence of such evidence is a demonstration to be temporarily made use of. No science is susceptible of demonstration throughout any more than a building can stand in the air; all its demonstrations must ulti-

mately rest upon what is perceived, and consequently
cannot be demonstrated, for the whole world of reflection rests upon and is rooted in the world of perception.
All primal, that is, original, *evidence* is a *perception*, as
the word itself indicates. Therefore it is either empirical
or founded upon the perception *a priori* of the conditions of possible experience. In both cases it affords
only immanent, not transcendent knowledge. Every concept has its worth and its existence only in its relation,
sometimes very indirect, to an idea of perception; what
is true of the concepts is also true of the judgments
constructed out of them, and of all science. Therefore
it must in some way be possible to know directly without
demonstrations or syllogisms every truth that is arrived
at through syllogisms and communicated by demonstrations. This is most difficult in the case of certain complicated mathematical propositions at which we only
arrive by chains of syllogisms; for example, the calculation of the chords and tangents to all arcs by deduction
from the proposition of Pythagoras. But even such a
truth as this cannot essentially and solely rest upon
abstract principles, and the space-relations which lie
at its foundation also must be capable of being so presented *a priori* in pure intuition or perception that the
truth of their abstract expression is directly established.
But of mathematical demonstration we shall speak more
fully shortly.

It is true we often hear men speak in a lofty strain
of sciences which rest entirely upon correct conclusions
drawn from sure premises, and which are consequently
unassailable. But through pure logical reasoning, however true the premises may be, we shall never receive
more than an articulate expression and exposition of
what lies already complete in the premises; thus we
shall only *explicitly* expound what was already *implicitly*

understood. The esteemed sciences referred to are, however, specially the mathematical sciences, particularly astronomy. But the certainty of astronomy arises from the fact that it has for its basis the intuition or perception of space, which is given *a priori,* and is therefore infallible. All space-relations, however, follow from each other with a necessity (ground of being) which affords *a priori* certainty, and they can therefore be safely deduced from each other. To these mathematical properties we have only to add one force of nature, gravity, which acts precisely in relation to the masses and the square of the distance; and, lastly, the law of inertia, which follows from the law of causality and is therefore true *a priori,* and with it the empirical datum of the motion impressed, once for all, upon each of these masses. This is the whole material of astronomy, which both by its simplicity and its certainty leads to definite results, which are highly interesting on account of the vastness and importance of the objects. For example, if I know the mass of a planet and the distance of its satellite from it, I can tell with certainty the period of the revolution of the latter according to Kepler's second law. But the ground of this law is, that with this distance only this velocity will both chain the satellite to the planet and prevent it from falling into it. Thus it is only upon such a geometrical basis, that is, by means of an intuition or perception *a priori,* and also under the application of a law of nature, that much can be arrived at by means of syllogisms, for here they are merely like bridges from *one* sensuous apprehension to others; but it is not so with mere pure syllogistic reasoning in the exclusively logical method. The source of the first fundamental truths of astronomy is, however, properly induction, that is, the comprehension of what is given in many perceptions in one true and directly founded judgment. From this, hypotheses are afterwards constructed, and their confirmation by experience, as induction approaching to completeness, affords the proof of the first judgment. For example, the apparent motion of the planets is known empirically; after many false hypotheses with regard to the spacial connection of this motion (planetary course) the right one was at last found, then the laws which it obeyed (the laws of Kepler), and, lastly, the cause of these laws (universal gravitation), and the empirically known agreement of all observed cases with the whole of the hypotheses, and with their consequences, that is to say, induction, established them with complete certainty. The invention of the hypotheses was the work of the judgment, which rightly comprehended the given facts and expressed them accordingly; but induction, that is, a multitude of perceptions, confirmed their truth. But their truth could also be known directly, and by a single empirical perception, if we could pass freely through space and had telescopic eyes. Therefore, here also syllogisms are not the essential and only source of knowledge, but really only a makeshift.

As a third example taken from a different sphere we may mention that the so-called metaphysical truths, that is, such truths as those to which Kant assigns the position of the metaphysical first principles of natural science, do not owe their evidence to demonstration. What is *a priori* certain we know directly; as the form of all knowledge, it is known to us with the most complete necessity. For example, that matter is permanent, that is, can neither come into being nor pass away, we know directly as negative truth; for our pure intuition or perception of space and time gives the possibility of motion; in the law of causality the understanding affords us the possibility of change of form and quality,

but we lack powers of the imagination for conceiving
the coming into being or passing away of matter. Therefore that truth has at all times been evident to all men
everywhere, nor has it ever been seriously doubted; and
this could not be the case if it had no other ground
of knowledge than the abstruse and exceedingly subtle
proof of Kant. But besides this, I have found Kant's
proof to be false (as is explained in the Appendix),
and have shown above that the permanence of matter
is to be deduced, not from the share which time has in
the possibility of experience, but from the share which
belongs to space. The true foundation of all truths
which in this sense are called metaphysical, that is,
abstract expressions of the necessary and universal
forms of knowledge, cannot itself lie in abstract principles; but only in the immediate consciousness of the
forms of the idea communicating itself in apodictic
assertions *a priori,* and fearing no refutation. But if
we yet desire to give a proof of them, it can only consist
in showing that what is to be proved is contained in
some truth about which there is no doubt, either as a
part of it or as a presupposition. Thus, for example,
I have shown that all empirical perception implies the
application of the law of causality, the knowledge of
which is hence a condition of all experience, and therefore cannot be first given and conditioned through experience as Hume thought. Demonstrations in general
are not so much for those who wish to learn as for those
who wish to dispute. Such persons stubbornly deny
directly established insight; now only the truth can be
consistent in all directions, and therefore we must show
such persons that they admit under *one* form and
indirectly, what they deny under another form and
directly; that is, the logically necessary connection between what is denied and what is admitted.

It is also a consequence of the scientific form, the subordination of everything particular under a general, and so on always to what is more general, that the truth of many propositions is only logically proved,—that is, through their dependence upon other propositions, through syllogisms, which at the same time appear as proofs. But we must never forget that this whole form of science is merely a means of rendering knowledge more easy, not a means to greater certainty. It is easier to discover the nature of an animal, by means of the species to which it belongs, and so on through the genus, family, order, and class, than to examine on every occasion the animal presented to us: but the truth of all propositions arrived at syllogistically is always conditioned by and ultimately dependent upon some truth which rests not upon reasoning but upon perception. If this perception were always as much within our reach as a deduction through syllogisms, then it would be in every respect preferable. For every deduction from concepts is exposed to great danger of error, on account of the fact we have considered above, that so many spheres lie partly within each other, and that their content is often vague or uncertain. This is illustrated by a multitude of demonstrations of false doctrines and sophisms of every kind. Syllogisms are indeed perfectly certain as regards form, but they are very uncertain on account of their matter, the concepts. For, on the one hand, the spheres of these are not sufficiently sharply defined, and, on the other hand, they intersect each other in so many ways that one sphere is in part contained in many others, and we may pass at will from it to one or another of these, and from this sphere again to others, as we have already shown. Or, in other words, the minor term and also the middle can always be subordinated to different concepts, from which we may choose at will the major and the middle, and the nature of the conclusion depends on this choice. Consequently immediate evidence is always much to be preferred to reasoned truth, and the latter is only to be accepted when the former is too remote, and not when it is as near or indeed nearer than the latter. Accordingly we saw above that, as a matter of fact, in the case of logic, in which the immediate knowledge in each individual case lies nearer to hand than deduced scientific knowledge, we always conduct our thought according to our immediate knowledge of the laws of thought, and leave logic unused.

§ 15. If now with our conviction that perception is the primary source of all evidence, and that only direct or indirect connection with it is absolute truth; and further, that the shortest way to this is always the surest, as every interposition of concepts means exposure to many deceptions; if, I say, we now turn with this conviction to mathematics, as it was established as a science by Euclid, and has remained as a whole to our own day, we cannot help regarding the method it adopts, as strange and indeed perverted. We ask that every logical proof shall be traced back to an origin in perception; but mathematics, on the contrary, is at great pains deliberately to throw away the evidence of perception which is peculiar to it, and always at hand, that it may substitute for it a logical demonstration. This must seem to us like the action of a man who cuts off his legs in order to go on crutches, or like that of the prince in the *Triumph of Sentiment* who flees from the beautiful reality of nature, to delight in a stage scene that imitates it. I must here refer to what I have said in the sixth chapter of the essay on the principle of sufficient reason, and take for granted that it is fresh and present in the memory of the reader; so that I may link my observa-

tions on to it without explaining again the difference
between the mere ground of knowledge of a mathematical truth, which can be given logically, and the
ground of being, which is the immediate connection of
the parts of space and time, known only in perception.
It is only insight into the ground of being that secures
satisfaction and thorough knowledge. The mere ground
of knowledge must always remain superficial; it can
afford us indeed rational knowledge *that* a thing is as it
is, but it cannot tell *why* it is so. Euclid chose the latter
way to the obvious detriment of the science. For just
at the beginning, for example, when he ought to show
once for all how in a triangle the angles and sides
reciprocally determine each other, and stand to each
other in the relation of reason and consequent, in accordance with the form which the principle of sufficient
reason has in pure space, and which there, as in every
other sphere, always affords the necessity that a thing
is as it is, because something quite different from it, is
as it is; instead of in this way giving a thorough insight
into the nature of the triangle, he sets up certain disconnected arbitrarily chosen propositions concerning the
triangle, and gives a logical ground of knowledge of
them, through a laborious logical demonstration, based
upon the principle of contradiction. Instead of an exhaustive knowledge of these space-relations we therefore receive merely certain results of them, imparted
to us at pleasure, and in fact we are very much in the
position of a man to whom the different effects of an
ingenious machine are shown, but from whom its inner
connection and construction are withheld. We are compelled by the principle of contradiction to admit that
what Euclid demonstrates is true, but we do not comprehend *why* it is so. We have therefore almost the
same uncomfortable feeling that we experience after

a juggling trick, and, in fact, most of Euclid's demonstrations are remarkably like such feats. The truth
almost always enters by the back door, for it manifests
itself through some contingent circumstance. Often a
reductio ad absurdum shuts all the doors one after another, until only one is left through which we are therefore compelled to enter. Often, as in the proposition of
Pythagoras, lines are drawn, we don't know why, and
it afterwards appears that they were traps which close
unexpectedly and take prisoner the assent of the astonished learner, who must now admit what remains wholly
inconceivable in its inner connection, so much so, that
he may study the whole of Euclid through and through
without gaining a real insight into the laws of space-
relations, but instead of them he only learns by heart
certain results which follow from them. This specially
empirical and unscientific knowledge is like that of the
doctor who knows both the disease and the cure for it,
but does not know the connection between them. But all
this is the necessary consequence if we capriciously
reject the special kind of proof and evidence of one
species of knowledge, and forcibly introduce in its stead
a kind which is quite foreign to its nature. However, in
other respects the manner in which this has been accomplished by Euclid deserves all the praise which has
been bestowed on him through so many centuries, and
which has been carried so far that his method of treating mathematics has been set up as the pattern of all
scientific exposition. Men tried indeed to model all the
sciences after it, but later they gave up the attempt
without quite knowing why. Yet in our eyes this method
of Euclid in mathematics can appear only as a very
brilliant piece of perversity. But when a great error in
life or in science has been intentionally and methodically carried out with universal applause, it is always

possible to discover its source in the philosophy which prevailed at the time.

In order to improve the method of mathematics, it is especially necessary to overcome the prejudice that demonstrated truth has any superiority over what is known through perception, or that logical truth founded upon the principle of contradiction has any superiority over metaphysical truth, which is immediately evident, and to which belongs the pure intuition or perception of space.

That which is most certain, and yet always inexplicable, is what is involved in the principle of sufficient reason, for this principle, in its different aspects, expresses the universal form of all our ideas and knowledge. All explanation consists of reduction to it, exemplification in the particular case of the connection of ideas expressed generally through it. It is thus the principle of all explanation, and therefore it is neither susceptible of an explanation itself, nor does it stand in need of it; for every explanation presupposes it, and only obtains meaning through it. Now, none of its forms are superior to the rest; it is equally certain and incapable of demonstration as the principle of the ground of being, or of change, or of action, or of knowing. The relation of reason and consequent is a necessity in all its forms, and indeed it is, in general, the source of the concept of necessity, for necessity has no other meaning. If the reason is given there is no other necessity than that of the consequent, and there is no reason that does not involve the necessity of the consequent. Just as surely then as the consequent expressed in the conclusion follows from the ground of knowledge given in the premises, does the ground of being in space determine its consequent in space: if I knew through perception the relation of these two, this certainty is just as great as any logical certainty. But every geometrical proposition is just as good an expression of such a relation as one of the twelve axioms; it is a metaphysical truth, and as such, just as certain as the principle of contradiction itself, which is a metalogical truth, and the common foundation of all logical demonstration. Whoever denies the necessity, exhibited for intuition or perception, of the space-relations expressed in any proposition, may just as well deny the axioms, or that the conclusion follows from the premises, or, indeed, he may as well deny the principle of contradiction itself, for all these relations are equally undemonstrable, immediately evident and known *a priori*. For any one to wish to derive the necessity of space-relations, known in intuition or perception, from the principle of contradiction by means of a logical demonstration is just the same as for the feudal superior of an estate to wish to hold it as the vassal of another. Yet this is what Euclid has done. His axioms only, he is compelled to leave resting upon immediate evidence; all the geometrical truths which follow are demonstrated logically, that is to say, from the agreement of the assumption made in the proposition with the axioms which are presupposed, or with some earlier proposition; or from the contradiction between the opposite of the proposition and the assumptions made in it, or the axioms, or earlier propositions, or even itself. But the axioms themselves have no more immediate evidence than any other geometrical problem, but only more simplicity on account of their smaller content.

When a criminal is examined, a *procès-verbal* is made of his statement in order that we may judge of its truth from its consistency. But this is only a makeshift, and we are not satisfied with it if it is possible to investigate the truth of each of his answers for itself; especially as he might lie consistently from the beginning. But Euclid investigated space according to this first method. He set about it, indeed, under the correct assumption that nature must everywhere be consistent, and that therefore it must also be so in space, its fundamental form. Since then the parts of space stand to each other in a relation of reason and consequent, no single property of space can be different from what it is without being in contradiction with all the others. But this is a very troublesome, unsatisfactory, and roundabout way to follow. It prefers indirect knowledge to direct, which is just as certain, and it separates the knowledge that a thing is from the knowledge why it is, to the great disadvantage of the science; and lastly, it entirely withholds from the beginner insight into the laws of space, and indeed renders him unaccustomed to the special investigation of the ground and inner connection of things, inclining him to be satisfied with a mere historical knowledge that a thing is as it is. The exercise of acuteness which this method is unceasingly extolled as affording consists merely in this, that the pupil practises drawing conclusions, i. e., he practises applying the principle of contradiction, but specially he exerts his memory to retain all those data whose agreement is to be tested.

Moreover, it is worth noticing that this method of proof was applied only to geometry and not to arithmetic. In arithmetic the truth is really allowed to come home to us through perception alone, which in it consists simply in counting. As the perception of numbers is in *time alone,* and therefore cannot be represented by a sensuous schema like the geometrical figure, the suspicion that perception is merely empirical, and possibly illusive, disappeared in arithmetic, and the introduction of the logical method of proof into geometry was en-

tirely due to this suspicion. As time has only one
dimension, counting is the only arithmetical operation,
to which all others may be reduced; and yet counting
is just intuition or perception *a priori,* to which there
is no hesitation in appealing here, and through which
alone everything else, every sum and every equation,
is ultimately proved. We prove, for example, not that
$\frac{7+9\times 8-2}{3} = 42$; but we refer to the pure perception
in time, counting thus makes each individual problem
an axiom. Instead of the demonstrations that fill geometry, the whole content of arithmetic and algebra is
thus simply a method of abbreviating counting. We
mentioned above that our immediate perception of numbers in time extends only to about ten. Beyond this an
abstract concept of the numbers, fixed by a word, must
take the place of the perception; which does not therefore actually occur any longer, but is only indicated
in a thoroughly definite manner. Yet even so, by the
important assistance of the system of figures which
enables us to represent all larger numbers by the same
small ones, intuitive or perceptive evidence of every
sum is made possible, even where we make such use of
abstraction that not only the numbers, but indefinite
quantities and whole operations are thought only in the
abstract and indicated as so thought, as $\sqrt{r^b}$. so that we
do not perform them, but merely symbolise them.

We might establish truth in geometry also, through
pure *a priori* perception, with the same right and
certainty as in arithmetic. It is in fact always this
necessity, known through perception in accordance with
the principle of sufficient reason of being, which gives
to geometry its principal evidence, and upon which in
the consciousness of every one, the certainty of its
propositions rests. The stilted logical demonstration is
always foreign to the matter, and is generally soon for-

gotten, without weakening our conviction. It might indeed be dispensed with altogether without diminishing the evidence of geometry, for this is always quite independent of such demonstration, which never proves anything we are not convinced of already, through another kind of knowledge. So far then it is like a cowardly soldier, who adds a wound to an enemy slain by another, and then boasts that he slew him himself.

After all this we hope there will be no doubt that the evidence of mathematics, which has become the pattern and symbol of all evidence, rests essentially not upon demonstration, but upon immediate perception, which is thus here, as everywhere else, the ultimate ground and source of truth. Yet the perception which lies at the basis of mathematics has a great advantage over all other perception, and therefore over empirical perception. It is *a priori,* and therefore independent of experience, which is always given only in successive parts; therefore everything is equally near to it, and we can start either from the reason or from the consequent, as we please. Now this makes it absolutely reliable, for in it the consequent is known from the reason, and this is the only kind of knowledge that has necessity; for example, the equality of the sides is known as established by the equality of the angles. All empirical perception, on the other hand, and the greater part of experience, proceeds conversely from the consequent to the reason, and this kind of knowledge is not infallible, for necessity only attaches to the consequent on account of the reason being given, and no necessity attaches to the knowledge of the reason from the consequent, for the same consequent may follow from different reasons. The latter kind of knowledge is simply induction, *i. e.,* from many consequents which point to one reason, the reason is accepted as certain; but as the cases can never be all before us, the truth here is not unconditionally certain. But all knowledge through sense-perception, and the great bulk of experience, has only this kind of truth. The affection of one of the senses induces the understanding to infer a cause of the effect, but, as a conclusion from the consequent to the reason is never certain, illusion, which is deception of the senses, is possible, and indeed often occurs, as was pointed out above. Only when several of the senses, or it may be all the five, receive impressions which point to the same cause, the possibility of illusion is reduced to a minimum; but yet it still exists, for there are cases, for example, the case of counterfeit money, in which all the senses are deceived. All empirical knowledge, and consequently the whole of natural science, is in the same position, except only the pure, or as Kant calls it, metaphysical part of it. Here also the causes are known from the effects, consequently all natural philosophy rests upon hypotheses, which are often false, and must then gradually give place to more correct ones. Only in the case of purposely arranged experiments, knowledge proceeds from the cause to the effect, that is, it follows the method that affords certainty; but these experiments themselves are undertaken in consequence of hypotheses. Therefore, no branch of natural science, such as physics, or astronomy, or physiology could be discovered all at once, as was the case with mathematics and logic, but required and requires the collected and compared experiences of many centuries. In the first place, repeated confirmation in experience brings the induction, upon which the hypothesis rests, so near completeness that in practice it takes the place of certainty, and is regarded as diminishing the value of the hypothesis, its source, just as little as the incommensurability of straight and curved lines diminishes

the value of the application of geometry, or that perfect
exactness of the logarithm, which is not attainable,
diminishes the value of arithmetic. For as the logarithm,
or the squaring of the circle, approaches infinitely near
to correctness through infinite fractions, so, through
manifold experience, the induction, i. e., the knowledge
of the cause from the effects, approaches, not infinitely
indeed, but yet so near mathematical evidence, i. e.,
knowledge of the effects from the cause, that the possibility of mistake is small enough to be neglected, but
yet the possibility exists; for example, a conclusion
from an indefinite number of cases to all cases, i. e., to
the unknown ground on which all depend, is an induction. What conclusion of this kind seems more certain
than that all men have the heart on the left side? Yet
there are extremely rare and quite isolated exceptions
of men who have the heart upon the right side. Sense-
perception and empirical science have, therefore, the
same kind of evidence. The advantage which mathematics, pure natural science, and logic have over them,
as *a priori* knowledge, rests merely upon this, that the
formal element in knowledge upon which all that is
a priori is based, is given as a whole and at once, and
therefore in it we can always proceed from the cause
to the effect, while in the former kind of knowledge we
are generally obliged to proceed from the effect to the
cause. In other respects, the law of causality, or the
principle of sufficient reason of change, which guides
empirical knowledge, is in itself just as certain as the
other forms of the principle of sufficient reason which
are followed by the *a priori* sciences referred to above.
Logical demonstrations from concepts or syllogisms
have the advantage of proceeding from the reason to the
consequent, just as much as knowledge through perception *a priori,* and therefore in themselves, i. e., ac-

cording to their form, they are infallible. This has greatly assisted to bring demonstration in general into such esteem. But this infallibility is merely relative; the demonstration merely subsumes under the first principles of the science, and it is these which contain the whole material truth of science, and they must not themselves be demonstrated, but must be founded on perception. In the few *a priori* sciences we have named above, this perception is pure, but everywhere else it is empirical, and is only raised to universality through induction. If, then, in the empirical sciences also, the particular is proved from the general, yet the general, on the other hand, has received its truth from the particular; it is only a store of collected material, not a self-constituted foundation.

As regards the *content* of the sciences generally, it is, in fact, always the relation of the phenomena of the world to each other, according to the principle of sufficient reason, under the guidance of the *why*, which has validity and meaning only through this principle. *Explanation* is the establishment of this relation. Therefore explanation can never go further than to show two ideas standing to each other in the relation peculiar to that form of the principle of sufficient reason which reigns in the class to which they belong. If this is done we cannot further be asked the question, *why:* for the relation proved is that one which absolutely cannot be imagined as other than it is, *i. e.,* it is the form of all knowledge. Therefore we do not ask why $2 + 2 = 4$; or why the equality of the angles of a triangle determines the equality of the sides; or why its effect follows any given cause; or why the truth of the conclusion is evident from the truth of the premises. Every explanation which does not ultimately lead to a relation of which no "why" can further be demanded, stops

at an accepted *qualitas occulta;* but this is the character of every original force of nature. Every explanation in natural science must ultimately end with such a
qualitas occulta, and thus with complete obscurity. It
must leave the inner nature of a stone just as much unexplained as that of a human being; it can give as little
account of the weight, the cohesion, the chemical qualities, &c., of the former, as of the knowing and acting
of the latter. Thus, for example, weight is a *qualitas
occulta,* for it can be thought away, and does not proceed as a necessity from the form of knowledge; which,
on the contrary, is not the case with the law of inertia,
for it follows from the law of causality, and is therefore
sufficiently explained if it is referred to that law. There
are two things which are altogether inexplicable,—that
is to say, do not ultimately lead to the relation which
the principle of sufficient reason expresses. These are,
first, the principle of sufficient reason itself in all its
four forms, because it is the principle of all explanation,
which has meaning only in relation to it; secondly, that
to which this principle does not extend, but which is the
original source of all phenomena; the thing-in-itself,
the knowledge of which is not subject to the principle of
sufficient reason. We must be content for the present not
to understand this thing-in-itself, for it can only be made
intelligible by means of the following book, in which we
shall resume this consideration of the possible achievements of the sciences. But at the point at which natural
science, and indeed every science, leaves things, because
not only its explanation of them, but even the principle
of this explanation, the principle of sufficient reason,
does not extend beyond this point; there philosophy
takes them up and treats them after its own method,
which is quite distinct from the method of science. In
my essay on the principle of sufficient reason, §51, I

have shown how in the different sciences the chief guiding clue is one or other form of that principle; and, in fact, perhaps the most appropriate classification of the sciences might be based upon this circumstance. Every explanation arrived at by the help of this clue is, as we have said, merely relative; it explains things in relation to each other, but something which indeed is presupposed is always left unexplained. In mathematics, for example, this is space and time; in mechanics, physics, and chemistry it is matter, qualities, original forces and laws of nature; in botany and zoology it is the difference of species, and life itself; in history it is the human race with all its properties of thought and will: in all it is that form of the principle of sufficient reason which is respectively applicable. It is peculiar to *philosophy* that it presupposes nothing as known, but treats everything as equally external and a problem; not merely the relations of phenomena, but also the phenomena themselves, and even the principle of sufficient reason to which the other sciences are content to refer everything. In philosophy nothing would be gained by such a reference, as one member of the series is just as external to it as another; and, moreover, that kind of connection is just as much a problem for philosophy as what is joined together by it, and the latter again is just as much a problem after its combination has been explained as before it. For, as we have said, just what the sciences presuppose and lay down as the basis and the limits of their explanation, is precisely and peculiarly the problem of philosophy, which may therefore be said to begin where science ends. It cannot be founded upon demonstrations, for they lead from known principles to unknown, but everything is equally unknown and external to philosophy. There can be no principle in consequence of which the world with all its phenomena first came into existence, and therefore it is not possible to construct, as Spinoza wished, a philosophy which demonstrates from self-evident principles. Philosophy is the most general rational knowledge, the first principles of which cannot therefore be derived from another principle still more general. The principle of contradiction establishes merely the agreement of concepts, but does not itself produce concepts. The principle of sufficient reason explains the connections of phenomena, but not the phenomena themselves; therefore philosophy cannot proceed upon these principles to seek an *efficient cause* or a *final cause* of the whole world. My philosophy, at least, does not by any means seek to know *whence* or *wherefore* the world exists, but merely *what* the world is. But the *why* is here subordinated to the *what,* for it already belongs to the world, as it arises and has meaning and validity only through the form of its phenomena, the principle of sufficient reason. We might indeed say that every one knows what the world is without help, for he is himself that subject of knowledge of which the world is the idea; and so far this would be true. But that knowledge is empirical, is in the concrete; the task of philosophy is to reproduce this in the abstract, to raise to permanent rational knowledge the successive changing perceptions, and in general, all that is contained under the wide concept of feeling and merely negatively defined as not abstract, distinct, rational knowledge. It must therefore consist of a statement in the abstract, of the nature of the whole world, of the whole, and of all the parts. In order then that it may not lose itself in the endless multitude of particular judgments, it must make use of abstraction and think everything individual in the universal, and its differences also in the universal. It must therefore partly separate and partly unite, in order to present to rational knowledge the whole manifold of the world generally, according to its nature, comprehended in a few abstract concepts. Through these concepts, in which it fixes the nature of the world, the whole individual must be known as well as the universal, the knowledge of both therefore must be bound together to the minutest point. Therefore the capacity for philosophy consists just in that in which Plato placed it, the knowledge of the one in the many, and the many in the one. Philosophy will therefore be a sum-total of general judgments, whose ground of knowledge is immediately the world itself in its entirety, without excepting anything; thus all that is to be found in human consciousness; it will be *a complete recapitulation, as it were, a reflection, of the world in abstract concepts,* which is only possible by the union of the essentially identical in *one* concept and the relegation of the different to another.

The agreement which all the sides and parts of the world have with each other, just because they belong to a whole, must also be found in this abstract copy of it. Therefore the judgments in this sum-total could to a certain extent be deduced from each other, and indeed always reciprocally so deduced. Yet to make the first judgment possible, they must all be present, and thus implied as prior to it in the knowledge of the world in the concrete, especially as all direct proof is more certain than indirect proof; their harmony with each other by virtue of which they come together into the unity of *one* thought, and which arises from the harmony and unity of the world of perception itself, which is their common ground of knowledge, is not therefore to be made use of to establish them, as that which is prior to them, but is only added as a confirmation of their truth. This problem itself can only become quite clear in being solved.

SECOND BOOK
THE WORLD AS WILL

FIRST ASPECT

THE OBJECTIFICATION OF THE WILL

II

§ 17. In the first book we considered the idea merely as such, that is, only according to its general form. It is true that as far as the abstract idea, the concept, is concerned, we obtained a knowledge of it in respect of its content also, because it has content and meaning only in relation to the idea of perception, without which it would be worthless and empty. Accordingly, directing our attention exclusively to the idea of perception, we shall now endeavour to arrive at a knowledge of its content, its more exact definition, and the forms which it presents to us. And it will specially interest us to find an explanation of its peculiar significance, that significance which is otherwise merely felt, but on account of which it is that these pictures do not pass by us entirely strange and meaningless, as they must otherwise do, but speak to us directly, are understood, and obtain an interest which concerns our whole nature.

We direct our attention to mathematics, natural science, and philosophy, for each of these holds out the hope that it will afford us a part of the explanation we desire. Now, taking philosophy first, we find that it is like a monster with many heads, each of which speaks a different language. They are not, indeed, all at variance on the point we are here considering, the significance of the idea of perception. For, with the ex-

ception of the Sceptics and the Idealists, the others, for
the most part, speak very much in the same way of an
object which constitutes the *basis* of the idea, and which
is indeed different in its whole being and nature from
the idea, but yet is in all points as like it as one egg is
to another. But this does not help us, for we are quite
unable to distinguish such an object from the idea; we
find that they are one and the same; for every object
always and for ever presupposes a subject, and therefore remains idea, so that we recognised objectivity as
belonging to the most universal form of the idea, which
is the division into subject and object. Further, the
principle of sufficient reason, which is referred to in
support of this doctrine, is for us merely the form of
the idea, the orderly combination of one idea with another, but not the combination of the whole finite or
infinite series of ideas with something which is not idea
at all, and which cannot therefore be presented in perception. Of the Sceptics and Idealists we spoke above,
in examining the controversy about the reality of the
outer world.

If we turn to mathematics to look for the fuller
knowledge we desire of the idea of perception, which we
have, as yet, only understood generally, merely in its
form, we find that mathematics only treats of these
ideas so far as they fill time and space, that is, so far as
they are quantities. It will tell us with the greatest accuracy the how-many and the how-much; but as this is
always merely relative, that is to say, merely a comparison of one idea with others, and a comparison only
in the one respect of quantity, this also is not the information we are principally in search of.

Lastly, if we turn to the wide province of natural
science, which is divided into many fields, we may, in
the first place, make a general division of it into two

parts. It is either the description of forms, which I call
Morphology, or the explanation of changes, which I call
Etiology. The first treats of the permanent forms, the
second of the changing matter, according to the laws of
its transition from one form to another. The first is
the whole extent of what is generally called natural
history. It teaches us, especially in the sciences of botany and zoology, the various permanent, organised, and
therefore definitely determined forms in the constant
change of individuals; and these forms constitute a
great part of the content of the idea of perception. In
natural history they are classified, separated, united, arranged according to natural and artificial systems, and
brought under concepts which make a general view and
knowledge of the whole of them possible. Further, an
infinitely fine analogy both in the whole and in the parts
of these forms, and running through them all (*unité de
plan*), is established, and thus they may be compared
to innumerable variations on a theme which is not given.
The passage of matter into these forms, that is to say,
the origin of individuals, is not a special part of natural science, for every individual springs from its like
by generation, which is everywhere equally mysterious,
and has as yet evaded definite knowledge. The little that
is known on the subject finds its place in physiology,
which belongs to that part of natural science I have
called etiology. Mineralogy also, especially where it becomes geology, inclines towards etiology, though it principally belongs to morphology. Etiology proper comprehends all those branches of natural science in which
the chief concern is the knowledge of cause and effect.
The sciences teach how, according to an invariable rule,
one condition of matter is necessarily followed by a certain other condition; how one change necessarily conditions and brings about a certain other change; this sort

of teaching is called *explanation*. The principal sciences in this department are mechanics, physics, chemistry, and physiology.

If, however, we surrender ourselves to its teaching, we soon become convinced that etiology cannot afford us the information we chiefly desire, any more than morphology. The latter presents to us innumerable and infinitely varied forms, which are yet related by an unmistakable family likeness. These are for us ideas, and when only treated in this way, they remain always strange to us, and stand before us like hieroglyphics which we do not understand. Etiology, on the other hand; teaches us that, according to the law of cause and effect, this particular condition of matter brings about that other particular condition, and thus it has explained it and performed its part. However, it really does nothing more than indicate the orderly arrangement according to which the states of matter appear in space and time, and teach in all cases what phenomenon must necessarily appear at a particular time in a particular place. It thus determines the position of phenomena in time and space, according to a law whose special content is derived from experience, but whose universal form and necessity is yet known to us independently of experience. But it affords us absolutely no information about the inner nature of any one of these phenomena: this is called a *force of nature,* and it lies outside the province of causal explanation, which calls the constant uniformity with which manifestations of such a force appear whenever their known conditions are present, *a law of nature*. But this law of nature, these conditions, and this appearance in a particular place at a particular time, are all that it knows or ever can know. The force itself which manifests itself, the inner nature of the phenomena which appear in accordance with these laws, remains always a secret to it, something entirely strange and unknown in the case of the simplest as well as of the most complex phenomena. For although as yet etiology has most completely achieved its aim in mechanics, and least completely in physiology, still the force on account of which a stone falls to the ground or one body repels another is, in its inner nature, not less strange and mysterious than that which produces the movements and the growth of an animal. The science of mechanics presupposes matter, weight, impenetrability, the possibility of communicating motion by impact, inertia and so forth as ultimate facts, calls them forces of nature, and their necessary and orderly appearance under certain conditions a law of nature. Only after this does its explanation begin, and it consists in indicating truly and with mathematical exactness, how, where and when each force manifests itself, and in referring every phenomenon which presents itself to the operation of one of these forces. Physics, chemistry, and physiology proceed in the same way in their province, only they presuppose more and accomplish less. Consequently the most complete etiological explanation of the whole of nature can never be more than an enumeration of forces which cannot be explained, and a reliable statement of the rule according to which phenomena appear in time and space, succeed, and make way for each other. But the inner nature of the forces which thus appear remains unexplained by such an explanation, which must confine itself to phenomena and their arrangement, because the law which it follows does not extend further. In this respect it may be compared to a section of a piece of marble which shows many veins beside each other, but does not allow us to trace the course of the veins from the interior of the marble to its surface. Or, if I may

use an absurd but more striking comparison, the philosophical investigator must always have the same feeling
towards the complete etiology of the whole of nature,
as a man who, without knowing how, has been brought
into a company quite unknown to him, each member of
which in turn presents another to him as his friend and
cousin, and therefore as quite well known, and yet the
man himself, while at each introduction he expresses
himself gratified, has always the question on his lips:
"But how the deuce do I stand to the whole company?"

Thus we see that, with regard to those phenomena
which we know only as our ideas, etiology can never
give us the desired information that shall carry us beyond this point. For, after all its explanations, they still
remain quite strange to us, as mere ideas whose significance we do not understand. The causal connection
merely gives us the rule and the relative order of their
appearance in space and time, but affords us no further
knowledge of that which so appears. Moreover, the law
of causality itself has only validity for ideas, for objects of a definite class, and it has meaning only in so
far as it presupposes them. Thus, like these objects
themselves, it always exists only in relation to a subject, that is, conditionally; and so it is known just as
well if we start from the subject, *i. e., a priori*, as if we
start from the object, *i. e., a posteriori*. Kant indeed has
taught us this.

But what now impels us to inquiry is just that we are
not satisfied with knowing that we have ideas, that they
are such and such, and that they are connected according to certain laws, the general expression of which is
the principle of sufficient reason. We wish to know the
significance of these ideas; we ask whether this world is
merely idea; in which case it would pass by us like an
empty dream or a baseless vision, not worth our notice;

or whether it is also something else, something more than idea, and if so, what. Thus much is certain, that this something we seek for must be completely and in its whole nature different from the idea; that the forms and laws of the idea must therefore be completely foreign to it; further, that we cannot arrive at it from the idea under the guidance of the laws which merely combine objects, ideas, among themselves, and which are the forms of the principle of sufficient reason.

Thus we see already that we can never arrive at the real nature of things from without. However much we investigate, we can never reach anything but images and names. We are like a man who goes round a castle seeking in vain for an entrance, and sometimes sketching the façades. And yet this is the method that has been followed by all philosophers before me.

§ 18. In fact, the meaning for which we seek of that world which is present to us only as our idea, or the transition from the world as mere idea of the knowing subject to whatever it may be besides this, would never be found if the investigator himself were nothing more than the pure knowing subject (a winged cherub without a body). But he is himself rooted in that world; he finds himself in it as an *individual*, that is to say, his knowledge, which is the necessary supporter of the whole world as idea, is yet always given through the medium of a body, whose affections are, as we have shown, the starting-point for the understanding in the perception of that world. His body is, for the pure knowing subject, an idea like every other idea, an object among objects. Its movements and actions are so far known to him in precisely the same way as the changes of all other perceived objects, and would be just as strange and incomprehensible to him if their meaning were not explained for him in an entirely dif-

ferent way. Otherwise he would see his actions follow
upon given motives with the constancy of a law of nature, just as the changes of other objects follow upon
causes, stimuli, or motives. But he would not understand
the influence of the motives any more than the connection between every other effect which he sees and its
cause. He would then call the inner nature of these
manifestations and actions of his body which he did
not understand a force, a quality, or a character, as he
pleased, but he would have no further insight into it.
But all this is not the case; indeed the answer to the
riddle is given to the subject of knowledge who appears
as an individual, and the answer is *will*. This and this
alone gives him the key to his own existence, reveals
to him the significance, shows him the inner mechanism
of his being, of his action, of his movements. The body
is given in two entirely different ways to the subject of
knowledge, who becomes an individual only through his
identity with it. It is given as an idea in intelligent
perception, as an object among objects and subject to
the laws of objects. And it is also given in quite a different way as that which is immediately known to every
one, and is signified by the word *will*. Every true act
of his will is also at once and without exception a movement of his body. The act of will and the movement of
the body are not two different things objectively known,
which the bond of causality unites; they do not stand
in the relation of cause and effect; they are one and
the same, but they are given in entirely different ways,—
immediately, and again in perception for the understanding. The action of the body is nothing but the act
of the will objectified, *i. e.*, passed into perception. It
will appear later that this is true of every movement
of the body, not merely those which follow upon motives, but also involuntary movements which follow

upon mere stimuli, and, indeed, that the whole body is nothing but objectified will, *i. e.,* will become idea. All this will be proved and made quite clear in the course of this work. In one respect, therefore, I shall call the body the *objectivity of will;* as in the previous book, and in the essay on the principle of sufficient reason, in accordance with the one-sided point of view intentionally adopted there (that of the idea), I called it *the immediate object.* Thus in a certain sense we may also say that will is the knowledge *a priori* of the body, and the body is the knowledge *a posteriori* of the will. Resolutions of the will which relate to the future are merely deliberations of the reason about what we shall will at a particular time, not real acts of will. Only the carrying out of the resolve stamps it as will, for till then it is never more than an intention that may be changed, and that exists only in the reason *in abstracto.* It is only in reflection that to will and to act are different; in reality they are one. Every true, genuine, immediate act of will is also, at once and immediately, a visible act of the body. And, corresponding to this, every impression upon the body is also, on the other hand, at once and immediately an impression upon the will. As such it is called pain when it is opposed to the will; gratification or pleasure when it is in accordance with it. The degrees of both are widely different. It is quite wrong, however, to call pain and pleasure ideas, for they are by no means ideas, but immediate affections of the will in its manifestation, the body; compulsory, instantaneous willing or not-willing of the impression which the body sustains. There are only a few impressions of the body which do not touch the will, and it is through these alone that the body is an immediate object of knowledge, for, as perceived by the understanding, it is already an indirect object like all others. These impressions are, therefore, to be treated directly as mere ideas, and excepted from what has been said. The impressions we refer to are the affections of the purely objective senses of sight, hearing, and touch, though only so far as these organs are affected in the way which is specially peculiar to their specific nature. This affection of them is so excessively weak an excitement of the heightened and specifically modified sensibility of these parts that it does not affect the will, but only furnishes the understanding with the data out of which the perception arises, undisturbed by any excitement of the will. But every stronger or different kind of affection of these organs of sense is painful, that is to say, against the will, and thus they also belong to its objectivity. Weakness of the nerves shows itself in this, that the impressions which have only such a degree of strength as would usually be sufficient to make them data for the understanding reach the higher degree at which they influence the will, that is to say, give pain or pleasure, though more often pain, which is, however, to some extent deadened and inarticulate, so that not only particular tones and strong light are painful to us, but there ensues a generally unhealthy and hypochondriacal disposition which is not distinctly understood. The identity of the body and the will shows itself further, among other ways, in the circumstance that every vehement and excessive movement of the will, *i. e.*, every emotion, agitates the body and its inner constitution directly, and disturbs the course of its vital functions.

Lastly, the knowledge which I have of my will, though it is immediate, cannot be separated from that which I have of my body. I know my will, not as a whole, not as a unity, not completely, according to its nature, but I know it only in its particular acts, and therefore in time, which is the form of the phenomenal aspect of my body, as of every object. Therefore the body is a condition of the knowledge of my will. Thus, I cannot really imagine this will apart from my body. In the essay on the principle of sufficient reason, the will, or rather the subject of willing, is treated as a special class of ideas or objects. But even there we saw this object become one with the subject; that is, we saw it cease to be an object. We there called this union the miracle *par excellence,* and the whole of the present work is to a certain extent an explanation of this. So far as I know my will specially as object, I know it as body. But then I am again at the first class of ideas laid down in that essay, *i. e.,* real objects. As we proceed we shall see always more clearly that these ideas of the first class obtain their explanation and solution from those of the fourth class given in the essay, which could no longer be properly opposed to the subject as object, and that, therefore, we must learn to understand the inner nature of the law of causality which is valid in the first class, and of all that happens in accordance with it from the law of motivation which governs the fourth class.

The identity of the will and the body, of which we have now given a cursory explanation, can only be proved in the manner we have adopted here. We have proved this identity for the first time, and shall do so more and more fully in the course of this work. By "proved" we mean raised from the immediate consciousness, from knowledge in the concrete to abstract knowledge of the reason, or carried over into abstract knowledge. On the other hand, from its very nature it can never be demonstrated, that is, deduced as indirect knowledge from some other more direct knowledge, just because it is itself the most direct knowledge; and if we do not apprehend it and stick to it as such, we shall

expect in vain to receive it again in some indirect way
as derivative knowledge. It is knowledge of quite a
special kind, whose truth cannot therefore properly be
brought under any of the four rubrics under which
I have classified all truth in the essay on the principle
of sufficient reason, § 29, the logical, the empirical, the
metaphysical, and the metalogical, for it is not, like all
these, the relation of an abstract idea to another idea,
or to the necessary form of perceptive or of abstract
ideation, but it is the relation of a judgment to the
connection which an idea of perception, the body, has
to that which is not an idea at all, but something *toto
genere* different, will. I should like therefore to distinguish this from all other truth, and call it *par excellence philosophical truth*. We can turn the expression
of this truth in different ways and say: My body and
my will are one;—or, What as an idea of perception
I call my body, I call my will, so far as I am conscious
of it in an entirely different way which cannot be compared to any other;—or, My body is the *objectivity*
of my will;—or, My body considered apart from the
fact that it is my idea is still my will, and so forth.

§ 19. In the first book we were reluctantly driven to
explain the human body as merely idea of the subject
which knows it, like all the other objects of this world
of perception. But it has now become clear that what
enables us consciously to distinguish our own body from
all other objects which in other respects are precisely
the same, is that our body appears in consciousness in
quite another way *toto genere* different from idea, and
this we denote by the world *will;* and that it is just this
double knowledge which we have of our own body
that affords us information about it, about its action and
movement following on motives, and also about what
it experiences by means of external impressions; in a

word, about what it is, not as idea, but as more than idea; that is to say, what it is *in itself.* None of this information have we got directly with regard to the nature, action, and experience of other real objects.

It is just because of this special relation to one body that the knowing subject is an individual. For regarded apart from this relation, his body is for him only an idea like all other ideas. But the relation through which the knowing subject is an *individual,* is just on that account a relation which subsists only between him and one particular idea of all those which he has. Therefore he is conscious of this one idea, not merely as an idea, but in quite a different way as a will. If, however, he abstracts from that special relation, from that twofold and completely heterogeneous knowledge of what is one and the same, then that *one,* the body, is an idea like all other ideas. Therefore, in order to understand the matter, the individual who knows must either assume that what distinguishes that one idea from others is merely the fact that his knowledge stands in this double relation to it alone; that insight in two ways at the same time is open to him only in the case of this one object of perception, and that this is to be explained not by the difference of this object from all others, but only by the difference between the relation of his knowledge to this one object, and its relation to all other objects. Or else he must assume that this object is essentially different from all others; that it alone of all objects is at once both will and idea, while the rest are only ideas, *i. e.,* only phantoms. Thus he must assume that his body is the only real individual in the world, *i. e.,* the only phenomenon of will and the only immediate object of the subject. That other objects, considered merely as *ideas,* are like his body, that is, like it, fill space (which itself can only be present as idea), and also, like it, are

causally active in space, is indeed demonstrably certain
from the law of causality which is *a priori* valid for
ideas, and which admits of no effect without a cause;
but apart from the fact that we can only reason from
an effect to a cause generally, and not to a similar cause,
we are still in the sphere of mere ideas, in which alone
the law of causality is valid, and beyond which it can
never take us. But whether the objects known to the
individual only as ideas are yet, like his own body,
manifestations of a will, is, as was said in the First
Book, the proper meaning of the question as to the
reality of the external world. To deny this is *theoretical
egoism,* which on that account regards all phenomena
that are outside its own will as phantoms, just as in
a practical reference exactly the same thing is done by
practical egoism. For in it a man regards and treats
himself alone as a person, and all other persons as mere
phantoms. Theoretical egoism can never be demonstrably refuted, yet in philosophy it has never been used
otherwise than as a sceptical sophism, *i. e.,* a pretence.
As a serious conviction, on the other hand, it could only
be found in a madhouse, and as such it stands in need
of a cure rather than a refutation. We do not therefore
combat it any further in this regard, but treat it as
merely the last stronghold of scepticism, which is always
polemical. Thus our knowledge, which is always bound
to individuality and is limited by this circumstance,
brings with it the necessity that each of us can only *be
one,* while, on the other hand, each of us can *know all;*
and it is this limitation that creates the need for philosophy. We therefore who, for this very reason, are
striving to extend the limits of our knowledge through
philosophy, will treat this sceptical argument of theoretical egoism which meets us, as an army would treat
a small frontier fortress. The fortress cannot indeed be

taken, but the garrison can never sally forth from it, and therefore we pass it by without danger, and are not afraid to have it in our rear.

The double knowledge which each of us has of the nature and activity of his own body, and which is given in two completely different ways, has now been clearly brought out. We shall accordingly make further use of it as a key to the nature of every phenomenon in nature, and shall judge of all objects which are not our own bodies, and are consequently not given to our consciousness in a double way but only as ideas, according to the analogy of our own bodies, and shall therefore assume that as in one aspect they are idea, just like our bodies, and in this respect are analogous to them, so in another aspect, what remains of objects when we set aside their existence as idea of the subject must in its inner nature be the same as that in us which we call *will*. For what other kind of existence or reality should we attribute to the rest of the material world? Whence should we take the elements out of which we construct such a world? Besides will and idea nothing is known to us or thinkable. If we wish to attribute the greatest known reality to the material world which exists immediately only in our idea, we give it the reality which our own body has for each of us; for that is the most real thing for every one. But if we now analyse the reality of this body and its actions, beyond the fact that it is idea, we find nothing in it except the will; with this its reality is exhausted. Therefore we can nowhere find another kind of reality which we can attribute to the material world. Thus if we hold that the material world is something more than merely our idea, we must say that besides being idea, that is, in itself and according to its inmost nature, it is that which we find immediately in ourselves as *will*. I say according to its inmost nature; but we must first come to know more accurately this real nature of the will, in order that we may be able to distinguish from it what does not belong to itself, but to its manifestation, which has many grades. Such, for example, is the circumstance of its being accompanied by knowledge, and the determination by motives which is conditioned by this knowledge. As we shall see farther on, this does not belong to the real nature of will, but merely to its distinct manifestation as an animal or a human being. If, therefore, I say,—the force which attracts a stone to the earth is according to its nature, in itself, and apart from all idea, will, I shall not be supposed to express in this proposition the insane opinion that the stone moves itself in accordance with a known motive, merely because this is the way in which will appears in man. We shall now proceed more clearly and in detail to prove, establish, and develop to its full extent what as yet has only been provisionally and generally explained.

§ 20. As we have said, the will proclaims itself primarily in the voluntary movements of our own body, as the inmost nature of this body, as that which it is besides being object of perception, idea. For these voluntary movements are nothing else than the visible aspect of the individual acts of will, with which they are directly coincident and identical, and only distinguished through the form of knowledge into which they have passed, and in which alone they can be known, the form of idea.

But these acts of will have always a ground or reason outside themselves in motives. Yet these motives never determine more than what I will at *this* time, in *this* place, and under *these* circumstances, not *that* I will in general, or *what* I will in general, that is, the maxims which characterise my volition generally. Therefore the inner nature of my volition cannot be explained from these motives; but they merely determine its manifestation at a given point of time: they are merely the occasion of my will showing itself; but the will itself lies outside the province of the law of motivation, which determines nothing but its appearance at each point of time. It is only under the presupposition of my empirical character that the motive is a sufficient ground of explanation of my action. But if I abstract from my character, and then ask, why, in general, I will this and not that, no answer is possible, because it is only the manifestation of the will that is subject to the principle of sufficient reason, and not the will itself, which in this respect is to be called *groundless*.

If now every action of my body is the manifestation of an act of will in which my will itself in general, and as a whole, thus my character, expresses itself under given motives, manifestation of the will must be the inevitable condition and presupposition of every action. For the fact of its manifestation cannot depend upon something which does not exist directly and only through it, which consequently is for it merely accidental, and through which its manifestation itself would be merely accidental. Now that condition is just the whole body itself. Thus the body itself must be manifestation of the will, and it must be related to my will as a whole, that is, to my intelligible character, whose phenomenal appearance in time is my empirical character, as the particular action of the body is related to the particular act of the will. The whole body, then, must be simply my will become visible, must be my will itself, so far as this is object of perception, an idea of the first class. It has already been advanced in confirmation of this that every impression upon my body also affects my will at once and immediately, and in this respect is called pain or pleasure, or, in its lower degrees, agreeable or disagreeable sensation; and also, conversely, that every violent movement of the will, every emotion or passion, convulses the body and disturbs the course of its functions. Indeed we can also give an etiological account, though a very incomplete one, of the origin of my body, and a somewhat better account of its development and conservation, and this is the substance of physiology. But physiology merely explains its theme in precisely the same way as motives explain action. Thus the physiological explanation of the functions of the body detracts just as little from the philosophical truth that the whole existence of this body and the sum total of its functions are merely the objectification of that will which appears in its outward actions in accordance with a motive, as the establishment of the individual action through the motive and the necessary sequence of the action from the motive conflicts with the fact that action in general, and according to its nature, is only the manifestation of a will which itself has no ground. If, however, physiology tries to refer even these outward actions, the immediate voluntary movements, to causes in the organism,—for example, if it explains the movement of the muscles as resulting from the presence of fluids, even supposing it really could give a thorough explanation of this kind, yet this would never invalidate the immediately certain truth that every voluntary motion is the manifestation of an act of will. Now, just as little can the physiological explanation of vegetative life, however far it may advance, ever invalidate the truth that the whole animal life which thus develops itself is the manifestation of will. In general, then, as we have shown above, no etiological explanation can ever give us more than the necessarily determined position in time and space of a particular manifestation, its necessary appearance there, according to a fixed law;

but the inner nature of everything that appears in this way remains wholly inexplicable, and is presupposed by every etiological explanation, and merely indicated by the names, force, or law of nature, or, if we are speaking of action, character or will. Thus, although every particular action, under the presupposition of the definite character, necessarily follows from the given motive, and although growth, the process of nourishment, and all the changes of the animal body take place according to necessarily acting causes (stimuli), yet the whole series of actions, and consequently every individual act, and also its condition, the whole body itself which accomplishes it, and therefore also the process through which and in which it exists, are nothing but the manifestation of the will, the becoming visible, *the objectification of the will.* Upon this rests the perfect suitableness of the human and animal body to the human and animal will in general, resembling, though far surpassing, the correspondence between an instrument made for a purpose and the will of the maker, and on this account appearing as design, *i. e.,* the teleological explanation of the body. The parts of the body must, therefore, completely correspond to the principal desires through which the will manifests itself; they must be the visible expression of these desires. Teeth, throat, and bowels are objectified hunger; the organs of generation are objectified sexual desire; the grasping hand, the hurrying feet, correspond to the more indirect desires of the will which they express. As the human form generally corresponds to the human will generally, so the individual bodily structure corresponds to the individually modified will, the character of the individual, and therefore it is throughout and in all its parts characteristic and full of expression.

§ 21. Whoever has now gained from all these expositions a knowledge *in abstracto,* and therefore clear and certain, of what every one knows directly *in concreto,* *i. e.,* as feeling, a knowledge that his will is the real inner nature of his phenomenal being, which manifests itself to him as idea, both in his actions and in their permanent substratum, his body, and that his will is that which is most immediate in his consciousness, though it has not as such completely passed into the form of idea in which object and subject stand over against each other, but makes itself known to him in a direct manner, in which he does not quite clearly distinguish subject and object, yet is not known as a whole to the individual himself, but only in its particular acts, —whoever, I say, has with me gained this conviction will find that of itself it affords him the key to the knowledge of the inmost being of the whole of nature; for he now transfers it to all those phenomena which are not given to him, like his own phenomenal existence, both in direct and indirect knowledge, but only in the latter, thus merely one-sidedly as *idea* alone. He will recognise this will of which we are speaking not only in those phenomenal existences which exactly resemble his own, in men and animals as their inmost nature, but the course of reflection will lead him to recognise the force which germinates and vegetates in the plant, and indeed the force through which the crystal is formed, that by which the magnet turns to the north pole, the force whose shock he experiences from the contact of two different kinds of metals, the force which appears in the elective affinites of matter as repulsion and attraction, decomposition and combination, and, lastly, even gravitation, which acts so powerfully throughout matter, draws the stone to the earth and the earth to the sun, —all these, I say, he will recognise as different only in their phenomenal existence, but in their inner nature as identical, as that which is directly known to him so

intimately and so much better than anything else, and
which in its most distinct manifestation is called *will*.
It is this application of reflection alone that prevents us
from remaining any longer at the phenomenon, and
leads us to the *thing in itself*. Phenomenal existence is
idea and nothing more. All idea, of whatever kind it may
be, all *object*, is *phenomenal* existence, but the *will*
alone is a *thing in itself*. As such, it is throughout not
idea, but *toto genere* different from it; it is that of
which all idea, all object, is the phenomenal appearance, the visibility, the objectification. It is the inmost
nature, the kernel, of every particular thing, and also
of the whole. It appears in every blind force of nature
and also in the preconsidered action of man; and the
great difference between these two is merely in the
degree of the manifestation, not in the nature of what
manifests itself.

§ 22. Now, if we are to think as an object this thing-
in-itself (we wish to retain the Kantian expression as
a standing formula), which, as such, is never object,
because all object is its mere manifestation, and therefore cannot be it itself, we must borrow for it the name
and concept of an object, of something in some way
objectively given, consequently of one of its own manifestations. But in order to serve as a clue for the
understanding, this can be no other than the most complete of all its manifestations, *i. e.*, the most distinct,
the most developed, and directly enlightened by knowledge. Now this is the human will. It is, however, well to
observe that here, at any rate, we only make use of a
denominatio a potiori, through which, therefore, the
concept of will receives a greater extension than it has
hitherto had. Knowledge of the identical in different
phenomena, and of difference in similar phenomena, is,
as Plato so often remarks, a *sine qua non* of philosophy.

But hitherto it was not recognised that every kind of active and operating force in nature is essentially identical with will, and therefore the multifarious kinds of phenomena were not seen to be merely different species of the same genus, but were treated as heterogeneous. Consequently there could be no word to denote the concept of this genus. I therefore name the genus after its most important species, the direct knowledge of which lies nearer to us and guides us to the indirect knowledge of all other species. But whoever is incapable of carrying out the required extension of the concept will remain involved in a permanent misunderstanding. For by the word *will* he understands only that species of it which has hitherto been exclusively denoted by it, the will which is guided by knowledge, and whose manifestation follows only upon motives, and indeed merely abstract motives, and thus takes place under the guidance of the reason. This, we have said, is only the most prominent example of the manifestation of will. We must now distinctly separate in thought the inmost essence of this manifestation which is known to us directly, and then transfer it to all the weaker, less distinct manifestations of the same nature, and thus we shall accomplish the desired extension of the concept of will. From another point of view I should be equally misunderstood by any one who should think that it is all the same in the end whether we denote this inner nature of all phenomena by the word *will* or by any other. This would be the case if the thing-in-itself were something whose existence we merely *inferred,* and thus knew indirectly and only in the abstract. Then, indeed, we might call it what we pleased; the name would stand merely as the symbol of an unknown quantity. But the word *will,* which, like a magic spell, discloses to us the inmost being of everything in nature, is by no means an

unknown quantity, something arrived at only by inference, but is fully and immediately comprehended, and is
so familiar to us that we know and understand what will
is far better than anything else whatever. The concept
of will has hitherto commonly been subordinated to that
of force, but I reverse the matter entirely, and desire
that every force in nature should be thought as will. It
must not be supposed that this is mere verbal quibbling
or of no consequence; rather, it is of the greatest significance and importance. For at the foundation of the
concept of force, as of all other concepts, there ultimately lies the knowledge in sense-perception of the
objective world, that is to say, the phenomenon, the
idea; and the concept is constructed out of this. It is
an abstraction from the province in which cause and
effect reign, *i. e.*, from ideas of perception, and means
just the causal nature of causes at the point at which
this causal nature is no further etiologically explicable,
but is the necessary presupposition of all etiological
explanation. The concept will, on the other hand, is of
all possible concepts the only one which has its source
not in the phenomenal, *not* in the mere idea of perception, but comes from within, and proceeds from the most
immediate consciousness of each of us, in which each of
us knows his own individuality, according to its nature,
immediately, apart from all form, even that of subject
and object, and which at the same time is this individuality, for here the subject and the object of knowledge
are one. If, therefore, we refer the concept of *force*
to that of *will*, we have in fact referred the less known
to what is infinitely better known; indeed, to the one
thing that is really immediately and fully known to us,
and have very greatly extended our knowledge. If, on
the contrary, we subsume the concept of will under that
of force, as has hitherto always been done, we renounce

the only immediate knowledge which we have of the inner nature of the world, for we allow it to disappear in a concept which is abstracted from the phenomenal, and with which we can therefore never go beyond the phenomenal.

§ 26. The lowest grades of the objectification of will are to be found in those most universal forces of nature which partly appear in all matter without exception, as gravity and impenetrability, and partly have shared the given matter among them, so that certain of them reign in one species of matter and others in another species, constituting its specific difference, as rigidity, fluidity, elasticity, electricity, magnetism, chemical properties and qualities of every kind. They are in themselves immediate manifestations of will, just as much as human action; and as such they are groundless, like human character. Only their particular manifestations are subordinated to the principle of sufficient reason, like the particular actions of men. They themselves, on the other hand, can never be called either effect or cause, but are the prior and presupposed conditions of all causes and effects through which their real nature unfolds and reveals itself. It is therefore senseless to demand a cause of gravity or electricity, for they are original forces. Their expressions, indeed, take place in accordance with the law of cause and effect, so that every one of their particular manifestations has a cause, which is itself again just a similar particular manifestation which determines that this force must express itself here, must appear in space and time; but the force itself is by no means the effect of a cause, nor the cause of an effect. It is therefore a mistake to say "gravity is the cause of a stone falling;" for the cause in this case is rather the nearness of the earth, because it attracts the stone. Take the earth away and the stone will not fall, al-

though gravity remains. The force itself lies quite outside the chain of causes and effects, which presupposes
time, because it only has meaning in relation to it; but
the force lies outside time. The individual change always
has for its cause another change just as individual as
itself, and not the force of which it is the expression.
For that which always gives its efficiency to a cause,
however many times it may appear, is a force of nature.
As such, it is groundless, i. e., it lies outside the chain
of causes and outside the province of the principle of
sufficient reason in general, and is philosophically known
as the immediate objectivity of will, which is the "in-
itself" of the whole of nature; but in etiology, which
in this reference is physics, it is set down as an original
force, i. e., a *qualitas occulta*.

In the higher grades of the objectivity of will we see
individuality occupy a prominent position, especially in
the case of man, where it appears as the great difference
of individual characters, i. e., as complete personality,
outwardly expressed in strongly marked individual
physiognomy, which influences the whole bodily form.
None of the brutes have this individuality in anything
like so high a degree, though the highest species of them
have a trace of it; but the character of the species completely predominates over it, and therefore they have
little individual physiognomy. The farther down we go,
the more completely is every trace of the individual
character lost in the common character of the species,
and the physiognomy of the species alone remains. We
know the physiological character of the species, and
from that we know exactly what is to be expected from
the individual; while, on the contrary, in the human
species every individual has to be studied and fathomed
for himself, which, if we wish to forecast his action with
some degree of certainty, is, on account of the possibility

of concealment that first appears with reason, a matter
of the greatest difficulty. It is probably connected with
this difference of the human species from all others, that
the folds and convolutions of the brain, which are entirely wanting in birds, and very weakly marked in
rodents, are even in the case of the higher animals far
more symmetrical on both sides, and more constantly
the same in each individual, than in the case of human
beings. It is further to be regarded as a phenomenon
of this peculiar individual character which distinguishes
men from all the lower animals, that in the case of the
brutes the sexual instinct seeks its satisfaction without
observable choice of objects, while in the case of man
this choice is, in a purely instinctive manner and independent of all reflection, carried so far that it rises
into a powerful passion. While then every man is to be
regarded as a specially determined and characterised
phenomenon of will, and indeed to a certain extent as
a special Idea, in the case of the brutes this individual
character as a whole is wanting, because only the species
has a special significance. And the farther we go from
man, the fainter becomes the trace of this individual
character, so that plants have no individual qualities
left, except such as may be fully explained from the
favourable or unfavourable external influences of soil,
climate, and other accidents. Finally, in the inorganic
kingdom of nature all individuality disappears. The
crystal alone is to be regarded as to a certain extent
individual. It is a unity of the tendency in definite directions, fixed by crystallisation, which makes the trace
of this tendency permanent. It is at the same time a
cumulative repetition of its primitive form, bound into
unity by an idea, just as the tree is an aggregate of
the single germinating fibre which shows itself in every
rib of the leaves, in every leaf, in every branch; which

repeats itself, and to some extent makes each of these appear as a separate growth, nourishing itself from the greater as a parasite, so that the tree, resembling the crystal, is a systematic aggregate of small plants, although only the whole is the complete expression of an individual Idea, *i. e.*, of this particular grade of the objectification of will. But the individuals of the same species of crystal can have no other difference than such as is produced by external accidents; indeed we can make at pleasure large or small crystals of every species. The individual, however, as such, that is, with traces of an individual character, does not exist further in unorganised nature. All its phenomena are expressions of general forces of nature, *i. e.*, of those grades of the objectification of will which do not objectify themselves (as is the case in organised nature), by means of the difference of the individualities which collectively express the whole of the Idea, but show themselves only in the species, and as a whole, without any variation in each particular example of it. Time, space, multiplicity, and existence conditioned by causes, do not belong to the will or to the Idea (the grade of the objectification of will), but only to their particular phenomena. Therefore such a force of nature as, for example, gravity or electricity, must show itself as such in precisely the same way in all its million phenomena, and only external circumstances can modify these. This unity of its being in all its phenomena, this unchangeable constancy of the appearance of these, whenever, under the guidance of causality, the necessary conditions are present, is called a *law of nature*. If such a law is once learned from experience, then the phenomenon of that force of nature, the character of which is expressed and laid down in it, may be accurately forecast and counted upon. But it is just this conformity to law of the phenomena of the lower grades of the objectification of will which gives them such a different aspect from the phenomena of the same will in the higher, *i. e.*, the more distinct, grades of its objectification, in animals, and in men and their actions, where the stronger or weaker influence of the individual character and the susceptibility to motives which often remain hidden from the spectator, because they lie in knowledge, has had the result that the identity of the inner nature of the two kinds of phenomena has hitherto been entirely overlooked.

If we start from the knowledge of the particular, and not from that of the Idea, there is something astonishing, and sometimes even terrible, in the absolute uniformity of the laws of nature. It might astonish us that nature never once forgets her laws; that if, for example, it has once been according to a law of nature that where certain materials are brought together under given conditions, a chemical combination will take place, or gas will be evolved, or they will go on fire; if these conditions are fulfilled, whether by our interposition or entirely by chance (and in this case the accuracy is the more astonishing because unexpected), to-day just as well as a thousand years ago, the determined phenomenon will take place at once and without delay. We are most vividly impressed with the marvellousness of this fact in the case of rare phenomena, which only occur under very complex circumstances, but which we are previously informed will take place if these conditions are fulfilled. For example, when we are told that if certain metals, when arranged alternately in fluid with which an acid has been mixed, are brought into contact, silver leaf brought between the extremities of this combination will suddenly be consumed in a green flame; or that under certain conditions the hard diamond turns into carbonic acid. It is the ghostly omnipresence

of natural forces that astonishes us in such cases, and
we remark here what in the case of phenomena which
happen daily no longer strikes us, how the connection
between cause and effect is really as mysterious as that
which is imagined between a magic formula and a spirit
that must appear when invoked by it. On the other
hand, if we have attained to the philosophical knowledge that a force of nature is a definite grade of the
objectification of will, that is to say, a definite grade
of that which we recognise as our own inmost nature,
and that this will, in itself, and distinguished from its
phenomena and their forms, lies outside time and space,
and that, therefore, the multiplicity, which is conditioned by time and space, does not belong to it, nor
directly to the grade of its objectification, *i. e.*, the
Idea, but only to the phenomena of the Idea; and if
we remember that the law of causality has significance
only in relation to time and space, inasmuch as it determines the position of the multitude of phenomena
of the different Ideas in which the will reveals itself,
governing the order in which they must appear; if, I
say, in this knowledge the inner meaning of the great
doctrine of Kant has been fully grasped, the doctrine
that time, space, and causality do not belong to the
thing-in-itself, but merely to the phenomenon, that they
are only the forms of our knowledge, not qualities of
things in themselves; then we shall understand that
this astonishment at the conformity to law and accurate
operation of a force of nature, this astonishment at the
complete sameness of all its million phenomena and the
infallibility of their occurrence, is really like that of a
child or a savage who looks for the first time through
a glass with many facets at a flower, and marvels at
the complete similarity of the innumerable flowers which
he sees, and counts the leaves of each of them sepa-
rately.

Thus every universal, original force of nature is nothing but a low grade of the objectification of will, and we call every such grade an eternal *Idea* in Plato's sense. But a *law of nature* is the relation of the Idea to the form of its manifestation. This form is time, space, and causality, which are necessarily and inseparably connected and related to each other. Through time and space the Idea multiplies itself in innumerable phenomena, but the order according to which it enters these forms of multiplicity is definitely determined by the law of causality; this law is as it were the norm of the limit of these phenomena of different Ideas, in accordance with which time, space, and matter are assigned to them. This norm is therefore necessarily related to the identity of the aggregate of existing matter, which is the common substratum of all those different phenomena. If all these were not directed to that common matter in the possession of which they must be divided, there would be no need for such a law to decide their claims. They might all at once and together fill a boundless space throughout an endless time. Therefore, because all these phenomena of the eternal Ideas are directed to one and the same matter, must there be a rule for their appearance and disappearance; for if there were not, they would not make way for each other. Thus the law of causality is essentially bound up with that of the permanence of substance; they reciprocally derive significance from each other. Time and space, again, are related to them in the same way. For time is merely the possibility of conflicting states of the same matter, and space is merely the possibility of the permanence of the same matter under all sorts of conflicting states. Accordingly, in the preceding book we explained matter as the union of space and time, and this union shows itself as change of the accidents in the permanence of the substance, of which causality or becoming is the universal possibility. And accordingly, we said that matter is through and through causality. We explained the understanding as the subjective correlative of causality, and said matter (and thus the whole world as idea) exists only for the understanding; the understanding is its condition, its supporters as its necessary correlative. I repeat all this in passing, merely to call to mind what was demonstrated in the First Book, for it is necessary for the complete understanding of these two books that their inner agreement should be observed, since what is inseparably united in the actual world as its two sides, will and idea, has, in order that we might understand each of them more clearly in isolation, been dissevered in these two books.

It may not perhaps be superfluous to elucidate further by an example how the law of causality has meaning only in relation to time and space, and the matter which consists in the union of the two. For it determines the limits in accordance with which the phenomena of the forces of nature divide themselves in the possession of matter, while the original forces of nature, as the immediate objectification of will, which, as a thing in itself, is not subordinated to the principle of sufficient reason, lie outside these forms, within which alone all etiological explanation has validity and meaning, and just on that account can never lead us to the inner reality of nature. For this purpose let us think of some kind of machine constructed according to the laws of mechanics. Iron weights begin the motion by their gravity; copper wheels resist by their rigidity, affect and raise each other and the lever by their impenetrability, and so on. Here gravity, rigidity, and impenetrability are original unexplained forces; mechanics only gives us the condition under which, and the manner in which, they manifest themselves, appear, and govern a definite matter, time, and place. If, now, a strong magnet is made to attract the iron of the weight, and overcome its gravity, the movement of the machine stops, and the matter becomes forthwith the scene of quite a different force of nature—magnetism, of which etiology again gives no further explanation than the condition under which it appears. Or let us suppose that the copper discs of such a machine are laid upon zinc plates, and an acid solution introduced between them. At once the same matter of the machine has become subject to another original force, galvanism, which now governs it according to its own laws, and reveals itself in it through its phenomena; and etiology can again tell us nothing about this force except the conditions under which, and the laws in accordance with which, it manifests itself. Let us now raise the temperature and add pure acid; the whole machine burns; that is to say, once more an entirely different force of nature, chemical energy, asserts at this time and in this place irresistible claims to this particular matter, and reveals itself in it as Idea, as a definite grade of the objectification of will. The calcined metal thus produced now unites with an acid, and a salt is obtained which forms itself into crystals. These are the phenomena of another Idea, which in itself is again quite inexplicable, while the appearance of its phenomena is dependent upon certain conditions which etiology can give us. The crystals dissolve, mix with other materials, and vegetation springs up from them—a new phenomenon of will: and so the same permanent matter may be followed *ad infinitum,* to observe how now this and now that natural force obtains a right to it and temporarily takes possession of it, in order to appear and reveal its own nature. The condition of this right, the point of time and space at which it becomes valid, is given by causality, but the explanation founded upon this law only extends thus far. The force itself is a manifestation of will, and as such is not subject to the forms of the principle of sufficient reason, that is, it is groundless. It lies outside all time, is omnipresent, and seems as it were to wait constantly till the circumstances occur under which it can appear and take possession of a definite matter, supplanting the forces which have reigned it in till then. All time exists only for the phenomena of such a force, and is without significance for the force itself. Through thousands of years chemical forces slumber in matter till the contact with the reagents sets them free; then they appear; but time exists only for the phenomena, not for the forces themselves. For thousands of years galvanism slumbered in copper and zinc, and they lay quietly beside silver, which must be consumed ·in flame as soon as all three are brought together under the required conditions. Even in the organic kingdom we see a dry seed preserve the slumbering force through three thousand years, and when at last the favourable circumstances occur, grow up as a plant.

If by this exposition the difference between a force of nature and all its phenomena has been made quite distinct; if we have seen clearly that the former is the will itself at this particular grade of its objectification, but that multiplicity comes to phenomena only through time and space, and that the law of causality is nothing but the determination of the position of these phenomena in time and space; then we shall recognise the complete truth and the deep meaning of Malebranche's doctrine of occasional causes (*causes occasionelles*).

Malebranche is right: every natural cause is only an

occasional cause. It only gives opportunity or occasion for the manifestation of the one indivisible will which is the "in-itself" of all things, and whose graduated objectification is the whole visible world. Only the appearance, the becoming visible, in this place, at this time, is brought about by the cause and is so far dependent on it, but not the whole of the phenomenon, nor its inner nature. This is the will itself, to which the principle of sufficient reason has not application, and which is therefore groundless. Nothing in the world has a sufficient cause of its existence generally, but only a cause of existence just here and just now. That a stone exhibits now gravity, now rigidity, now electricity, now chemical qualities, depends upon causes, upon impressions upon it from without, and is to be explained from these. But these qualities themselves, and thus the whole inner nature of the stone which consists in them, and therefore manifests itself in all the ways referred to; thus, in general, that the stone is such as it is, that it exists generally—all this, I say, has no ground, but is the visible appearance of the groundless will. Every cause is thus an occasional cause. We have found it to be so in nature, which is without knowledge, and it is also precisely the same when motives and not causes or stimuli determine the point at which the phenomena are to appear, that is to say, in the actions of animals and human beings. For in both cases it is one and the same will which appears; very different in the grades of its manifestation, multiplied in the phenomena of these grades, and, in respect of these, subordinated to the principle of sufficient reason, but in itself free from all this. Motives do not determine the character of man, but only the phenomena of his character, that is, his actions; the outward fashion of his life, not its inner meaning and content. These proceed from the character which is the immediate manifestation of the will, and is therefore groundless. That one man is bad and another good, does not depend upon motives or outward influences, such as teaching and preaching, and is in this sense quite inexplicable. But whether a bad man shows his badness in petty acts of injustice, cowardly tricks, and low knavery which he practises in the narrow sphere of his circumstances, or whether as a conqueror he oppresses nations, throws a world into lamentation, and sheds the blood of millions; this is the outward form of his manifestation, that which is unessential to it, and depends upon the circumstances in which fate has placed him, upon his surroundings, upon external influences, upon motives; but his decision upon these motives can never be explained from them; it proceeds from the will, of which this man is a manifestation. Of this we shall speak in the Fourth Book. The manner in which the character discloses its qualities is quite analogous to the way in which those of every material body in unconscious nature are disclosed. Water remains water with its intrinsic qualities, whether as a still lake it reflects its banks, or leaps in foam from the cliffs, or, artificially confined, spouts in a long jet into the air. All that depends upon external causes; the one form is as natural to it as the other, but it will always show the same form in the same circumstances; it is equally ready for any, but in every case true to its character, and at all times revealing this alone. So will every human character under all circumstances reveal itself, but the phenomena which proceed from it will always be in accordance with the circumstances.

§ 27. I wish it had been possible for me to dispel by clearness of explanation the obscurity which clings to the subject of these thoughts; but I see very well that the reader's own consideration of the matter must ma-

terially aid me if I am not to remain uncomprehended
or misunderstood. According to the view I have expressed, the traces of chemical and physical modes of
operation will indeed be found in the organism, but it
can never be explained from them; because it is by no
means a phenomenon even accidentally brought about
through the united actions of such forces, but a higher
Idea which has overcome these lower ideas by *sub-
duing assimilation;* for the *one* will which objectifies
itself in all Ideas always seeks the highest possible objectification, and has therefore in this case given up
the lower grades of its manifestation after a conflict,
in order to appear in a higher grade, and one so much
the more powerful. No victory without conflict: since
the higher Idea or objectification of will can only appear
through the conquest of the lower, it endures the opposition of these lower Ideas, which, although brought into
subjection, still constantly strive to obtain an independent and complete expression of their being. The
magnet that has attracted a piece of iron carries on a
perpetual conflict with gravitation, which, as the lower
objectification of will, has a prior right to the matter of
the iron; and in this constant battle the magnet indeed
grows stronger, for the opposition excites it, as it were,
to greater effort. In the same way every manifestation
of the will, including that which expresses itself in the
human organism, wages a constant war against the
many physical and chemical forces which, as lower
Ideas, have a prior right to that matter. Thus the arm
falls which for a while, overcoming gravity, we have
held stretched out; thus the pleasing sensation of health,
which proclaims the victory of the Idea of the self-conscious organism over the physical and chemical laws,
which originally governed the humours of the body, is
so often interrupted, and is indeed always accompanied

by greater or less discomfort, which arises from the resistance of these forces, and on account of which the
vegetative part of our life is constantly attended by
slight pain. Thus also digestion weakens all the animal
functions, because it requires the whole vital force to
overcome the chemical forces of nature by assimilation.
Hence also in general the burden of physical life, the
necessity of sleep, and, finally, of death; for at last
these subdued forces of nature, assisted by circumstances, win back from the organism, wearied even by
the constant victory, the matter it took from them, and
attain to an unimpeded expression of their being. We
may therefore say that every organism expresses the
Idea of which it is the image, only after we have sub-
tracted the part of its force which is expended in sub-
duing the lower Ideas that strive with it for matter.
This seems to have been running in the mind of Jacob
Böhm when he says somewhere that all the bodies of
men and animals, and even all plants, are really half
dead. According as the subjection in the organism of
these forces of nature, which express the lower grades
of the objectification of will, is more or less successful,
the more or the less completely does it attain to the expression of its Idea; that is to say, the nearer it is to
the *ideal* or the further from it—the *ideal* of beauty in
its species.

Thus everywhere in nature we see strife, conflict, and
alternation of victory, and in it we shall come to recognise more distinctly that variance with itself which is
essential to the will. Every grade of the objectification
of will fights for the matter, the space, and the time of
the others. The permanent matter must constantly change
its form; for under the guidance of causality, mechanical, physical, chemical, and organic phenomena, eagerly
striving to appear, wrest the matter from each other,

for each desires to reveal its own Idea. This strife may
be followed through the whole of nature; indeed nature
exists only through it. Yet this strife itself is only the
revelation of that variance with itself which is essential
to the will. This universal conflict becomes most distinctly visible in the animal kingdom. For animals have
the whole of the vegetable kingdom for their food, and
even within the animal kingdom every beast is the prey
and the food of another; that is, the matter in which its
Idea expresses itself must yield itself to the expression of another Idea, for each animal can only maintain its existence by the constant destruction of some
other. Thus the will to live everywhere preys upon itself,
and in different forms is its own nourishment, till finally
the human race, because it subdues all the others, regards nature as a manufactory for its use. Yet even the
human race, as we shall see in the Fourth Book, reveals
in itself with most terrible distinctness this conflict, this
variance with itself of the will. Meanwhile we can recognise this strife, this subjugation, just as well in the
lower grades of the objectification of will. Many insects (especially ichneumon-flies) lay their eggs on the
skin, and even in the body of the larvæ of other insects,
whose slow destruction is the first work of the newly
hatched brood. The young hydra, which grows like a
bud out of the old one, and afterwards separates itself
from it, fights while it is still joined to the old one for
the prey that offers itself, so that the one snatches it out
of the mouth of the other. But the bulldog-ant of Aus-
tralia affords us the most extraordinary example of this
kind; for if it is cut in two, a battle begins between the
head and the tail. The head seizes the tail with its
teeth, and the tail defends itself bravely by stinging the
head: the battle may last for half an hour, until they
die or are dragged away by other ants. This contest

takes place every time the experiment is tried. On the banks of the Missouri one sometimes sees a mighty oak the stem and branches of which are so encircled, fettered, and interlaced by a gigantic wild vine, that it withers as if choked. The same thing shows itself in the lowest grades; for example, when water and carbon are changed into vegetable sap, or vegetables or bread into blood by organic assimilation; and so also in every case in which animal secretion takes place, along with the restriction of chemical forces to a subordinate mode of activity. This also occurs in unorganised nature, when, for example, crystals in process of formation meet, cross, and mutually disturb each other to such an extent that they are unable to assume the pure crystalline form, so that almost every cluster of crystals is an image of such a conflict of will at this low grade of its objectification; or again, when a magnet forces its magnetism upon iron, in order to express its Idea in it; or when galvanism overcomes chemical affinity, decomposes the closest combinations, and so entirely suspends the laws of chemistry that the acid of a decomposed salt at the negative pole must pass to the positive pole without combining with the alkalies through which it goes on its way, or turning red the litmus paper that touches it. On a large scale it shows itself in the relation between the central body and the planet, for although the planet is in absolute dependence, yet it always resists, just like the chemical forces in the organism; hence arises the constant tension between centripetal and centrifugal force, which keeps the globe in motion, and is itself an example of that universal essential conflict of the manifestation of will which we are considering. For as every body must be regarded as the manifestation of a will, and as will necessarily ·expresses itself as a struggle, the original condition of every world that is formed into a globe cannot

be rest, but motion, a striving forward in boundless space
without rest and without end. Neither the law of inertia
nor that of causality is opposed to this: for as, according to the former, matter as such is alike indifferent to
rest and motion, its original condition may just as well
be the one as the other, therefore if we first find it in
motion, we have just as little right to assume that this
was preceded by a condition of rest, and to inquire into
the cause of the origin of the motion, as, conversely,
if we found it at rest, we would have to assume a previous motion and inquire into the cause of its suspension.
It is, therefore, not needful to seek for a first impulse
for centrifugal force, for, according to the hypothesis
of Kant and Laplace, it is, in the case of the planets,
the residue of the original rotation of the central body,
from which the planets have separated themselves as it
contracted. But to this central body itself motion is
essential; it always continues its rotation, and at the
same time rushes forward in endless space, or perhaps
circulates round a greater central body invisible to us.
This view entirely agrees with the conjecture of astron-
omers that there is a central sun, and also with the
observed advance of our whole solar system, and perhaps of the whole stellar system to which our sun belongs. From this we are finally led to assume a general
advance of fixed stars, together with the central sun,
and this certainly loses all meaning in boundless space
(for motion in absolute space cannot be distinguished
from rest), and becomes, as is already the case from its
striving and aimless flight, an expression of that nothingness, that failure of all aim, which, at the close of
this book, we shall be obliged to recognise in the striving
of will in all its phenomena. Thus boundless space and
endless time must be the most universal and essential
forms of the collective phenomena of will, which exist

for the expression of its whole being. Lastly, we can recognise that conflict which we are considering of all phenomena of will against each other in simple matter regarded as such; for the real characteristic of matter is correctly expressed by Kant as repulsive and attractive force; so that even crude matter has its existence only in the strife of conflicting forces. If we abstract from all chemical differences in matter, or go so far back in the chain of causes and effects that as yet there is no chemical difference, there remains mere matter,—the world rounded to a globe, whose life, *i. e.*, objectification of will, is now constituted by the conflict between attractive and repulsive forces, the former as gravitation pressing from all sides towards the centre, the latter as impenetrability always opposing the former either as rigidity or elasticity; and this constant pressure and resistance may be regarded as the objectivity of will in its very lowest grade, and even there it expresses its character.

THIRD BOOK

THE WORLD AS IDEA

SECOND ASPECT

THE IDEA INDEPENDENT OF THE PRINCIPLE OF SUFFICIENT REASON: THE PLATONIC IDEA: THE OBJECT OF ART

III

§ 30. In the First Book the world was explained as mere *idea*, object for a subject. In the Second Book we considered it from its other side, and found that in this aspect it is *will*, which proved to be simply that which this world is besides being idea. In accordance with this knowledge we called the world as idea, both as a whole and in its parts, the *objectification of will*, which therefore means the will become object, *i. e.*, idea. Further, we remember that this objectification of will was found to have many definite grades, in which, with gradually increasing distinctness and completeness, the nature of will appears in the idea, that is to say, presents itself as object. In these grades we already recognised the Platonic Ideas, for the grades are just the determined species, or the original unchanging forms and qualities of all natural bodies, both organised and unorganised, and also the general forces which reveal themselves according to natural laws. These Ideas, then, as a whole express themselves in innumerable individuals and particulars, and are related to these as archetypes to their copies. The multiplicity of such individuals is only conceivable through time and space, their appearing and passing away through causality, and in all these forms we recognise merely the different modes of the principle of sufficient reason, which is the ultimate principle of all that is finite, of all individual existence, and the universal form of the idea as it appears in the knowledge of the individual as such. The Platonic Idea, on the other hand, does not come under this principle, and has therefore neither multiplicity nor change. While the individuals in which it expresses itself are innumerable, and unceasingly come into being and pass away, it remains unchanged as one and the same, and the principle of sufficient reason has for it no meaning. As, however, this is the form under which all knowledge of the subject comes, so far as the subject knows as an *individual,* the Ideas lie quite outside the sphere of its knowledge. If, therefore, the Ideas are to become objects of knowledge, this can only happen by transcending the individuality of the knowing subject. The more exact and detailed explanation of this is what will now occupy our attention.

§ 33. Since now, as individuals, we have no other knowledge than that which is subject to the principle of sufficient reason, and this form of knowledge excludes the Ideas, it is certain that if it is possible for us to raise ourselves from the knowledge of particular things to that of the Ideas, this can only happen by an alteration taking place in the subject which is analogous and corresponds to the great change of the whole nature of the object, and by virtue of which the subject, so far as it knows an Idea, is no more individual.

It will be remembered from the preceding book that knowledge in general belongs to the objectification of will at its higher grades, and sensibility, nerves, and brain, just like the other parts of the organised being, are the expression of the will at this stage of its ob-

jectivity, and therefore the idea which appears through
them is also in the same way bound to the service of
will as a means for the attainment of its now complicated aims for sustaining a being of manifold requirements. Thus originally and according to its nature,
knowledge is completely subject to the will, and, like
the immediate object, which, by means of the application of the law of causality, is its starting-point, all
knowledge which proceeds in accordance with the principle of sufficient reason remains in a closer or more
distant relation to the will. For the individual finds his
body as an object among objects, to all of which it is
related and connected according to the principle of sufficient reason. Thus all investigations of these relations
and connections lead back to his body, and consequently
to his will. Since it is the principle of sufficient reason
which places the objects in this relation to the body,
and, through it, to the will, the one endeavour of the
knowledge which is subject to this principle will be to
find out the relations in which objects are placed to
each other through this principle, and thus to trace their
innumerable connections in space, time, and causality.
For only through these is the object *interesting* to the
individual, *i. e.,* related to the will. Therefore the knowledge which is subject to the will knows nothing further
of objects than their relations, knows the objects only
so far as they exist at this time, in this place, under
these circumstances, from these causes, and with these
effects—in a word, as particular things; and if all these
relations were to be taken away, the objects would also
have disappeared for it, because it knew nothing more
about them. We must not disguise the fact that what
the sciences consider in things is also in reality nothing
more, than this; their relations, the connections of time
and space, the causes of natural changes, the resem-

blance of forms, the motives of actions,—thus merely relations. What distinguishes science from ordinary knowledge is merely its systematic form, the facilitating of knowledge by the comprehension of all particulars in the universal, by means of the subordination of concepts, and the completeness of knowledge which is thereby attained. All relation has itself only a relative existence; for example, all being in time is also non-being; for time is only that by means of which opposite determinations can belong to the same thing; therefore every phenomenon which is in time again is not, for what separates its beginning from its end is only time, which is essentially a fleeting, inconstant, and relative thing, here called duration. But time is the most universal form of all objects of the knowledge which is subject to the will, and the prototype of its other forms.

Knowledge now, as a rule, remains always subordinate to the service of the will, as indeed it originated for this service, and grew, so to speak, to the will, as the head of the body. In the case of the brutes this subjection of knowledge to the will can never be abolished. In the case of men it can be abolished only in exceptional cases, which we shall presently consider more closely. This distinction between man and brute is outwardly expressed by the difference of the relation of the head to the body. In the case of the lower brutes both are deformed: in all brutes the head is directed towards the earth, where the objects of its will lie; even in the higher species the head and the body are still far more one than in the case of man, whose head seems freely set upon his body, as if only carried by and not serving it. This human excellence is exhibited in the highest degree by the Apollo of Belvedere; the head of the god of the Muses, with eyes fixed on the far distance, stands so freely on his shoulders that it seems wholly delivered from the body, and no more subject to its cares.

§ 34. The transition which we have referred to as possible, but yet to be regarded as only exceptional, from the common knowledge of particular things to the knowledge of the Idea, takes place suddenly; for knowledge breaks free from the service of the will, by the subject ceasing to be merely individual, and thus becoming the pure will-less subject of knowledge, which no longer traces relations in accordance with the principle of sufficient reason, but rests in fixed contemplation of the object presented to it, out of its connection with all others, and rises into it.

A full explanation is necessary to make this clear, and the reader must suspend his surprise for a while, till he has grasped the whole thought expressed in this work, and then it will vanish of itself.

If, raised by the power of the mind, a man relinquishes the common way of looking at things, gives up tracing, under the guidance of the forms of the principle of sufficient reason, their relations to each other, the final goal of which is always a relation to his own will; if he thus ceases to consider the where, the when, the why, and the whither of things, and looks simply and solely at the *what;* if, further, he does not allow abstract thought, the concepts of the reason, to take possession of his consciousness, but, instead of all this, gives the whole power of his mind to perception, sinks himself entirely in this, and lets his whole consciousness be filled with the quiet contemplation of the natural object actually present, whether a landscape, a tree, a mountain, a building, or whatever it may be; inasmuch as he *loses* himself in this object (to use a pregnant German idiom), *i. e.,* forgets even his individuality, his will, and only continues to exist as the pure subject, the clear

mirror of the object, so that it is as if the object alone
were there, without any one to perceive it, and he can
no longer separate the perceiver from the perception,
but both have become one, because the whole consciousness is filled and occupied with one single sensuous picture; if thus the object has to such an extent passed out
of all relation to something outside it, and the subject
out of all relation to the will, then that which is so
known is no longer the particular thing as such; but it
is the *Idea,* the eternal form, the immediate objectivity
of the will at this grade; and, therefore, he who is sunk
in this perception is no longer individual, for in such
perception the individual has lost himself; but he is
pure, will-less, painless, timeless *subject of knowledge.*
In such contemplation the particular thing becomes at
once the *Idea* of its species, and the perceiving individual becomes *pure subject of knowledge.* The individual, as such, knows only particular things; the pure
subject of knowledge knows only Ideas. For the individual is the subject of knowledge in its relation to a
definite particular manifestation of will, and in subjection to this. This particular manifestation of will is, as
such, subordinated to the principle of sufficient reason
in all its forms; therefore, all knowledge which relates
itself to it also follows the principle of sufficient reason,
and no other kind of knowledge is fitted to be of use
to the will but this, which always consists merely of
relations to the object. The knowing individual as such,
and the particular things known by him, are always in
some place, at some time, and are links in the chain of
causes and effects. The pure subject of knowledge and
his correlative, the Idea, have passed out of all these
forms of the principle of sufficient reason: time, place,
the individual that knows, and the individual that is
known, have for them no meaning. When an individual

knower has raised himself in the manner described to be pure subject of knowledge, and at the same time has raised the observed object to the Platonic Idea, the *world as idea* appears complete and pure, and the full objectification of the will takes place, for the Platonic Idea alone is its *adequate objectivity*. The Idea includes object and subject in like manner in itself, for they are its one form; but in it they are absolutely of equal importance; for as the object is here, as elsewhere, simply the idea of the subject, the subject, which passes entirely into the perceived object has thus become this object itself, for the whole consciousness is nothing but its perfectly distinct picture. Now this consciousness constitutes the whole *world as idea,* for one imagines the whole of the Platonic Ideas, or grades of the objectivity of will, in their series passing through it. The particular things of all time and space are nothing but Ideas multiplied through the principle of sufficient reason (the form of the knowledge of the individual as such), and thus obscured as regards their pure objectivity. When the Platonic Idea appears, in it subject and object are no longer to be distinguished, for the Platonic Idea, the adequate objectivity of will, the true world as idea, arises only when the subject and object reciprocally fill and penetrate each other completely; and in the same way the knowing and the known individuals, as things in themselves, are not to be distinguished. For if we look entirely away from the true *world as idea,* there remains nothing but *the world as will*. The will is the "in-itself" of the Platonic Idea, which fully objectifies it; it is also the "in-itself" of the particular thing and of the individual that knows it, which objectify it incompletely. As will, outside the idea and all its forms, it is one and the same in the object contemplated and in the individual, who soars aloft in this contemplation, and becomes conscious of himself as pure subject. These two are, therefore, in themselves not different, for in themselves they are will, which here knows itself; and multiplicity and difference exist only as the way in which this knowledge comes to the will, *i. e.,* only in the phenomenon, on account of its form, the principle of sufficient reason.

Now the known thing, without me as the subject of knowledge, is just as little an object, and not mere will, blind effort, as without the object, without the idea, I am a knowing subject and not mere blind will. This will is in itself, *i. e.,* outside the idea, one and the same with mine: only in the world as idea, whose form is always at least that of subject and object, we are separated as the known and the knowing individual. As soon as knowledge, the world as idea, is abolished, there remains nothing but mere will, blind effort. That it should receive objectivity, become idea, supposes at once both subject and object; but that this should be pure, complete, and adequate objectivity of the will, supposes the object as Platonic Idea, free from the forms of the principle of sufficient reason, and the subject as the pure subject of knowledge, free from individuality and subjection to the will.

Whoever now, has, after the manner referred to, become so absorbed and lost in the perception of nature that he only continues to exist as the pure knowing subject, becomes in this way directly conscious that, as such, he is the condition, that is, the supporter, of the world and all objective existence; for this now shows itself as dependent upon his existence. Thus he draws nature into himself, so that he sees it to be merely an accident of his own being. In this sense Byron says—

"Are not the mountains, waves, and skies, a part
Of me and of my soul, as I of them?"

But how shall he who feels this, regard himself as absolutely transitory, in contrast to imperishable nature?

§ 35. In order to gain a deeper insight into the nature of the world, it is absolutely necessary that we should learn to distinguish the will as thing-in-itself from its adequate objectivity, and also the different grades in which this appears more and more distinctly and fully, *i. e.*, the Ideas themselves, from the merely phenomenal existence of these Ideas in the forms of the principle of sufficient reason, the restricted method of knowledge of the individual. We shall then agree with Plato when he attributes actual being only to the Ideas, and allows only an illusive, dream-like existence to things in space and time, the real world for the individual. Then we shall understand how one and the same Idea reveals itself in so many phenomena, and presents its nature only bit by bit to the individual, one side after another. Then we shall also distinguish the Idea itself from the way in which its manifestation appears in the observation of the individual, and recognise the former as essential and the latter as unessential. Let us consider this with the help of examples taken from the most insignificant things, and also from the greatest. When the clouds move, the figures which they form are not essential, but indifferent to them; but that as elastic vapour they are pressed together, drifted along, spread out, or torn asunder by the force of the wind: this is their nature, the essence of the forces which objectify themselves in them, the Idea; their actual forms are only for the individual observer. To the brook that flows over stones, the eddies, the waves, the foam-flakes which it forms are indifferent and unessential; but that it follows the attraction of gravity, and behaves as inelastic, perfectly mobile, formless, transparent fluid: this is its nature; this, *if known through perception,* is its Idea;

these accidental forms are only for us so long as we
know as individuals. The ice on the window-pane forms
itself into crystals according to the laws of crystallisation, which reveal the essence of the force of nature that
appears here, exhibit the Idea; but the trees and flowers
which it traces on the pane are unessential, and are only
there for us. What appears in the clouds, the brook, and
the crystal is the weakest echo of that will which appears more fully in the plant, more fully still in the
beast, and most fully in man. But only the essential
in all these grades of its objectification constitutes the
Idea; on the other hand, its unfolding or development,
because broken up in the forms of the principle of sufficient reason into a multiplicity of many-sided phenomena, is unessential to the Idea, lies merely in the kind
of knowledge that belongs to the individual and has
reality only for this. The same thing necessarily holds
good of the unfolding of that Idea which is the completest objectivity of will. Therefore, the history of the
human race, the throng of events, the change of times,
the multifarious forms of human life in different lands
and countries, all this is only the accidental form of the
manifestations of the Idea, does not belong to the Idea
itself, in which alone lies the adequate objectivity of
the will, but only to the phenomenon which appears
in the knowledge of the individual, and is just as foreign, unessential, and indifferent to the Idea itself as the
figures which they assume are to the clouds, the form
of its eddies and foam-flakes to the brook, or its trees
and flowers to the ice.

To him who has thoroughly grasped this, and can distinguish between the will and the Idea, and between the
Idea and its manifestation, the events of the world will
have significance only so far as they are the letters out
of which we may read the Idea of man, but not in and

for themselves. He will not believe with the vulgar that time may produce something actually new and significant; that through it, or in it, something absolutely real may attain to existence, or indeed that it itself as a whole has beginning and end, plan and development, and in some way has for its final aim the highest perfection (according to their conception) of the last generation of man, whose life is a brief thirty years. Therefore he will just as little, with Homer, people a whole Olympus with gods to guide the events of time, as, with Ossian, he will take the forms of the clouds for individual beings; for, as we have said, both have just as much meaning as regards the Idea which appears in them. In the manifold forms of human life and in the unceasing change of events, he will regard the Idea only as the abiding and essential, in which the will to live has its fullest objectivity, and which shows its different sides in the capacities, the passions, the errors and the excellences of the human race; in self-interest, hatred, love, fear, boldness, frivolity, stupidity, slyness, wit, genius, and so forth, all of which crowding together and combining in thousands of forms (individuals), continually create the history of the great and the little world, in which it is all the same whether they are set in motion by nuts or by crowns. Finally, he will find that in the world it is the same as in the dramas of Gozzi, in all of which the same persons appear, with like intention, and with a like fate; the motives and incidents are certainly different in each piece, but the spirit of the incidents is the same; the actors in one piece know nothing of the incidents of another, although they performed in it themselves; therefore, after all experience of former pieces, Pantaloon has become no more agile or generous, Tartaglia no more conscientious, Brighella no more courageous, and Columbine no more modest.

Suppose we were allowed for once a clearer glance into the kingdom of the possible, and over the whole chain of causes and effects; if the earth-spirit appeared and showed us in a picture all the greatest men, enlighteners of the world, and heroes, that chance destroyed before they were ripe for their work; then the great events that would have changed the history of the world and brought in periods of the highest culture and enlightenment, but which the blindest chance, the most insignificant accident, hindered at the outset; lastly, the splendid powers of great men, that would have enriched whole ages of the world, but which, either misled by error or passion, or compelled by necessity, they squandered uselessly on unworthy or unfruitful objects, or even wasted in play. If we saw all this, we would shudder and lament at the thought of the lost treasures of whole periods of the world. But the earth-spirit would smile and say, "The source from which the individuals and their powers proceed is inexhaustible and unending as time and space; for, like these forms of all phenomena, they also are only phenomena, visibility of the will. No finite measure can exhaust that infinite source; therefore an undiminished eternity is always open for the return of any event or work that was nipped in the bud. In this world of phenomena true loss is just as little possible as true gain. The will alone is; it is the thing in-itself, and the source of all these phenomena. Its self-knowledge and its assertion or denial, which is then decided upon, is the only event in-itself."

§ 36. History follows the thread of events; it is pragmatic so far as it deduces them in accordance with the law of motivation, a law that determines the self-manifesting will wherever it is enlightened by knowledge. At the lowest grades of its objectivity, where it still acts without knowledge, natural science, in the form of etiology, treats of the laws of the changes of its phenomena, and, in the form of morphology, of what is permanent in them. This almost endless task is lightened by the aid of concepts, which comprehend what is general in order that we may deduce what is particular from it. Lastly, mathematics treats of the mere forms, time and space, in which the Ideas, broken up into multiplicity, appear for the knowledge of the subject as individual. All these, of which the common name is science, proceed according to the principle of sufficient reason in its different forms, and their theme is always the phenomenon, its laws, connections, and the relations which result from them. But what kind of knowledge is concerned with that which is outside and independent of all relations, that which alone is really essential to the world, the true content of its phenomena, that which is subject to no change, and therefore is known with equal truth for all time, in a word, the *Ideas,* which are the direct and adequate objectivity of the thing in-itself, the will? We answer, *Art,* the work of genius. It repeats or reproduces the eternal Ideas grasped through pure contemplation, the essential and abiding in all the phenomena of the world; and according to what the material is in which it reproduces, it is sculpture or painting, poetry or music. Its one source is the knowledge of Ideas; its one aim the communication of this knowledge. While science, following the unresting and inconstant stream of the fourfold forms of reason and consequent, with each end attained sees further, and can never reach a final goal nor attain full satisfaction, any more than by running we can reach the place where the clouds touch the horizon; art, on the contrary, is everywhere at its goal. For it plucks the object of its contemplation out of the stream of the world's course, and has it isolated before it. And this particular thing, which in that stream was a small perishing part, becomes to art the representative of the whole, an equivalent of the endless multitude in space and time. It therefore pauses at this particular thing; the course of time stops; the relations vanish for it; only the essential, the Idea, is its object. We may, therefore, accurately define it as the *way of viewing things independent of the principle of sufficient reason,* in opposition to the way of viewing them which proceeds in accordance with that principle, and which is the method of experience and of science. This last method of considering things may be compared to a line infinitely extended in a horizontal direction, and the former to a vertical line which cuts it at any point. The method of viewing things which proceeds in accordance with the principle of sufficient reason is the rational method, and it alone is valid and of use in practical life and in science. The method which looks away from the content of this principle is the method of genius, which is only valid and of use in art. The first is the method of Aristotle; the second is, on the whole, that of Plato. The first is like the mighty storm, that rushes along without beginning and without aim, bending, agitating, and carrying away everything before it; the second is like the silent sunbeam, that pierces through the storm quite unaffected by it. The first is like the innumerable showering drops of the waterfall, which, constantly changing, never rest for an instant; the second is like the rainbow, quietly resting on this raging torrent. Only through the pure contemplation described above, which ends entirely in the object, can Ideas be comprehended; and the nature of *genius* consists in pre-eminent capacity for such contemplation. Now, as this requires that a man should entirely forget himself and the relations in which he stands, *genius* is simply the completest *objectivity,* i. e., the objective tendency of the mind, as opposed to the subjective, which is directed to one's own self—in other words, to the will. Thus genius is the faculty of continuing in the state of pure perception, of losing oneself in perception, and of enlisting in this service the knowledge which originally existed only for the service of the will; that is to say, genius is the power of leaving one's own interest, wishes, and aims entirely out of sight, thus of entirely renouncing one's own personality for a time, so as to remain *pure knowing subject,* clear vision of the world; and this not merely at moments, but for a sufficient length of time, and with sufficient consciousness, to enable one to reproduce by deliberate art what has thus been apprehended, and "to fix in lasting thoughts the wavering images that float before the mind." It is as if, when genius appears in an individual, a far larger measure of the power of knowledge falls to his lot than is necessary for the service of an individual will; and this superfluity of knowledge, being free, now becomes subject purified from will, a clear mirror of the inner nature of the world. This explains the activity, amounting even to disquietude, of men of genius, for the present can seldom satisfy them, because it does not fill their consciousness. This gives them that restless aspiration, that unceasing desire for new things, and for the contemplation of lofty things, and also that longing that is hardly ever satisfied, for men of similar nature and of like stature, to whom they might communicate themselves; whilst the common mortal, entirely filled and satisfied by the common present, ends in it, and finding everywhere his like, enjoys that peculiar satisfaction in daily life that is denied to genius.

Imagination has rightly been recognised as an essential element of genius; it has sometimes even been regarded as identical with it; but this is a mistake. As the objects of genius are the eternal Ideas, the permanent, essential forms of the world and all its phenomena, and as the knowledge of the Idea is necessarily knowledge through perception, is not abstract, the knowledge of the genius would be limited to the Ideas of the objects actually present to his person, and dependent upon the chain of circumstances that brought these objects to him, if his imagination did not extend his horizon far beyond the limits of his actual personal existence, and thus enable him to construct the whole out of the little that comes into his own actual apperception, and so to let almost all possible scenes of life pass before him in his own consciousness. Further, the actual objects are almost always very imperfect copies of the Ideas expressed in them; therefore the man of genius requires imagination in order to see in things, not that which Nature has actually made, but that which she endeavoured to make, yet could not because of that conflict of her forms among themselves which we referred to in the last book. We shall return to this farther on in treating of sculpture. The imagination then extends the intellectual horizon of the man of genius beyond the objects which actually present themselves to him, both as regards quality and quantity. Therefore extraordinary strength of imagination accompanies, and is indeed a necessary condition of genius. But the converse does not hold, for strength of imagination does not indicate genius; on the contrary, men who have no touch of genius may have much imagination. For as it is possible to consider a real object in two opposite ways, purely objectively, the way of genius grasping its Idea, or in the common way, merely in the relations in which it stands to other objects and to one's own will, in accordance with the principle of sufficient reason, it is also possible to perceive an imaginary object in both of these

ways. Regarded in the first way, it is a means to the
knowledge of the Idea, the communication of which is
the work of art; in the second case, the imaginary object
is used to build castles in the air congenial to egotism
and the individual humour, and which for the moment
delude and gratify; thus only the relations of the phantasies so linked together are known. The man who
indulges in such an amusement is a dreamer; he will
easily mingle those fancies that delight his solitude with
reality, and so unfit himself for real life: perhaps he
will write them down, and then we shall have the ordinary novel of every description, which entertains those
who are like him and the public at large, for the readers
imagine themselves in the place of the hero, and then
find the story very agreeable.

The common mortal, that manufacture of Nature
which she produces by the thousand every day, is, as we
have said, not capable, at least not continuously so, of
observation that in every sense is wholly disinterested,
as sensuous contemplation, strictly so called, is. He can
turn his attention to things only so far as they have
some relation to his will, however indirect it may be.
Since in this respect, which never demands anything but
the knowledge of relations, the abstract conception of
the thing is sufficient, and for the most part even better
adapted for use; the ordinary man does not linger long
over the mere perception, does not fix his attention long
on one object, but in all that is presented to him hastily
seeks merely the concept under which it is to be brought,
as the lazy man seeks a chair, and then it interests him
no further. This is why he is so soon done with everything, with works of art, objects of natural beauty, and
indeed everywhere with the truly significant contemplation of all the scenes of life. He does not linger; only
seeks to know his own way in life, together with all

that might at any time become his way. Thus he makes
topographical notes in the widest sense; over the consideration of life itself as such he wastes no time. The
man of genius, on the other hand, whose excessive power
of knowledge frees it at times from the service of will,
dwells on the consideration of life itself, strives to comprehend the Idea of each thing, not its relations to other
things; and in doing this he often forgets to consider his
own path in life, and therefore for the most part pursues
it awkwardly enough. While to the ordinary man his
faculty of knowledge is a lamp to lighten his path, to
the man of genius it is the sun which reveals the world.
This great diversity in their way of looking at life soon
becomes visible in the outward appearance both of the
man of genius and of the ordinary mortal. The man in
whom genius lives and works is easily distinguished by
his glance, which is both keen and steady, and bears the
stamp of perception, of contemplation. This is easily
seen from the likenesses of the few men of genius whom
Nature has produced here and there among countless
millions. On the other hand, in the case of an ordinary
man, the true object of his contemplation, what he is
prying into, can be easily seen from his glance, if indeed
it is not quite stupid and vacant, as is generally the case.
Therefore the expression of genius in a face consists in
this, that in it a decided predominance of knowledge
over will is visible, and consequently there also shows
itself in it a knowledge that is entirely devoid of relation
to will, i. e., pure knowing. On the contrary, in ordinary
countenances there is a predominant expression of will;
and we see that knowledge only comes into activity
under the impulse of will, and thus is directed merely
by motives.

Since the knowledge that pertains to genius, or the
knowledge of Ideas, is that knowledge which does not

follow the principle of sufficient reason, so, on the other hand, the knowledge which does follow that principle is that which gives us prudence and rationality in life, and which creates the sciences. Thus men of genius are affected with the deficiencies entailed in the neglect of this latter kind of knowledge. Yet what I say in this regard is subject to the limitation that it only concerns them in so far as and while they are actually engaged in that kind of knowledge which is peculiar to genius; and this is by no means at every moment of their lives, for the great though spontaneous exertion which is demanded for the comprehension of Ideas free from will must necessarily relax, and there are long intervals during which men of genius are placed in very much the same position as ordinary mortals, both as regards advantages and deficiencies. On this account the action of genius has always been regarded as an inspiration, as indeed the name indicates, as the action of a superhuman being distinct from the individual himself, and which takes possession of him only periodically. The disinclination of men of genius to direct their attention to the content of the principle of sufficient reason will first show itself, with regard to the ground of being, as dislike of mathematics; for its procedure is based upon the most universal forms of the phenomenon, space and time, which are themselves merely modes of the principle of sufficient reason, and is consequently precisely the opposite of that method of thought which seeks merely the content of the phenomenon, the Idea which expresses itself in it apart from all relations. The logical method of mathematics is also antagonistic to genius, for it does not satisfy but obstructs true insight, and presents merely a chain of conclusions in accordance with the principle of the ground of knowing. The mental faculty upon which it makes the greatest claim is memory, for it is necessary to recollect all the earlier propositions which are referred to. Experience has also proved that men of great artistic genius have no faculty for mathematics; no man was ever very distinguished for both. Alfieri relates that he was never able to understand the fourth proposition of Euclid. Goethe was constantly reproached with his want of mathematical knowledge by the ignorant opponents of his theory of colours. Here certainly, where it was not a question of calculation and measurement upon hypothetical data, but of direct knowledge by the understanding of causes and effects, this reproach was so utterly absurd and inappropriate, that by making it they have exposed their entire want of judgment, just as much as by the rest of their ridiculous arguments. The fact that up to the present day, nearly half a century after the appearance of Goethe's theory of colours, even in Germany the Newtonian fallacies still have undisturbed possession of the professorial chair, and men continue to speak quite seriously of the seven homogeneous rays of light and their different refrangibility, will some day be numbered among the great intellectual peculiarities of men generally, and especially of Germans. From the same cause as we have referred to above, may be explained the equally well-known fact that, conversely, admirable mathematicians have very little susceptibility for works of fine art. This is very naïvely expressed in the well-known anecdote of the French mathematician, who, after having read Racine's "Iphigenia," shrugged his shoulders and asked, *"Qu'est ce que cela prouve?"* Further, as quick comprehension of relations in accordance with the laws of causality and motivation is what specially constitutes prudence or sagacity, a prudent man, so far as and while he is so, will not be a genius, and a man of genius, so far as and while he is so, will not be a prudent man.

Lastly, perceptive knowledge generally, in the province of which the Idea always lies, is directly opposed to rational or abstract knowledge, which is guided by the principle of the ground of knowing. It is also well known that we seldom find great genius united with pre-eminent reasonableness; on the contrary, persons of genius are often subject to violent emotions and irrational passions. But the ground of this is not weakness of reason, but partly unwonted energy of that whole phenomenon of will—the man of genius—which expresses itself through the violence of all his acts of will, and partly preponderance of the knowledge of perception through the senses and understanding over abstract knowledge, producing a decided tendency to the perceptible, the exceedingly lively impressions of which so far outshine colourless concepts, that they take their place in the guidance of action, which consequently becomes irrational. Accordingly the impression of the present moment is very strong with such persons, and carries them away into unconsidered action, violent emotions and passions. Moreover, since, in general, the knowledge of persons of genius has to some extent freed itself from the service of will, they will not in conversation think so much of the person they are addressing as of the thing they are speaking about, which is vividly present to them; and therefore they are likely to judge or narrate things too objectively for their own interests; they will not pass over in silence what would more prudently be concealed, and so forth. Finally, they are given to soliloquising, and in general may exhibit certain weaknesses which are actually akin to madness. It has often been remarked that there is a side at which genius and madness touch, and even pass over into each other, and indeed poetical inspiration has been called a kind of madness: *amabilis insania,* Horace calls it (Od.

iii. 4), and Wieland in the introduction to "Oberon" speaks of it as "amiable madness." Even Aristotle, as quoted by Seneca (De Tranq. Animi, 15, 16), is reported to have said: There has been no great genius without a mixture of madness. Plato expresses it in the figure of the dark cave, referred to above (De Rep. 7), when he says: "Those who, outside the cave, have seen the true sunlight and the things that have true being (Ideas), cannot afterwards see properly down in the cave, because their eyes are not accustomed to the darkness; they cannot distinguish the shadows, and are jeered at for their mistakes by those who have never left the cave and its shadows." In the "Phædrus" also (p. 317), he distinctly says that there can be no true poet without a certain madness; in fact, (p. 327), that every one appears mad who recognises the eternal Ideas in fleeting things. Cicero also quotes: Democritus denied that a poet could be great without madness, even as Plato said (De Divin., i. 37). And, lastly, Pope says—

"Great wits to madness sure are near allied,
And thin partitions do their bounds divide."

Especially instructive in this respect is Goethe's "Torquato Tasso," in which he shows us not only the suffering, the martyrdom of genius as such, but also how it constantly passes into madness. Finally, the fact of the direct connection of genius and madness is established by the biographies of great men of genius, such as Rousseau, Byron, and Alfieri, and by anecdotes from the lives of others. On the other hand, I must mention that, by a diligent search in lunatic asylums, I have found individual cases of patients who were unquestionably endowed with great talents, and whose genius distinctly appeared through their madness, which, however, had completely gained the upper hand. Now this cannot be ascribed to chance, for on the one hand the number of mad persons is relatively very small, and on the other hand a person of genius is a phenomenon which is rare beyond all ordinary estimation, and only appears in nature as the greatest exception. It will be sufficient to convince us of this if we compare the number of really great men of genius that the whole of civilised Europe has produced, both in ancient and modern times, with the two hundred and fifty millions who are always living in Europe, and who change entirely every thirty years. In estimating the number of men of outstanding genius, we must of course only count those who have produced works which have retained through all time an enduring value for mankind. I shall not refrain from mentioning, that I have known some persons of decided, though not remarkable, mental superiority, who also showed a slight trace of insanity. It might seem from this that every advance of intellect beyond the ordinary measure, as an abnormal development, disposes to madness. In the meantime, however, I will explain as briefly as possible my view of the purely intellectual ground of the relation between genius and madness, for this will certainly assist the explanation of the real nature of genius, that is to say, of that mental endowment which alone can produce genuine works of art. But this necessitates a brief explanation of madness itself.

A clear and complete insight into the nature of madness, a correct and distinct conception of what constitutes the difference between the sane and the insane, has, as far as I know, not as yet been found. Neither reason nor understanding can be denied to madmen, for they talk and understand, and often draw very accurate conclusions; they also, as a rule, perceive what is pres-

ent quite correctly, and apprehend the connection between cause and effect. Visions, like the phantasies of
delirium, are no ordinary symptom of madness: delirium
falsifies perception, madness the thoughts. For the most
part, madmen do not err in the knowledge of what is
immediately *present;* their raving always relates to what
is *absent* and *past,* and only through these to their connection with what is present. Therefore it seems to me
that their malady specially concerns the memory; not
indeed that memory fails them entirely, for many of
them know a great deal by heart, and sometimes recognise persons whom they have not seen for a long time;
but rather that the thread of memory is broken, the con-
tinuity of its connection destroyed, and no uniformly
connected recollection of the past is possible. Particular scenes of the past are known correctly, just like the
particular present; but there are gaps in their recollection which they fill up with fictions, and these are either
always the same, in which case they become fixed ideas,
and the madness that results is called monomania or
melancholy; or they are always different, momentary
fancies, and then it is called folly, *fatuitas.* This is why
it is so difficult to find out their former life from lunatics
when they enter an asylum. The true and the false are
always mixed up in their memory. Although the immediate present is correctly known, it becomes falsified
through its fictitious connection with an imaginary past;
they therefore regard themselves and others as identical
with persons who exist only in their imaginary past;
they do not recognise some of their acquaintances at all,
and thus while they perceive correctly what is actually
present, they have only false conceptions of its relations
to what is absent. If the madness reaches a high degree,
there is complete absence of memory, so that the madman is quite incapable of any reference to what is ab-

sent or past, and is only determined by the caprice of
the moment in connection with the fictions which, in his
mind, fill the past. In such a case, we are never for a
moment safe from violence or murder, unless we constantly make the madman aware of the presence of superior force. The knowledge of the madman has this in
common with that of the brute, both are confined to the
present. What distinguishes them is that the brute has
really no idea of the past as such, though the past acts
upon it through the medium of custom, so that, for example, the dog recognises its former master even after
years, that is to say, it receives the wonted impression
at the sight of him; but of the time that has passed since
it saw him it has no recollection. The madman, on the
other hand, always carries about in his reason an abstract past, but it is a false past, which exists only for
him, and that either constantly, or only for the moment.
The influence of this false past prevents the use of the
true knowledge of the present which the brute is able
to make. The fact that violent mental suffering or unexpected and terrible calamities should often produce
madness, I explain in the following manner. All such
suffering is as an actual event confined to the present.
It is thus merely transitory, and is consequently never
excessively heavy; it only becomes unendurably great
when it is lasting pain; but as such it exists only in
thought, and therefore lies in the *memory*. If now such
a sorrow, such painful knowledge or reflection, is so
bitter that it becomes altogether unbearable, and the individual is prostrated under it, then, terrified Nature
seizes upon *madness* as the last resource of life; the
mind so fearfully tortured at once destroys the thread of
its memory, fills up the gaps with fictions, and thus seeks
refuge in madness from the mental suffering that exceeds its strength, just as we cut off a mortified limb

and replace it with a wooden one. The distracted Ajax, King Lear, and Ophelia may be taken as examples; for the creations of true genius, to which alone we can refer here, as universally known, are equal in truth to real persons; besides, in this case, frequent actual experience shows the same thing. A faint analogy of this kind of transition from pain to madness is to be found in the way in which all of us often seek, as it were mechanically, to drive away a painful thought that suddenly occurs to us by some loud exclamation or quick movement—to turn ourselves from it, to distract our minds by force.

We see, from what has been said, that the madman has a true knowledge of what is actually present, and also of certain particulars of the past, but that he mistakes the connection, the relations, and therefore falls into error and talks nonsense. Now this is exactly the point at which he comes into contact with the man of genius; for he also leaves out of sight the knowledge of the connection of things, since he neglects that knowledge of relations which conforms to the principle of sufficient reason, in order to see in things only their Ideas, and to seek to comprehend their true nature, which manifests itself to perception, and in regard to which *one thing* represents its whole species, in which way, as Goethe says, one case is valid for a thousand. The particular object of his contemplation, or the present which is perceived by him with extraordinary vividness, appear in so strong a light that the other links of the chain to which they belong are at once thrown into the shade, and this gives rise to phenomena which have long been recognized as resembling those of madness. That which in particular given things exists only incompletely and weakened by modifications, is raised by the man of genius, through his way of contemplating

it, to the Idea of the thing, to completeness: he therefore sees everywhere extremes, and therefore his own action tends to extremes; he cannot hit the mean, he lacks
soberness, and the result is what we have said. He knows
the Ideas completely but not the individuals. Therefore
it has been said that a poet may know mankind deeply
and thoroughly, and may yet have a very imperfect
knowledge of men. He is easily deceived, and is a tool
in the hands of the crafty.

§ 37. Genius, then, consists, according to our explanation, in the capacity for knowing, independently of
the principle of sufficient reason, not individual things,
which have their existence only in their relations, but
the Ideas of such things, and of being oneself the correlative of the Idea, and thus no longer an individual,
but the pure subject of knowledge. Yet this faculty must
exist in all men in a smaller and different degree; for
if not, they would be just as incapable of enjoying works
of art as of producing them; they would have no susceptibility for the beautiful or the sublime; indeed, these
words could have no meaning for them. We must therefore assume that there exists in all men this power of
knowing the Ideas in things, and consequently of transcending their personality for the moment, unless indeed
there are some men who are capable of no æsthetic
pleasure at all. The man of genius excels ordinary men
only by possessing this kind of knowledge in a far higher
degree and more continuously. Thus, while under its
influence he retains the presence of mind which is necessary to enable him to repeat in a voluntary and intentional work what he has learned in this manner; and this
repetition is the work of art. Through this he communicates to others the Idea he has grasped. This Idea remains unchanged and the same, so that æsthetic pleasure
is one and the same whether it is called forth by a work

of art or directly by the contemplation of nature and life. The work of art is only a means of facilitating the knowledge in which this pleasure consists. That the Idea comes to us more easily from the work of art than directly from nature and the real world, arises from the fact that the artist, who knew only the Idea, no longer the actual, has reproduced in his work the pure Idea, has abstracted it from the actual, omitting all disturbing accidents. The artist lets us see the world through his eyes. That he has these eyes, that he knows the inner nature of things apart from all their relations, is the gift of genius, is inborn; but that he is able to lend us this gift, to let us see with his eyes, is acquired, and is the technical side of art. Therefore, after the account which I have given in the preceding pages of the inner nature of æsthetical knowledge in its most general outlines, the following more exact philosophical treatment of the beautiful and the sublime will explain them both, in nature and in art, without separating them further. First of all we shall consider what takes place in a man when he is affected by the beautiful and the sublime; whether he derives this emotion directly from nature, from life, or partakes of it only through the medium of art, does not make any essential, but merely an external, difference.

§ 38. In the æsthetical mode of contemplation we have found *two inseparable constituent parts*—the knowledge of the object, not as individual thing but as Platonic Idea, that is, as the enduring form of this whole species of things; and the self-consciousness of the knowing person, not as individual, but as *pure will-less subject of knowledge.* The condition under which both these constituent parts appear always united was found to be the abandonment of the method of knowing which is bound to the principle of sufficient reason, and which, on the other hand, is the only kind of knowledge that is of value for the service of the will and also for science. Moreover, we shall see that the pleasure which is produced by the contemplation of the beautiful arises from these two constituent parts, sometimes more from the one, sometimes more from the other, according to what the object of the æsthetical contemplation may be.

All *willing* arises from want, therefore from deficiency, and therefore from suffering. The satisfaction of a wish ends it; yet for one wish that is satisfied there remain at least ten which are denied. Further, the desire lasts long, the demands are infinite; the satisfaction is short and scantily measured out. But even the final satisfaction is itself only apparent; every satisfied wish at once makes room for a new one; both are illusions; the one is known to be so, the other not yet. No attained object of desire can give lasting satisfaction, but merely a fleeting gratification; it is like the alms thrown to the beggar, that keeps him alive today that his misery may be prolonged till the morrow. Therefore, so long as our consciousness is filled by our will, so long as we are given up to the throng of desires with their constant hopes and fears, so long as we are the subject of willing, we can never have lasting happiness nor peace. It is essentially all the same whether we pursue or flee, fear injury or seek enjoyment; the care for the constant demands of the will, in whatever form it may be, continually occupies and sways the consciousness; but without peace no true well-being is possible. The subject of willing is thus constantly stretched on the revolving wheel of Ixion, pours water into the sieve of the Danaids, is the ever-longing Tantalus.

But when some external cause or inward disposition lifts us suddenly out of the endless stream of willing, delivers knowledge from the slavery of the will, the attention is no longer directed to the motives of willing, but comprehends things free from their relation to the will, and thus observes them without personal interest, without subjectivity, purely objectively, gives itself entirely up to them so far as they are ideas, but not in so far as they are motives. Then all at once the peace which we were always seeking, but which always fled from us on the former path of the desires, comes to us of its own accord, and it is well with us. It is the painless state which Epicurus prized as the highest good and as the state of the gods; for we are for the moment set free from the miserable striving of the will; we keep the Sabbath of the penal servitude of willing; the wheel of Ixion stands still.

But this is just the state which I described above as necessary for the knowledge of the Idea, as pure contemplation, as sinking oneself in perception, losing oneself in the object, forgetting all individuality, surrendering that kind of knowledge which follows the principle of sufficient reason, and comprehends only relations; the state by means of which at once and inseparably the perceived particular thing is raised to the Idea of its whole species, and the knowing individual to the pure subject of will-less knowledge, and as such they are both taken out of the stream of time and all other relations. It is then all one whether we see the sun set from the prison or from the palace.

Inward disposition, the predominance of knowing over willing, can produce this state under any circumstances. This is shown by those admirable Dutch artists who directed this purely objective perception to the most insignificant objects, and established a lasting monument of their objectivity and spiritual peace in their pictures of *still life,* which the æsthetic beholder does not look on without emotion; for they present to him the

peaceful, still, frame of mind of the artist, free from
will, which was needed to contemplate such insignificant
things so objectively, to observe them so attentively, and
to repeat this perception so intelligently; and as the
picture enables the onlooker to participate in this state,
his emotion is often increased by the contrast between it
and the unquiet frame of mind, disturbed by vehement
willing, in which he finds himself. In the same spirit,
landscape-painters, and particularly Ruisdael, have
often painted very insignificant country scenes, which
produce the same effect even more agreeably.

All this is accomplished by the inner power of an artistic nature alone; but that purely objective disposition
is facilitated and assisted from without by suitable objects, by the abundance of natural beauty which invites
contemplation, and even presses itself upon us. Whenever it discloses itself suddenly to our view, it almost
always succeeds in delivering us, though it may be only
for a moment, from subjectivity, from the slavery of the
will, and in raising us to the state of pure knowing.
This is why the man who is tormented by passion, or
want, or care, is so suddenly revived, cheered, and re-
stored by a single free glance into nature: the storm of
passion, the pressure of desire and fear, and all the
miseries of willing are then at once, and in a marvellous
manner, calmed and appeased. For at the moment at
which, freed from the will, we give ourselves up to pure
will-less knowing, we pass into a world from which
everything is absent that influenced our will and moved
us so violently through it. This freeing of knowledge lifts
us as wholly and entirely away from all that, as do
sleep and dreams; happiness and unhappiness have disappeared; we are no longer individual; the individual
is forgotten; we are only pure subject of knowledge;
we are only that *one* eye of the world which looks out

from all knowing creatures, but which can become perfectly free from the service of will in man alone. Thus all difference of individuality so entirely disappears, that it is all the same whether the perceiving eye belongs to a mighty king or to a wretched beggar; for neither joy nor complaining can pass that boundary with us. So near us always lies a sphere in which we escape from all our misery; but who has the strength to continue long in it? As soon as any single relation to our will, to our person, even of these objects of our pure contemplation, comes again into consciousness, the magic is at an end; we fall back into the knowledge which is governed by the principle of sufficient reason; we know no longer the Idea, but the particular thing, the link of a chain to which we also belong, and we are again abandoned to all our woe. Most men remain almost always at this standpoint because they entirely lack objectivity, *i. e.,* genius. Therefore they have no pleasure in being alone with nature; they need company, or at least a book. For their knowledge remains subject to their will; they seek, therefore, in objects, only some relation to their will, and whenever they see anything that has no such relation, there sounds within them, like a ground bass in music, the constant inconsolable cry, "It is of no use to me;" thus in solitude the most beautiful surroundings have for them a desolate, dark, strange, and hostile appearance.

Lastly, it is this blessedness of will-less perception which casts an enchanting glamour over the past and distant, and presents them to us in so fair a light by means of self-deception. For as we think of days long gone by, days in which we lived in a distant place, it is only the objects which our fancy recalls, not the subject of will, which bore about with it then its incurable sorrows just as it bears them now; but they are forgotten, because since then they have often given place to others. Now, objective perception acts with regard to what is remembered just as it would in what is present, if we let it have influence over us, if we surrendered ourselves to it free from will. Hence it arises that, especially when we are more than ordinarily disturbed by some want, the remembrance of past and distant scenes suddenly flits across our minds like a lost paradise. The fancy recalls only what was objective, not what was individually subjective, and we imagine that that objective stood before us then just as pure and undisturbed by any relation to the will as its image stands in our fancy now; while in reality the relation of the objects to our will gave us pain then just as it does now. We can deliver ourselves from all suffering just as well through present objects as through distant ones whenever we raise ourselves to a purely objective contemplation of them, and so are able to bring about the illusion that only the objects are present and not we ourselves. Then, as the pure subject of knowledge, freed from the miserable self, we become entirely one with these objects, and, for the moment, our wants are as foreign to us as they are to them. The world as idea alone remains, and the world as will has disappeared.

§ 39. All these reflections are intended to bring out the subjective part of æsthetic pleasure; that is to say, that pleasure so far as it consists simply of delight in perceptive knowledge as such, in opposition to will. And as directly connected with this, there naturally follows the explanation of that disposition or frame of mind which has been called the sense of the *sublime*.

We have already remarked above that the transition to the state of pure perception takes place most easily when the objects bend themselves to it, that is, when by their manifold and yet definite and distinct form they

easily become representatives of their Ideas, in which
beauty, in the objective sense, consists. This quality belongs pre-eminently to natural beauty, which thus affords even to the most insensible at least a fleeting æsthetic satisfaction: indeed it is so remarkable how
especially the vegetable world invites æsthetic observa·
tion, and, as it were, presses itself upon it, that one
might say, that these advances are connected with the
fact that these organisms, unlike the bodies of animals,
are not themselves immediate objects of knowledge, and
therefore require the assistance of a foreign intelligent
individual in order to rise out of the world of blind will
and enter the world of idea, and that thus they long, as
it were, for this entrance, that they may attain at least
indirectly what is denied them directly. But I leave this
suggestion which I have hazarded, and which borders
perhaps upon extravagance, entirely undecided, for only
a very intimate and devoted consideration of nature can
raise or justify it. As long as that which raises us from
the knowledge of mere relations subject to the will, to
æsthetic contemplation, and thereby exalts us to the
position of the subject of knowledge free from will, is
this fittingness of nature, this significance and distinctness of its forms, on account of which the Ideas individu-
alized in them readily present themselves to us; so long
is it merely *beauty* that affects us and the sense of the
beautiful that is excited. But if these very objects whose
significant forms invite us to pure contemplation, have
a hostile relation to the human will in general, as it
exhibits itself in its objectivity, the human body, if they
are opposed to it, so that it is menaced by the irresistible predominance of their power, or sinks into insignificance before their immeasurable greatness; if, nevertheless, the beholder does not direct his attention to this
eminently hostile relation to his will, but, although per-

ceiving and recognising it, turns consciously away from it, forcibly detaches himself from his will and its relations, and, giving himself up entirely to knowledge, quietly contemplates those very objects that are so terrible to the will, comprehends only their Idea, which is foreign to all relation, so that he lingers gladly over its contemplation, and is thereby raised above himself, his person, his will, and all will:—in that case he is filled with the sense of the *sublime,* he is in the state of spiritual exaltation, and therefore the object producing such a state is called *sublime.* Thus what distinguishes the sense of the sublime from that of the beautiful is this: in the case of the beautiful, pure knowledge has gained the upper hand without a struggle, for the beauty of the object, *i. e.,* that property which facilitates the knowledge of its Idea, has removed from consciousness without resistance, and therefore imperceptibly, the will and the knowledge of relations which is subject to it, so that what is left is the pure subject of knowledge without even a remembrance of will. On the other hand, in the case of the sublime that state of pure knowledge is only attained by a conscious and forcible breaking away from the relations of the same object to the will, which are recognised as unfavourable, by a free and conscious transcending of the will and the knowledge related to it.

This exaltation must not only be consciously won, but also consciously retained, and it is therefore accompanied by a constant remembrance of will; yet not of a single particular volition, such as fear or desire, but of human volition in general, so far as it is universally expressed in its objectivity, the human body. If a single real act of will were to come into consciousness, through actual personal pressure and danger from the object, then the individual will thus actually influenced would at once gain the upper hand, the peace of contemplation would become impossible, the impression of the sublime would be lost, because it yields to the anxiety, in which the effort of the individual to right itself has sunk every other thought. A few examples will help very much to elucidate this theory of the æsthetic sublime and remove all doubt with regard to it; at the same time they will bring out the different degrees of this sense of the sublime. It is in the main identical with that of the beautiful, with pure will-less knowing, and the knowledge, that necessarily accompanies it of Ideas out of all relation determined by the principle of sufficient reason, and it is distinguished from the sense of the beautiful only by the additional quality that it rises above the known hostile relation of the object contemplated to the will in general. Thus there come to be various degrees of the sublime, and transitions from the beautiful to the sublime, according as this additional quality is strong, bold, urgent, near, or weak, distant, and merely indicated. I think it is more in keeping with the plan of my treatise, first to give examples of these transitions, and of the weaker degrees of the impression of the sublime, although persons whose æsthetical susceptibility in general is not very great, and whose imagination is not very lively, will only understand the examples given later of the higher and more distinct grades of that impression; and they should therefore confine themselves to these, and pass over the examples of the very weak degrees of the sublime that are to be given first.

As man is at once impetuous and blind striving of will (whose pole or focus lies in the genital organs), and eternal, free, serene subject of pure knowing (whose pole is the brain); so, corresponding to this antithesis, the sun is both the source of *light*, the condition of the

most perfect kind of knowledge, and therefore of the
most delightful of things—and the source of *warmth,*
the first condition of life, *i. e.,* of all phenomena of will
in its higher grades. Therefore, what warmth is for the
will, light is for knowledge. Light is the largest gem in
the crown of beauty, and has the most marked influence
on the knowledge of every beautiful object. Its presence
is an indispensable condition of beauty; its favourable
disposition increases the beauty of the most beautiful.
Architectural beauty more than any other object is enhanced by favourable light, though even the most insignificant things become through its influence most
beautiful. If, in the dead of winter, when all nature is
frozen and stiff, we see the rays of the setting sun reflected by masses of stone, illuminating without warm-
ing, and thus favourable only to the purest kind of
knowledge, not to the will; the contemplation of the
beautiful effect of the light upon these masses lifts us, as
does all beauty, into a state of pure knowing. But, in
this case, a certain transcending of the interests of the
will is needed to enable us to rise into the state of pure
knowing, because there is a faint recollection of the lack
of warmth from these rays, that is, an absence of the
principle of life; there is a slight challenge to persist
in pure knowing, and to refrain from all willing, and
therefore it is an example of a transition from the sense
of the beautiful to that of the sublime. It is the faintest
trace of the sublime in the beautiful; and beauty itself
is indeed present only in a slight degree. The following
is almost as weak an example.

Let us imagine ourselves transported to a very lonely
place, with unbroken horizon, under a cloudless sky,
trees and plants in the perfectly motionless air, no animals, no men, no running water, the deepest silence.
Such surroundings are, as it were, a call to seriousness

and contemplation, apart from all will and its cravings;
but this is just what imparts to such a scene of desolate
stillness a touch of the sublime. For, because it affords
no object, either favourable or unfavourable, for the
will which is constantly in need of striving and attaining, there only remains the state of pure contemplation,
and whoever is incapable of this, is ignominiously abandoned to the vacancy of unoccupied will, and the misery
of ennui. So far it is a test of our intellectual worth, of
which, generally speaking, the degree of our power of
enduring solitude, or our love of it, is a good criterion.
The scene we have sketched affords us, then, an example of the sublime in a low degree, for in it, with the
state of pure knowing in its peace and all-sufficiency,
there is mingled, by way of contrast, the recollection of
the dependence and poverty of the will which stands in
need of constant action. This is the species of the sublime for which the sight of the boundless prairies of the
interior of North America is celebrated.

But let us suppose such a scene, stripped also of vegetation, and showing only naked rocks; then from the
entire absence of that organic life which is necessary
for existence, the will at once becomes uneasy, the desert
assumes a terrible aspect, our mood becomes more tragic;
the elevation to the sphere of pure knowing takes place
with a more decided tearing of ourselves away from the
interests of the will; and because we persist in continuing in the state of pure knowing, the sense of the sublime distinctly appears.

The following situation may occasion this feeling in a
still higher degree: Nature convulsed by a storm; the
sky darkened by black threatening thunder-clouds; stupendous, naked, overhanging cliffs, completely shutting
out the view; rushing, foaming torrents; absolute desert;
the wail of the wind sweeping through the clefts of the

rocks. Our dependence, our strife with hostile nature, our will broken in the conflict, now appears visibly before our eyes. Yet, so long as the personal pressure does not gain the upper hand, but we continue in æsthetic contemplation, the pure subject of knowing gazes unshaken and unconcerned through that strife of nature, through that picture of the broken will, and quietly comprehends the Ideas even of those objects which are threatening and terrible to the will. In this contrast lies the sense of the sublime.

But the impression becomes still stronger, if, when we have before our eyes, on a large scale, the battle of the raging elements, in such a scene we are prevented from hearing the sound of our own voice by the noise of a falling stream; or, if we are abroad in the storm of tempestuous seas, where the mountainous waves rise and fall, dash themselves furiously against steep cliffs, and toss their spray high into the air; the storm howls, the sea boils, the lightning flashes from black clouds, and the peals of thunder drown the voice of storm and sea. Then, in the undismayed beholder, the two-fold nature of his consciousness reaches the highest degree of distinctness. He perceives himself, on the one hand, as an individual, as the frail phenomenon of will, which the slightest touch of these forces can utterly destroy, helpless against powerful nature, dependent, the victim of chance, a vanishing nothing in the presence of stupendous might; and, on the other hand, as the eternal, peaceful, knowing subject, the condition of the object, and, therefore, the supporter of this whole world; the terrific strife of nature only his idea; the subject itself free and apart from all desires and necessities, in the quiet comprehension of the Ideas. This is the complete impression of the sublime. Here he obtains a glimpse of a power beyond all comparison superior to the individual, threatening it with annihilation.

The impression of the sublime may be produced in quite another way, by presenting a mere immensity in space and time; its immeasurable greatness dwindles the individual to nothing. Adhering to Kant's nomenclature and his accurate division, we may call the first kind the dynamical, and the second the mathematical sublime, although we entirely dissent from his explanation of the inner nature of the impression, and can allow no share in it either to moral reflections, or to hypostases from scholastic philosophy.

If we lose ourselves in the contemplation of the infinite greatness of the universe in space and time, meditate on the thousands of years that are past or to come, or if the heavens at night actually bring before our eyes innumerable worlds and so force upon our consciousness the immensity of the universe, we feel ourselves dwindle to nothing; as individuals, as living bodies, as transient phenomena of will, we feel ourselves pass away and vanish into nothing like drops in the ocean. But at once there rises against this ghost of our own nothingness, against such lying impossibility, the immediate consciousness that all these worlds exist only as our idea, only as modifications of the eternal subject of pure knowing, which we find ourselves to be as soon as we forget our individuality, and which is the necessary supporter of all worlds and all times the condition of their possibility. The vastness of the world which disquieted us before, rests now in us; our dependence upon it is annulled by its dependence upon us. All this, however, does not come at once into reflection, but shows itself merely as the felt consciousness that in some sense or other (which philosophy alone can explain) we are one with the world, and therefore not oppressed, but exalted by its immensity.

We receive this impression of the mathematical-sublime, quite directly, by means of a space which is small indeed as compared with the world, but which has become directly perceptible to us, and affects us with its whole extent in all its three dimensions, so as to make our own body seem almost infinitely small. An empty space can never be thus perceived, and therefore never an open space, but only space that is directly perceptible in all its dimensions by means of the limits which enclose it; thus for example a very high, vast dome, like that of St. Peter's at Rome, or St. Paul's in London. The sense of the sublime here arises through the consciousness of the vanishing nothingness of our own body in the presence of a vastness which, from another point of view, itself exists only in our idea, and of which we are as knowing subject, the supporter. Thus here as everywhere it arises from the contrast between the insignificance and dependence of ourselves as individuals, as phenomena of will, and the consciousness of ourselves as pure subject of knowing. Even the vault of the starry heaven produces this if it is contemplated without reflection; but just in the same way as the vault of stone, and only by its apparent, not its real extent. Some objects of our perception excite in us the feeling of the sublime because, not only on account of their spatial vastness, but also of their great age, that is, their temporal duration, we feel ourselves dwarfed to insignificance in their presence, and yet revel in the pleasure of contemplating them: of this kind are very high mountains, the Egyptian pyramids, and colossal ruins of great antiquity.

Our explanation of the sublime applies also to the ethical, to what is called the sublime character. Such a character arises from this, that the will is not excited by objects which are well calculated to excite it, but that knowledge retains the upper hand in their presence. A man of sublime character will accordingly consider men in a purely objective way, and not with reference to the relations which they might have to his will; he will, for example, observe their faults, even their hatred and injustice to himself, without being himself excited to hatred; he will behold their happiness without envy; he will recognise their good qualities without desiring any closer relations with them; he will perceive the beauty of women, but he will not desire them. His personal happiness or unhappiness will not greatly affect him, he will rather be as Hamlet describes Horatio:—

". . . for thou hast been,
As one, in suffering all, that suffers nothing;
A man that fortune's buffets and rewards
Hast ta'en with equal thanks," &c. (A. 3. Sc. 2.)

For in the course of his own life and its misfortunes, he will consider less his individual lot than that of humanity in general, and will therefore conduct himself in its regard, rather as knowing than as suffering.

§ 40. Opposites throw light upon each other, and therefore the remark may be in place here, that the proper opposite of the sublime is something which would not at the first glance be recognised, as such: *the charming* or *attractive*. By this, however, I understand, that which excites the will by presenting to it directly its fulfilment, its satisfaction. We saw that the feeling of the sublime rises from the fact that something entirely unfavourable to the will becomes the object of pure contemplation, so that such contemplation can only be maintained by persistently turning away from the will, and transcending its interests; this constitutes the sublimity of the character. The charming or attractive, on the contrary, draws the beholder away from the pure contemplation which is demanded by all apprehension of the beautiful, because it necessarily excites this will, by objects which directly appeal to it, and thus he no longer remains pure subject of knowing, but becomes the needy and dependent subject of will. That every beautiful thing which is bright or cheering should be called charming, is the result of a too general concept, which arises from a want of accurate discrimination, and which I must entirely set aside, and indeed condemn. But in the sense of the word which has been given and explained, I find only two species of the charming or attractive in the province of art, and both of them are unworthy of it. The one species, a very low one, is found in Dutch paintings of still life, when they err by representing articles of food, which by their deceptive likeness necessarily excite the appetite for the things they represent, and this is just an excitement of the will, which puts an end to all æsthetic contemplation of the object. Painted fruit is yet admissible, because we may regard it as the further development of the flower, and as a beautiful product of nature in form and colour, without being obliged to think of it as eatable; but unfortunately we often find, represented with deceptive naturalness, prepared and served dishes, oysters, herrings, crabs, bread and butter, beer, wine, and so forth, which is altogether to be condemned. In historical painting and in sculpture the charming consists in naked figures, whose position, drapery, and general treatment are calculated to excite the passions of the beholder, and thus pure æsthetical contemplation is at once annihilated, and the aim of art is defeated. This mistake corresponds exactly to that which we have just censured in the Dutch paintings. The ancients are almost always free from this fault in their representations of beauty and complete nakedness of form, because the artist himself created them in a purely objective spirit, filled with ideal beauty, not in the spirit of subjective, and base sensuality. The charming is thus everywhere to be avoided in art.

There is also a negative species of the charming or exciting which is even more reprehensible than the positive form which has been discussed; this is the disgusting or the loathsome. It arouses the will of the beholder, just as what is properly speaking charming, and therefore disturbs pure æsthetic contemplation. But it is an active aversion and opposition which is excited by it; it arouses the will by presenting to it objects which it abhors. Therefore it has always been recognised that it is altogether inadmissible in art, where even what is ugly, when it is not disgusting, is allowable in its proper place, as we shall see later.

§ 42. I return to the exposition of the æsthetic impression. The knowledge of the beautiful always supposes at once and inseparably the pure knowing subject and the known Idea as object. Yet the source of æsthetic satisfaction will sometimes lie more in the comprehension of the known Idea, sometimes more in the blessedness and spiritual peace of the pure knowing subject freed from all willing, and therefore from all individuality, and the pain that proceeds from it. And, indeed, this predominance of one or the other constituent part of æsthetic feeling will depend upon whether the intuitively grasped Idea is a higher or a lower grade of the objectivity of will. Thus in æsthetic contemplation (in the real, or through the medium of art) of the beauty of nature in the inorganic and vegetable worlds, or in works of architecture, the pleasure of pure willless knowing will predominate, because the Ideas which are here apprehended are only low grades of the objectivity of will, and are therefore not manifestations of deep significance and rich content. On the other hand, if animals and man are the objects of æsthetic contemplation or representation, the pleasure will consist rather in the comprehension of these Ideas, which are the most distinct revelation of will; for they exhibit the greatest multiplicity of forms, the greatest richness and deep significance of phenomena, and reveal to us most completely the nature of will, whether in its violence, its terribleness, its satisfaction or its aberration (the latter in tragic situations), or finally in its change and self-surrender, which is the peculiar theme of christian painting; as the Idea of the will enlightened by full knowledge is the object of historical painting in general, and of the drama. We shall now go through the fine arts one by one, and this will give completeness and distinctness to the theory of the beautiful which we have advanced.

§ 43. Matter as such cannot be the expression of an Idea. For, as we found in the first book, it is throughout nothing but causality: its being consists in its causal action. But causality is a form of the principle of sufficient reason; knowledge of the Idea, on the other hand, absolutely excludes the content of that principle. We also found, in the second book, that matter is the common substratum of all particular phenomena of the Ideas, and consequently is the connecting link between the Idea and the phenomenon, or the particular thing. Accordingly for both of these reasons it is impossible that matter can for itself express any Idea. This is confirmed *a posteriori* by the fact that it is impossible to have a perceptible idea of matter as such, but only an abstract conception; in the former, *i. e.*, in perceptible ideas are exhibited only the forms and qualities of which matter is the supporter, and in all of which Ideas reveal themselves. This corresponds also with the fact, that causality (the whole essence of matter) cannot for itself be presented perceptibly, but is merely a definite causal connection. On the other hand, *every phenomenon* of an Idea, because as such it has entered the form of the principle of sufficient reason, or the principle of individuation, must exhibit itself in matter, as one of its qualities. So far then matter is, as we have said, the connecting link between the Idea and the principle of individuation, which is the form of knowledge of the individual, or the principle of sufficient reason. Plato is therefore perfectly right in his enumeration, for after the Idea and the phenomenon, which include all other things in the world, he gives matter only, as a third thing which is different from both (Timaus, p. 345). The individual, as a phenomenon of the Idea, is always matter. Every quality of matter is also the phenomenon of an Idea, and as such it may always be an object of æsthetic contemplation, *i. e.,* the Idea expressed in it may always be recognized. This holds good of even the most universal qualities of matter, without which it never appears, and which are the weakest objectivity of will. Such are gravity, cohesion, rigidity, fluidity, sensitiveness to light, and so forth.

If now we consider *architecture* simply as a fine art and apart from its application to useful ends, in which it serves the will and not pure knowledge, and therefore ceases to be art in our sense; we can assign to it no other aim than that of bringing to greater distinctness some of those ideas, which are the lowest grades of the objectivity of will; such as gravity, cohesion, rigidity, hardness, those universal qualities of stone, those first, simplest, most inarticulate manifestations of will; the bass notes of nature; and after these light, which in many respects is their opposite. Even at these low grades of the objectivity of will we see its nature revealing itself in discord; for properly speaking the conflict between gravity and rigidity is the sole æsthetic material of architecture; its problem is to make this conflict appear with perfect distinctness in a multitude of different ways. It solves it by depriving these indestructible forces of the shortest way to their satisfaction, and conducting them to it by a circuitous route, so that the conflict is lengthened and the inexhaustible efforts of both forces become visible in many different ways. The whole mass of the building, if left to its original tendency, would exhibit a mere heap or clump, bound as closely as possible to the earth, to which gravity, the form in which the will appears here, continually presses, while rigidity, also objectivity of will, resists. But this very tendency, this effort, is hindered by architecture from obtaining direct satisfaction, and only allowed to reach it indirectly and by roundabout ways. The roof, for example, can only press the earth through columns, the arch must support itself, and can only satisfy its tendency towards the earth through the medium of the pillars, and so forth. But just by these enforced digressions, just by these restrictions, the forces which reside in the crude mass of stone unfold themselves in the most distinct and multifarious ways; and the purely æsthetic aim of architecture can go no further than this. Therefore the beauty, at any rate, of a building lies in the obvious adaptation of every part, not to the outward arbitrary end of man (so far the work belongs to practical architecture), but directly to the stability of the whole, to which the position, dimensions, and form of every part must have so necessary a relation that, where it is possible, if any one part were taken away, the whole would fall to pieces. For just because each part bears just as much as it conveniently can, and each is supported just where it requires to be and just to the necessary extent, this opposition unfolds itself, this conflict between rigidity and gravity, which constitutes the life, the manifestation of will, in the stone, becomes completely visible, and these lowest grades of the objectivity of will reveal themselves distinctly. In the same way the form of each part must not be determined arbitrarily, but by its end, and its relation to the whole. The column is the simplest form of support, determined simply by its end: the twisted column is tasteless; the four-cornered pillar is in fact not so simple as the round column, though it happens that it is easier to make it. The forms also of frieze, rafter, roof, and dome are entirely determined by their immediate end, and explain themselves from it. The decoration of capitals, &c., belongs to sculpture, not to architecture, which admits it merely as extraneous ornament, and could dispense with it. According to what has been said, it is absolutely necessary, in order to understand the æsthetic satisfaction afforded by a work of architecture, to have immediate knowledge through perception of its matter as regards its weight, rigidity, and cohesion, and our pleasure in such a work would suddenly be very much diminished by the discovery that the material used was pumice-stone; for then it would appear to us as a kind of sham building. We would be affected in almost the same way if we were told that it was made of wood, when we had supposed it to be of stone, just because this alters and destroys the relation between rigidity and gravity, and consequently the significance and necessity of all the parts, for these natural forces reveal themselves in a far weaker degree in a wooden building. Therefore no real work of architecture as a fine art can be made of wood, although it assumes all forms so easily; this can only be explained by our theory. If we were distinctly told that a building, the sight of which gave us pleasure, was made of different kinds of material of very unequal weight and consistency, but not distinguishable to the eye, the whole building would become as utterly incapable of affording us pleasure as a poem in an unknown language. All this proves that architecture does not affect us mathematically, but also dynamically, and that what speaks to us through it, is not mere form and symmetry, but rather those fundamental forces of nature, those first Ideas, those lowest grades of the objectivity of will. The regularity of the building and its parts is partly produced by the direct adaptation of each member to the stability of the whole, partly it serves to facilitate the survey and comprehension of the whole, and finally, regular figures to some extent enhance the beauty because they reveal the constitution of space as such. But all this is of subordinate value and necessity, and by no means the chief concern; indeed, symmetry is not invariably demanded, as ruins are still beautiful.

Works of architecture have further quite a special relation to light; they gain a double beauty in the full sunshine, with the blue sky as a background, and again they have quite a different effect by moonlight. Therefore, when a beautiful work of architecture is to be erected, special attention is always paid to the effects of the light and to the climate. The reason of all this is, indeed, principally that all the parts and their relations are only made clearly visible by a bright, strong light; but besides this I am of opinion that it is the function of architecture to reveal the nature of light just as it reveals that of things so opposite to it as gravity and rigidity. For the light is intercepted, confined, and reflected by the great opaque, sharply outlined, and variously formed masses of stone, and thus it unfolds its nature and qualities in the purest and clearest way, to the great pleasure of the beholders, for light is the most joy-giving of things, as the condition and the objective correlative of the most perfect kind of knowledge of perception.

Now, because the Ideas which architecture brings to clear perception, are the lowest grades of the objectivity of will, and consequently their objective significance, which architecture reveals to us, is comparatively small; the æsthetic pleasure of looking at a beautiful building in a good light will lie, not so much in the comprehension of the Idea, as in the subjective correlative which accompanies this comprehension; it will consist pre-eminently in the fact that the beholder, set free from the kind of knowledge that belongs to the individual, and which serves the will and follows the principle of sufficient reason, is raised to that of the pure subject of knowing free from will. It will consist then principally in pure contemplation itself, free from all the suffering of will and of individuality. In this respect the opposite of architecture, and the other extreme of the series of the fine arts, is the drama, which brings to knowledge the most significant Ideas. Therefore in the æsthetic pleasure afforded by the drama the objective side is throughout predominant.

Architecture has this distinction from plastic art and poetry: it does not give us a copy but the thing itself. It does not repeat, as they do, the known Idea, so that the artist lends his eyes to the beholder, but in it the artist merely presents the object to the beholder, and facilitates for him the comprehension of the Idea by bringing the actual, individual object to a distinct and complete expression of its nature.

Unlike the works of the other arts, those of architecture are very seldom executed for purely æsthetic ends. These are generally subordinated to other useful ends which are foreign to art itself. Thus the great merit of the architect consists in achieving and attaining the pure æsthetic ends, in spite of their subordination to other ends which are foreign to them. This he does by cleverly adapting them in a variety of ways to the arbitrary ends in view, and by rightly judging which form of æsthetical architectonic beauty is compatible and may be associated with a temple, which with a palace, which with a prison, and so forth. The more a harsh climate increases these demands of necessity and utility, determines them definitely, and prescribes them more inevitably, the less free play has beauty in architecture. In the mild climate of India, Egypt, Greece, and Rome, where the demands of necessity were fewer and less definite, architecture could follow its æsthetic ends with the greatest freedom. But under a northern sky this was sorely hindered. Here, when caissons, pointed roofs and towers were what was demanded, architecture could only unfold its own beauty within very narrow limits, and therefore it was obliged to make amends by resorting all the more to the borrowed ornaments of sculpture, as is seen in Gothic architecture.

We thus see that architecture is greatly restricted by the demands of necessity and utility; but on the other hand it has in them a very powerful support, for, on account of the magnitude and costliness of its works, and the narrow sphere of its æsthetic effect, it could not continue to exist merely as a fine art, if it had not also, as a useful and necessary profession, a firm and honourable place among the occupations of men. It is the want of this that prevents another art from taking its place beside architecture as a sister art, although in an æsthetical point of view it is quite properly to be classed along with it as its counterpart; I mean artistic arrangements of water. For what architecture accomplishes for the Idea of gravity when it appears in connection with that of rigidity, hydraulics accomplishes for the same Idea, when it is connected with fluidity, i. e., formlessness, the greatest mobility and transparency. Leaping waterfalls foaming and tumbling over rocks, cataracts dispersed into floating spray, springs gushing up as high columns of water, and clear reflecting lakes, reveal the Ideas of fluid and heavy matter, in precisely the same way as the works of architecture unfold the Ideas of rigid matter. Artistic hydraulics, however, obtains no support from practical hydraulics, for, as a rule, their ends cannot be combined; yet, in exceptional cases, this happens; for example, in the Cascata di Trevi at Rome.

§ 45. The great problem of historical painting and sculpture is to express directly and for perception the Idea in which the will reaches the highest grade of its objectification. The objective side of the pleasure afforded by the beautiful is here always predominant, and the subjective side has retired into the background. It is further to be observed that at the next grade below this, animal painting, the characteristic is entirely one with the beautiful; the most characteristic lion, wolf, horse, sheep, or ox, was always the most beautiful also. The reason of this is that animals have only the character of their species, no individual character. In the representation of men the character of the species is separated from that of the individual; the former is now called beauty (entirely in the objective sense), but the latter retains the name, character, or expression, and the new difficulty arises of representing both, at once and completely, in the same individual.

Human beauty is an objective expression, which means the fullest objectification of will at the highest grade at which it is knowable, the Idea of man in general, completely expressed in the sensible form. But however much the objective side of the beautiful appears here, the subjective side still always accompanies it. And just because no object transports us so quickly into pure æsthetic contemplation, as the most beautiful human countenance and form, at the sight of which we are instantly filled with unspeakable satisfaction, and raised above ourselves and all that troubles us; this is only possible because this most distinct and purest knowledge of will raises us most easily and quickly to the state of pure knowing, in which our personality, our will with its constant pain, disappears, so long as the pure æsthetic pleasure lasts. Therefore it is that Goethe says: "No evil can touch him who looks on human beauty; he feels himself at one with himself and with the world." That a beautiful human form is produced by nature must be explained in this way. At this its highest grade the will objectifies itself in an individual; and therefore through circumstances and its own power it completely overcomes all the hindrances and opposition which the phenomena of the lower grades present to it. Such are the forces of nature, from which the will must always first extort and win back the matter that belongs to all its manifestations. Further, the phenomenon of will at its higher grades always has multiplicity in its form. Even the tree is only a systematic aggregate of innumerably repeated sprouting fibres. This combination assumes greater complexity in higher forms, and the human body is an exceedingly complex system of different parts, each of which has a peculiar life of its own, *vita propria,* subordinate to the whole. Now that all these parts are in the proper fashion subordinate to the whole, and co-ordinate to each other, that they all work together harmoniously for the expression of the whole, nothing superfluous, nothing restricted; all these are the rare conditions, whose result is beauty, the completely expressed character of the species. So is it in nature. But how in art? One would suppose that art achieved the beautiful by imitating nature. But how is the artist to recognise the perfect work which is to be imitated, and distinguish it from the failures, if he does not anticipate the beautiful *before experience?* And be-

sides this, has nature ever produced a human being perfectly beautiful in all his parts? It has accordingly been
thought that the artist must seek out the beautiful parts,
distributed among a number of different human beings,
and out of them construct a beautiful whole; a perverse
and foolish opinion. For it will be asked, how is he to
know that just these forms and not others are beautiful?
We also see what kind of success attended the efforts of
the old German painters to achieve the beautiful by imitating nature. Observe their naked figures. No knowledge
of the beautiful is possible purely *a posteriori*, and from
mere experience; it is always, at least in part, *a priori*,
although quite different in kind, from the forms of the
principle of sufficient reason, of which we are conscious
a priori. These concern the universal form of phenomena
as such, as it constitutes the possibility of knowledge in
general, the universal *how* of all phenomena, and from
this knowledge proceed mathematics and pure natural
science. But this other kind of knowledge *a priori*, which
makes it possible to express the beautiful, concerns, not
the form but the content of phenomena, not the *how* but
the *what* of the phenomenon. That we all recognise human beauty when we see it, but that in the true artist
this takes place with such clearness that he shows it as
he has never seen it, and surpasses nature in his representation; this is only possible because *we ourselves are* the
will whose adequate objectification at its highest grade is
here to be judged and discovered. Thus alone have we in
fact an anticipation of that which nature (which is
just the will that constitutes our own being) strives
to express. And in the true genius this anticipation is accompanied by so great a degree of intelligence that he
recognises the Idea in the particular thing, and thus, as
it were, *understands the half-uttered speech of nature*,
and articulates clearly what she only stammered forth.

He expresses in the hard marble that beauty of form which in a thousand attempts she failed to produce, he presents it to nature, saying, as it were, to her, "That is what you wanted to say!" And whoever is able to judge replies, "Yes, that is it." Only in this way was it possible for the genius of the Greeks to find the type of human beauty and establish it as a canon for the school of sculpture; and only by virtue of such an anticipation is it possible for all of us to recognise beauty, when it has actually been achieved by nature in the particular case. This anticipation is the *Ideal*. It is the *Idea* so far as it is known *a priori*, at least half, and it becomes practical for art, because it corresponds to and completes what is given *a posteriori* through nature. The possibility of such an anticipation of the beautiful *a priori* in the artist, and of its recognition *a posteriori* by the critic, lies in the fact that the artist and the critic are themselves the "in-itself" of nature, the will which objectifies itself. For, as Empedocles said, like can only be known by like: only nature can understand itself: only nature can fathom itself: but only spirit also can understand spirit.

The opinion, which is absurd, although expressed by the Socrates of Xenophon that the Greeks discovered the established ideal of human beauty empirically, by collecting particular beautiful parts, uncovering and noting here a knee, there an arm, has an exact parallel in the art of poetry. The view is entertained, that Shakespeare, for example, observed, and then gave forth from his own experience of life, the innumerable variety of the characters in his dramas, so true, so sustained, so profoundly worked out. The impossibility and absurdity of such an assumption need not be dwelt upon. It is obvious that the man of genius produces the works of poetic art by means of an anticipation of what is characteristic, just as he produces the works of plastic and pictorial art by means of a prophetic anticipation of the beautiful; yet both require experience as a pattern or model, for thus alone can that which is dimly known *a priori* be called into clear consciousness, and an intelligent representation of it becomes possible.

§ 48. *Historical painting* has for its principal object, besides beauty and grace, character. By character we mean generally, the representation of will at the highest grade of its objectification, when the individual, as giving prominence to a particular side of the Idea of humanity, has special significance, and shows this not merely by his form, but makes it visible in his bearing and occupation, by action of every kind, and the modifications of knowing and willing that occasion and accompany it. The Idea of man must be exhibited in these circumstances, and therefore the unfolding of its many-sidedness must be brought before our eyes by means of representative individuals, and these individuals can only be made visible in their significance through various scenes, events, and actions. This is the endless problem of the historical painter, and he solves it by placing before us scenes of life of every kind, of greater or less significance. No individual and no action can be without significance; in all and through all the Idea of man unfolds itself more and more. Therefore no event of human life is excluded from the sphere of painting. It is thus a great injustice to the excellent painters of the Dutch school, to prize merely their technical skill, and to look down upon them in other respects, because, for the most part, they represent objects of common life, whereas it is assumed that only the events of the history of the world, or the incidents of biblical story, have significance. We ought first to bethink ourselves that the inward significance of an action is quite different from its outward significance, and that these are often separated from each other. The outward signifi-

cance is the importance of an action in relation to its result for and in the actual world; thus according to the
principle of sufficient reason. The inward significance is
the depth of the insight into the Idea of man which it
reveals, in that it brings to light sides of that Idea which
rarely appear, by making individuals who assert themselves distinctly and decidedly, disclose their peculiar
characteristics by means of appropriately arranged circumstances. Only the inward significance concerns art;
the outward belongs to history. They are both completely
independent of each other; they may appear together,
but may each appear alone. An action which is of the
highest significance for history may in inward significance be a very ordinary and common one; and conversely, a scene of ordinary daily life may be of great inward
significance, if human individuals, and the inmost recesses of human action and will, appear in it in a clear
and distinct light. Further, the outward and the inward
significance of a scene may be equal and yet very different. Thus, for example, it is all the same, as far as inward significance is concerned, whether ministers discuss
the fate of countries and nations over a map, or boors
wrangle in a beer-house over cards and dice, just as it is
all the same whether we play chess with golden or
wooden pieces. But apart from this, the scenes and events
that make up the life of so many millions of men, their
actions, their sorrows, their joys, are on that account important enough to be the object of art, and by their rich
variety they must afford material enough for unfolding
the many-sided Idea of man. Indeed the very transitoriness of the moment which art has fixed in such a picture
(now called *genre*-painting) excites a slight and peculiar
sensation; for to fix the fleeting, ever-changing world in
the enduring picture of a single event, which yet repre-

sents the whole, is an achievement of the art of painting
by which it seems to bring time itself to a standstill, for
it raises the individual to the Idea of its species. Finally,
the historical and outwardly significant subjects of painting have often the disadvantage that just what is significant in them cannot be presented to perception, but must
be arrived at by thought. In this respect the nominal significance of the picture must be distinguished from its
real significance. The former is the outward significance,
which, however, can only be reached as a conception; the
latter is that side of the Idea of man which is made visible to the onlooker in the picture. For example, Moses
found by the Egyptian princess is the nominal significance of a painting; it represents a moment of the greatest importance in history; the real significance, on the
other hand, that which is really given to the onlooker, is
a foundling child rescued from its floating cradle by a
great lady, an incident which may have happened more
than once. The costume alone can here indicate the particular historical case to the learned; but the costume is
only of importance to the nominal significance, and is a
matter of indifference to the real significance; for the latter knows only the human being as such, not the arbitrary forms. Subjects taken from history have no advantage over those which are taken from mere possibility,
and which are therefore to be called, not individual, but
merely general. For what is peculiarly significant in the
former is not the individual, not the particular event as
such, but the universal in it, the side of the Idea of humanity which expresses itself through it. But, on the
other hand, definite historical subjects are not on this account to be rejected, only the really artistic view of such
subjects, both in the painter and in the beholder, is never
directed to the individual particulars in them, which
properly constitute the historical, but to the universal

which expresses itself in them, to the Idea. And only
those historical subjects are to be chosen the chief point
of which can actually be represented, and not merely arrived at by thought, otherwise the nominal significance
is too remote from the real; what is merely thought in
connection with the picture becomes of most importance,
and interferes with what is perceived. If even on the
stage it is not right that the chief incident of the plot
should take place behind the scenes (as in French tragedies), it is clearly a far greater fault in a picture. Historical subjects are distinctly disadvantageous only when
they confine the painter to a field which has not been
chosen for artistic but for other reasons, and especially
when this field is poor in picturesque and significant objects—if, for example, it is the history of a small, isolated, capricious, hierarchical (*i. e.*, ruled by error), obscure people, like the Jews, despised by the great contemporary nations of the East and the West. Since the
wandering of the tribes lies between us and all ancient nations, as the change of the bed of the ocean lies between
the earth's surface as it is to-day and as it was when
those organisations existed which we only know from fos-
sil remains, it is to be regarded generally as a great misfortune that the people whose culture was to be the principal basis of our own were not the Indians or the
Greeks, or even the Romans, but these very Jews. But it
was especially a great misfortune for the Italian painters
of genius in the fifteenth and sixteenth centuries that, in
the narrow sphere to which they were arbitrarily driven
for the choice of subjects, they were obliged to have recourse to miserable beings of every kind. For the New
Testament, as regards its historical part, is almost more
unsuitable for painting than the Old, and the subsequent
history of martyrs and doctors of the church is a very
unfortunate subject. Yet of the pictures, whose subject

is the history or mythology of Judaism and Christianity, we must carefully distinguish those in which the peculiar, *i. e.,* the ethical spirit of Christianity is revealed for perception, by the representation of men who are full of this spirit. These representations are in fact the highest and most admirable achievements of the art of painting; and only the greatest masters of this art succeeded in this, particularly Raphael and Correggio, and especially in their earlier pictures. Pictures of this kind are not properly to be classed as historical: for, as a rule, they represent no event, no action; but are merely groups of saints, with the Saviour himself, often still a child, with His mother, angels, &c. In their countenances, and especially in the eyes, we see the expression, the reflection, of the completest knowledge, that which is not directed to particular things, but has fully grasped the Ideas, and thus the whole nature of the world and life. And this knowledge in them, reacting upon the will, does not, like other knowledge, convey *motives* to it, but on the contrary has become a *quieter* of all will, from which proceeded the complete resignation, which is the innermost spirit of Christianity, as of the Indian philosophy; the surrender of all volition, conversion, the suppression of will, and with it of the whole inner being of this world, that is to say, salvation. Thus these masters of art, worthy of eternal praise, expressed perceptibly in their works the highest wisdom. And this is the summit of all art. It has followed the will in its adequate objectivity, the Ideas, through all its grades, in which it is affected and its nature unfolded in so many ways, first by causes, then by stimuli, and finally by motives. And now art ends with the representation of the free self-suppression of will, by means of the great peace which it gains from the perfect knowledge of its own nature.

§ 49. The truth which lies at the foundation of all that we have hitherto said about art, is that the object of art, the representation of which is the aim of the artist, and the knowledge of which must therefore precede his work as its germ and source, is an Idea in Plato's sense, and never anything else; not the particular thing, the object of common apprehension, and not the concept, the object of rational thought and of science. Although the Idea and the concept have something in common, because both represent as unity a multiplicity of real things; yet the great difference between them has no doubt been made clear and evident enough by what we have said about concepts in the first book, and about Ideas in this book. I by no means wish to assert, however, that Plato really distinctly comprehended this difference; indeed many of his examples of Ideas, and his discussions of them, are applicable only to concepts. Meanwhile we leave this question alone and go on our own way, glad when we come upon traces of any great and noble mind, yet not following his footsteps but our own aim. The *concept* is abstract, discursive, undetermined within its own sphere, only determined by its limits, attainable and comprehensible by him who has only reason, communicable by words without any other assistance, entirely exhausted by its definition. The *Idea* on the contrary, although defined as the adequate representative of the concept, is always object of perception, and although representing an infinite number of particular things, is yet thoroughly determined. It is never known by the individual as such, but only by him who has raised himself above all willing and all individuality to the pure subject of knowing. Thus it is only attainable by the man of genius, and by him who, for the most part through the assistance of the works of genius, has reached an exalted frame of mind, by increasing his power of pure knowing. It is therefore not absolutely but only conditionally communicable, because the Idea, comprehended and repeated in the work of art, appeals to every one only according to the measure of his own intellectual worth. So that just the most excellent works of every art, the noblest productions of genius, must always remain sealed books to the dull majority of men, inaccessible to them, separated from them by a wide gulf, just as the society of princes is inaccessible to the common people. It is true that even the dullest of them accept on authority recognisedly great works, lest otherwise they should argue their own incompetence; but they wait in silence, always ready to express their condemnation, as soon as they are allowed to hope that they may do so without being left to stand alone; and then their long-restrained hatred against all that is great and beautiful, and against the authors of it, gladly relieves itself; for such things never appealed to them, and for that very reason were humiliating to them. For as a rule a man must have worth in himself in order to recognise it and believe in it willingly and freely in others. On this rests the necessity of modesty in all merit, and the disproportionately loud praise of this virtue, which alone of all its sisters is always included in the eulogy of every one who ventures to praise any distinguished man, in order to appease and quiet the wrath of the unworthy. What then is modesty but hypocritical humility, by means of which, in a world swelling with base envy, a man seeks to obtain pardon for excellences and merits from those who have none? For whoever attributes to himself no merits, because he actually has none, is not modest but merely honest.

The *Idea* is the unity that falls into multiplicity on account of the temporal and spatial form of our intuitive apprehension; the *concept,* on the contrary, is the unity

reconstructed out of multiplicity by the abstraction of
our reason; the latter may be defined as *unitas post rem,*
the former as *unitas ante rem.* Finally, we may express
the distinction between the Idea and the concept, by a
comparison, thus: the *concept* is like a dead receptacle,
in which, whatever has been put, actually lies side by
side, but out of which no more can be taken (by analytical judgment) than was put in (by synthetical reflection); the (Platonic) *Idea,* on the other hand, develops,
in him who has comprehended it, ideas which are new
as regards the concept of the same name; it resembles
a living organism, developing itself and possessed of the
power of reproduction, which brings forth what was not
put into it.

It follows from all that has been said, that the concept, useful as it is in life, and serviceable, necessary
and productive as it is in science, is yet always barren
and unfruitful in art. The comprehended Idea, on the
contrary, is the true and only source of every work of
art. In its powerful originality it is only derived from
life itself, from nature, from the world, and that only
by the true genius, or by him whose momentary inspiration reaches the point of genius. Genuine and immortal
works of art spring only from such direct apprehension.
Just because the Idea is and remains object of perception, the artist is not conscious in the abstract of the
intention and aim of his work; not a concept, but an
Idea floats before his mind; therefore he can give no
justification of what he does. He works, as people say,
from pure feeling, and unconsciously, indeed instinctively. On the contrary, imitators, mannerists, start,
in art, from the concept; they observe what pleases and
affects us in true works of art; understand it clearly,
fix it in a concept, and thus abstractly, and then imi-
tate it, openly or disguisedly, with dexterity and inten-

tionally. They suck their nourishment, like parasite plants, from the works of others, and like polypi, they become the colour of their food. We might carry comparison further, and say that they are like machines which mince fine and mingle together whatever is put into them, but can never digest it, so that the different constituent parts may always be found again if they are sought out and separated from the mixture; the man of genius alone resembles the organised, assimilating, transforming and reproducing body. For he is indeed educated and cultured by his predecessors and their works; but he is really fructified only by life and the world directly, through the impression of what he perceives; therefore the highest culture never interferes with his originality. All imitators, all mannerists, apprehend in concepts the nature of representative works of art; but concepts can never impart inner life to a work. The age, *i. e.,* the dull multitude of every time, knows only concepts, and sticks to them, and therefore receives mannered works of art with ready and loud applause: but after a few years these works become insipid, because the spirit of the age, *i. e.,* the prevailing concepts, in which alone they could take root, have changed. Only true works of art, which are drawn directly from nature and life, have eternal youth and enduring power, like nature and life themselves. For they belong to no age, but to humanity, and as on that account they are coldly received by their own age, to which they disdain to link themselves closely, and because indirectly and negatively they expose the existing errors, they are slowly and unwillingly recognized; on the other hand, they cannot grow old, but appear to us ever fresh and new down to the latest ages. Then they are no longer exposed to neglect and ignorance, for they are crowned and sanctioned by the praise of the few men capable of judging, who appear singly and rarely in the course of ages, and give in their votes, whose slowly growing number constitutes the authority, which alone is the judgment-seat we mean when we appeal to posterity. It is these successively appearing individuals, for the mass of posterity will always be and remain just as perverse and dull as the mass of contemporaries always was and always is. We read the complaints of great men in every century about the customs of their age. They always sound as if they referred to our own age, for the race is always the same. At every time and in every art, mannerisms have taken the place of the spirit, which was always the possession of a·few individuals, but mannerisms are just the old cast-off garments of the last manifestation of the spirit that existed and was recognised. From all this it appears that, as a rule, the praise of posterity can only be gained at the cost of the praise of one's contemporaries, and *vice versa*.

§ 51. If now, with the exposition which has been given of art in general, we turn from plastic and pictorial art to poetry, we shall have no doubt that its aim also is the revelation of the Ideas, the grades of the objectification of will, and the communication of them to the hearer with the distinctness and vividness with which the poetical sense comprehends them. Ideas are essentially perceptible; if, therefore, in poetry only abstract conceptions are directly communicated through words, it is yet clearly the intention to make the hearer perceive the Ideas of life in the representatives of these conceptions, and this can only take place through the assistance of his own imagination. But in order to set the imagination to work for the accomplishment of this end, the abstract conceptions, which are the immediate material of poetry as of dry prose, must be so arranged

that their spheres intersect each other in such a way
that none of them can remain in its abstract universality;
but, instead of it, a perceptible representative appears
to the imagination; and this is always further modified
by the words of the poet according to what his intention
may be. As the chemist obtains solid precipitates by combining perfectly clear and transparent fluids; the poet
understands how to precipitate, as it were, the concrete,
the individual, the perceptible idea, out of the abstract
and transparent universality of the concepts by the manner in which he combines them. For the Idea can only be
known by perception; and knowledge of the Idea is the
end of art. The skill of a master, in poetry as in chemistry, enables us always to obtain the precise precipitate
we intended. This end is assisted by the numerous epi-
thets in poetry, by means of which the universality of
every concept is narrowed more and more till we reach
the perceptible.

"Where gentle winds from the blue heavens sigh,
There stand the myrtles still, the laurel high,"—

calls up before the imagination by means of a few concepts the whole delight of a southern clime.

Rhythm and rhyme are quite peculiar aids to poetry.
I can give no other explanation of their incredibly
powerful effect than that our faculties of perception
have received from time, to which they are essentially
bound, some quality on account of which we inwardly
follow, and, as it were, consent to each regularly recurring sound. In this way rhythm and rhyme are
partly a means of holding our attention, because we
willingly follow the poem read, and partly they produce in us a blind consent to what is read prior to any
judgment, and this gives the poem a certain emphatic
power of convincing independent of all reasons.

From the general nature of the material, that is, the concepts, which poetry uses to communicate the Ideas, the extent of its province is very great. The whole of nature, the Ideas of all grades, can be represented by means of it, for it proceeds according to the Idea it has to impart, so that its representations are sometimes descriptive, sometimes narrative, and sometimes directly dramatic. If, in the representation of the lower grades of the objectivity of will, plastic and pictorial art generally surpass it, because lifeless nature, and even brute nature, reveals almost its whole being in a single well-chosen moment; man, on the contrary, so far as he does not express himself by the mere form and expression of his person, but through a series of actions and the accompanying thoughts and emotions, is the principal object of poetry, in which no other art can compete with it, for here the progress or movement which cannot be represented in plastic or pictorial art just suits its purpose.

The revelation of the Idea, which is the highest grade of the objectivity of will, the representation of man in the connected series of his efforts and actions, is thus the great problem of poetry. It is true that both experience and history teach us to know man; yet oftener men than man, *i. e.*, they give us empirical notes of the behaviour of men to each other, from which we may frame rules for our own conduct, oftener than they afford us deep glimpses of the inner nature of man. The latter function, however, is by no means entirely denied them; but as often as it is the nature of mankind itself that discloses itself to us in history or in our own experience, we have comprehended our experience, and the historian has comprehended history, with artistic eyes, poetically, *i. e.*, according to the Idea, not the phenomenon, in its inner nature, not in its relations. Our own experience is the indispensable condition of understanding poetry as of understanding history; for it is, so to speak, the dictionary of the language that both speak. But history is related to poetry as portrait-painting is related to historical painting; the one gives us the true in the individual, the other the true in the universal; the one has the truth of the phenomenon, and can therefore verify it from the phenomenal, the other has the truth of the Idea, which can be found in no particular phenomenon, but yet speaks to us from them all. The poet from deliberate choice represents significant characters in significant situations; the historian takes both as they come. Indeed, he must regard and select the circumstances and the persons, not with reference to their inward and true significance, which expresses the Idea, but according to the outward, apparent, and relatively important significance with regard to the connection and the consequences. He must consider nothing in and for itself in its essential character and expression, but must look at everything in its relations, in its connection, in its influence upon what follows, and especially upon its own age. Therefore he will not overlook an action of a king, though of little significance, and in itself quite common, because it has results and influence. And, on the other hand, actions of the highest significance of particular and very eminent individuals are not to be recorded by him if they have no consequences. For his treatment follows the principle of sufficient reason, and apprehends the phenomenon, of which this principle is the form. But the poet comprehends the Idea, the inner nature of man apart from all relations, outside all time, the adequate objectivity of the thing-in-itself, at its highest grade. Even in that method of treatment which is necessary for the historian, the inner nature and significance of the phenomena, the kernel of all these shells, can never be entirely lost. He who seeks for it, at any rate, may find it and recognise it. Yet that which is significant in itself, not in its relations, the real unfolding of the Idea, will be found far more accurately and distinctly in poetry than in history, and, therefore, however paradoxical it may sound, far more really genuine inner truth is to be attributed to poetry than to history. For the historian must accurately follow the particular event, according to life, as it develops itself in time in the manifold tangled chains of causes and effects. It is, however, impossible that he can have all the data for this; he cannot have seen all and discovered all. He is forsaken at every moment by the original of his picture, or a false one substitutes itself for it, and this so constantly that I think I may assume that in all history the false outweighs the true. The poet, on the contrary, has comprehended the Idea of man from some definite side which is to be represented; thus it is the nature of his own self that objectifies itself in it for him. His knowledge, as we explained above when speaking of sculpture, is half *a priori;* his ideal stands before his mind firm, distinct, brightly illuminated, and cannot forsake him; therefore he shows us, in the mirror of his mind, the Idea pure and distinct, and his delineation of it down to the minutest particular is true as life itself. The great ancient historians are, therefore, in those particulars in which their data fail them, for example, in the speeches of their heroes—poets; indeed their whole manner of handling their material approaches to the epic. But this gives their representations unity, and enables them to retain inner truth, even when outward truth was not accessible, or indeed was falsified. And as we compared history to partrait-painting, in contradistinction to poetry, which corresponds to historical painting, we find that Winckelmann's maxim, that the portrait ought to be the ideal of the individual, was followed by the ancient historians, for they represent the individual in such a way as to bring out that side of the Idea of man which is expressed in it. Modern historians, on the contrary, with few exceptions, give us in general only "a dust-bin and a lumber-room, and at the most a chronicle of the principal political events." Therefore, whoever desires to know man in his inner nature, identical in all its phenomena and developments, to know him according to the Idea, will find that the works of the great, immortal poet present a far truer, more distinct picture, than the historians can ever give. For even the best of the historians are, as poets, far from the first; and moreover their hands are tied. In this aspect the relation between the historian and the poet may be illustrated by the following comparison. The mere, pure historian, who works only according to data, is like a man, who without any knowledge of mathematics, has investigated the relations of certain figures, which he has accidentally found, by measuring them; and the problem thus empirically solved is affected of course by all the errors of the drawn figure. The poet, on the other hand, is like the mathematician, who constructs these relations *a priori* in pure perception, and expresses them not as they actually are in the drawn figure, but as they are in the Idea, which the drawing is intended to render for the senses. Therefore Schiller says:—

> "What has never anywhere come to pass,
> That alone never grows old."

Indeed I must attribute greater value to biographies, and especially to autobiographies, in relation to the knowledge of the nature of man, than to history proper, at least as it is commonly handled. Partly because in the former the data can be collected more accurately and completely than in the latter; partly, because in history proper, it is not so much men as nations and heroes that act, and the individuals who do appear, seem so far off, surrounded with such pomp and circumstance, clothed in the stiff robes of state, or heavy, inflexible armour, that it is really hard through all this to recognise the human movements. On the other hand, the life of the individual when described with truth, in a narrow sphere, shows the conduct of men in all its forms and subtilties, the excellence, the virtue, and even holiness of a few, the perversity, meanness, and knavery of most, the dissolute profligacy of some. Besides, in the only aspect we are considering here, that of the inner significance of the phenomenal, it is quite the same whether the objects with which the action is concerned, are, relatively considered, trifling or important, farm-houses or kingdoms: for all these things in themselves are without significance, and obtain it only in so far as the will is moved by them. The motive has significance only through its relation to the will, while the relation which it has as a thing to other things like itself, does not concern us here. As a circle of one inch in diameter, and a circle of forty million miles in diameter, have precisely the same geometrical properties, so are the events and the history of a village and a kingdom essentially the same; and we may study and learn to know mankind as well in the one as in the other. It is also a mistake to suppose that autobiographies are full of deceit and dissimulation. On the contrary, lying (though always possible) is perhaps more difficult there than elewhere. Dissimulation is easiest in mere conversation; indeed, though it may sound paradoxical, it is really more difficult even in a letter. For in the case of a letter the writer is alone, and looks into himself, and not out on the world, so that what is strange and distant does not easily approach him; and he has not the test of the impression made upon another before his eyes. But the receiver of the letter peruses it quietly in a mood unknown to the writer, reads it repeatedly and at different times, and thus easily finds out the concealed intention. We also get to know an author as a man most easily from his books, because all these circumstances act here still more strongly and permanently. And in an autobiography it is so difficult to dissimulate, that perhaps there does not exist a single one that is not, as a whole, more true, than any history that ever was written. The man who writes his own life surveys it as a whole, the particular becomes small, the near becomes distant, the distant becomes near again, the motives that influenced him shrink; he seats himself at the confessional, and has done so of his own free will; the spirit of lying does not so easily take hold of him here, for there is also in every man an inclination to truth which has first to be overcome whenever he lies, and which here has taken up a specially strong position. The relation between biography and the history of nations may be made clear for perception by means of the following comparison: History shows us mankind as a view from a high mountain shows us nature; we see much at a time, wide stretches, great masses, but nothing is distinct nor recognisable in all the details of its own peculiar nature. On the other hand, the representation of the life of the individual shows us the man, as we see nature if we go about among her trees, plants, rocks, and waters. But in landscape-painting in which the artist lets us look at nature with his eyes, the knowledge of the Ideas, and the condition of pure will-less knowing, which is demanded by these, is made much easier for us; and, in the same way, poetry is far superior both to history and biography, in the representation of the

Ideas which may be looked for in all three. For here also genius holds up to us the magic glass, in which all that is essential and significant appears before us collected and placed in the clearest light, and what is accidental and foreign is left out.

The representation of the Idea of man, which is the work of the poet, may be performed, so that what is represented is also the representer. This is the case in lyrical poetry, in songs, properly so called, in which the poet only perceives vividly his own state and describes it. Thus a certain subjectivity is essential to this kind of poetry from the nature of its object. Again, what is to be represented may be entirely different from him who represents it, as is the case in all other kinds of poetry, in which the poet more or less conceals himself behind his representation, and at last disappears altogether. In the ballad the poet still expresses to some extent his own state through the tone and proportion of the whole; therefore, though much more objective than the lyric, it has yet something subjective. This becomes less in the idyll, still less in the romantic poem, almost entirely disappears in the true epic, and even to the last vestige in the drama, which is the most objective and, in more than one respect, the completest and most difficult form of poetry. The lyrical form of poetry is consequently the easiest, and although art, as a whole, belongs only to the true man of genius, who so rarely appears, even a man who is not in general very remarkable may produce a beautiful song if, by actual strong excitement from without, some inspiration raises his mental powers; for all that is required for this is a lively perception of his own state at a moment of emotional excitement. This is proved by the existence of many single songs by individuals who have otherwise remained unknown; especially the German national

songs, of which we have an exquisite collection in the
"Wunderhorn;" and also by innumerable love-songs and
other songs of the people in all languages;—for to seize
the mood of a moment and embody it in a song is the
whole achievement of this kind of poetry. Yet in the
lyrics of true poets the inner nature of all mankind is
reflected, and all that millions of past, present, and
future men have found, or will find, in the same situations, which are constantly recurring, finds its exact
expression in them. And because these situations, by constant recurrence, are permanent as man himself and
always call up the same sensations, the lyrical productions of genuine poets remain through thousands of years
true, powerful, and fresh. But if the poet is always the
universal man, then all that has ever moved a human
heart, all that human nature in any situation has ever
produced from itself, all that dwells and broods in any
human breast—is his theme and his material, and also
all the rest of nature. Therefore the poet may just as
well sing of voluptuousness as of mysticism, be Anacreon
or Angelus Silesius, write tragedies or comedies, represent the sublime or the common mind—according to
humour or vocation. And no one has the right to prescribe to the poet what he ought to be—noble and sublime, moral, pious, Christian, one thing or another, still
less to reproach him because he is one thing and not
another. He is the mirror of mankind, and brings to its
consciousness what it feels and does.

If we now consider more closely the nature of the
lyric proper, and select as examples exquisite and pure
models, not those that approach in any way to some
other form of poetry, such as the ballad, the elegy, the
hymn, the epigram, &c., we shall find that the peculiar
nature of the lyric, in the narrowest sense, is this: It is
the subject of will, *i. e.*, his own volition, which the con-

sciousness of the singer feels; often as a released and
satisfied desire (joy), but still oftener as a restricted
desire (grief), always as an emotion, a passion, a
moved frame of mind. Besides this, however, and along
with it, by the sight of surrounding nature, the singer
becomes conscious of himself as the subject of pure, will-
less knowing, whose unbroken blissful peace now appears, in contrast to the stress of desire which is always
restricted and always needy. The feeling of this contrast, this alternation, is really what the lyric as a whole
expresses, and what principally constitutes the lyrical
state of mind. In it pure knowing comes to us, as it were,
to deliver us from desire and its stain; we follow, but
only for an instant; desire, the remembrance of our own
personal ends, tears us anew from peaceful contemplation; yet ever again the next beautiful surrounding in
which the pure will-less knowledge presents itself to
us, allures us away from desire. Therefore, in the lyric
and the lyrical mood, desire (the personal interest of
the ends), and pure perception of the surroundings presented, are wonderfully mingled with each other; connections between them are sought for and imagined;
the subjective disposition, the affection of the will, imparts its own hue to the perceived surroundings, and conversely, the surroundings communicate the reflex of their
colour to the will. The true lyric is the expression of
the whole of this mingled and divided state of mind. In
order to make clear by examples this abstract analysis
of a frame of mind that is very far from all abstraction,
any of the immortal songs of Goethe may be taken. As
specially adapted for this end I shall recommend only
a few: "The Shepherd's Lament," "Welcome and Fare-
well," "To the Moon," "On the Lake," "Autumn;" also
the songs in the "Wunderhorn" are excellent examples;
particularly the one which begins, "O Bremen, I must

now leave thee." As a comical and happy parody of
the lyrical character a song of Voss strikes me as remarkable. It describes the feeling of a drunk plumber
falling from a tower, who observes in passing that the
clock on the tower is at half-past eleven, a remark which
is quite foreign to his condition, and thus belongs to
knowledge free from will. Whoever accepts the view
that has been expressed of the lyrical frame of mind, will
also allow, that it is the sensuous and poetical knowledge
of the principle which I established in my essay on the
Principle of Sufficient Reason, and have also referred to
in this work, that the identity of the subject of knowing
with that of willing may be called the miracle *par excellence*, so that the poetical effect of the lyric rests finally
on the truth of that principle. In the course of life these
two subjects, or, in popular language, head and heart,
are ever becoming further apart; men are always separating more between their subjective feeling and their
objective knowledge. In the child the two are still entirely blended together; it scarcely knows how to distinguish itself from its surroundings, it is at one with them.
In the young man all perception chiefly affects feeling
and mood, and even mingles with it, as Byron very beau-
tifully expresses—

> "I live not in myself, but I become
> Portion of that around me; and to me
> High mountains are a feeling."

This is why the youth clings so closely to the perceptible
and outward side of things; this is why he is only fit for
lyrical poetry, and only the full-grown man is capable of
the drama. The old man we can think of as at the most
an epic poet, like Ossian, and Homer for narration is
characteristic of old age.

In the more objective kinds of poetry, especially in the

romance, the epic, and the drama, the end, the revelation of the Idea of man, is principally attained by two means, by true and profound representation of significant characters, and by the invention of pregnant situations in which they disclose themselves. For as it is incumbent upon the chemist not only to exhibit the simple elements, pure and genuine, and their principal compounds, but also to expose them to the influence of such reagents as will clearly and strikingly bring out their peculiar qualities, so is it incumbent on the poet not only to present to us significant characters truly and faithfully as nature itself; but, in order that we may get to know them, he must place them in those situations in which their peculiar qualities will fully unfold themselves, and appear distinctly in sharp outline; situations which are therefore called significant. In real life, and in history, situations of this kind are rarely brought about by chance, and they stand alone, lost and concealed in the multitude of those which are insignificant. The complete significance of the situations ought to distinguish the romance, the epic, and the drama from real life as completely as the arrangement and selection of significant characters. In both, however, absolute truth is a necessary condition of their effect, and want of unity in the characters, contradiction either of themselves or of the nature of humanity in general, as well as impossibility, or very great improbability in the events, even in mere accessories, offend just as much in poetry as badly drawn figures, false perspective, or wrong lighting in painting. For both in poetry and painting we demand the faithful mirror of life, of man, of the world, only made more clear by the representation, and more significant by the arrangement. For there is only one end of all the arts, the representation of the Ideas; and their essential difference lies simply in the different grades of the objectification of will to which the

Ideas that are to be represented belong. This also determines the material of the representation. Thus the arts
which are most widely separated may yet throw light on
each other. For example, in order to comprehend fully
the Ideas of water it is not sufficient to see it in the quiet
pond or in the evenly-flowing stream; but these Ideas disclose themselves fully only when the water appears under
all circumstances and exposed to all kinds of obstacles.
The effects of the varied circumstances and obstacles give
it the opportunity of fully exhibiting all its qualities.
This is why we find it beautiful when it tumbles, rushes,
and foams, or leaps into the air, or falls in a cataract of
spray; or, lastly, if artificially confined it springs up in
a fountain. Thus showing itself different under different
circumstances, it yet always faithfully asserts its character; it is just as natural to it to sprout up as to lie in
glassy stillness; it is as ready for the one as for the other
as soon as the circumstances appear. Now, what the en-
gineer achieves with the fluid matter of water, the architect achieves with the rigid matter of stone, and just this
the epic or dramatic poet achieves with the Idea of man.
Unfolding and rendering distinct the Idea expressing itself in the object of every art, the Idea of the will which
objectifies itself at each grade, is the common end of all
the arts. The life of man, as it shows itself for the most
part in the real world, is like the water, as it is generally
seen in the pond and the river; but in the epic, the romance, the tragedy, selected characters are placed in
those circumstances in which all their special qualities
unfold themselves, the depths of the human heart are revealed, and become visible in extraordinary and very significant actions. Thus poetry objectifies the Idea of man,
an Idea which has the peculiarity of expressing itself in
highly individual characters.

Tragedy is to be regarded, and is recognised as the

summit of poetical art, both on account of the greatness
of its effect and the difficulty of its achievement. It is
very significant for our whole system, and well worthy of
observation, that the end of this highest poetical achievement is the representation of the terrible side of life. The
unspeakable pain, the wail of humanity, the triumph of
evil, the scornful mastery of chance, and the irretrievable
fall of the just and innocent, is here presented to us; and
in this lies a significant hint of the nature of the world
and of existence. It is the strife of will with itself, which
here, completely unfolded at the highest grade of its objectivity, comes into fearful prominence. It becomes visible in the suffering of men, which is now introduced,
partly through chance and error, which appear as the
rulers of the world, personified as fate, on account of
their insidiousness, which even reaches the appearance
of design; partly it proceeds from man himself, through
the self-mortifying efforts of a few, through the wickedness and perversity of most. It is one and the same will
that lives and appears in them all, but whose phenomena
fight against each other and destroy each other. In one
individual it appears powerfully, in another more weakly;
in one more subject to reason, and softened by the light
of knowledge, in another less so, till at last, in some single
case, this knowledge, purified and heightened by suffering itself, reaches the point at which the phenomenon,
the veil of Maya, no longer deceives it. It sees through
the form of the phenomenon, the principle of individuation. The egoism which rests on this perishes with it,
so that now the *motives* that were so powerful before
have lost their might, and instead of them the complete
knowledge of the nature of the world, which has a *quiet-
ing* effect on the will, produces resignation, the surrender
not merely of life, but of the very will to live. Thus we
see in tragedies the noblest men, after long conflict and

suffering, at last renounce the ends they have so keenly followed, and all the pleasures of life for ever, or else freely and joyfully surrender life itself. So is it with the steadfast prince of Calderon; with Gretchen in "Faust"; with Hamlet, whom his friend Horatio would willingly follow, but is bade remain a while, and in this harsh world draw his breath in pain, to tell the story of Hamlet, and clear his memory; so also is it with the Maid of Orleans, the Bride of Messina; they all die purified by suffering, *i. e.*, after the will to live which was formerly in them is dead. In the "Mohammed" of Voltaire this is actually expressed in the concluding words which the dying Palmira addresses to Mohammed: "The world is for tyrants: live!" On the other hand, the demand for so-called poetical justice rests on entire misconception of the nature of tragedy, and, indeed, of the nature of the world itself. It boldly appears in all its dulness in the criticisms which Dr. Samuel Johnson made on particular plays of Shakespeare, for he very naïvely laments its entire absence. And its absence is certainly obvious, for in what has Ophelia, Desdemona, or Cordelia offended? But only the dull, optimistic, Protestant-rationalistic, or peculiarly Jewish view of life will make the demand for poetical justice, and find satisfaction in it. The true sense of tragedy is the deeper insight, that it is not his own individual sins that the hero atones for, but original sin, *i. e.*, the crime of existence itself:

> "Pues el delito mayor
> Del hombre es haber nacido;"

> ("For the greatest crime of man
> Is that he was born;")

as Calderon exactly expresses it.

I shall allow myself only one remark, more closely concerning the treatment of tragedy. The representation of a great misfortune is alone essential to tragedy. But the many different ways in which this is introduced by the poet may be brought under three specific conceptions. It may happen by means of a character of extraordinary wickedness, touching the utmost limits of possibility, who becomes the author of the misfortune; examples of this kind are Richard III., Iago in "Othello," Shylock in "The Merchant of Venice," Franz Moor, Phædra of Euripides, Creon in the "Antigone," &c., &c. Secondly, it may happen through blind fate, *i. e.*, chance and error; a true pattern of this kind is the Œdipus Rex of Sophocles, the "Trachiniæ" also; and in general most of the tragedies of the ancients belong to this class. Among modern tragedies, "Romeo and Juliet," "Tancred" by Voltaire, and "The Bride of Messina," are examples. Lastly, the misfortune may be brought about by the mere position of the *dramatis personæ* with regard to each other, through their relations; so that there is no need either for a tremendous error or an unheard-of accident, nor yet for a character whose wickedness reaches the limits of human possibility; but characters of ordinary morality, under circumstances such as often occur, are so situated with regard to each other that their position compels them, knowingly and with their eyes open, to do each other the greatest injury, without any one of them being entirely in the wrong. This last kind of tragedy seems to me far to surpass the other two, for it shows us the greatest misfortune, not as an exception, not as something occasioned by rare circumstances or monstrous characters, but as arising easily and of itself out of the actions and characters of men, indeed almost as essential to them, and thus brings it terribly near to us. In the other two kinds we may look on the prodigious fate and the horrible wickedness as terrible powers which certainly threaten us, but only from afar, which we may very well escape without taking refuge in renunciation. But in the last kind of tragedy we see that those powers which destroy happiness and life are such that their path to us also is open at every moment; we see the greatest sufferings brought about by entanglements that our fate might also partake of, and through actions that perhaps we also are capable of performing, and so could not complain of injustice; then shuddering we feel ourselves already in the midst of hell. This last kind of tragedy is also the most difficult of achievement; for the greatest effect has to be produced in it with the least use of means and causes of movement, merely through the position and distribution of the characters; therefore even in many of the best tragedies this difficulty is evaded. Yet one tragedy may be referred to as a perfect model of this kind, a tragedy which in other respects is far surpassed by more than one work of the same great master; it is "Clavigo." "Hamlet" belongs to a certain extent to this class, as far as the relation of Hamlet to Laertes and Ophelia is concerned. "Wallenstein" has also this excellence. "Faust" belongs entirely to this class, if we regard the events connected with Gretchen and her brother as the principal action; also the "Cid" of Corneille, only that it lacks the tragic conclusion, while on the contrary the analogous relation of Max to Thecla has it.

§ 52. I gave my mind entirely up to the impression of music in all its forms, and then returned to reflection and the system of thought expressed in the present work, and thus I arrived at an explanation of the inner nature of music and of the nature of its imitative relation to the world—which from analogy had necessarily to be presupposed—an explanation which is quite sufficient for myself, and satisfactory to my investigation, and which will doubtless be equally evident to any one who has followed me thus far and has agreed with my view of the world. Yet I recognise the fact that it is essentially impossible to prove this explanation, for it assumes and establishes a relation of music, as idea, to that which from its nature can never be idea, and music will have to be regarded as the copy of an original which can never itself be directly presented as idea. I can therefore do no more than state here, at the conclusion of this third book, which has been principally devoted to the consideration of the arts, the explanation of the marvellous art of music which satisfies myself, and I must leave the acceptance or denial of my view to the effect produced upon each of my readers both by music itself and by the whole system of thought communicated in this work. Moreover, I regard it as necessary, in order to be able to assent with full conviction to the exposition of the significance of music I am about to give, that one should often listen to music with constant reflection upon my theory concerning it, and for this again it is necessary to be very familiar with the whole of my system of thought.

The (Platonic) Ideas are the adequate objectification of will. To excite or suggest the knowledge of these by means of the representation of particular things (for works of art themselves are always representations of particular things) is the end of all the other arts, which can only be attained by a corresponding change in the knowing subject. Thus all these arts objectify the will indirectly only by means of the Ideas; and since our world is nothing but the manifestation of the Ideas in multiplicity, though their entrance into the principle of individuality (the form of the knowledge possible for the individual as such), music also, since it passes over the Ideas, is entirely independent of the phenomenal world, ignores it altogether, could to a certain extent exist if there was no world at all, which cannot be said of the other arts. Music is as *direct* an objectification and copy of the whole *will* as the world itself, nay, even as the Ideas, whose multiplied manifestation constitutes the world of individual things. Music is thus by no means like the other arts, the copy of the Ideas, but the *copy of the will itself*, whose objectivity the Ideas are. This is why the effect of music is so much more powerful and penetrating than that of the other arts, for they speak only of shadows, but it speaks of the thing itself. Since, however, it is the same will which objectifies itself both in the Ideas and in music, though in quite different ways, there must be, not indeed a direct likeness, but yet a parallel, an analogy, between music and the Ideas whose manifestation in multiplicity and incompleteness is the visible world. The establishing of this analogy will facilitate, as an illustration, the understanding of this exposition, which is so difficult on account of the obscurity of the subject.

I recognise in the deepest tones of harmony, in the bass, the lowest grades of the objectification of will, unorganised nature, the mass of the planet. It is well known that all the high notes which are easily sounded, and die away more quickly, are produced by the vibration in their vicinity of the deep bass-notes. When, also, the low notes sound, the high notes always sound faintly, and it is a law of harmony that only those high notes may accompany a bass-note which actually already sound along with it of themselves on account of its vibration. This is analogous to the fact that the whole of the bodies and organisations of nature must be regarded as having come into existence through gradual development out of the mass of the planet; this is both their supporter and their source, and the same relation subsists between the high notes and the bass. There is a limit of depth, below which no sound is audible. This corresponds to the fact

that no matter can be perceived without form and quality, *i. e.*, without the manifestation of a force which cannot be further explained, in which an Idea expresses itself, and, more generally, that no matter can be entirely
without will. Thus, as a certain pitch is inseparable from
the note as such, so a certain grade of the manifestation
of will is inseparable from matter. Bass is thus, for us,
in harmony what unorganised nature, the crudest mass,
upon which all rests, and from which everything orig-
inates and develops, is in the world. Now, further, in the
whole of the complemental parts which make up the harmony between the bass and the leading voice singing the
melody, I recognise the whole gradation of the Ideas in
which the will objectifies itself. Those nearer to the bass
are the lower of these grades, the still unorganised, but
yet manifold phenomenal things; the higher represent to
me the world of plants and beasts. The definite intervals
of the scale are parallel to the definite grades of the objectification of will, the definite species in nature. The
departure from the arithmetical correctness of the intervals, through some temperament, or produced by the key
selected, is analogous to the departure of the individual
from the type of the species. Indeed, even the impure
discords, which give no definite interval, may be compared to the monstrous abortions produced by beasts of
two species, or by man and beast. But to all these bass
and complemental parts which make up the *harmony*
there is wanting that connected progress which belongs
only to the high voice singing the melody, and it alone
moves quickly and lightly in modulations and runs, while
all these others have only a slower movement without a
connection in each part for itself. The deep bass moves
most slowly, the representative of the crudest mass. Its
rising and falling occurs only by large intervals, in
thirds, fourths, fifths, never by *one* tone, unless it is a

base inverted by double counterpoint. This slow movement is also physically essential to it; a quick run or
shake in the low notes cannot even be imagined. The
higher complemental parts, which are parallel to animal
life, move more quickly, but yet without melodious connection and significant progress. The disconnected course
of all the complemental parts, and their regulation by
definite laws, is analogous to the fact that in the whole
irrational world, from the crystal to the most perfect
animal, no being has a connected consciousness of its own
which would make its life into a significant whole, and
none experiences a succession of mental developments,
none perfects itself by culture, but everything exists always in the same way according to its kind, determined
by fixed law. Lastly, in the *melody*, in the high, singing,
principal voice leading the whole and progressing with
unrestrained freedom, in the unbroken significant connection of *one* thought from beginning to end representing a whole, I recognise the highest grade of the objectification of will, the intellectual life and effort of man.
As he alone, because endowed with reason, constantly
looks before and after on the path of his actual life and
its innumerable possibilities, and so achieves a course of
life which is intellectual, and therefore connected as a
whole; corresponding to this, I say, the *melody* has significant intentional connection from beginning to end.
It records, therefore, the history of the intellectually enlightened will. This will expresses itself in the actual
world as the series of its deeds; but melody says more, it
records the most secret history of this intellectually enlightened will, pictures every excitement, every effort,
every movement of it, all that which the reason collects
under the wide and negative concept of feeling, and
which it cannot apprehend further through its abstract
concepts. Therefore it has always been said that music is

the language of feeling and of passion, as words are the
language of reason.

Now the nature of man consists in this, that his will
strives, is satisfied and strives anew, and so on for ever.
Indeed, his happiness and well-being consist simply in
the quick transition from wish to satisfaction, and from
satisfaction to a new wish. For the absence of satisfaction is suffering, the empty longing for a new wish, languor, *ennui*. And corresponding to this the nature of melody is a constant digression and deviation from the key-
note in a thousand ways, not only to the harmonious intervals to the third and dominant, but to every tone, to
the dissonant sevenths and to the superfluous degrees;
yet there always follows a constant return to the key-
note. In all these deviations melody expresses the multifarious efforts of will, but always its satisfaction also by
the final return to an harmonious interval, and still more,
to the key-note. The composition of melody, the disclo-
sure in it of all the deepest secrets of human willing and
feeling, is the work of genius, whose action, which is
more apparent here than anywhere else, lies far from all
reflection and conscious intention, and may be called an
inspiration. The conception is here, as everywhere in art,
unfruitful. The composer reveals the inner nature of the
world, and expresses the deepest wisdom in a language
which his reason does not understand; as a person under
the influence of mesmerism tells things of which he has
no conception when he awakes. Therefore in the composer, more than in any other artist, the man is entirely
separated and distinct from the artist. Even in the explanation of this wonderful art, the concept shows its
poverty and limitation. I shall try, however, to complete
our analogy. As quick transition from wish to satisfaction, and from satisfaction to a new wish, is happiness
and well-being, so quick melodies without great devia-

tions are cheerful; slow melodies, striking painful discords, and only winding back through many bars to the
key-note are, as analogous to the delayed and hardly won
satisfaction, sad. The delay of the new excitement of
will, languor, could have no other expression than the
sustained key-note, the effect of which would soon be unbearable; very monotonous and unmeaning melodies approach this effect. The short intelligible subjects of
quick dance-music seem to speak only of easily attained
common pleasure. On the other hand, the *Allegro maes-
toso*, in elaborate movements, long passages, and wide
deviations, signifies a greater, nobler effort towards a
more distant end, and its final attainment. The *Adagio*
speaks of the pain of a great and noble effort which de-
spises a trifling happiness. But how wonderful is the
effect of the *minor* and *major*! How astounding that the
change of half a tone, the entrance of a minor third instead of a major, at once and inevitably forces upon us
an anxious painful feeling, from which again we are just
as instantaneously delivered by the major. The *Adagio*
lengthens in the minor the expression of the keenest pain,
and becomes even a convulsive wail. Dance-music in the
minor seems to indicate the failure of that trifling happiness which we ought rather to despise, seems to speak of
the attainment of a lower end with toil and trouble. The
inexhaustibleness of possible melodies corresponds to the
inexhaustibleness of Nature in difference of individuals,
physiognomies, and courses of life. The transition from
one key to an entirely different one, since it altogether
breaks the connection with what went before, is like
death, for the individual ends in it; but the will which
appeared in this individual lives after him as before him,
appearing in other individuals, whose consciousness, however, has no connection with his.

But it must never be forgotten, in the investigation of all these analogies I have pointed out, that music has no direct, but merely an indirect relation to them, for it never expresses the phenomenon, but only the inner nature, the in-itself of all phenomena, the will itself. It does not therefore express this or that particular and definite joy, this or that sorrow, or pain, or horror, or delight, or merriment, or peace of mind; but joy, sorrow, pain, horror, delight, merriment, peace of mind *themselves*, to a certain extent in the abstract, their essential nature, without accessories, and therefore without their motives. Yet we completely understand them in this extracted quintessence. Hence it arises that our imagination is so easily excited by music, and now seeks to give form to that invisible yet actively moved spirit-world which speaks to us directly, and clothe it with flesh and blood, *i. e.*, to embody it in an analogous example. This is the origin of the song with words, and finally of the opera, the text of which should therefore never forsake that subordinate position in order to make itself the chief thing and the music a mere means of expressing it, which is a great misconception and a piece of utter perversity; for music always expresses only the quintessence of life and its events, never these themselves, and therefore their differences do not always affect it. It is precisely this universality, which belongs exclusively to it, together with the greatest determinateness, that gives music the high worth which it has as the panacea for all our woes. Thus, if music is too closely united to the words, and tries to form itself according to the events, it is striving to speak a language which is not its own. No one has kept so free from this mistake as Rossini; therefore his music speaks *its own language* so distinctly and purely that it requires no words, and produces its full effect when rendered by instruments alone.

According to all this, we may regard the phenomenal world, or nature, and music as two different expressions of the same thing, which is therefore itself the only medium of their analogy, so that a knowledge of it is demanded in order to understand that analogy. Music, therefore, if regarded as an expression of the world, is in the highest degree a universal language, which is related indeed to the universality of concepts, much as they are related to the particular things. Its universality, however, is by no means that empty universality of abstraction, but quite of a different kind, and is united with thorough and distinct definiteness. In this respect it resembles geometrical figures and numbers, which are the universal forms of all possible objects of experience and applicable to them all *a priori,* and yet are not abstract but perceptible and thoroughly determined. All possible efforts, excitements, and manifestations of will, all that goes on in the heart of man and that reason includes in the wide, negative concept of feeling, may be expressed by the infinite number of possible melodies, but always in the universal, in the mere form, without the material, always according to the thing-in-itself, not the phenomenon, the inmost soul, as it were, of the phenomenon, without the body. This deep relation which music has to the true nature of all things also explains the fact that suitable music played to any scene, action, event, or surrounding seems to disclose to us its most secret meaning, and appears as the most accurate and distinct commentary upon it. This is so truly the case, that whoever gives himself up entirely to the impression of a symphony, seems to see all the possible events of life and the world take place in himself, yet if he reflects, he can find no likeness between the music and the things that passed before his mind. For, as we have said, music is distinguished from all

the other arts by the fact that it is not a copy of the
phenomenon, or, more accurately, the adequate objectivity of will, but is the direct copy of the will itself,
and therefore exhibits itself as the metaphysical to
everything physical in the world, and as the thing-in-
itself to every phenomenon. We might, therefore, just
as well call the world embodied music as embodied will;
and this is the reason why music makes every picture,
and indeed every scene of real life and of the world,
at once appear with higher significance, certainly all
the more in proportion as its melody is analogous to the
inner spirit of the given phenomenon. It rests upon this
that we are able to set a poem to music as a song, or a
perceptible representation as a pantomime, or both as an
opera. Such particular pictures of human life, set to
the universal language of music, are never bound to it
or correspond to it with stringent necessity; but they
stand to it only in the relation of an example chosen at
will to a general concept. In the determinateness of the
real, they represent that which music expresses in the
universality of mere form. For melodies are to a certain
extent, like general concepts, an abstraction from the
actual. This actual world, then, the world of particular
things, affords the object of perception, the special and
individual, the particular case, both to the universality
of the concepts and to the universality of the melodies.
But these two universalities are in a certain respect opposed to each other; for the concepts contain particulars
only as the first forms abstracted from perception, as it
were, the separated shell of things; thus they are,
strictly speaking, *abstracta;* music, on the other hand,
gives the inmost kernel which precedes all forms, or
the heart of things. This relation may be very well expressed in the language of the schoolmen by saying the
concepts are the *universalia post rem,* but music gives

the *universalia ante rem,* and the real world the *universalia in re.* To the universal significance of a melody to which a poem has been set, it is quite possible to set other equally arbitrarily selected examples of the universal expressed in this poem corresponding to the significance of the melody in the same degree. This is why the same composition is suitable to many verses; and this is also what makes the *vaudeville* possible. But that in general a relation is possible between a composition and a perceptible representation rests, as we have said, upon the fact that both are simply different expressions of the same inner being of the world. When now, in the particular case, such a relation is actually given, that is to say, when the composer has been able to express in the universal language of music the emotions of will which constitute the heart of an event, then the melody of the song, the music of the opera, is expressive. But the analogy discovered by the composer between the two must have proceeded from the direct knowledge of the nature of the world unknown to his reason, and must not be an imitation produced with conscious intention by means of conceptions, otherwise the music does not express the inner nature of the will itself, but merely gives an inadequate imitation of its phenomenon. All specially imitative music does this; for example, "The Seasons," by Haydn; also many passages of his "Creation," in which phenomena of the external world are directly imitated; also all battle-pieces. Such music is entirely to be rejected.

The unutterable depth of all music by virtue of which it floats through our consciousness as the vision of a paradise firmly believed in yet ever distant from us, and by which also it is so fully understood and yet so inexplicable, rests on the fact that it restores to us all the emotions of our inmost nature, but entirely without reality and far removed from their pain. So also the seriousness which is essential to it, which excludes the absurd from its direct and peculiar province, is to be explained by the fact that its object is not the idea, with reference to which alone deception and absurdity are possible; but its object is directly the will, and this is essentially the most serious of all things, for it is that on which all depends. How rich in content and full of significance the language of music is, we see from the repetitions, as well as the *Da capo,* the like of which would be unbearable in works composed in a language of words, but in music are very appropriate and beneficial, for, in order to comprehend it fully, we must hear it twice.

In the whole of this exposition of music I have been trying to bring out clearly that it expresses in a perfectly universal language, in a homogeneous material, mere tones, and with the greatest determinateness and truth, the inner nature, the in-itself of the world, which we think under the concept of will, because will is its most distinct manifestation. Further, according to my view and contention, philosophy is nothing but a complete and accurate repetition or expression of the nature of the world in very general concepts, for only in such is it possible to get a view of that whole nature which will everywhere be adequate and applicable. Thus, whoever has followed me and entered into my mode of thought, will not think it so very paradoxical if I say, that supposing it were possible to give a perfectly accurate, complete explanation of music, extending even to particulars, that is to say, a detailed repetition in concepts of what it expresses, this would also be a sufficient repetition and explanation of the world in concepts, or at least entirely parallel to such an explanation, and thus it would be the true philosophy.

I might still have something to say about the way in which music is perceived, namely, in and through time alone, with absolute exclusion of space, and also apart from the influence of the knowledge of causality, thus without understanding; for the tones make the æsthetic impression as effect, and without obliging us to go back to their causes, as in the case of perception. I do not wish, however, to lengthen this discussion, as I have perhaps already gone too much into detail with regard to some things in this Third Book, or have dwelt too much on particulars. But my aim made it necessary, and it will be the less disapproved if the importance and high worth of art, which is seldom sufficiently recognised, be kept in mind. For if, according to our view, the whole visible world is just the objectification, the mirror, of the will, conducting it to knowledge of itself, and, indeed, as we shall soon see, to the possibility of its deliverance; and if, at the same time, the world as idea, if we regard it in isolation, and, freeing ourselves from all volition, allow it alone to take possession of our consciousness, is the most joy-giving and the only innocent side of life; we must regard art as the higher ascent, the more complete development of all this, for it achieves essentially just what is achieved by the visible world itself, only with greater concentration, more perfectly, with intention and intelligence, and therefore may be called, in the full significance of the word, the flower of life. If the whole world as idea is only the visibility of will, the work of art is to render this visibility more distinct. It is the *camera obscura* which shows the objects more purely, and enables us to survey them and comprehend them better. It is the play within the play, the stage upon the stage in "Hamlet."

The pleasure we receive from all beauty, the consolation which art affords, the enthusiasm of the artist, which enables him to forget the cares of life,—the latter an advantage of the man of genius over other men, which alone repays him for the suffering that increases in proportion to the clearness of consciousness, and for the desert loneliness among men of a different race,— all this rests on the fact that the in-itself of life, the will, existence itself, is, as we shall see farther on, a constant sorrow, partly miserable, partly terrible; while, on the contrary, as idea alone, purely contemplated, or copied by art, free from pain, it presents to us a drama full of significance. This purely knowable side of the world, and the copy of it in any art, is the element of the artist. He is chained to the contemplation of the play, the objectification of will; he remains beside it, does not get tired of contemplating it and representing it in copies; and meanwhile he bears himself the cost of the production of that play, i. e., he himself is the will which objectifies itself, and remains in constant suffering. That pure, true, and deep knowledge of the inner nature of the world becomes now for him an end in itself: he stops there. Therefore it does not become to him a quieter of the will, as, we shall see in the next book, it does in the case of the saint who has attained to resignation; it does not deliver him for ever from life, but only at moments, and is therefore not for him a path out of life, but only an occasional consolation in it, till his power, increased by this contemplation and at last tired of the play, lays hold on the real. The St. Cecilia of Raphael may be regarded as a representation of this transition. To the real, then, we now turn in the following book.

FOURTH BOOK

THE WORLD AS WILL

———

SECOND ASPECT

THE ASSERTION AND DENIAL OF THE WILL TO LIVE, WHEN
SELF—CONSCIOUSNESS HAS BEEN ATTAINED

§ 54. The first three books will, it is hoped, have con-
veyed the distinct and certain knowledge that the world
as idea is the complete mirror of the will, in which
it knows itself in ascending grades of distinctness and
completeness, the highest of which is man, whose nature,
however, receives its complete expression only through
the whole connected series of his actions. The self-conscious connection of these actions is made possible by
reason, which enables a man constantly to survey the
whole in the abstract.

The will, which, considered purely in itself, is without knowledge, and is merely a blind incessant impulse,
as we see it appear in unorganised and vegetable nature
and their laws, and also in the vegetative part of our
own life, receives through the addition of the world as
idea, which is developed in subjection to it, the knowledge of its own willing and of what it is that it wills.
And this is nothing else than the world as idea, life,
precisely as it exists. Therefore we called the phenomenal world the mirror of the will, its objectivity. And
since what the will wills is always life, just because
life is nothing but the representation of that willing
for the idea, it is all one and a mere pleonism if, in-

189

stead of simply saying "the will," we say "the will to live."

Will is the thing-in-itself, the inner content, the essence of the world. Life, the visible world, the phenomenon, is only the mirror of the will. Therefore life accompanies the will as inseparably as the shadow accompanies the body; and if will exists, so will life, the world, exist. Life is, therefore, assured to the will to live; and so long as we are filled with the will to live we need have no fear for our existence, even in the presence of death. It is true we see the individual come into being and pass away; but the individual is only phenomenal, exists only for the knowledge which is bound to the principle of sufficient reason, to the principle of individuation. Certainly, for this kind of knowledge, the individual receives his life as a gift, rises out of nothing, then suffers the loss of this gift through death, and returns again to nothing. But we desire to consider life philosophically, i. e., according to its Ideas, and in this sphere we shall find that neither the will, the thing-in-itself in all phenomena, nor the subject of knowing, that which perceives all phenomena, is affected at all by birth or by death. Birth and death belong merely to the phenomenon of will, thus to life; and it is essential to this to exhibit itself in individuals which come into being. and pass away, as fleeting phenomena appearing in the form of time—phenomena of that which in itself knows no time, but must exhibit itself precisely in the way we have said, in order to objectify its peculiar nature. Birth and death belong in like manner to life, and hold the balance as reciprocal conditions of each other, or, if one likes the expression, as poles of the whole phenomenon of life. The wisest of all mythologies, the Indian, expresses this by giving to the very god that symbolises destruction, death (as Brahma, the most sinful and the

lowest god of the Trimurti, symbolises generation, coming into being, and Vishnu maintaining or preserving),
by giving, I say, to Siva as an attribute not only the
necklace of skulls, but also the lingam, the symbol of
generation, which appears here as the counterpart of
death, thus signifying that generation and death are
essentially correlatives, which reciprocally neutralise
and annul each other. It was precisely the same sentiment that led the Greeks and Romans to adorn their
costly sarcophagi, just as we see them now, with feasts,
dances, marriages, the chase, fights of wild beasts, bac-
chanalians, &c.; thus with representations of the full
ardour of life, which they place before us not only in
such revels and sports, but also in sensual groups, and
even go so far as to represent the sexual intercourse of
satyrs and goats. Clearly the aim was to point in the
most impressive manner away from the death of the
mourned individual to the immortal life of nature, and
thus to indicate, though without abstract knowledge,
that the whole of nature is the phenomenon and also
the fulfilment of the will to live. The form of this
phenomenon is time, space, and causality, and by means
of these individuation, which carries with it that the
individual must come into being and pass away. But
this no more affects the will to live, of whose manifestation the individual is, as it were, only a particular example or specimen, than the death of an individual injures
the whole of nature. For it is not the individual, but
only the species that Nature cares for, and for the preservation of which she so earnestly strives, providing
for it with the utmost prodigality through the vast sur-
plus of the seed and the great strength of the fructi-
fying impulse. The individual, on the contrary, neither
has nor can have any value for Nature, for her kingdom is infinite time and infinite space, and in these in-

finite multiplicity of possible individuals. Therefore she is always ready to let the individual fall, and hence it is not only exposed to destruction in a thousand ways by the most insignificant accident, but originally destined for it, and conducted towards it by Nature herself from the moment it has served its end of maintaining the species. Thus Nature naïvely expresses the great truth that only the Ideas, not the individuals, have, properly speaking, reality, i. e., are complete objectivity of the will. Now, since man is Nature itself, and indeed Nature at the highest grade of its self-consciousness, but Nature is only the objectified will to live, the man who has comprehended and retained this point of view may well console himself, when contemplating his own death and that of his friends, by turning his eyes to the immortal life of Nature, which he himself is.

That generation and death are to be regarded as something belonging to life, and essential to this phenomenon of the will, arises also from the fact that they both exhibit themselves merely as higher powers of the expression of that in which all the rest of life consists. This is through and through nothing else than the constant change of matter in the fixed permanence of form; and this is what constitutes the transitoriness of the individual and the permanence of the species. Constant nourishment and renewal differ from generation only in degree, and constant excretion differs only in degree from death. The first shows itself most simply and distinctly in the plant. The plant is throughout a constant recurrence of the same impulse of its simplest fibre, which groups itself into leaf and branch. It is a systematic aggregate of similar plants supporting each other, whose constant reproduction is its single impulse. It ascends to the full satisfaction of this tendency through the grades of its metamorphosis, finally to the blossom and fruit, that compendium of its existence and effort in which it now attains, by a short way, to that which is its single aim, and at a stroke produces a thousand-fold what, up till then, it effected only in the particular case—the repetition of itself. Its earlier growth and development stands in the same relation to its fruit as writing stands to printing. With the animal it is clearly quite the same. The process of nourishing is a constant reproduction; the process of reproduction is a higher power of nourishing. The pleasure which accompanies the act of procreation is a higher power of the agreeableness of the sense of life. On the other hand, excretion, the constant exhalation and throwing off of matter, is the same as that which, at a higher power, death, is the contrary of generation. And if here we are always content to retain the form without lamenting the discarded matter, we ought to bear ourselves in the same way if in death the same thing happens, in a higher degree and to the whole, as takes place daily and hourly in a partial manner in excretion: if we are indifferent to the one, we ought not to shrink from the other. Therefore, from this point of view, it appears just as perverse to desire the continuance of an individuality which will be replaced by other individuals as to desire the permanence of matter which will be replaced by other matter. It appears just as foolish to embalm the body as it would be carefully to preserve its excrement. As to the individual consciousness which is bound to the individual body, it is absolutely interrupted every day by sleep. Deep sleep is, while it lasts, in no way different from death, into which, in fact, it often passes continuously, as in the case of freezing to death. It differs only with regard to the future, the awaking. Death is a sleep in which individuality is forgotten; everything else wakes again, or rather never slept.

Above all things, we must distinctly recognise that the

form of the phenomenon of will, the form of life or reality, is really only the *present*, not the future nor the past. The latter are only in the conception, exist only in the connection of knowledge, so far as it follows the principle of sufficient reason. No man has ever lived in the past, and none will live in the future; the *present* alone is the form of all life, and is its sure possession which can never be taken from it. The present always exists, together with its content. Both remain fixed without wavering, like the rainbow on the waterfall. For life is firm and certain in the will, and the present is firm and certain in life. Certainly, if we reflect on the thousands of years that are past, of the millions of men who lived in them, we ask, What were they? what has become of them? But, on the other hand, we need only recall our own past life and renew its scenes vividly in our imagination, and then ask again, What was all this? what has become of it? As it is with it, so is it with the life of those millions. Or should we suppose that the past could receive a new existence because it has been sealed by death? Our own past, the most recent part of it, and even yesterday, is now no more than an empty dream of the fancy, and such is the past of all those millions. What was? What is? The will, of which life is the mirror, and knowledge free from will, which beholds it clearly in that mirror. Whoever has not yet recognised this, or will not recognise it, must add to the question asked above as to the fate of past generations of men this question also: Why he, the questioner, is so fortunate as to be conscious of this costly, fleeting, and only real present, while those hundreds of generations of men, even the heroes and philosophers of those ages, have sunk into the night of the past, and have thus become nothing; but he, his insignificant ego, actually exists? or more shortly, though somewhat strangely: Why this now, his now, *is* just now and *was* not long ago? Since he asks such strange questions, he regards his existence and his time as independent of each other, and the former as projected into the latter. He assumes indeed two nows—one which belongs to the object, the other which belongs to the subject, and marvels at the happy accident of their coincidence. But in truth, only the point of contact of the object, the form of which is time, with the subject, which has no mode of the principle of sufficient reason as its form, constitutes the present, as is shown in the essay on the principle of sufficient reason. Now all object is the will so far as it has become idea, and the subject is the necessary correlative of the object. But real objects are only in the present; the past and the future contain only conceptions and fancies, therefore the present is the esssential form of the phenomenon of the will, and inseparable from it. The present alone is that which always exists and remains immovable. That which, empirically apprehended, is the most transitory of all, presents itself to the metaphysical vision, which sees beyond the forms of empirical perception, as that which alone endures, the *nunc stans* of the schoolmen. The source and the supporter of its content is the will to live or the thing-in-itself,—which we are. That which constantly becomes and passes away, in that it has either already been or is still to be, belongs to the phenomenon as such on account of its forms, which make coming into being and passing away possible. Accordingly, we must think:—What has been?—What is. What will be?—What was; and take it in the strict meaning of the words; thus understand not similar but the same. For life is certain to the will, and the present is certain to life. Thus it is that every one can say, "I am once for all lord of the present, and through all eternity it will accompany me as my shadow: therefore I do not wonder where it has come from, and how it happens that it is exactly now." We might compare time to a constantly revolving sphere; the half that was always sinking would be the past, that which was always rising would be the future; but the indivisible point at the top, where the tangent touches, would be the extensionless present. As the tangent does not revolve with the sphere, neither does the present, the point of contact of the object, the form of which is time, with the subject, which has no form, because it does not belong to the knowable, but is the condition of all that is knowable. Or, time is like an unceasing stream, and the present a rock on which the stream breaks itself, but does not carry away with it. The will, as thing-in-itself, is just as little subordinate to the principle of sufficient reason as the subject of knowledge, which, finally, in a certain regard is the will itself or its expression. And as life, its own phenomenon, is assured to the will, so is the present, the single form of real life. Therefore we have not to investigate the past before life, nor the future after death: we have rather to know the *present*, the one form in which the will manifects itself. It will not escape from the will, but neither will the will escape from it. If, therefore, life as it is satisfies, whoever affirms it in every way may regard it with confidence as endless, and banish the fear of death as an illusion that inspires him with the foolish dread that he can ever be robbed of the present, and foreshadows a time in which there is no present; an illusion with regard to time analogous to the illusion with regard to space through which every one imagines the position on the globe he happens to occupy as above, and all other places as below. In the same way every one links the present to his own individuality, and imagines that all present is extinguished with it; that then past and future might be without a present. But as on the surface of the globe every place is above, so the form of all life is the *present,* and to fear death because it robs us of the present, is just as foolish as to fear that we may slip down from the round globe upon which we have now the good fortune to occupy the upper surface. The present is the form essential to the objectification of the will. It cuts time, which extends infinitely in both directions, as a mathematical point, and stands immovably fixed, like an everlasting mid-day with no cool evening, as the actual sun burns without intermission, while it only seems to sink into the bosom of night. Therefore, if a man fears death as his annihilation, it is just as if he were to think that the sun cries out at evening, "Woe is me! for I go down into eternal night." And conversely, whoever is oppressed with the burden of life, whoever desires life and affirms it, but abhors its torments, and especially can no longer endure the hard lot that has fallen to himself, such a man has no deliverance to hope for from death, and cannot right himself by suicide. The cool shades of Orcus allure him only with the false appearance of a haven of rest. The earth rolls from day into night, the individual dies, but the sun itself shines without intermission, an eternal noon. Life is assured to the will to live; the form of life is an endless present, no matter how the individuals, the phenomena of the Idea, arise and pass away in time, like fleeting dreams. Thus even already suicide appears to us as a vain and therefore a foolish action; when we have carried our investigation further it will appear to us in a still less favourable light.

Dogmas change and our knowledge is deceptive; but Nature never errs, her procedure is sure, and she never conceals it. Everything is entirely in Nature, and Nature is entire in everything. She has her centre in every brute. It has surely found its way into existence, and it will surely find its way out of it. In the meantime it lives, fearless and without care, in the presence of annihilation, supported by the consciousness that it is Nature herself, and imperishable as she is. Man alone carries about with him, in abstract conceptions, the certainty of his death; yet this can only trouble him very rarely, when for a single moment some occasion calls it up to his imagination. Against the mighty voice of Nature reflection can do little. In man, as in the brute which does not think, the certainty that springs from his inmost consciousness that he himself is Nature, the world, predominates as a lasting frame of mind; and on account of this no man is observably disturbed by the thought of certain and never-distant death, but lives as if he would live for ever. Indeed this is carried so far that we may say that no one has really a lively conviction of the certainty of his death, otherwise there would be no great difference between his frame of mind and that of a condemned criminal. Every one recognises that certainty in the abstract and theoretically, but lays it aside like other theoretical truths which are not applicable to practice, without really receiving it into his living consciousness. Whoever carefully considers this peculiarity of human character will see that the psychological explanations of it, from habit and acquiescence in the inevitable, are by no means sufficient, and that its true explanation lies in the deeper ground we have given. The same fact explains the circumstance that at all times and among all peoples dogmas of some kind or other relating to the continued existence of the individual after death arise, and are believed in, although the evidence in support of them must always be very insufficient, and the evidence against them forcible and varied. But, in truth, this really requires no proof, but is recognised by the healthy understanding as a fact, and confirmed by the confidence that Nature never lies any more than she errs, but openly exhibits and naïvely expresses her action and her nature,

while only we ourselves obscure it by our folly, in order
to establish what is agreeable to our limited point of
view.

But this that we have brought to clearest consciousness, that although the particular phenomenon of the
will has a temporal beginning and end, the will itself as
thing-in-itself is not affected by it, nor yet the correlative of all object, the knowing but never known subject,
and that life is always assured to the will to live—this is
not to be numbered with the doctrines of immortality.
For permanence has no more to do with the will or with
the pure subject of knowing, the eternal eye of the world,
than transitoriness, for both are predicates that are only
valid in time, and the will and the pure subject of knowing lie outside time. Therefore the egoism of the individual (this particular phenomenon of will enlightened
by the subject of knowing) can extract as little nourishment and consolation for his wish to endure through endless time from the view we have expressed, as he could
from the knowledge that after his death the rest of the
eternal world would continue to exist, which is just the
expression of the same view considered objectively, and
therefore temporally. For every individual is transitory
only as phenomenon, but as thing-in-itself is timeless,
and therefore endless. But it is also only as phenomenon
that an individual is distinguished from the other things
of the world; as thing-in-itself he is the will which appears in all, and death destroys the illusion which separates his consciousness from that of the rest: this is immortality. His exemption from death, which belongs to
him only as thing-in-itself, is for the phenomenon one
with the immortality of the rest of the external world.
Hence also, it arises that although the inward and merely
felt consciousness of that which we have raised to distinct knowledge is indeed, as we have said, sufficient to

prevent the thought of death from poisoning the life of the rational being, because this consciousness is the basis of that love of life which maintains everything living, and enables it to live on at ease as if there were no such thing as death, so long as it is face to face with life, and turns its attention to it, yet it will not prevent the individual from being seized with the fear of death, and trying in every way to escape from it, when it presents itself to him in some particular real case, or even only in his imagination, and he is compelled to contemplate it. For just as, so long as his knowledge was directed to life as such, he was obliged to recognise immortality in it, so when death is brought before his eyes, he is obliged to recognise it as that which it is, the temporal end of the particular temporal phenomenon. What we fear in death is by no means the pain, for it lies clearly on this side of death, and, moreover, we often take refuge in death from pain, just as, on the contrary, we sometimes endure the most fearful suffering merely to escape death for a while, although it would be quick and easy. Thus we distinguish pain and death as two entirely different evils. What we fear in death is the end of the individual, which it openly professes itself to be, and since the individual is a particular objectification of the will to live itself, its whole nature struggles against death. Now when feeling thus exposes us helpless, reason can yet step in and for the most part overcome its adverse influence, for it places us upon a higher standpoint, from which we no longer contemplate the particular but the whole. Therefore a philosophical knowledge of the nature of the world, which extended to the point we have now reached in this work but went no farther, could even at this point of view overcome the terror of death in the measure in which reflection had power over direct feeling in the given individual. A man who had thoroughly assimilated

the truths we have already advanced, but had not come
to know, either from his own experience or from a deeper
insight, that constant suffering is essential to life, who
found satisfaction and all that he wished in life, and
could calmly and deliberately desire that his life, as he
had hitherto known it, should endure for ever or repeat
itself ever anew, and whose love of life was so great that
he willingly and gladly accepted all the hardships and
miseries to which it is exposed for the sake of its pleasures,—such a man would stand "with firm-knit bones
on the well-rounded, enduring earth," and would have
nothing to fear. Armed with the knowledge we have given
him, he would await with indifference the death that hastens towards him on the wings of time. He would regard
it as a false illusion, an impotent spectre, which fright-
ens the weak but has no power over him who knows that
he is himself the will of which the whole world is the
objectification or copy, and that therefore he is always
certain of life, and also of the present, the peculiar and
only form of the phenomenon of the will. He could not
be terrified by an endless past or future in which he
would not be, for this he would regard as the empty delusion of the web of Maya. Thus he would no more fear
death than the sun fears the night. In the "Bhagavad-
Gita" Krishna thus raises the mind of his young pupil
Arjuna, when, seized with compunction at the sight of
the arrayed hosts (somewhat as Xerxes was), he loses
heart and desires to give up the battle in order to avert
the death of so many thousands. Krishna leads him to
this point of view, and the death of those thousands can
no longer restrain him; he gives the sign for battle. This
point of view is also expressed by Goethe's Prometheus,
especially when he says—

"Here sit I, form mankind
In my own image,

A race like to myself,
To suffer and to weep,
Rejoice, enjoy,
And heed thee not,
As I."

The philosophy of Bruno and that of Spinoza might also lead any one to this point of view whose conviction was not shaken and weakened by their errors and imperfections. That of Bruno has properly no ethical theory at all, and the theory contained in the philosophy of Spinoza does not really proceed from the inner nature of his doctrine, but is merely tacked on to it by means of weak and palpable sophisms, though in itself it is praiseworthy and beautiful. Finally, there are many men who would occupy this point of view if their knowledge kept pace with their will, i. e., if, free from all illusion, they were in a position to become clearly and distinctly themselves. For this is, for knowledge, the point of view of the complete *assertion of the will to live.*

That the will asserts itself means, that while in its objectivity, i. e., in the world and life, its own nature is completely and distinctly given it as idea, this knowledge does not by any means check its volition; but this very life, so known, is willed as such by the will with knowledge, consciously and deliberately, just as up to this point it willed it as blind effort without knowledge. The opposite of this, the *denial of the will to live,* shows itself if, when that knowledge is attained, volition ends, because the particular known phenomena no longer act as *motives* for willing, but the whole knowledge of the nature of the world, the mirror of the will, which has grown up through the comprehension of the *Ideas,* becomes a *quieter* of the will; and thus free, the will suppresses itself. These quite unfamiliar conceptions are difficult to understand when expressed in this general way, but it is hoped they will become clear through the exposition we shall give presently, with special reference to action, of the phenomena in which, on the one hand, the assertion in its different grades, and, on the other hand, the denial, expresses itself. For both proceed from knowledge, yet not from abstract knowledge, which is expressed in words, but from living knowledge, which is expressed in action and behaviour alone, and is independent of the dogmas which at the same time occupy the reason as abstract knowledge. To exhibit them both, and bring them to distinct knowledge of the reason, can alone be my aim, and not to prescribe or recommend the one or the other, which would be as foolish as it would be useless; for the will in itself is absolutely free and entirely self-determining, and for it there is no law. But before we go on to the exposition referred to, we must first explain and more exactly define this *freedom* and its relation to necessity. And also, with regard to the life, the assertion and denial of which is our problem, we must insert a few general remarks connected with the will and its objects. Through all this we shall facilitate the apprehension of the inmost nature of the knowledge we are aiming at, of the ethical significance of methods of action.

§ 55. That the will as such is *free*, follows from the fact that, according to our view, it is the thing-in-itself, the content of all phenomena. The phenomena, on the other hand, we recognise as absolutely subordinate to the principle of sufficient reason in its four forms. And since we know that necessity is throughout identical with following from given grounds, and that these are convertible conceptions, all that belongs to the phenomenon, i. e., all that is object for the knowing subject as individual, is in one aspect reason, and in another aspect consequent; and in this last capacity is determined with absolute necessity, and can, therefore, in no respect be other than it is. The whole content of Nature, the collective sum of its phenomena, is thus throughout necessary, and the necessity of every part, of every phenomenon, of every event, can always be proved, because it must be possible to find the reason from which it follows as a consequent. This admits of no exception: it follows from the unrestricted validity of the principle of sufficient reason. In another aspect, however, the same world is for us, in all its phenomena, objectivity of will. And the will, since it is not phenomenon, is not idea or object, but thing-in-itself, and is not subordinate to the principle of sufficient reason, the form of all object; thus is not determined as a consequent through any reason, knows no necessity, *i. e.*, is *free*. The concept of freedom is thus properly a negative concept, for its content is merely the denial of necessity, *i. e.*, the relation of consequent to its reason, according to the principle of sufficient reason. Now here lies before us in its most distinct form the solution of that great contradiction, the union of freedom with necessity, which has so often been discussed in recent times, yet, so far as I know, never clearly and adequately. Everything is as phenomenon, as object, absolutely necessary; *in itself* it is will, which is perfectly free to all eternity. The phenomenon, the object, is necessarily and unalterably determined in that chain of causes and effects which admits of no interruption. But the existence in general of this object, and its specific nature, *i. e.*, the Idea which reveals itself in it, or, in other words, its character, is a direct manifestation of will. Thus, in conformity with the freedom of this will, the object might not be at all, or it might be originally and essentially something quite different from what it is, in which case, however, the whole chain of which it is a link, and which is itself a manifestation of the same will,

would be quite different also. But once there and existing, it has entered the chain of causes and effects, is always necessarily determined in it, and can, therefore,
neither become something else, *i. e.*, change itself, nor
yet escape from the chain, *i. e.*, vanish. Man, like every
other part of Nature, is objectivity of the will; therefore
all that has been said holds good of him. As everything
in Nature has its forces and qualities, which react in a
definite way when definitely affected, and constitute its
character, man also has his *character*, from which the
motives call forth his actions with necessity. In this manner of conduct his empirical character reveals itself, but
in this again his intelligible character, the will in itself,
whose determined phenomenon he is. But man is the most
complete phenomenon of will, and, as we explained in
the Second Book, he had to be enlightened with so high
a degree of knowledge in order to maintain himself in
existence, that in it a perfectly adequate copy or repetition of the nature of the world under the form of the
idea became possible: this is the comprehension of the
Ideas, the pure mirror of the world, as we learnt in the
Third Book. Thus in man the will can attain to full self-
consciousness, to distinct and exhaustive knowledge of
its own nature, as it mirrors itself in the whole world.
We saw in the preceding book that art springs from the
actual presence of this degree of knowledge; and at the
end of our whole work it will further appear that,
through the same knowledge, in that the will relates it
to itself, a suppression and self-denial of the will in its
most perfect manifestation is possible. So that the freedom which otherwise, as belonging to the thing-in-itself,
can never show itself in the phenomenon, in such a case
does also appear in it, and, by abolishing the nature
which lies at the foundation of the phenomenon, while
the latter itself still continues to exist in time, it brings

about a contradiction of the phenomenon with itself, and in this way exhibits the phenomena of holiness and self-renunciation. But all this can only be fully understood at the end of this book. What has just been said merely affords a preliminary and general indication of how man is distinguished from all the other phenomena of will by the fact that freedom, *i. e.*, independence of the principle of sufficient reason, which only belongs to the will as thing-in-itself, and contradicts the phenomenon, may yet possibly, in his case, appear in the phenomenon also, where, however, it necessarily exhibits itself as a contradiction of the phenomenon with itself. In this sense, not only the will in itself, but man also may certainly be called free, and thus distinguished from all other beings. But how this is to be understood can only become clear through all that is to follow, and for the present we must turn away from it altogether. For, in the first place, we must beware of the error that the action of the individual definite man is subject to no necessity, *i. e.*, that the power of the motive is less certain than the power of the cause, or the following of the conclusion from the premises. The freedom of the will as thing-in-itself, if, as has been said, we abstract from the entirely exceptional case mentioned above, by no means extends directly to its phenomenon, not even in the case in which this reaches the highest grade of its visibility, and thus does not extend to the rational animal endowed with individual character, *i. e.*, the person. The person is never free although he is the phenomenon of a free will; for he is already the determined phenomenon of the free volition of this will, and, because he enters the form of every object, the principle of sufficient reason, he develops indeed the unity of that will in a multiplicity of actions, but on account of the timeless unity of that volition in itself, this multiplicity exhibits in itself the regu-

lar conformity to law of a force of Nature. Since, however, it is that free volition that becomes visible in the
person and the whole of his conduct, relating itself to
him as the concept to the definition, every individual action of the person is to be ascribed to the free will, and
directly proclaims itself as such in consciousness. Therefore, as was said in the Second Book, every one regards
himself *a priori* (*i. e.*, here in this original feeling) as
free in his individual actions, in the sense that in every
given case every action is possible for him, and he only
recognises *a posteriori* from experience and reflection
upon experience that his actions take place with absolute
necessity from the coincidence of his character with his
motives. Hence it arises that every uncultured man, following his feeling, ardently defends complete freedom
in particular actions, while the great thinkers of all ages,
and indeed the more profound systems of religion, have
denied it. But whoever has come to see clearly that the
whole nature of man is will, and he himself only a phenomenon of this will, and that such a phenomenon has,
even from the subject itself, the principle of sufficient
reason as its necessary form, which here appears as the
law of motivation,—such a man will regard it as just as
absurd to doubt the inevitable nature of an action when
the motive is presented to a given character, as to doubt
that the three angles of any triangle are together equal
to two right angles. Priestly has very sufficiently proved
the necessity of the individual action in his "Doctrine of
Philosophical Necessity"; but Kant, whose merit in this
respect is specially great, first proved the coexistence of
this necessity with the freedom of the will in itself, *i. e.*,
apart from the phenomenon,[1] by establishing the distinction between the intelligible and the empirical char-

[1] "Critique of Pure Reason," first edition, pp. 532–558; fifth
edition, pp. 560–586; and "Critique of Practical Reason,"
fourth edition, pp. 169–179; Rosenkranz's edition, pp. 224–231.

acter. I entirely adhere to this distinction, for the former is the will as thing-in-itself so far as it appears in a definite individual in a definite grade, and the latter is this phenomenon itself as it exhibits itself in time in the mode of action, and in space in the physical structure. In order to make the relation of the two comprehensible, the best expression is that which I have already used in the introductory essay, that the intelligible character of every man is to be regarded as an act of will outside time, and therefore indivisible and unchangeable, and the manifestation of this act of will developed and broken up in time and space and all the forms of the principle of sufficient reason is the empirical character as it exhibits itself for experience in the whole conduct and life of this man. As the whole tree is only the constantly repeated manifestation of one and the same tendency, which exhibits itself in its simplest form in the fibre, and recurs and is easily recognised in the construction of the leaf, shoot, branch, and trunk, so all a man's deeds are merely the constantly repeated expression, somewhat varied in form, of his intelligible character, and the induction based on the sum of all these expressions gives us his empirical character. For the rest, I shall not at this point repeat in my own words Kant's masterly exposition, but presuppose it as known.

Apart from the fact that the will as the true thing-in-itself is actually original and independent, and that the feeling of its originality and absoluteness must accompany its acts in self-consciousness, though here they are already determined, there arises the illusion of an empirical freedom of the will (instead of the transcendental freedom which alone is to be attributed to it), and thus a freedom of its particular actions, from that attitude of the intellect towards the will which is explained, separated, and subordinated in the nineteenth chapter of the supplement, especially under No. 3. The intellect knows the conclusions of the will only *a posteriori* and empirically; therefore when a choice is presented, it has no data as to how the will is to decide. For the intelligible character, by virtue of which, when motives are given, only *one* decision is possible and is therefore necessary, does not come within the knowledge of the intellect, but merely the empirical character is known to it through the succession of its particular acts. Therefore it seems to the intellect that in a given case two opposite decisions are possible for the will. But this is just the same thing as if we were to say of a perpendicular beam that has lost its balance, and is hesitating which way to fall, "It can fall either to the right hand or the left." This *can* has merely a subjective significance, and really means "as far as the data known to us are concerned." Objectively, the direction of the fall is necessarily determined as soon as the equilibrium is lost. Accordingly, the decision of one's own will is undetermined only to the beholder, one's own intellect, and thus merely relatively and subjectively for the subject of knowing. In itself and objectively, on the other hand, in every choice presented to it, its decision is at once determined and necessary. But this determination only comes into consciousness through the decision that follows upon it. Indeed, we receive an empirical proof of this when any difficult and important choice lies before us, but only under a condition which is not yet present, but merely hoped for, so that in the meanwhile we can do nothing, but must remain passive. Now we consider how we shall decide when the circumstances occur that will give us a free activity and choice. Generally the foresight of rational deliberation recommends one decision, while direct inclination leans rather to the other. So long as we are compelled to remain passive, the side of reason seems to wish to keep the upperhand; but we see beforehand how strongly the other side will influence us when the opportunity for action arises. Till then we are eagerly concerned to place the motives on both sides in the clearest light, by calm meditation on the *pro et contra,* so that every motive may exert its full influence upon the will when the time arrives, and it may not be misled by a mistake on the part of the intellect to decide otherwise than it would have done if all the motives had their due influence upon it. But this distinct unfolding of the motives on both sides is all that the intellect can do to assist the choice. It awaits the real decision just as passively and with the same intense curiosity as if it were that of a foreign will. Therefore from its point of view both decisions must seem to it equally possible; and this is just the illusion of the empirical freedom of the will. Certainly the decision enters the sphere of the intellect altogether empirically, as the final conclusion of the matter; but yet it proceeded from the inner nature, the intelligible character, of the individual will in its conflict with given motives, and therefore with complete necessity. The intellect can do nothing more than bring out clearly and fully the nature of the motives; it cannot determine the will itself; for the will is quite inaccessible to it, and, as we have seen, cannot be investigated.

If, under the same circumstances, a man could act now one way and now another, it would be necessary that his will itself should have changed in the meantime, and thus that it should lie in time, for change is only possible in time; but then either the will would be a mere phenomenon, or time would be a condition of the thing-in-itself. Accordingly the dispute as to the freedom of the particular action, the freedom of indifference, really turns on the question whether the will lies in time or not. If, as both Kant's doctrine and the whole of my system

necessitates, the will is the thing-in-itself outside time
and outside every form of the principle of sufficient reason, not only must the individual act in the same way in
the same circumstances, and not only must every bad
action be the sure warrant of innumerable others, which
the individual *must* perform and *cannot* leave, but, as
Kant said, if only the empirical character and the motives were completely given, it would be possible to calculate the future conduct of a man just as we can calculate an eclipse of the sun or moon. As Nature is consistent, so is the character; every action must take place
in accordance with it, just as every phenomenon takes
place according to a law of Nature; the causes in the
latter case and the motives in the former are merely the
occasional causes, as was shown in the Second Book. The
will, whose phenomenon is the whole being and life of
man, cannot deny itself in the particular case, and what
the man wills on the whole, that will he also will in the
particular case.

The assertion of an empirical freedom of the will, a
freedom of indifference, agrees precisely with the doctrine that places the inner nature of man in a *soul*, which
is originally a *knowing*, and indeed really an abstract
thinking nature, and only in consequence of this a *willing*
nature—a doctrine which thus regards the will as of a
secondary or derivative nature, instead of knowledge
which is really so. The will indeed came to be regarded
as an act of thought, and to be identified with the judgment, especially by Descartes and Spinoza. According
to this doctrine every man must become what he is only
through his knowledge; he must enter the world as a
moral cipher come to know the things in it, and there-
upon determine to be this or that, to act thus or thus,
and may also through new knowledge achieve a new
course of action, that is to say, become another person.

Further, he must first know a thing to be *good*, and in consequence of this will it, instead of first *willing* it, and in consequence of this calling it *good*. According to my fundamental point of view, all this is a reversal of the true relation. Will is first and original; knowledge is merely added to it as an instrument belonging to the phenomenon of will. Therefore every man is what he is through his will, and his character is original, for willing is the basis of his nature. Through the knowledge which is added to it he comes to know in the course of experience *what he is, i. e.,* he learns his character. Thus he *knows* himself in consequence of and in accordance with the nature of his will, instead of *willing* in consequence of and in accordance with his knowing. According to the latter view, he would only require to consider how he would like best to be, and he would be it; that is its doctrine of the freedom of the will. Thus it consists really in this, that a man is his own work guided by the light of knowledge. I, on the contrary, say that he is his own work before all knowledge, and knowledge is merely added to it to enlighten it. Therefore he cannot resolve to be this or that, nor can he become other than he is; but he *is* once for all, and he knows in the course of experience *what* he is. According to one doctrine he *wills* what he knows, and according to the other he *knows* what he wills.

The motives which determine the manifestation of the character or conduct influence it through the medium of knowledge. But knowledge is changeable, and often vacillates between truth and error, yet, as a rule, is rectified more and more in the course of life, though certainly in very different degrees. Therefore the conduct of a man may be observably altered without justifying us in concluding that his character has been changed. What the man really and in general wills, the striving of his

inmost nature, and the end he pursues in accordance
with it, this we can never change by influence upon him
from without by instruction, otherwise we could transform him. From without the will can only be affected by
motives. But these can never change the will itself; for
they have power over it only under the presupposition
that it is precisely such as it is. All that they can do is
thus to alter the direction of its effort, *i. e.*, bring it
about that it shall seek in another way than it has hitherto done that which it invariably seeks. Therefore instruction, improved knowledge, in other words, influence
from without, may indeed teach the will that it erred in
the means it employed, and can therefore bring it about
that the end after which it strives once for all according
to its inner nature shall be pursued on an entirely different path and in an entirely different object from what
has hitherto been the case. But it can never bring about
that the will shall will something actually different from
what it has hitherto willed; this remains unchangeable,
for the will is simply this willing itself, which would
have to be abolished. The former, however, the possible
modification of knowledge, and through knowledge of
conduct, extends so far that the will seeks to attain its
unalterable end, for example, Mohammed's paradise, at
one time in the real world, at another time in a world of
imagination, adapting the means to each, and thus in the
first case applying prudence, might, and fraud, and in
the second case, abstinence, justice, alms, and pilgrimages to Mecca. But its effort itself has not therefore
changed, still less the will itself. Thus, although its action certainly shows itself very different at different
times, its willing has yet remained precisely the same.

For motives to act, it is necessary not only that they
should be present, but that they should be known. For
example, in order that the relation may appear that

exists in a given man between egoism and sympathy, it is not sufficient that he should possess wealth and see others in want, but he must also know what he can do with his wealth, both for himself and for others: not only must the suffering of others be presented to him, but he must know both what suffering and also what pleasure is. Perhaps, on a first occasion, he did not know all this so well as on a second; and if, on a similar occasion, he acts differently, this arises simply from the fact that the circumstances were really different, as regards the part of them that depends on his knowing them, although they seem to be the same. As ignorance of actually existing circumstances robs them of their influence, so, on the other hand, entirely imaginary circumstances may act as if they were real, not only in the case of a particular deception, but also in general and continuously. For example, if a man is firmly persuaded that every good action will be repaid him a hundredfold in a future life, such a conviction affects him in precisely the same way as a good bill of exchange at a very long date, and he can give from mere egoism, as from another point of view he would take from egoism. He has not changed himself. It is on account of this great influence of knowledge upon action, while the will remains unchangeable, that the character develops and its different features appear only little by little. Therefore it shows itself different at every period of life, and an impetuous, wild youth may be succeeded by a staid, sober, manly age. Especially what is bad in the character will always come out more strongly with time, yet sometimes it occurs that passions which a man gave way to in his youth are afterwards voluntarily restrained, simply because the motives opposed to them have only then come into knowledge. Hence, also, we are all innocent to begin with, and this merely means that neither we nor others know the evil of our own nature; it only appears with the motives, and only in time do the motives appear in knowledge. Finally we come to know ourselves as quite different from what *a priori* we supposed ourselves to be, and then we are often terrified at ourselves.

Repentance never proceeds from a change of the will (which is impossible), but from a change of knowledge. The essential and peculiar in what I have always willed I must still continue to will; for I myself am this will which lies outside time and change. I can therefore never repent of what I have willed, though I can repent of what I have done; because, led by false conceptions, I did something that was not in conformity with my will. The discovery of this through fuller knowledge is *repentance*. This extends not merely to worldly wisdom, to the choice of the means, and the judgment of the appropriateness of the end to my own will, but also to what is properly ethical. For example, I may have acted more egotistically than is in accordance with my character, led astray by exaggerated ideas of the need in which I myself stood, or of the craft, falseness, and wickedness of others, or because I hurried too much, *i. e.,* acted without deliberation, determined not by motives distinctly known *in abstracto,* but by merely perceived motives, by the present and the emotion which it excited, and which was so strong that I had not properly the use of my reason; but the return of reflection is thus here also merely corrected knowledge, and from this repentance may proceed, which always proclaims itself by making amends for the past, as far as is possible. Yet it must be observed that, in order to deceive themselves, men prearrange what seem to be hasty errors, but are really secretly considered actions. For we deceive and flatter no one through such fine devices as ourselves. The converse of the case we have given may also occur. I may be misled by too good opinion of others, or want of knowledge of the relative value of the good things of life, or some abstract dogma in which I have since lost faith, and thus I may act less egotistically t' n is in keeping with my character, and lay up for myself repentance of another kind. Thus repentance is always corrected knowledge of the relation of an act to its special intention. When the will reveals its Ideas in space alone, *i. e.*, through mere form, the matter in which other Ideas—in this case natural forces —already reign, resists the will, and seldom allows the form that is striving after visibility to appear in perfect purity and distinctness, *i. e.*, in perfect beauty. And there is an analogous hindrance to the will as it reveals itself in time alone, *i. e.*, through actions, in the knowledge which seldom gives it the data quite correctly, so that the action which takes place does not accurately correspond to the will, and leads to repentance. Repentance thus always proceeds from corrected knowledge, not from the change of the will, which is impossible. Anguish of conscience for past deeds is anything but repentance. It is pain at the knowledge of oneself in one's inmost nature, *i. e.*, as will. It rests precisely on the certainty that we have still the same will. If the will were changed, and therefore the anguish of conscience mere repentance, it would cease to exist. The past could then no longer give us pain, for it exhibited the expressions of a will which is no longer that of him who has repented. We shall explain the significance of anguish of conscience in detail farther on.

The influence which knowledge, as the medium of motives, exerts, not indeed upon the will itself, but upon its appearance in actions, is also the source of the principal distinction between the action of men and that of brutes, for their methods of knowledge are different.

The brute has only knowledge of perception, the man, through reason, has also abstract ideas, conceptions. Now, although man and brute are with equal necessity determined by their motives, yet man, as distinguished from the brute, has a complete *choice,* which has often been regarded as a freedom of the will in particular actions, although it is nothing but the possibility of a thoroughly-fought-out battle between several motives, the strongest of which then determines it with necessity. For this the motives must have assumed the form of abstract thoughts, because it is really only by means of these that deliberation, *i. e.,* a weighing of opposite reasons for action, is possible. In the case of the brute there can only be a choice between perceptible motives presented to it, so that the choice is limited to the narrow sphere of its present sensuous perception. Therefore the necessity of the determination of the will by the motive, which is like that of the effect by the cause, can be exhibited perceptibly and directly only in the case of the brutes, because here the spectator has the motives just as directly before his eyes as their effect; while in the case of man the motives are almost always abstract ideas, which are not communicated to the spectator, and even for the actor himself the necessity of their effect is hidden behind their conflict. For only *in abstracto* can several ideas, as judgments and chains of conclusions, lie beside each other in consciousness, and then, free from all determination of time, work against each other till the stronger overcomes the rest and determines the will. This is the complete *choice* or power of deliberation which man has as distinguished from the brutes, and on account of which freedom of the will has been attributed to him, in the belief that his willing is a mere result of the operations of his intellect, without a definite tendency which serves as its basis; while, in

truth, the motives only work on the foundation and
under the presupposition of his definite tendency, which
in his case is individual, *i. e.*, a character. For the rest,
this power of deliberation which man possesses is one
of those things that makes his existence so much more
miserable than that of the brute. For in general our
greatest sufferings do not lie in the present as ideas of
perception or as immediate feelings; but in the reason,
as abstract conceptions, painful thoughts, from which
the brute, which lives only in the present, and therefore in enviable carelessness, is entirely free.

The distinction we have established between the ways
in which the brutes and man are respectively moved by
motives exerts a very wide influence upon the nature of
both, and has most to do with the complete and obvious
differences of their existence. While an idea of perception is in every case the motive which determines the
brute, the man strives to exclude this kind of motivation
altogether, and to determine himself entirely by abstract
ideas. Thus he uses his prerogative of reason to the
greatest possible advantage. Independent of the present,
he neither chooses nor avoids the passing pleasure or
pain, but reflects on the consequences of both. In most
cases, setting aside quite insignificant actions, we are
determined by abstract, thought motives, not present
impressions. Therefore all particular privation for the
moment is for us comparatively light, but all renunciation is terribly hard; for the former only concerns
the fleeting present, but the latter concerns the future,
and includes in itself innumerable privations, of which
it is the equivalent. The causes of our pain, as of our
pleasure, lie for the most part, not in the real present,
but merely in abstract thoughts. It is these which are
often unbearable to us—inflict torments in comparison
with which all the sufferings of the animal world are

very small; for even our own physical pain is not felt at all when they are present. Indeed, in the case of keen mental suffering, we even inflict physical suffering on ourselves merely to distract our attention from the former to the latter. This is why, in great mental anguish, men tear their hair, beat their breasts, lacerate their faces, or roll on the floor, for all these are in reality only violent means of diverting the mind from an unbearable thought. Just because mental pain, being much greater, makes us insensible to physical pain, suicide is very easy to the person who is in despair, or who is consumed by morbid depression, even though formerly, in comfortable circumstances, he recoiled at the thought of it. In the same way care and passion (thus the play of thought) wear out the body oftener and more than physical hardships. Eulenspiegel admirably bantered human nature, for going uphill he laughed, and going downhill he wept. Indeed, children who have hurt themselves often cry, not at the pain, but at the thought of the pain which is awakened when some one condoles with them. Such great differences in conduct and in life arise from the diversity between the methods of knowledge of the brutes and man. Further, the appearance of the distinct and decided individual character, the principal distinction between man and the brute, which has scarcely more than the character of the species, is conditioned by the choice between several motives, which is only possible through abstract conceptions. For only after a choice has been made are the resolutions, which vary in different individuals, an indication of the individual character which is different in each; while the action of the brute depends only upon the presence or absence of the impression, supposing this impression to be in general a motive for its species. And, finally, in the case of man, only the resolve, and not the mere wish, is a valid indication of his character both for himself and for others; but the resolve becomes for himself, as for others, a certain fact only through the deed. The wish is merely the necessary consequence of the present impression, whether of the outward stimulus, or the inward passing mood; and is therefore as immediately necessary and devoid of consideration as the action of the brutes. Therefore, like the action of the brutes, it merely expresses the character of the species, not that of the individual, *i. e.,* it indicates merely what *man in general,* not what the individual who experiences the wish, is capable of doing. The deed alone,—because as human action it always requires a certain deliberation, and because as a rule a man has command of his reason, is considerate, *i. e.,* decides in accordance with considered and abstract motives,—is the expression of the intelligible maxims of his conduct, the result of his inmost willing, and is related as a letter to the word that stands for his empirical character, itself merely the temporal expression of his intelligible character. In a healthy mind, therefore, only deeds oppress the conscience, not wishes and thoughts; for it is only our deeds that hold up to us the mirror of our will. The deed referred to above, that is entirely unconsidered and is really committed in blind passion, is to a certain extent an intermediate thing between the mere wish and the resolve. Therefore, by true repentance, which, however, shows itself as action also, it can be obliterated, as a falsely drawn line, from that picture of our will which our course of life is. I may insert the remark here, as a very good comparison, that the relation between wish and deed has a purely accidental but accurate analogy with that between the accumulation and discharge of electricity.

As the result of the whole of this discusion of the freedom of the will and what relates to it, we find that although the will may, in itself and apart from the phenomenon, be called free and even omnipotent, yet in its particular phenomena enlightened by knowledge, as in men and brutes, it is determined by motives to which the special character regularly and necessarily responds, and always in the same way. We see that because of the possession on his part of abstract or rational knowledge, man, as distinguished from the brutes, has a *choice,* which only makes him the scene of the conflict of his motives, without withdrawing him from their control. This choice is therefore certainly the condition of the possibility of the complete expression of the individual character, but is by no means to be regarded as freedom of the particular volition, *i. e.,* independence of the law of causality, the necessity of which extends to man as to every other phenomenon. Thus the difference between human volition and that of the brutes, which is introduced by reason or knowledge through concepts, extends to the point we have indicated, and no farther. But, what is quite a different thing, there may arise a phenomenon of the human will which is quite impossible in the brute creation, if man altogether lays aside the knowledge of particular things as such which is subordinate to the principle of sufficient reason, and by means of his knowledge of the Ideas sees through the *principle of individuation.* Then an actual appearance of the real freedom of the will as a thing-in-itself is possible, by which the phenomenon comes into a sort of contradiction with itself, as is indicated by the word self-renunciation; and, finally, the "in-itself" of its nature suppresses itself. But this, the one, real, and direct expression of the freedom of the will in itself in the phenomenon, cannot be distinctly explained here, but will form the subject of the concluding part of our work.

Now that we have shown clearly in these pages the

unalterable nature of the empirical character, which is just the unfolding of the intelligible character that lies outside time, together with the necessity with which actions follow upon its contact with motives, we hasten to anticipate an argument which may very easily be drawn from this in the interest of bad dispositions. Our character is to be regarded as the temporal unfolding of an extra-temporal, and therefore indivisible and unalterable, act of will, or an intelligible character. This necessarily dtermines all that is essential in our conduct in life, *i. e.*, its ethical content, which must express itself in accordance with it in its phenomenal appearance, the empirical character; while only what is unessential in this, the outward form of our course of life, depends upon the forms in which the motives present themselves. It might, therefore, be inferred that it is a waste of trouble to endeavour to improve one's character, and that it is wiser to submit to the inevitable, and gratify every inclination at once, even if it is bad. But this is precisely the same thing as the theory of an inevitable fate which is called in more recent times Turkish faith. Its true refutation, as it is supposed to have been given by Chrysippus, is explained by Cicero in his book *De Fato*, ch. 12, 13.

Though everything may be regarded as irrevocably predetermined by fate, yet it is so only through the medium of the chain of causes; therefore in no case can it be determined that an effect shall appear without its cause. Thus it is not simply the event that is predetermined, but the event as the consequence of preceding causes; so that fate does not decide the consequence alone, but also the means as the consequence of which it is destined to appear. Accordingly, if some means is not present, it is certain that the consequence also will not be present: each is always present in accordance with the determination of fate, but this is never known to us till afterwards.

As events always take place according to fate, *i. e.*, according to the infinite concatenation of causes, so our actions always take place according to our intelligible character. But just as we do not know the former beforehand, so no *a priori* insight is given us into the latter, but we only come to know ourselves as we come to know other persons *a posteriori* through experience. If the intelligible character involved that we could only form a good resolution after a long conflict with a bad disposition, this conflict would have to come first and be waited for. Reflection on the unalterable nature of the character, on the unity of the source from which all our actions flow, must not mislead us into claiming the decision of the character in favour of one side or the other; it is in the resolve that follows that we shall see what manner of men we are, and mirror ourselves in our actions. This is the explanation of the satisfaction or the anguish of soul with which we look back on the course of our past life. Both are experienced, not because these past deeds have still an existence; they are past, they have been, and now are no more; but their great importance for us lies in their significance, lies in the fact that these deeds are the expression of the character, the mirror of the will, in which we look and recognise our inmost self, the kernel of our will. Because we experience this not before, but only after, it behoves us to strive and fight in time, in order that the picture we produce by our deeds may be such that the contemplation of it may calm us as much as possible, instead of harassing us. The significance of this consolation or anguish of soul will, as we have said, be inquired into farther on; but to this place there belongs the inquiry which follows, and which stands by itself.

Besides the intelligible and the empirical character, we must mention a third which is different from them both, the *acquired character,* which one only receives in life through contact with the world, and which is referred to when one is praised as a man of character or censured as being without character. Certainly one might suppose that, since the empirical character, as the phenomenon of the intelligible, is unalterable, and, like every natural phenomenon, is consistent with itself, man would always have to appear like himself and consistent, and would therefore have no need to acquire a character artificially by experience and reflection. But the case is otherwise, and although a man is always the same, yet he does not always understand himself, but often mistakes himself, till he has in some degree acquired real self-knowledge. The empirical character, as a mere natural tendency, is in itself irrational; nay, more, its expressions are disturbed by reason, all the more so the more intellect and power of thought the man has; for these always keep before him what becomes *man in general* as the character of the species, and what is possible for him both in will and in deed. This makes it the more difficult for him to see how much his individuality enables him to will and to accomplish. He finds in himself the germs of all the various human pursuits and powers, but the difference of degree in which they exist in his individuality is not clear to him in the absence of experience; and if he now applies himself to the pursuits which alone correspond to his character, he yet feels, especially at particular moments and in particular moods, the inclination to directly opposite pursuits which cannot be combined with them, but must be entirely suppressed if he desires to follow the former undisturbed. For as our physical path upon earth is always merely a line, not an extended surface, so in life, if we desire to grasp and possess one thing, we must renounce and leave innumerable others on the right hand and on the left. If we cannot make up our minds to this, but, like children at the fair, snatch at everything that attracts us in passing, we are making the perverse endeavour to change the line of our path into an extended surface; we run in a zigzag, skip about like a will o' the wisp, and attain to nothing. Or, to use another comparison, as according to Hobbes' philosophy of law, every one has an original right to everything but an exclusive right to nothing, yet can obtain an exclusive right to particular things by renouncing his right to all the rest, while others, on their part, do likewise with regard to what he has chosen; so is it in life, in which some definite pursuit, whether it be pleasure, honour, wealth, science, art, or virtue, can only be followed with seriousness and success when all claims that are foreign to it are given up, when everything else is renounced. Accordingly, the mere will and the mere ability are not sufficient, but a man must also *know* what he wills, and *know* what he can do; only then will he show character, and only then can he accomplish something right. Until he attains to that, notwithstanding the natural consistency of the empirical character, he is without character. And although, on the whole, he must remain true to himself, and fulfil his course, led by his dæmon, yet his path will not be a straight line, but wavering and uneven. He will hesitate, deviate, turn back, lay up for himself repentance and pain. And all this is because, in great and small, he sees before him all that is possible and attainable for man in general, but does not know what part of all this is alone suitable for him, can be accomplished by him, and and is alone enjoyable by him. He will, therefore, envy many men on account of a position and circumstances which are yet only suitable to their characters and not to his, and in which he would feel unhappy, if indeed he found them endurable at all. For as a fish is only at home in water, a bird in the air, a mole in the earth, so every man is only at home in the atmosphere suitable to him. For example, not all men can breathe the air of court life. From deficiency of proper insight into all this, many a man will make all kinds of abortive attempts, will do violence to his character in particulars, and yet, on the whole, will have to yield to it again; and what he thus painfully attains will give him no pleasure; what he thus learns will remain dead; even in an ethical regard, a deed that is too noble for his character, that has not sprung from pure, direct impulse, but from a concept, a dogma, will lose all merit, even in his own eyes, through subsequent egoistical repentance. We only become conscious of the inflexibility of another person's character through experience, and till then we childishly believe that it is possible, by means of rational ideas, by prayers and entreaties, by example and noble-mindedness, ever to persuade any one to leave his own way, to change his course of conduct, to depart from his mode of thinking, or even to extend his capacities: so is it also with ourselves. We must first learn from experience what we desire and what we can do. Till then we know it not, we are without character, and must often be driven back to our own way by hard blows from without. But if we have finally learnt it, then we have attained to what in the world is called character, the *acquired character*. This is accordingly nothing but the most perfect knowledge possible of our own individuality. It is the abstract, and consequently distinct, knowledge of the unalterable qualities of our own empirical character, and of the measure and direction of our mental and physical powers, and thus of the whole strength and weakness of our own individuality. This places us in a position to carry out deliberately and methodically the rôle which belongs to our own person, and to fill up the gaps which caprices or weaknesses produce in it, under the guidance of fixed conceptions. This rôle is in itself unchangeably determined once for all, but hitherto we have allowed it to follow its natural course without any rule. We have now brought to distinct conscious maxims which are always present to us the form of conduct which is necessarily determined by our own individual nature, and now we conduct it in accordance with them as deliberately as if we had learned it; without ever falling into error through the passing influence of the mood or the impression of the present, without being checked by the bitterness or sweetness of some particular thing we meet with on our path, without delay, without hesitation, without inconsistency. We shall now no longer, as novices, wait, attempt, and grope about in order to see what we really desire and are able to do, but we know this once for all, and in every choice we have only to apply general principles to particular cases, and arrive at once at a decision. We know our will in general, and do not allow ourselves to be led by the passing mood or by solicitations from without to resolve in particular cases what is contrary to it as a whole. We know in the same way the nature and the measure of our strength and our weakness, and thereby are spared much suffering. For we experience no real pleasure except in the use and feeling of our own powers, and the greatest pain is the conscious deficiency of our powers where we need them. If, now, we have discovered where our strength and our weakness lie, we will endeavour to cultivate, employ, and in every way make use of those talents which are naturally prominent in us. We will always turn to those occupations in which they are valuable and to the purpose, and entirely avoid, even with self-renunciation, those pursuits for which we have naturally little aptitude; we will beware of attempting that in which we have no chance of succeeding. Only he who has attained to this will constantly and with full consciousness be completely himself, and will never fail himself at the critical moment, because he will always have known what he could expect from himself. He will often enjoy the satisfaction of feeling his strength, and seldom experience the pain of being reminded of his weakness. The latter is mortification, which causes perhaps the greatest of mental sufferings; therefore it is far more endurable to have our misfortune brought clearly before us than our incapacity. And, further, if we are thus fully acquainted with our strength and our weakness, we will not attempt to make a show of powers which we do not possess; we will not play with base coin, for all such dissimulation misses the mark in the end. For since the whole man is only the phenomenon of his will, nothing can be more perverse than to try, by means of reflection, to become something else than one is, for this is a direct contradiction of the will with itself. The imitation of the qualities and idiosyncrasies of others is much more shameful than to dress in other people's clothes; for it is the judgment of our own worthlessness pronounced by ourselves. Knowledge of our own mind and its capacities of every kind, and their unalterable limits, is in this respect the surest way to the attainment of the greatest possible contentment with ourselves. For it holds good of inward as of outward circumstances that there is for us no consolation so effective as the complete certainty of unalterable necessity. No evil that befalls us pains us so much as the thought of the circumstances by which it might have been warded off. There-

fore nothing comforts us so effectually as the consideration of what has happened from the standpoint of necessity, from which all accidents appear as tools in the
hand of an over-ruling fate, and we therefore recognise the evil that has come to us as inevitably produced
by the conflict of inner and outer circumstances; in
other words, fatalism. We really only complain and
storm so long as we hope either to affect others or to
excite ourselves to unheard-of efforts. But children and
grown-up people know very well to yield contentedly
as soon as they clearly see that it absolutely cannot be
otherwise. We are like the entrapped elephants, that
rage and struggle for many days, till they see that it is
useless, and then suddenly offer their necks quietly to
the yoke, tamed for ever. We are like King David, who,
as long as his son still lived, unceasingly importuned
Jehovah with prayers, and behaved himself as if in
despair; but as soon as his son was dead, thought no
longer about it. Hence it arises that innumerable permanent ills, such as lameness, poverty, low estate, ugliness, a disagreeable dwelling-place, are borne with indifference by innumerable persons, and are no longer
felt, like healed wounds, just because these persons
know that inward or outward necessity renders it impossible that any change can take place in these things;
while those who are more fortunate cannot understand
how such misfortunes can be borne. Now as with outward necessity, so also with inward; nothing reconciles
so thoroughly as a distinct knowledge of it. If we have
once for all distinctly recognised not only our good
qualities and our strength, but also our defects and
weakness, established our aim accordingly, and rest
satisfied concerning what cannot be attained, we thus
escape in the surest way, as far as our individuality
permits, the bitterest of all sorrows, discontentment with

ourselves, which is the inevitable result of ignorance of
our own individuality, of false conceit and the audacity
that proceeds from it.

§ 57. At every grade that is enlightened by knowledge,
the will appears as an individual. The human individual
finds himself as finite in infinite space and time, and
consequently as a vanishing quantity compared with
them. He is projected into them, and, on account of
their unlimited nature, he has always a merely relative, never absolute *when* and *where* of his existence;
for his place and duration are finite parts of what is
infinite and boundless. His real existence is only in the
present, whose unchecked flight into the past is a constant transition into death, a constant dying. For his
past life, apart from its possible consequences for the
present, and the testimony regarding the will that is
expressed in it, is now entirely done with, dead, and
no longer anything; and, therefore, it must be, as a matter of reason, indifferent to him whether the content of
that past was pain or pleasure. But the present is always passing through his hands into the past; the future
is quite uncertain and always short. Thus his existence,
even when we consider only its formal side, is a constant
hurrying of the present into the dead past, a constant
dying. But if we look at it from the physical side; it
is clear that, as our walking is admittedly merely a
constantly prevented falling, the life of our body is only
a constantly prevented dying, an ever-postponed death:
finally, in the same way, the activity of our mind is a
constantly deferred ennui. Every breath we draw wards
off the death that is constantly intruding upon us. In
this way we fight with it every moment, and again, at
longer intervals, through every meal we eat, every
sleep we take, every time we warm ourselves, &c. In the
end, death must conquer, for we became subject to him

through birth, and he only plays for a little while with his prey before he swallows it up. We pursue our life, however, with great interest and much solicitude as long as possible, as we blow out a soap-bubble as long and as large as possible, although we know perfectly well that it will burst.

We saw that the inner being of unconscious nature is a constant striving without end and without rest. And this appears to us much more distinctly when we consider the nature of brutes and man. Willing and striving is its whole being, which may be very well compared to an unquenchable thirst. But the basis of all willing is need, deficiency, and thus pain. Consequently, the nature of brutes and man is subject to pain originally and through its very being. If, on the other hand, it lacks objects of desire, because it is at once deprived of them by a too easy satisfaction, a terrible void and ennui comes over it, *i. e.,* its being and existence itself becomes an unbearable burden to it. Thus its life swings like a pendulum backwards and forwards between pain and ennui. This has also had to express itself very oddly in this way; after man had transferred all pain and torments to hell, there then remained nothing over for heaven but ennui.

But the constant striving which constitutes the inner nature of every manifestation of will obtains its primary and most general foundation at the higher grades of objectification, from the fact that here the will manifests itself as a living body, with the iron command to nourish it; and what gives strength to this command is just that this body is nothing but the objectified will to live itself. Man, as the most complete objectification of that will, is in like measure also the most necessitous of all beings: he is through and through concrete willing and needing; he is a concretion of a thousand necessities.

With these he stands upon the earth, left to himself, uncertain about everything except his own need and misery. Consequently the care for the maintenance of that existence under exacting demands, which are renewed every day, occupies, as a rule, the whole of human life. To this is directly related the second claim, that of the propagation of the species. At the same time he is threatened from all sides by the most different kinds of dangers, from which it requires constant watchfulness to escape. With cautious steps and casting anxious glances round him he pursues his path, for a thousand accidents and a thousand enemies lie in wait for him. Thus he went while yet a savage, thus he goes in civilised life; there is no security for him. The life of the great majority is only a constant struggle for this existence itself, with the certainty of losing it at last. But what enables them to endure this wearisome battle is not so much the love of life as the fear of death, which yet stands in the background as inevitable, and may come upon them at any moment. Life itself is a sea, full of rocks and whirlpools, which man avoids with the greatest care and solicitude, although he knows that even if he succeeds in getting through with all his efforts and skill, he yet by doing so comes nearer at every step to the greatest, the total, inevitable, and irremediable shipwreck, death; nay, even steers right upon it: this is the final goal of the laborious voyage, and worse for him than all the rocks from which he has escaped.

Now it is well worth observing that, on the one hand, the suffering and misery of life may easily increase to such an extent that death itself, in the flight from which the whole of life consists, becomes desirable, and we hasten towards it voluntarily; and again, on the other hand, that as soon as want and suffering permit rest to a man, ennui is at once so near that he necessarily re-

quires diversion. The striving after existence is what
occupies all living things and maintains them in motion. But when existence is assured, then they know not
what to do with it; thus the second thing that sets them
in motion is the effort to get free from the burden of
existence, to make it cease to be felt, "to kill time,"
i. e., to escape from ennui. Accordingly we see that almost all men who are secure from want and care, now
that at last they have thrown off all other burdens, become a burden to themselves, and regard as a gain every
hour they succeed in getting through, and thus every
diminution of the very life which, till then, they have
employed all their powers to maintain as long as possible. Ennui is by no means an evil to be lightly
esteemed; in the end it depicts on the countenance real
despair. It makes beings who love each other so little
as men do, seek each other eagerly, and thus becomes
the source of social intercourse. Moreover, even from
motives of policy, public precautions are everywhere
taken against it, as against other universal calamities.
For this evil may drive men to the greatest excesses, just
as much as its opposite extreme, famine: the people require *panem et circenses* ("bread and circuses"). The
strict penitentiary system of Philadelphia makes use
of ennui alone as a means of punishment, through soli-
tary confinement and idleness, and it is found so terrible that it has even led prisoners to commit suicide. As
want is the constant scourge of the people, so ennui is
that of the fashionable world. In middle-class life ennui
is represented by the Sunday, and want by the six
week-days.

Thus between desiring and attaining all human life
flows on throughout. The wish is, in its nature, pain;
the attainment soon begets satiety: the end was only
apparent; possession takes away the charm; the wish,

the need, presents itself under a new form; when it does not, then follows desolateness, emptiness, ennui, against which the conflict is just as painful as against want. That wish and satisfaction should follow each other neither too quickly nor too slowly reduces the suffering, which both occasion to the smallest amount, and constitutes the happiest life. For that which we might otherwise call the most beautiful part of life, its purest joy, if it were only because it lifts us out of real existence and transforms us into disinterested spectators of it—that is, pure knowledge, which is foreign to all willing, the pleasure of the beautiful, the true delight in art— this is granted only to a very few, because it demands rare talents, and to these few only as a passing dream. And then, even these few, on account of their higher intellectual power, are made susceptible of far greater suffering than duller minds can ever feel, and are also placed in lonely isolation by a nature which is obviously different from that of others; thus here also accounts are squared. But to the great majority of men purely intellectual pleasures are not accessible. They are almost quite incapable of the joys which lie in pure knowledge. They are entirely given up to willing. If, therefore, anything is to win their sympathy, to be *interesting* to them, it must (as is implied in the meaning of the word) in some way excite their *will*, even if it is only through a distant and merely problematical relation to it; the will must not be left altogether out of the question, for their existence lies far more in willing than in knowing,—action and reaction is their one element. We may find in trifles and everyday occurrences the naïve expressions of this quality. Thus, for example, at any place worth seeing they may visit, they write their names, in order thus to react, to affect the place since it does not affect them. Again, when they see a strange rare animal, they cannot easily confine themselves to merely observing it; they must rouse it, tease it, play with it, merely to experience action and reaction; but this need for excitement of the will manifests itself very specially in the discovery and support of card-playing, which is quite peculiarly the expression of the miserable side of humanity.

§ 58. All satisfaction, or what is commonly called happiness, is always really and essentially only *negative,* and never positive. It is not an original gratification coming to us of itself, but must always be the satisfaction of a wish. The wish, *i. e.,* some want, is the condition which precedes every pleasure. But with the satisfaction the wish and therefore the pleasure cease. Thus the satisfaction or the pleasing can never be more than the deliverance from a pain, from a want; for such is not only every actual, open sorrow, but every desire, the importunity of which disturbs our peace, and, indeed, the deadening ennui also that makes life a burden to us. It is, however, so hard to attain or achieve anything; difficulties and troubles without end are opposed to every purpose, and at every step hindrances accumulate. But when finally everything is overcome and attained, nothing can ever be gained but deliverance from some sorrow or desire, so that we find ourselves just in the same position as we occupied before this sorrow or desire appeared. All that is even directly given us is merely the want, *i. e.,* the pain. The satisfaction and the pleasure we can only know indirectly through the remembrance of the preceding suffering and want, which ceases with its appearance. Hence it arises that we are not properly conscious of the blessings and advantages we actually possess, nor do we prize them, but think of them merely as a matter of course, for they gratify us only negatively by restraining suffering. Only when we have lost them do we become sensible of their value; for the want, the privation, the sorrow, is the positive, communicating itself directly to us. Thus also we are pleased by the remembrance of past need, sickness, want, and such like, because this is the only means of enjoying the present blessings. And, further, it cannot be denied that in this respect, and from this standpoint of egoism, which is the form of the will to live, the sight or the description of the sufferings of others affords us satisfaction and pleasure. Yet we shall see farther on that this kind of pleasure, through knowledge of our own well-being obtained in this way, lies very near the source of real, positive wickedness.

That all happiness is only of a negative not a positive nature, that just on this account it cannot be lasting satisfaction and gratification, but merely delivers us from some pain or want which must be followed either by a new pain, or by languor, empty longing, and ennui; this finds support in art, that true mirror of the world and life, and especially in poetry. Every epic and dramatic poem can only represent a struggle, an effort, and fight for happiness, never enduring and complete happiness itself. It conducts its heroes through a thousand difficulties and dangers to the goal; as soon as this is reached, it hastens to let the curtain fall; for now there would remain nothing for it to do but to show that the glittering goal in which the hero expected to find happiness had only disappointed him, and that after its attainment he was no better off than before. Because a genuine enduring happiness is not possible, it cannot be the subject of art. Certainly the aim of the idyll is the description of such a happiness, but one also sees that the idyll as such cannot continue. The poet always finds that it either becomes epical in his hands, and in this case it is a very insignificant epic, made up of trifling sorrows, trifling delights, and trifling efforts—this is the common-est case—or else it becomes a merely descriptive poem, describing the beauty of nature, *i. e.*, pure knowing free from will, which certainly, as a matter of fact, is the only pure happiness, which is neither preceded by suffer-ing or want, nor necessarily followed by repentance, sor-row, emptiness, or satiety; but this happiness cannot fill the whole life, but is only possible at moments. What we see in poetry we find again in music; in the melodies of which we have recognised the universal expression of the inmost history of the self-conscious will, the most secret life, longing, suffering, and delight; the ebb and flow of the human heart. Melody is always a deviation from the keynote through a thousand capricious wander-ings, even to the most painful discord, and then a final return to the keynote which expresses the satisfaction and appeasing of the will, but with which nothing more can then be done, and the continuance of which any longer would only be a wearisome and unmeaning monot-ony corresponding to ennui.

All that we intend to bring out clearly through these investigations, the impossibility of attaining lasting sat-isfaction and the negative nature of all happiness, finds its explanation in what is shown at the conclusion of the Second Book: that the will, of which human life, like every phenomenon, is the objectification, is a striving without aim or end. We find the stamp of this endless-ness imprinted upon all the parts of its whole manifes-tation, from its most universal form, endless time and space, up to the most perfect of all phenomena, the life and efforts of man. We may theoretically assume three extremes of human life, and treat them as elements of actual human life. First, the powerful will, the strong passions (Radscha-Guna). It appears in great historical characters; it is described in the epic and the drama.

But it can also show itself in the little world, for the size of the objects is measured here by the degree in which they influence the will, not according to their external relations. Secondly, pure knowing, the comprehension of the Ideas, conditioned by the freeing of knowledge from the service of will: the life of genius (Satwa-Guna). Thirdly and lastly, the greatest lethargy of the will, and also of the knowledge attaching to it, empty longing, life-benumbing languor (Tama-Guna). The life of the individual, far from becoming permanently fixed in one of these extremes, seldom touches any of them, and is for the most part only a weak and wavering approach to one or the other side, a needy desiring of trifling objects, constantly recurring, and so escaping ennui. It is really incredible how meaningless and void of significance when looked at from without, how dull and unenlightened by intellect when felt from within, is the course of the life of the great majority of men. It is a weary longing and complaining, a dreamlike staggering through the four ages of life to death, accompanied by a series of trivial thoughts. Such men are like clockwork, which is wound up, and goes it knows not why; and every time a man is begotten and born, the clock of human life is wound up anew, to repeat the same old piece it has played innumerable times before, passage after passage, measure after measure, with insignificant variations. Every individual, every human being and his course of life, is but another short dream of the endless spirit of nature, of the persistent will to live; is only another fleeting form, which it carelessly sketches on its infinite page, space and time; allows to remain for a time so short that it vanishes into nothing in comparison with these, and then obliterates to make new room. And yet, and here lies the serious side of life, every one of these fleeting forms, these empty fancies, must be paid for by the whole will to live, in all its activity, with many and deep sufferings, and finally with a bitter death, long feared and coming at last. This is why the sight of a corpse makes us suddenly so serious.

The life of every individual, if we survey it as a whole and in general, and only lay stress upon its most significant features, is really always a tragedy, but gone through in detail, it has the character of a comedy. For the deeds and vexations of the day, the restless irritation of the moment, the desires and fears of the week, the mishaps of every hour, are all through chance, which is ever bent upon some jest, scenes of a comedy. But the never-satisfied wishes, the frustrated efforts, the hopes unmercifully crushed by fate, the unfortunate errors of the whole life, with increasing suffering and death at the end, are always a tragedy. Thus, as if fate would add derision to the misery of our existence, our life must contain all the woes of tragedy, and yet we cannot even assert the dignity of tragic characters, but in the broad detail of life must inevitably be the foolish characters of a comedy.

But however much great and small trials may fill human life, they are not able to conceal its insufficiency to satisfy the spirit; they cannot hide the emptiness and superficiality of existence, nor exclude ennui, which is always ready to fill up every pause that care may allow. Hence it arises that the human mind, not content with the cares, anxieties, and occupations which the actual world lays upon it, creates for itself an imaginary world also in the form of a thousand different superstitions, then finds all manner of employment with this, and wastes time and strength upon it, as soon as the real world is willing to grant it the rest which it is quite incapable of enjoying. This is accordingly most markedly the case with nations for which life is made easy by the

congenial nature of the climate and the soil, most of all
with the Hindus, then with the Greeks, the Romans, and
later with the Italians, the Spaniards, &c. Demons, gods,
and saints man creates in his own image; and to them he
must then unceasingly bring offerings, prayers, temple
decorations, vows and their fulfilment, pilgrimages, salu-
tations, ornaments for their images, &c. Their service
mingles everywhere with the real, and, indeed, obscures
it. Every event of life is regarded as the work of these
beings; the intercourse with them occupies half the time
of life, constantly sustains hope, and by the charm of
illusion often becomes more interesting than intercourse
with real beings. It is the expression and symptom of
the actual need of mankind, partly for help and support,
partly for occupation and diversion; and if it often
works in direct opposition to the first need, because when
accidents and dangers arise valuable time and strength,
instead of being directed to warding them off, are uselessly wasted on prayers and offerings; it serves the second end all the better by this imaginary converse with a
visionary spirit world; and this is the by no means contemptible gain of all superstitions.

§ 61. It may be remembered from the Second Book
that in the whole of nature, at all the grades of the objectification of will, there was a necessary and constant conflict between the individuals of all species; and in this
way was expressed the inner contradiction of the will to
live with itself. At the highest grade of the objectification, this phenomenon, like all others, will exhibit itself
with greater distinctness, and will therefore be more
easily explained. With this aim we shall next attempt to
trace the source of *egoism* as the starting-point of all
conflict.

We have called time and space the principle of individuation, because only through them and in them is mul-

tiplicity of the homogeneous possible. They are the essential forms of natural knowledge, *i. e.,* knowledge
springing from the will. Therefore the will everywhere
manifests itself in the multiplicity of individuals. But
this multiplicity does not concern the will as thing-in-
itself, but only its phenomena. The will itself is present,
whole and undivided, in every one of these, and beholds
around it the innumerably repeated image of its own nature; but this nature itself, the actually real, it finds directly only in its inner self. Therefore every one desires
everything for himself, desires to possess, or at least to
control, everything, and whatever opposes it it would like
to destroy. To this is added, in the case of such beings as
have knowledge, that the individual is the supporter of
the knowing subject, and the knowing subject is the supporter of the world, *i. e.,* that the whole of Nature outside the knowing subject, and thus also all other individuals, exist only in its idea; it is only conscious of
them as its idea, thus merely indirectly as something
which is dependent on its own nature and existence; for
with its consciousness the world necessarily disappears
for it, *i. e.,* its being and non-being become synonymous
and indistinguishable. Every knowing individual is thus
in truth, and finds itself as the whole will to live, or the
inner being of the world itself, and also as the complemental condition of the world as idea, consequently as a
microcosm which is of equal value with the macrocosm.
Nature itself, which is everywhere and always truthful,
gives him this knowledge, originally and independently
of all reflection, with simple and direct certainty. Now
from these two necessary properties we have given the
fact may be explained that every individual, though vanishing altogether and diminished to nothing in the boundless world, yet makes itself the centre of the world, has
regard for its own existence and well-being before every-

thing else; indeed, from the natural standpoint, is ready
to sacrifice everything else for this—is ready to anni-
hilate the world in order to maintain its own self, this
drop in the ocean, a little longer. This disposition is *egoism*, which is essential to everything in Nature. Yet it is
just through egoism that the inner conflict of the will
with itself attains to such a terrible revelation; for this
egoism has its continuance and being in that opposition
of the microcosm and macrocosm, or in the fact that the
objectification of will has the principle of individuation
for its form, through which the will manifests itself in
the same way in innumerable individuals, and indeed entire and completely in both aspects (will and idea) in
each. Thus, while each individual is given to itself directly as the whole will and the whole subject of ideas,
other individuals are only given it as ideas. Therefore its
own being, and the maintenance of it, is of more importance to it than that of all others together. Every one
looks upon his own death as upon the end of the world,
while he accepts the death of his acquaintances as a matter of comparative indifference, if he is not in some way
affected by it. In the consciousness that has reached the
highest grade, that of man, egoism, as well as knowledge,
pain and pleasure, must have reached its highest grade
also, and the conflict of individuals which is conditioned
by it must appear in its most terrible form. And indeed
we see this everywhere before our eyes, in small things
as in great. Now we see its terrible side in the lives of
great tyrants and miscreants, and in world-desolating
wars; now its absurd side, in which it is the theme of
comedy, and very specially appears as self-conceit and
vanity. Rochefoucault understood this better than any
one else, and presented it in the abstract. We see it both
in the history of the world and in our own experience.
But it appears most distinctly of all when any mob of

men is set free from all law and order; then there shows
itself at once in the distinctest form the "war of all
against all" which Hobbes has so admirably described
in the first chapter *De Cive*. We see not only how every
one tries to seize from the other what he wants himself,
but how often one will destroy the whole happiness or
life of another for the sake of an insignificant addition
to his own happiness. This is the highest expression of
egoism, the manifestations of which in this regard are
only surpassed by those of actual wickedness, which
seeks, quite disinterestedly, the hurt and suffering of
others, without any advantage to itself. Of this we shall
speak soon.

A chief source of that suffering which we found above
to be essential and inevitable to all life is, when it really
appears in a definite form, that *Eris*, the conflict of all
individuals, the expression of the contradiction, with
which the will to live is affected in its inner self, and
which attains a visible form through the principle of individuation. Wild-beast fights are the most cruel means
of showing this directly and vividly. In this original discord lies an unquenchable source of suffering, in spite
of the precautions that have been taken against it, and
which we shall now consider more closely.

§ 63. We have recognised *temporal justice*, which has
its seat in the state, as requiting and punishing, and have
seen that this only becomes justice through a reference
to the *future*. For without this reference all punishing
and requiting would be an outrage without justification,
and indeed merely the addition of another evil to that
which has already occurred, without meaning or significance. But it is quite otherwise with *eternal justice*,
which was referred to before, and which rules not the
state but the world, is not dependent upon human insti-
tutions, is not subject to chance and deception, is not

uncertain, wavering, and erring, but infallible, fixed, and sure. The conception of requital implies that of time; therefore *eternal justice* cannot be requital. Thus it cannot, like temporal justice, admit of respite and delay, and require time in order to triumph, equalising the evil deed by the evil consequences only by means of time. The punishment must here be so bound up with the offence that both are one.

Now that such an eternal justice really lies in the nature of the world will soon become completely evident to whoever has grasped the whole of the thought which we have hitherto been developing.

The world, in all the multiplicity of its parts and forms, is the manifestation, the objectivity, of the one will to live. Existence itself, and the kind of existence, both as a collective whole and in every part, proceeds from the will alone. The will is free, the will is almighty. The will appears in everything, just as it determines itself in itself and outside time. The world is only the mirror of this willing; and all finitude, all suffering, all miseries, which it contains, belong to the expression of that which the will wills, are as they are because the will so wills. Accordingly with perfect right every being supports existence in general, and also the existence of its species and its peculiar individuality, entirely as it is and in circumstances as they are, in a world such as it is, swayed by chance and error, transient, ephemeral, and constantly suffering; and in all that it experiences, or indeed can experience, it always gets its due. For the will belongs to it; and as the will is, so is the world. Only this world itself can bear the responsibility of its own existence and nature—no other; for by what means could another have assumed it? Do we desire to know what men, morally considered, are worth as a whole and in general, we have only to consider their fate as a

whole and in general. This is want, wretchedness, affliction, misery, and death. Eternal justice reigns; if they
were not, as a whole, worthless, their fate, as a whole,
would not be so sad. In this sense we may say, the world
itself is the judgment of the world. If we could lay all
the misery of the world in one scale of the balance, and
all the guilt of the world in the other, the needle would
certainly point to the centre.

Certainly, however, the world does not exhibit itself
to the knowledge of the individual as such, developed for
the service of the will, as it finally reveals itself to the
inquirer as the objectivity of the one and only will to
live, which he himself is. But the sight of the uncultured
individual is clouded, as the Hindus say, by the veil of
Mâyâ. He sees not the thing-in-itself but the phenomenon in time and space, the principle of individuation,
and in the other forms of the principle of sufficient reason. And in this form of his limited knowledge he sees
not the inner nature of things, which is one, but its phenomena as separated, disunited, innumerable, very different, and indeed opposed. For to him pleasure appears
as one thing and pain as quite another thing: one man
as a tormentor and a murderer, another as a martyr and
a victim; wickedness as one thing and evil as another.
He sees one man live in joy, abundance, and pleasure,
and even at his door another die miserably of want and
cold. Then he asks, Where is the retribution? And he
himself, in the vehement pressure of will which is his
origin and his nature, seizes upon the pleasures and
enjoyments of life, firmly embraces them, and knows not
that by this very act of his will he seizes and hugs all
those pains and sorrows at the sight of which he shudders. He sees the ills and he sees the wickedness in the
world, but far from knowing that both of these are but
different sides of the manifestation of the one will to

live, he regards them as very different, and indeed quite opposed, and often seeks to escape by wickedness, *i. e.*, by causing the suffering of another, from ills, from the suffering of his own individuality, for he is involved in the principle of individuation, deluded by the veil of Mâyâ. Just as a sailor sits in a boat trusting to his frail barque in a stormy sea, unbounded in every direction, rising and falling with the howling mountainous waves; so in the midst of a world of sorrows the individual man sits quietly, supported by and trusting to the principle of individuation, or the way in which the individual knows things as phenomena. The boundless world, everywhere full of suffering in the infinite past, in the infinite future, is strange to him, indeed is to him but a fable; his ephemeral person, his extensionless present, his momentary satisfaction, this alone has reality for him; and he does all to maintain this, so long as his eyes are not opened by a better knowledge. Till then, there lives only in the inmost depths of his consciousness a very obscure presentiment that all that is after all not really so strange to him, but has a connection with him, from which the principle of individuation cannot protect him. From this presentiment arises that ineradicable *awe* common to all men (and indeed perhaps even to the most sensible of the brutes) which suddenly seizes them if by any chance they become puzzled about the principle of individuation, because the principle of sufficient reason in some one of its forms seems to admit of an exception. For example, if it seems as if some change took place without a cause, or some one who is dead appears again, or if in any other way the past or the future becomes present or the distant becomes near. The fearful terror at anything of the kind is founded on the fact that they suddenly become puzzled about the forms of knowledge of the phenomenon, which alone separate their own in-

dividuality from the rest of the world. But even this
separation lies only in the phenomenon, and not in the
thing-in-itself; and on this rests eternal justice. In fact,
all temporal happiness stands, and all prudence proceeds,
upon ground that is undermined. They defend the person from accidents and supply its pleasures; but the person is merely phenomenon, and its difference from other
individuals, and exemption from the sufferings which
they endure, rests merely in the form of the phenomenon, the principle of individuation. According to the
true nature of things, every one has all the suffering of
the world as his own, and indeed has to regard all merely
possible suffering as for him actual, so long as he is the
fixed will to live, i. e., asserts life with all his power. For
the knowledge that sees through the principle of individuation, a happy life in time, the gift of chance or won
by prudence, amid the sorrows of innumerable others, is
only the dream of a beggar in which he is a king, but
from which he must awake and learn from experience
that only a fleeting illusion had separated him from the
suffering of his life.

Eternal justice withdraws itself from the vision that
is involved in the knowledge which follows the principle
of sufficient reason in the principle of individuation; such
vision misses it altogether unless it vindicates it in some
way by fictions. It sees the bad, after misdeeds and cruel-
ties of every kind, live in happiness and leave the world
unpunished. It sees the oppressed drag out a life full of
suffering to the end without an avenger, a requiter appearing. But that man only will grasp and comprehend
eternal justice who raises himself above the knowledge
that proceeds under the guidance of the principle of sufficient reason, bound to the particular thing, and recognises the Ideas, sees through the principle of individuation, and becomes conscious that the forms of the phe-

nomenon do not apply to the thing-in-itself. Moreover,
he alone, by virtue of the same knowledge, can understand the true nature of virtue, as it will soon disclose
itself to us in connection with the present inquiry, although for the practice of virtue this knowledge in the
abstract is by no means demanded. Thus it becomes clear
to whoever has attained to the knowledge referred to,
that because the will is the in-itself of all phenomena,
the misery which is awarded to others and that which he
experiences himself, the bad and the evil, always concerns only that one inner being which is everywhere the
same, although the phenomena in which the one and the
other exhibits itself exist as quite different individuals,
and are widely separated by time and space. He sees that
the difference between him who inflicts the suffering and
him who must bear it is only the phenomenon, and does
not concern the thing-in-itself, for this is the will living
in both, which here, deceived by the knowledge which is
bound to its service, does not recognise itself, and seeking an increased happiness in *one* of its phenomena, produces great suffering in *another*, and thus, in the pressure of excitement, buries its teeth in its own flesh, not
knowing that it always injures only itself, revealing in
this form, through the medium of individuality, the conflict with itself which it bears in its inner nature. The
inflicter of suffering and the sufferer are one. The former errs in that he believes he is not a partaker in the
suffering; the latter, in that he believes he is not a partaker in the guilt. If the eyes of both were opened, the
inflicter of suffering would see that he lives in all that
suffers pain in the wide world, and which, if endowed
with reason, in vain asks why it was called into existence
for such great suffering, its desert of which it does not
understand. And the sufferer would see that all the wick-

edness which is or ever was committed in the world proceeds from that will which constitutes *his* own nature also, appears also in *him,* and that through this phenomenon and its assertion he has taken upon himself all the sufferings which proceed from such a will and bears them as his due, so long as he is this will. From this knowledge speaks the profound poet Calderon in "Life a Dream"—

> "Pues el delito mayor
> Del hombre es haber nacido."
>
> ("For the greatest crime of man
> Is that he ever was born.")

Why should it not be a crime, since, according to an eternal law, death follows upon it? Calderon has merely expressed in these lines the Christian dogma of original sin.

The living knowledge of eternal justice, of the balance that inseparably binds together the evil of crime with the evil of punishment, demands the complete transcending of individuality and the principle of its possibility. Therefore it will always remain unattainable to the majority of men, as will also be the case with the pure and distinct knowledge of the nature of all virtue, which is akin to it, and which we are about to explain. Accordingly the wise ancestors of the Hindu people have directly expressed it in the Vedas, which are only allowed to the three regenerate castes, or in their esoteric teaching, so far at any rate as conception and language comprehend it, and their method of exposition, which always remains pictorial and even rhapsodical, admits; but in the religion of the people, or exoteric teaching, they only communicate it by means of myths. The direct exposition we find in the Vedas, the fruit of the highest human knowledge and wisdom, the kernel of which has at last reached us in the Upanishads as the greatest gift of this century. It is expressed in various ways, but especially by making all the beings in the world, living and lifeless, pass successively before the view of the student, and pronouncing over every one of them that word which has become a formula, and as such has been called the Mahavakya: Tatoumes,—more correctly, Tat twam asi, —which means, "This thou art." But for the people, that great truth, so far as in their limited condition they could comprehend it, was translated into the form of knowledge which follows the principle of sufficient reason. This form of knowledge is indeed, from its nature, quite incapable of apprehending that truth pure and in itself, and even stands in contradiction to it, yet in the form of a myth it received a substitute for it which was sufficient as a guide for conduct. For the myth enables the method of knowledge, in accordance with the principle of sufficient reason, to comprehend by figurative representation the ethical significance of conduct, which itself is ever foreign to it. This is the aim of all systems of religion, for as a whole they are the mythical clothing of the truth which is unattainable to the uncultured human intellect. In this sense this myth might, in Kant's language, be called a postulate of the practical reason; but regarded as such, it has the great advantage that it contains absolutely no elements but such as lie before our eyes in the course of actual experience, and can therefore support all its conceptions with perceptions. What is here referred to is the myth of the transmigration of souls. It teaches that all sufferings which in life one inflicts upon other beings must be expiated in a subsequent life in this world, through precisely the same sufferings; and this extends so far, that he who only kills a brute must, some time in endless time, be born as the same kind of brute and suffer the same death. It teaches that wicked conduct involves a future life in this world in suffering and despised creatures, and, accordingly, that one will then be born again in lower castes, or as a woman, or as a brute, as Pariah or Tschandala, as a leper, or as a crocodile, and so forth. All the pains which the myth threatens it supports with perceptions from actual life, through suffering creatures which do not know how they have merited their misery, and it does not require to call in the assistance of any other hell. As a reward, on the other hand, it promises re-birth in better, nobler forms, as Brahmans, wise men, or saints. The highest reward, which awaits the noblest deeds and the completest resignation, which is also given to the woman who in seven successive lives has voluntarily died on the funeral pile of her husband, and not less to the man whose pure mouth has never uttered a single lie,—this reward the myth can only express negatively in the language of this world by the promise, which is so often repeated, that they shall never be born again, or, as the Buddhists, who recognise neither Vedas nor castes, express it, "Thou shalt attain to Nirvâna," *i. e.*, to a state in which four things no longer exist—birth, age, sickness, and death.

Never has a myth entered, and never will one enter, more closely into the philosophical truth which is attainable to so few than this primitive doctrine of the noblest and most ancient nation. Broken up as this nation now is into many parts, this myth yet reigns as the universal belief of the people, and has the most decided influence upon life to-day, as four thousand years ago. Therefore Pythagoras and Plato have seized with admiration on that *ne plus ultra* of mythical representation, received it from India or Egypt, honoured it, made use of it, and, we know not how far, even believed it. We, on the contrary, now send the Brahmans English clergymen and evangelical linen-weavers to set them right out of sympathy, and to show them that they are created out of nothing, and ought thankfully to rejoice in the fact. But it is just the same as if we fired a bullet against a cliff. In India our religions will never take root. The ancient wisdom of the human race will not be displaced by what happened in Galilee. On the contrary, Indian philosophy streams back to Europe, and will produce a fundamental change in our knowledge and thought.

§ 65. In all the preceding investigations of human action, we have been leading up to the final investigation, and have to a considerable extent lightened the task of raising to abstract and philosophical clearness, and exhibiting as a branch of our central thought that special ethical significance of action which in life is with perfect understanding denoted by the words *good* and *bad*.

First, however, I wish to trace back to their real meaning those conceptions of *good* and *bad* which have been treated by the philosophical writers of the day, very extraordinarily, as simple conceptions, and thus incapable of analysis; so that the reader may not remain involved in the senseless delusion that they contain more than is actually the case, and express in and for themselves all that is here necessary. I am in a position to do this because in ethics I am no more disposed to take refuge behind the word *good* than formerly behind the words *beautiful* and *true*, in order that by the adding a "ness," I might induce the belief that by uttering three such words I had done more than denote three very wide and abstract, and consequently empty conceptions, of very different origin and significance. Who is there, indeed, who has made himself acquainted with the books of our own day to whom these three words, admirable as are the things to which they originally refer, have not become an aversion after he has seen for the thousandth time how those who are least capable of thinking believe that they have only to utter these three words with open mouth and the air of an intelligent sheep, in order to have spoken the greatest wisdom?

The explanation of the concept *true* has already been given in the essay on the principle of sufficient reason, chap. v. § 29 *et seq*. The content of the concept *beautiful* found for the first time its proper explanation through the whole of the Third Book of the present work. We now wish to discover the significance of the concept *good*, which can be done with very little trouble. This concept is essentially relative, and signifies *the conformity of an object to any definite effort of the will*. Accordingly everything that corresponds to the will in any of its expressions and fulfils its end is thought through the concept *good*, however different such things may be in other respects. Thus we speak of good eating, good roads, good weather, good weapons, good omens, and so on; in short, we call everything good that is just as we wish it to be; and therefore that may be good in the eyes of one man which is just the reverse in those of another. The conception of the good divides itself into two sub-species —that of the direct and present satisfaction of any volition, and that of its indirect satisfaction which has reference to the future, *i. e.*, the agreeable and the useful. The conception of the opposite, so long as we are speaking of unconscious existence, is expressed by the word *bad*, more rarely and abstractly by the word *evil*, which thus denotes everything that does not correspond to any effort of the will. Like all other things that can come into relation to the will, men who are favourable to the ends which happen to be desired, who further and befriend them, are called good, in the same sense, and always with that relative limitation, which shows itself, for example, in the expression, "I find this good, but you don't." Those, however, who are naturally disposed not to hinder the endeavours of others, but rather to assist them, and who are thus consistently helpful, benevolent, friendly, and charitable, are called *good* men, on account of this relation of their conduct to the will of others in general. In the case of conscious beings (brutes and men) the contrary conception is denoted in German, and, within the last hundred years or so, in French also, by a different word from that which is used in speaking of unconscious existence; in German, *böse;* in French, *méchant;* while in almost all other languages this distinction does not exist; and κακος, *malus, cattivo, bad,* are used of men, as of lifeless things, which are opposed to the ends of a definite individual will. Thus, having started entirely from the passive element in the good, the inquiry could only proceed later to the active element, and investigate the conduct of the man who is called good, no longer with reference to others, but to himself; specially setting itself the task of explaining both the purely objective respect which such conduct produces in others, and the peculiar contentment with himself which it clearly produces in the man himself, since he purchases it with sacrifices of another kind; and also, on the other hand, the inner pain which accompanies the bad disposition, whatever outward advantages it brings to him who entertains it. It was from this source that the ethical systems, both the philosophical and those which are supported by systems of religion, took their rise. Both seek constantly in some way or other to connect happiness with virtue, the former either by means of the principle of contradiction or that of sufficient reason, and thus to make happiness either identical with or the consequence of virtue, always sophistically; the latter, by asserting the existence of other worlds than that which alone can be known to experience. In our system, on the contrary, virtue will show itself, not as a striving after happiness, that is, well-being and life, but as an effort in quite an opposite direction.

It follows from what has been said above, that the *good* is, according to its concept, essentially relative, for its being consists in its relation to a desiring will. *Absolute good* is, therefore, a contradiction in terms; highest good, *summum bonum*, really signifies the same thing—a final satisfaction of the will, after which no new desire could arise,—a last motive, the attainment of which would afford enduring satisfaction of the will. But, according to the investigations which have already been conducted in this Fourth Book, such a consummation is not even thinkable. The will can just as little cease from willing altogether on account of some particular satisfaction, as time can end or begin; for it there is no such thing as a permanent fulfilment which shall completely and for ever satisfy its craving. It is the vessel of the Danaides; for it there is no highest good, no absolute good, but always a merely temporary good. If, however, we wish to give an honorary position, as it were emeritus, to an old expression, which from custom we do not like to discard altogether, we may, metaphorically and figuratively, call the complete self-effacement and denial of the will, the true absence of will, which alone for ever stills and silences its struggle, alone gives that contentment which can never again be disturbed, alone redeems the world, and which we shall now soon consider at the close of our whole investigation—the absolute good, the *summum bonum*—and regard it as the only radical cure of the disease of which all other means are only palliations or anodynes. In this sense the Greek τελος and and also *finis bonorum* correspond to the thing still better. So much for the words *good* and *bad;* now for the thing itself.

If a man is always disposed to do *wrong* whenever the opportunity presents itself, and there is no external power to restrain him, we call him *bad.* According to our doctrine of wrong, this means that such a man does not merely assert the will to live as it appears in his own body, but in this assertion goes so far that he denies the will which appears in other individuals. This is shown by the fact that he desires their powers for the service of his own will, and seeks to destroy their existence when they stand in the way of its efforts. The ultimate source of this is a high degree of egoism, the nature of which has been already explained. Two things are here apparent. In the first place, that in such a man an excessively vehement will to live expresses itself, extending far beyond the assertion of his own body; and, in the second place, that his knowledge, entirely given up to the principle of sufficient reason and involved in the principle of individuation, cannot get beyond the difference which this latter principle establishes between his own person and every one else. Therefore he seeks his own well-being alone, completely indifferent to that of all others, whose existence is to him altogether foreign and divided from his own by a wide gulf, and who are indeed regarded by him as mere masks with no reality behind them. And these two qualities are the constituent elements of the bad character.

This great intensity of will is in itself and directly a constant source of suffering. In the first place, because all volition as such arises from want; that is, suffering. (Therefore, as will be remembered, from the Third Book, the momentary cessation of all volition, which takes place whenever we give ourselves up to æsthetic contemplation, as pure will-less subject of knowledge, the correlative of the Idea, is one of the principal elements in our pleasure in the beautiful.) Secondly, because, through the causal connection of things, most of our desires must remain unfulfilled, and the will is oftener crossed than satisfied, and therefore much intense volition carries with it much intense suffering. For all suffering is simply unfulfilled and crossed volition; and even the pain of the body when it is injured or destroyed is as such only possible through the fact that the body is nothing but the will itself become object. Now on this account, because much intense suffering is inseparable from much intense volition, very bad men bear the stamp of inward suffering in the very expression of the countenance; even when they have attained every external happiness, they always look unhappy so long as they are not transported by some momentary ecstasy and are not dissembling. From this inward torment, which is absolutely and directly essential to them, there finally proceeds that delight in the suffering of others which does not spring from mere egoism, but is disinterested, and which constitutes *wickedness* proper, rising to the pitch of *cruelty*. For this the suffering of others is not a means for the attainment of the ends of its own will, but an end in itself. The more definite explanation of this phenomenon is as follows:—Since man is a manifestation of will illuminated by the clearest knowledge, he is always contrasting the actual and felt satisfaction of his will with the merely possible satisfacion of it which knowledge presents to him. Hence arises envy: every privation is infinitely increased by the enjoyment of others, and relieved by the knowledge that others also suffer the same privation. Those ills which are common to all and inseparable from human life trouble us little, just as those which belong to the climate, to the whole country. The recollection of greater

sufferings than our own stills our pain; the sight of the
sufferings of others soothes our own. If, now, a man
is filled with an exceptionally intense pressure of will,—
if with burning eagerness he seeks to accumulate everything to slake the thirst of his egoism, and thus experiences, as he inevitably must, that all satisfaction is
merely apparent, that the attained end never fulfils
the promise of the desired object, the final appeasing of
the fierce pressure of will, but that when fulfilled the
wish only changes its form, and now torments him in a
new one; and indeed that if at last all wishes are exhausted, the pressure of will itself remains without any
conscious motive, and makes itself known to him with
fearful pain as a feeling of terrible desolation and
emptiness; if from all this, which in the case of the
ordinary degrees of volition is only felt in a small measure, and only produces the ordinary degree of melancholy, in the case of him who is a manifestation of will
reaching the point of extraordinary wickedness, there
necessarily springs an excessive inward misery, an
eternal unrest, an incurable pain; he seeks indirectly
the alleviation which directly is denied him,—seeks to
mitigate his own suffering by the sight of the suffering
of others, which at the same time he recognises as an expression of his power. The suffering of others now becomes for him an end in itself, and is a spectacle in
which he delights; and thus arises the phenomenon of
pure cruelty, blood-thirstiness, which history exhibits
so often in the Neros and Domitians, in the African Deis,
in Robespierre, and the like.

The desire of revenge is closely related to wickedness. It recompenses evil with evil, not with reference
to the future, which is the character of punishment, but
merely on account of what has happened, what is past,
as such, thus disinterestedly, not as a means, but as an

end, in order to revel in the torment which the avenger himself has inflicted on the offender. What distinguishes revenge from pure wickedness, and to some extent excuses it, is an appearance of justice. For if the same act, which is now revenge, were to be done legally, that is, according to a previously determined and known rule, and in a society which had sanctioned this rule, it would be punishment, and thus justice.

Besides the suffering which has been described, and which is inseparable from wickedness, because it springs from the same root, excessive vehemence of will, another specific pain quite different from this is connected with wickedness, which is felt in the case of every bad action, whether it be merely injustice proceeding from egoism or pure wickedness, and according to the length of its duration is called *the sting of conscience* or *remorse.* Now, whoever remembers and has present in his mind the content of the preceding portion of this Fourth Book, and especially the truth explained at the beginning of it, that life itself is always assured to the will to live, as its mere copy or mirror, and also the exposition of eternal justice, will find that the sting of conscience can have no other meaning than the following, *i. e.,* its content, abstractly expressed, is what follows, in which two parts are distinguished, which again, however, entirely coincide. and must be thought as completely united.

However closely the veil of Mâyâ may envelop the mind of the bad man, *i. e.,* however firmly he may be involved in the principle of individuation, according to which he regards his person as absolutely different and separated by a wide gulf from all others, a knowledge to which he clings with all his might, as it alone suits and supports his egoism, so that knowledge is almost always corrupted by will, yet there arises in the inmost depths of his consciousness the secret presentiment that such an order of things is only phenomenal, and that their real constitution is quite different. He has a dim foreboding that, however much time and space may separate him from other individuals and the innumerable miseries which they suffer, and even suffer through him, and may represent them as quite foreign to him, yet in themselves, and apart from the idea and its forms, it is the one will to live appearing in them all, which here failing to recognise itself, turns its weapons against itself, and, by seeking increased happiness in one of its phenomena, imposes the greatest suffering upon another. He dimly sees that he, the bad man, is himself this whole will; that consequently he is not only the inflicter of pain but also the endurer of it, from whose suffering he is only separated and exempted by an illusive dream, the form of which is space and time, which, however, vanishes away; that he must in reality pay for the pleasure with the pain, and that all suffering which he only knows as possible really concerns him as the will to live, inasmuch as the possible and actual, the near and the distant in time and space, are only different for the knowledge of the individual, only by means of the principle of individuation, not in themselves. This is the truth which mythically, *i. e.,* adapted to the principle of sufficient reason, and so translated into the form of the phenomenal, is expressed in the transmigration of souls. Yet it has its purest expression, free from all foreign admixture, in that obscurely felt yet inconsolable misery called remorse. But this springs also from a second immediate knowledge, which is closely bound to the first—the knowledge of the strength with which the will to live asserts itself in the wicked individual, which extends far beyond his own individual phenomenon, to the absolute denial of the same will appearing in other individuals. Consequently the inward horror of the

wicked man at his own deed, which he himself tries
to conceal, contains, besides that presentment of the
nothingness, the mere illusiveness of the principle of individuation, and of the distinction established by it between him and others; also the knowledge of the vehemence of his own will, the intensity with which he has
seized upon life and attached himself closely to it, even
that life whose terrible side he sees before him in the
misery of those who are oppressed by him, and with
which he is yet so firmly united, that just on this account the greatest atrocity proceeds from him himself,
as a means for the fuller assertion of his own will. He
recognises himself as the concentrated manifestation of
the will to live, feels to what degree he is given up to
life, and with it also to innumerable sufferings which
are essential to it, for it has infinite time and infinite
space to abolish the distinction between the possible and
the actual, and to change all the sufferings which as yet
are merely *known* to him into sufferings he has *experienced*. The millions of years of constant rebirth certainly exist, like the whole past and future, only in
conception; occupied time, the form of the phenomenon
of the will, is only the present, and for the individual
time is ever new: it seems to him always as if he had
newly come into being. For life is inseparable from the
will to live, and the only form of life is the present.
Death (the repetition of the comparison must be ex-
cused) is like the setting of the sun, which is only apparently swallowed up by the night, but in reality, itself the source of all light, burns without intermission,
brings new days to new worlds, is always rising and always setting. Beginning and end only concern the individual through time, the form of the phenomenon for
the idea. Outside time lies only the will, Kant's thing-
in-itself, and its adequate objectification, the Idea of

Plato. Therefore suicide affords no escape; what every one in his inmost consciousness *wills,* that must he *be;* and what every one *is,* that he *wills.* Thus, besides the merely felt knowledge of the illusiveness and nothingness of the forms of the idea which separate individuals, it is the self-knowledge of one's own will and its degree that gives the sting to conscience. The course of life draws the image of the empirical character, whose original is the intelligible character, and horrifies the wicked man by this image. He is horrified all the same whether the image is depicted in large characters, so that the world shares his horror, or in such small ones that he alone sees it, for it only concerns him directly. The past would be a matter of indifference, and could not pain the conscience if the character did not feel itself free from all time and unalterable by it, so long as it does not deny itself. Therefore things which are long past still weigh on the conscience. The prayer, "Lead me not into temptation," means, "Let me not see what manner of person I am." In the might with which the bad man asserts life, and which exhibits itself to him in the sufferings which he inflicts on others, he measures how far he is from the surrender and denial of that will, the only possible deliverance from the world and its miseries. He sees how far he belongs to it, and how firmly he is bound to it; the *known* suffering of others has no power to move him; he is given up to life and *felt* suffering. It remains hidden whether this will ever break and overcome the vehemence of his will.

This exposition of the significance and inner nature of the *bad,* which as mere feeling, *i. e.,* not as distinct, abstract knowledge, is the content of *remorse,* will gain distinctness and completeness by the similar consideration of the *good* as a quality of human will, and finally of absolute resignation and holiness, which proceeds from it when it has attained its highest grade. For opposites always throw light upon each other, and the day at once reveals both itself and the night, as Spinoza admirably remarks.

§ 66. Before we speak of the *good* proper, in opposition to the *bad*, which has been explained, we must touch on an intermediate grade, the mere negation of the bad; this is *justice*. The nature of right and wrong has been fully explained above; therefore we may briefly say here, that he who voluntarily recognises and observes those merely moral limits between wrong and right, even where this is not secured by the state or any other external power, thus he who, according to our explanation, never carries the assertion of his own will so far as to deny the will appearing in another individual, is *just*. Thus, in order to increase his own well-being, he will not inflict suffering upon others, *i. e.,* he will commit no crime, he will respect the rights and the property of others. We see that for such a just man the principle of individuation is no longer, as in the case of the bad man, an absolute wall of partition. We see that he does not, like the bad man, merely assert his own manifestation of will and deny all others; that other persons are not for him mere masks, whose nature is quite different from his own; but he shows in his conduct that he also recognises his own nature—the will to live as a thing-in-itself, in the foreign manifestation which is only given to him as idea. Thus he finds himself again in that other manifestation, up to a certain point, that of doing no wrong, *i. e.,* abstaining from injury. To this extent, therefore, he sees through the principle of individuation, the veil of Mâyâ; so far he sets the being external to him on a level with his own—he does it no injury.

If we examine the inmost nature of this justice, there

already lies in it the resolution not to go so far in the assertion of one's own will as to deny the manifestations of will of others, by compelling them to serve one's own. One will therefore wish to render to others as much as one receives from them. The highest degree of this justice of disposition, which is, however, always united with goodness proper, whose character is no longer merely negative, extends so far that a man doubts his right to inherited property, wishes to support his body only by his own powers, mental and physical, feels every service of others and every luxury a reproach, and finally embraces voluntary poverty. Thus we see how Pascal, when he became an ascetic, would no longer permit any services to be rendered him, although he had servants enough; in spite of his constant bad health he made his bed himself, brought his own food from the kitchen, &c. ("Vie de Pascal, par sa Sœur," p. 19). Quite in keeping with this, it is reported that many Hindus, even Rajas with great wealth, expend it merely on the maintenance of their position, their court and attendants, and themselves observe with the greatest scrupulousness the maxim that a man should eat nothing that he has not himself both sowed and reaped. Yet a certain misunderstanding lies at the bottom of this; for one man, just because he is rich and powerful, can render such signal services to the whole of human society that they counterbalance the wealth he has inherited, for the secure possession of which he is indebted to society. In reality that excessive justice of such Hindus is already more than justice; it is actual renunciation, denial of the will to live,—asceticism, of which we shall speak last. On the other hand, pure idleness and living through the exertions of others, in the case of inherited wealth, without accomplishing anything, may be regarded as morally wrong, even if it must remain right according to positive laws.

We have found that voluntary justice has its inmost source in a certain degree of penetration of the principle of individuation, while the unjust remain entirely involved in this principle. This penetration may exist not only in the degree which is required for justice, but also in the higher degree which leads to benevolence and well-doing, to love of mankind. And this may take place however strong and energetic in itself the will which appears in such an individual may be. Knowledge can always counterbalance it in him, teach him to resist the tendency to wrong, and even produce in him every degree of goodness, and indeed of resignation. Thus the good man is by no means to be regarded as originally a weaker manifestation of will than the bad man, but it is knowledge which in him masters the blind striving of will. There are certainly individuals who merely seem to have a good disposition on account of the weakness of the will appearing in them, but what they are soon appears from the fact that they are not capable of any remarkable self-conquest in order to perform a just or good deed.

If, however, as a rare exception, we meet a man who possesses a considerable income, but uses very little of it for himself and gives all the rest to the poor, while he denies himself many pleasures and comforts, and we seek to explain the action of this man, we shall find, apart altogether from the dogmas through which he tries to make his action intelligible to his reason, that the simplest general expression and the essential character of his conduct is that *he makes less distinction than is usually made between himself and others.* This distinction is so great in the eyes of many that the suffering of others is a direct pleasure to the wicked and a welcome means of happiness to the unjust. The merely just man is content not to cause it; and, in general, most men know and are acquainted with innumerable sufferings of others in their vicinity, but do not determine to mitigate them, because to do so would involve some self-denial on their part. Thus, in each of all these a strong distinction seems to prevail between his own ego and that of others; on the other hand, to the noble man we have imagined, this distinction is not so significant. The principle of individuation, the form of the phenomenon, no longer holds him so tightly in its grasp, but the suffering which he sees in others touches him almost as closely as his own. He therefore tries to strike a balance between them, denies himself pleasures, practises renunciation, in order to mitigate the suffering of others. He sees that the distinction between himself and others, which to the bad man is so great a gulf, only belongs to a fleeting and illusive phenomenon. He recognises directly and without reasoning that the in-itself of his own manifestation is also that of others, the will to live, which constitutes the inner nature of everything and lives in all; indeed, that this applies also to the brutes and the whole of nature, and therefore he will not cause suffering even to a brute.

He is now just as little likely to allow others to starve, while he himself has enough and to spare, as any one would be to suffer hunger one day in order to have more the next day than he could enjoy. For to him who does works of love the veil of Mâyâ has become transparent, the illusion of the principle of individuation has left him. He recognises himself, his will, in every being, and consequently also in the sufferer. He is now free from the perversity with which the will to live, not recognising itself, here in one individual enjoys a fleeting and precarious pleasure, and there in another pays for it with suffering and starvation, and thus both inflicts and endures misery, not knowing that, like Thyestes, it eagerly devours its own flesh; and then, on the

one hand, laments its undeserved suffering, and on the
other hand transgresses without fear of Nemesis, always merely because, involved in the principle of individuation, thus generally in the kind of knowledge
which is governed by the principle of sufficient reason,
it does not recognise itself in the foreign phenomenon,
and therefore does not perceive eternal justice. To be
cured of this illusion and deception of Mâyâ, and to do
works of love, are one and the same. But the latter is
the necessary and inevitable symptom of that knowledge.

The opposite of the sting of conscience, the origin
and significance of which is explained above, is the *good
conscience,* the satisfaction which we experience after
every disinterested deed. It arises from the fact that
such a deed, as it proceeds from the direct recognition
of our own inner being in the phenomenon of another,
affords us also the verification of this knowledge, the
knowledge that our true self exists not only in our own
person, this particular manifestation, but in everything
that lives. By this the heart feels itself enlarged, as by
egoism it is contracted. For as the latter concentrates
our interest upon the particular manifestation of our
own individuality, upon which knowledge always presents to us the innumerable dangers which constantly
threaten this manifestation, and anxiety and care becomes the key-note of our disposition; the knowledge
that everything living is just as much our own inner
nature, as is our own person, extends our interest to
everything living; and in this way the heart in enlarged. Thus through the diminished interest in our own
self, the anxious care for the self is attacked at its very
root and limited; hence the peace, the unbroken serenity, which a virtuous disposition and a good conscience
affords, and the more distinct appearance of this with
every good deed, for it proves to ourselves the depth

of that disposition. The egoist feels himself surrounded
by strange and hostile individuals, and all his hope is
centred in his own good. The good man lives in a world
of friendly individuals, the well-being of any of whom
he regards as his own. Therefore, although the knowledge of the lot of mankind generally does not make his
disposition a joyful one, yet the permanent knowledge
of his own nature in all living beings, gives him a certain evenness, and even serenity of disposition. For the
interest which is extended to innumerable manifestations cannot cause such anxiety as that which is concentrated upon one. The accidents which concern individuals collectively, equalise themselves, while those
which happen to the particular individual constitute good
or bad fortune.

Thus, though others have set up moral principles
which they give out as prescriptions for virtue, and laws.
which it was necessary to follow, I, as has already been
said, cannot do this because I have no "ought" or law
to prescribe to the eternally free-will. Yet on the other
hand, in the connection of my system, what to a certain
extent corresponds and is analogous to that undertaking
is the purely theoretical truth, of which my whole exposition may be regarded as merely an elaboration, that
the will is the in-itself of every phenomenon, but itself,
as such, is free from the forms of the phenomenal, and
consequently from multiplicity; a truth, which, with
reference to action, I do not know how to express better
than by the formula of the Vedas already quoted: "Tat
twam asi!" (This thou art!) Whoever is able to say
this to himself, with regard to every being with whom
he comes in contact, with clear knowledge and firm inward conviction, is certain of all virtue and blessedness,
and is on the direct road to salvation.

But before I go further, and, as the conclusion of my

exposition, show how love, the origin and nature of which we recognised as the penetration of the principle of individuation, leads to salvation, to the entire surrender of the will to live, *i. e.*, of all volition, and also how another path, less soft but more frequented, leads men to the same goal, a paradoxical proposition must first be stated and explained; not because it is paradoxical, but because it is true, and is necessary to the completeness of the thought I have present. It is this: "All love (αγαπη, *caritas*) is sympathy."

§ 68. We saw before that hatred and wickedness are conditioned by egoism, and egoism rests on the entanglement of knowledge in the principle of individuation. Thus we found that the penetration of that principle of individuation is the source and the nature of justice, and when it is carried further, even to its fullest extent, it is the source and nature of love and nobility of character. For this penetration alone, by abolishing the distinction between our own individuality and that of others, renders possible and explains perfect goodness of disposition, extending to disinterested love and the most generous self-sacrifice for others.

If, however, this penetration of the principle of individuation, this direct knowledge of the identity of will in all its manifestations, is present in a high degree of distinctness, it will at once show an influence upon the will which extends still further. If that veil of Mâyâ, the principle of individuation, is lifted from the eyes of a man to such an extent that he no longer makes the egotistical distinction between his person and that of others, but takes as much interest in the sufferings of other individuals as in his own, and therefore is not only benevolent in the highest degree, but even ready to sacrifice his own individuality whenever such a sacrifice will save a number of other persons, then it clearly follows that such a man, who recognises in all beings his own inmost and true self, must also regard the infinite suffering of all suffering beings as his own, and take on himself the pain of the whole world. No suffering is any longer strange to him. All the miseries of others which he sees and is so seldom able to alleviate, all the miseries he knows directly, and even those which he only knows as possible, work upon his mind like his own. It is no longer the changing joy and sorrow of his own person that he has in view, as is the case with him who is still involved in egoism; but, since he sees through the principle of individuation, all lies equally near him. He knows the whole, comprehends its nature, and finds that it consists in a constant passing away, vain striving, inward conflict, and continual suffering. He sees wherever he looks suffering humanity, the suffering brute creation, and a world that passes away. But all this now lies as near him as his own person lies to the egoist. Why should he now, with such knowledge of the world, assert this very life through constant acts of will, and thereby bind himself ever more closely to it, press it ever more firmly to himself? Thus he who is still involved in the principle of individuation, in egoism, only knows particular things and their relation to his own person, and these constantly become new *motives* of his volition. But, on the other hand, that knowledge of the whole, of the nature of the thing-in-itself which has been described, becomes a *quieter* of all and every volition. The will now turns away from life; it now shudders at the pleasures in which it recognises the assertion of life. Man now attains to the state of voluntary renunciation, resignation, true indifference, and perfect will-lessness. If at times, in the hard experience of our own suffering, or in the vivid recognition of that of others, the knowledge of the vanity and bitterness of life draws nigh to us also who are still wrapt in the veil of Mâyâ, and we would like to destroy the sting of the desires, close the entrance against all suffering, and purify and sanctify ourselves by complete and final renunciation; yet the illusion of the phenomenon soon entangles us again, and its motives influence the will anew; we cannot tear ourselves free. The allurement of hope, the flattery of the present, the sweetness of pleasure, the well-being which falls to our lot, amid the lamentations of a suffering world governed by chance and error, draws us back to it and rivets our bonds anew. Therefore Jesus says: "It is easier for a camel to go through the eye of a needle, than for a rich man to enter into the kingdom of God."

If we compare life to a course or path through which we must unceasingly run—a path of red-hot coals, with a few cool places here and there; then he who is entangled in delusion is consoled by the cool places, on which he now stands, or which he sees near him, and sets out to run through the course. But he who sees through the principle of individuation, and recognises the real nature of the thing-in-itself, and thus the whole, is no longer susceptible of such consolation; he sees himself in all places at once, and withdraws. His will turns round, no longer asserts its own nature, which is reflected in the phenomenon, but denies it. The phenomenon by which this change is marked, is the transition from virtue to asceticism. That is to say, it no longer suffices for such a man to love others as himself, and to do as much for them as for himself; but there arises within him a horror of the nature of which his own phenomenal existence is an expression, the will to live, the kernel and inner nature of that world which is recognised as full of misery. He therefore disowns this nature which appears in him, and is already expressed through his body, and his action gives the lie to his phenomenal existence, and appears in open contradiction to it. Essentially nothing else but a manifestation of will, he ceases to will anything, guards against attaching his will to anything, and seeks to confirm in himself the greatest indifference to everything. His body, healthy and strong, expresses through the genitals, the sexual impulse; but he denies the will and gives the lie to the body; he desires no sensual gratification under any condition. Voluntary and complete chastity is the first step in asceticism or the denial of the will to live. It thereby denies the assertion of the will which extends beyond the individual life, and gives the assurance that with the life of this body, the will, whose manifestation it is, ceases. Nature, always true and naïve, declares that if this maxim became universal, the human race would die out; and I think I may assume, in accordance with what was said in the Second Book about the connection of all manifestations of will, that with its highest manifestation, the weaker reflection of it would also pass away, as the twilight vanishes along with the full light. With the entire abolition of knowledge, the rest of the world would of itself vanish into nothing; for without a subject there is no object.

Asceticism then shows itself further in voluntary and intentional poverty, which not only arises *per accidens,* because the possessions are given away to mitigate the sufferings of others, but is here an end in itself, is meant to serve as a constant mortification of will, so that the satisfaction of the wishes, the sweet of life, shall not again arouse the will, against which self-knowledge has conceived a horror. He who has attained to this point, still always feels, as a living body, as concrete manifestation of will, the natural disposition for every kind of volition; but he intentionally suppresses it, for he compels himself to refrain from doing all that he would like to do, and to do all that he would like not to do, even if this has no further end than that of serving as a mortification of will. Since he himself denies the will which appears in his own person, he will not resist if another does the same, *i. e.,* inflicts wrongs upon him. Therefore every suffering coming to him from without through chance or the wickedness of others, is welcome to him, every injury, ignominy, and insult; he receives them gladly as the opportunity of learning with certainty that he no longer asserts the will, but gladly sides with every enemy of the manifestation of will which is his own person. Therefore he bears such ignominy and suffering with inexhaustible patience and meekness, returns good for evil without ostentation, and allows the fire of anger to rise within him just as little as that of the desires. And he mortifies not only the will itself, but also its visible form, its objectivity, the body. He nourishes it sparingly, lest its excessive vigour and prosperity should animate and excite more strongly the will, of which it is merely the expression and the mirror. So he practises fasting, and even resorts to chastisement and self-inflicted torture, in order that, by constant privation and suffering, he may more and more break down and destroy the will, which he recognises and abhors as the source of his own suffering existence and that of the world. If at last death comes, which puts an end to this manifestation of that will, whose existence here has long since perished through free denial of itself, with the exception of the weak residue of it which appears as the life of this body; it is most welcome, and is gladly received as a longed-for deliverance. Here it is not, as in the case of others, merely the manifestation which ends with death; but the inner nature itself is abolished, which here existed only in the manifestation, and that in a very weak degree; this

last slight bond is now broken. For him who thus ends,
the world has ended also.

And what I have here described with feeble tongue
and only in general terms, is no philosophical fable, invented by myself, and only of to-day; no, it was the
enviable life of so many saints and beautiful souls among
Christians, and still more among Hindus and Buddhists,
and also among the believers of other religions. However different were the dogmas impressed on their reason, the same inward, direct, intuitive knowledge, from
which alone all virtue and holiness proceed, expressed
itself in precisely the same way in the conduct of life.
For here also the great distinction between intuitive and
abstract knowledge shows itself; a distinction which is
of such importance and universal application in our
whole investigation, and which has hitherto been too
little attended to. There is a wide gulf between the two,
which can only be crossed by the aid of philosophy, as
regards the knowledge of the nature of the world. Intuitively or *in concreto,* every man is really conscious of
all philosophical truths, but to bring them to abstract
knowledge, to reflection, is the work of philosophy,
which neither ought nor is able to do more than this.

Thus it may be that the inner nature of holiness, self-
renunciation, mortification of our own will, asceticism, is
here for the first time expressed abstractly, and free
from all mythical elements, as *denial of the will to live,*
appearing after the complete knowledge of its own nature has become a quieter of all volition. On the other
hand, it has been known directly and realised in practice by saints and ascetics, who had all the same inward knowledge, though they used very different language with regard to it, according to the dogmas which
their reason had accepted, and in consequence of which
an Indian, a Christian, or a Lama saint must each give

a very different account of his conduct, which is, however, of no importance as regards the fact. A saint may
be full of the absurdest superstition, or, on the contrary, he may be a philosopher, it is all the same. His
conduct alone certifies that he is a saint, for, in a moral
regard, it proceeds from knowledge of the world and its
nature, which is not abstractly but intuitively and directly apprehended, and is only expressed by him in any
dogma for the satisfaction of his reason. It is therefore
just as little needful that a saint should be a philosopher
as that a philosopher should be a saint; just as it is not
necessary that a perfectly beautiful man should be a
great sculptor, or that a great sculptor should himself
be a beautiful man. In general, it is a strange demand
upon a moralist that he should teach no other virtue
than that which he himself possesses. To repeat the whole
nature of the world abstractly, universally, and distinctly in concepts, and thus to store up, as it were, a
reflected image of it in permanent concepts always at
the command of the reason; this and nothing else is
philosophy.

It will be remembered from the Third Book that the
æsthetic pleasure in the beautiful consists in great measure in the fact that in entering the state of pure contemplation we are lifted for the moment above all willing, i. e., all wishes and cares; we become, as it were,
freed from ourselves. We are no longer the individual
whose knowledge is subordinated to the service of its
constant willing, the correlative of the particular thing
to which objects are motives, but the eternal subject of
knowing purified from will, the correlative of the Platonic Idea. And we know that these moments in which,
delivered from the ardent strain of will, we seem to rise
out of the heavy atmosphere of earth, are the happiest
which we experience. From this we can understand how

blessed the life of a man must be whose will is silenced, not merely for a moment, as in the enjoyment of the beautiful, but for ever, indeed altogether extinguished, except as regards the last glimmering spark that retains the body in life, and will be extinguished with its death. Such a man, who, after many bitter struggles with his own nature, has finally conquered entirely, continues to exist only as a pure, knowing being, the undimmed mirror of the world. Nothing can trouble him more, nothing can move him, for he has cut all the thousand cords of will which hold us bound to the world, and, as desire, fear, envy, anger, drag us hither and thither in constant pain. He now looks back smiling and at rest on the delusions of this world, which once were able to move and agonise his spirit also, but which now stand before him as utterly indifferent to him, as the chess-men when the game is ended, or as, in the morning, the cast-off masquerading dress which worried and disquieted us in a night in Carnival. Life and its forms now pass before him as a fleeting illusion, as a light morning dream before half-waking eyes, the real world already shining through it so that it can no longer deceive; and like this morning dream, they finally vanish altogether without any violent transition. From this we can understand the meaning of Madame Guion when towards the end of her autobiography she often expresses herself thus: "Everything is alike to me; I *cannot* will anything more: often I know not whether I exist or not." In order to express how, after the extinction of the will, the death of the body (which is indeed only the manifestation of the will, and therefore loses all significance when the will is abolished) can no longer have any bitterness, but is very welcome, I may be allowed to quote the words of that holy penitent, although they are not very elegantly turned: "*Midi de la gloire; jour où il n'y a plus de nuit;*

vie qui ne craint plus la mort, dans la mort même: par-
ceque la mort a vaincu la mort, et que celui qui a souffert
la première mort, ne goutera plus la seconde mort." (Vie
de Mad. de Guion, vol. ii, p. 13).

We must not, however, suppose that when, by means
of the knowledge which acts as a quieter of will, the
denial of the will to live has once appeared, it never
wavers or vacillates, and that we can rest upon it as on
an assured possession. Rather, it must ever anew be attained by a constant battle. For since the body is the will
itself only in the form of objectivity or as manifestation
in the world as idea, so long as the body lives, the whole
will to live exists potentially, and constantly strives to
become actual, and to burn again with all its ardour.
Therefore that peace and blessedness in the life of holy
men which we have described is only found as the flower
which proceeds from the constant victory over the will,
and the ground in which it grows is the constant battle
with the will to live, for no one can have lasting peace
upon earth. We therefore see the histories of the inner
life of saints full of spiritual conflicts, temptations, and
absence of grace, *i. e.,* the kind of knowledge which
makes all motives ineffectual, and as an universal quieter
silences all volition, gives the deepest peace and opens
the door of freedom. Therefore also we see those who
have once attained to the denial of the will to live strive
with all their might to keep upon this path, by enforced
renunciation of every kind, by penance and severity of
life, and by selecting whatever is disagreeable to them,
all in order to suppress the will, which is constantly
springing up anew. Hence, finally, because they already
know the value of salvation, their anxious carefulness to
retain the hard-won blessing, their scruples of conscience
about every innocent pleasure, or about every little excitement of their vanity, which here also dies last, the

most immovable, the most active, and the most foolish of all the inclinations of man. By the term *asceticism*, which I have used so often, I mean in its narrower sense this *intentional* breaking of the will by the refusal of what is agreeable and the selection of what is disagreeable, the voluntarily chosen life of penance and self-chastisement for the continual mortification of the will.

We see this practised by him who has attained to the denial of the will in order to enable him to persist in it; but suffering in general, as it is inflicted by fate, is a second way of attaining to that denial. Indeed, we may assume that most men only attain to it in this way, and that it is the suffering which is personally experienced, not that which is merely known, which most frequently produces complete resignation, often only at the approach of death. For only in the case of a few is the mere knowledge which, seeing through the principle of individuation, first produces perfect goodness of disposition and universal love of humanity, and finally enables them to regard all the suffering of the world as their own; only in the case of a few, I say, is this knowledge sufficient to bring about the denial of the will. Even with him who approaches this point, it is almost invariably the case that the tolerable condition of his own body, the flattery of the moment, the delusion of hope, and the satisfaction of the will, which is ever presenting itself anew, *i. e.*, lust, is a constant hindrance to the denial of the will, and a constant temptation to the renewed assertion of it. Therefore in this respect all these illusions have been personified as the devil. Thus in most cases the will must be broken by great personal suffering before its self-conquest appears. Then we see the man who has passed through all the increasing degrees of affliction with the most vehement resistance, and is finally brought to the verge of despair, suddenly retire into himself, know himself and the world, change his whole nature, rise above himself and all suffering, as if purified and sanctified by it, in inviolable peace, blessedness, and sublimity, willingly renounce everything he previously desired with all his might, and joyfully embrace death. It is the refined silver of the denial of the will to live that suddenly comes forth from the purifying flame of suffering. It is salvation. Sometimes we see even those who were very wicked purified to this degree by great grief; they have become new beings and are completely changed. Therefore their former misdeeds trouble their consciences no more, yet they willingly atone for them by death, and gladly see the end of the manifestation of that will which is now foreign to them and abhored by them. The great Goethe has given us a distinct and visible representation of this denial of the will, brought about by great misfortunes and despair of all deliverance, in his immortal masterpiece "Faust," in the story of the sufferings of Gretchen. I know no parallel to this in poetry. It is a perfect example of the second path that leads to the denial of the will, not, as the first, through the mere knowledge of the sufferings of a whole world which one has voluntarily acquired, but through excessive suffering experienced in one's own person. Many tragedies certainly end by conducting their strong-willed heroes to the point of entire resignation, and then generally the will to live and its manifestation end together, but no representation that is known to me brings what is essential to that change so distinctly before us, free from all that is extraneous, as the part of "Faust" I have referred to.

§ 71. I now end the general account of ethics, and with it the whole development of that one thought which it has been my object to impart; and I by no means desire to conceal here an objection which concerns this last part of my exposition, but rather to point out that it lies in the nature of the question, and that it is quite impossible to remove it. It is this, that after our investigation has brought us to the point at which we have before our eyes perfect holiness, the denial and surrender of all volition, and thus the deliverance from a world whose whole existence we have found to be suffering, this appears to us as a passing away into empty nothingness.

Before us there is certainly only nothingness. But that which resists this passing into nothing, our nature, is indeed just the will to live, which we ourselves are as it is our world. That we abhor annihilation so greatly, is simply another expression of the fact that we so strenuously will life, and are nothing but this will, and know nothing besides it. But if we turn our glance from our own needy and embarrassed condition to those who have overcome the world, in whom the will, having attained to perfect self-knowledge, found itself again in all, and then freely denied itself, and who then merely wait to see the last trace of it vanish with the body which it animates; then, instead of the restless striving and effort, instead of the constant transition from wish to fruition, and from joy to sorrow, instead of the never-satisfied and never-dying hope which constitutes the life of the man who wills, we shall see that peace which is above all reason, that perfect calm of the spirit, that deep rest, that inviolable confidence and serenity, the mere reflection of which in the countenance, as Raphael and Correggio have represented it, is an entire and certain gospel; only knowledge remains, the will has vanished. We look with deep and painful longing upon this state, beside which the misery and wretchedness of our own is brought out clearly by the contrast. Yet this is the only consideration which can afford us lasting consolation, when, on the one hand, we have recognised incurable suffering and endless misery as essential to the manifestation of will, the world; and, on the other hand, see the world pass away with the abolition of will, and retain before us only empty nothingness. Thus, in this way, by contemplation of the life and conduct of saints, whom it is certainly rarely granted us to meet with in our own experience, but who are brought before our eyes by their written history, and, with the stamp of inner truth, by art, we must banish the dark impression of that nothingness which we discern behind all virtue and holiness as their final goal, and which we fear as children fear the dark; we must not even evade it like the Indians, through myths and meaningless words, such as reabsorption in Brahma or the Nirvana of the Buddhists. Rather do we freely acknowledge that what remains after the entire abolition of will is for all those who are still full of will certainly nothing; but, conversely, to those in whom the will has turned and has denied itself, this our world, which is so real, with all its suns and milky-ways—is nothing.

SUPPLEMENTS TO "THE WORLD AS WILL AND IDEA"

SELECTIONS

CHAPTER XVII[1]

ON MAN'S NEED OF METAPHYSICS

WITH the exception of man, no being wonders at its own existence; but it is to them all so much a matter of course that they do not observe it. The wisdom of nature speaks out of the peaceful glance of the brutes; for in them the will and the intellect are not yet so widely separated that they can be astonished at each other when they meet again. Thus here the whole phenomenon is still firmly attached to the stem of nature from which it has come, and is partaker of the unconscious omniscience of the great mother. Only after the inner being of nature (the will to live in its objectification) has ascended, vigorous and cheerful, through the two series of unconscious existences, and then through the long and broad series of animals, does it attain at last to reflection for the first time on the entrance of reason, thus in man. Then it marvels at its own works, and asks itself what it itself is. Its wonder however is the more serious, as it here stands for the first time consciously in the presence of *death*, and besides the finiteness of all existence, the vanity of all effort forces itself more or less upon it. With this reflection and this wonder there arises therefore in man alone, the need *for a metaphysic;* he is accordingly an *animal metaphysicum*. At the beginning of his consciousness certainly he also accepts himself as a mat-

[1] This chapter is connected with § 15 of the first volume.

ter of course. This does not last long however, but very
early, with the first dawn of reflection, that wonder already appears, which is some day to become the mother
of metaphysics. In agreement with this Aristotle also
says at the beginning of his metaphysics: "Because of
wonder, now and in the beginning, men have been induced to philosophize." Moreover, the special philosophical disposition consists primarily in this, that a
man is capable of wonder beyond the ordinary and
everyday degree, and is thus induced to make the *universal* of the phenomenon his problem, while the investigators in the natural sciences wonder only at exquisite
or rare phenomena, and their problem is merely to refer
these to phenomena which are better known. The lower
a man stands in an intellectual regard the less of a problem is existence itself for him; everything, how it is,
and that it is, appears to him rather a matter of course.
This rests upon the fact that his intellect still remains
perfectly true to its original destiny of being serviceable
to the will as the medium of motives, and therefore is
closely bound up with the world and nature, as an in-
tegral part of them. Consequently it is very far from
comprehending the world in a purely objective manner,
freeing itself, so to speak, from the whole of things, opposing itself to this whole, and so for a while becoming
as if self-existent. On the other hand, the philosophical
wonder which springs from this is conditioned in the
individual by higher development of the intellect, yet in
general not by this alone; but without doubt it is the
knowledge of death, and along with this the consideration of the suffering and misery of life, which gives the
strongest impulse to philosophical reflection and metaphysical explanation of the world. If our life were endless and painless, it would perhaps occur to no one to
ask why the world exists, and is just the kind of world it

is; but everything would just be taken as a matter of course. In accordance with this we find that the interest which philosophical and also religious systems inspire has always its strongest hold in the dogma of some kind of existence after death; and although the most recent systems seem to make the existence of their gods the main point, and to defend this most zealously, yet in reality this is only because they have connected their special dogma of immortality with this, and regard the one as inseparable from the other: only on this account is it of importance to them. For if one could establish their doctrine of immortality for them in some other way, their lively zeal for their gods would at once cool, and it would give place almost to complete indifference if, conversely, the absolute impossibility of immortality were proved to them; for the interest in the existence of the gods would vanish with the hope of a closer acquaintance with them, to the residuum which might connect itself with their possible influence on the events of this present life. But if one could prove that continued existence after death is incompatible with the existence of gods, because, let us say, it pre-supposes originality of being, they would soon sacrifice the gods to their own immortality and become zealous for Atheism. The fact that the materialistic systems, properly so-called, and also absolute scepticism, have never been able to obtain a general or lasting influence, depends upon the same grounds.

Temples and churches, pagodas and mosques, in all lands and in all ages, in splendour and vastness, testify to the metaphysical need of man, which strong and ineradicable, follows close upon his physical need. Certainly whoever is satirically inclined might add that this metaphysical need is a modest fellow who is content with poor fare. It sometimes allows itself to be satisfied with clumsy fables and insipid tales. If only imprinted early enough, they are for a man adequate explanations of his existence and supports of his morality. Consider, for example, the Koran. This wretched book was sufficient to found a religion of the world, to satisfy the metaphysical need of innumerable millions of men for twelve hundred years, to become the foundation of their morality, and of no small contempt for death, and also to inspire them to bloody wars and most extended conquests. We find in it the saddest and the poorest form of Theism. Much may be lost through the translations; but I have not been able to discover one single valuable thought in it. Such things show that metaphysical capacity does not go hand in hand with the metaphysical need. Yet it will appear that in the early ages of the present surface of the earth this was not the case, and that those who stood considerably nearer than we do to the beginning of the human race and the source of organic nature, had also both greater energy of the intuitive faculty of knowledge, and a truer disposition of mind, so that they were capable of a purer, more direct comprehension of the inner being of nature, and were thus in a position to satisfy the metaphysical need in a more worthy manner. Thus originated in the primitive ancestors of the Brahmans, the Rishis, the almost superhuman conceptions which were afterwards set down in the Upanishads of the Vedas.

On the other hand, there have never been wanting persons who were interested in deriving their living from that metaphysical need, and in making the utmost they could out of it. Therefore among all nations there are monopolists and farmers-general of it—the priests. Yet their trade had everywhere to be assured to them in this way, that they received the right to impart their metaphysical dogmas to men at a very early age, before the judgment has awakened from its morning slumber, thus in early childhood; for then every well-impressed dogma, however senseless it may be, remains for ever. If they had to wait till the judgment is ripe, their privileges could not continue.

A second, though not a numerous class of persons, who derive their support from the metaphysical need of man, is constituted by those who live by *philosophy*. By the Greeks they were called Sophists, by the moderns they are called Professors of Philosophy. Aristotle (*Metaph.*, ii. 2) without hesitation numbers Aristippus among the Sophists. In Diogenes Laertius (ii. 65) we find that the reason of this is that he was the first of the Socratics who accepted payment for his philosophy; on account of which Socrates also returned him his present. Among the moderns also those who live *by* philosophy are not only, as a rule, and with the rarest exceptions, quite different from those who live *for* philosophy, but they are very often the opponents, the secret and irreconcilable enemies of the latter. For every true and important philosophical achievement will overshadow their own too much, and, moreover, cannot adapt itself to the views and limitations of their guild. Therefore it is always their endeavour to prevent such a work from making its way; and for this purpose, according to the age and circumstances in each case, the customary means are suppressing, concealing, hushing up, ignoring and keeping secret, or denying, disparaging, censuring, slandering and distorting, or, finally, denouncing and persecuting. Hence many a great man has had to drag himself wearily through life unknown, unhonoured, unrewarded, till at last, after his death, the world became undeceived as to him and as to them. In the meanwhile they had attained their end, had been accepted by preventing him from being accepted, and, with wife and

child, had lived *by* philosophy, while he lived *for* it.
But if he is dead, then the thing is reversed; the new
generation of the former class, which always exists, now
becomes heir to his achievements, cuts them down to its
own measure, and now lives *by* him. That Kant could
yet live both *by* and *for* philosophy depended on the
rare circumstance that, for the first time since *Divus
Antoninus* and *Divus Julianus,* a philosopher sat on the
throne. Only under such auspices could the "Critique
of Pure Reason" have seen the light. Scarcely was the
king dead than we see that Kant also, seized with fear,
because he belonged to the guild, modified, expurgated,
and spoiled his masterpiece in the second edition, and
yet was soon in danger of losing his place; so that
Campe invited him to come to him, in Brunswick, and
live with him as the instructor of his family (Ring.,
Ansichten aus Kant's Leben, p. 68). University philosophy, is, as a rule, mere juggling. Its real aim is to impart
to the students, in the deepest ground of their thought,
that tendency of mind which the ministry that appoints to
the professorships regards as consistent with its views.
The ministry may also be perfectly right in this from a
statesman's point of view; only the result of it is that
such philosophy of the chair cannot be regarded as serious philosophy, but as the mere jest of it. Moreover, it
is at any rate just that such inspection or guidance
should extend only to the philosophy of the chair, and
not to the real philosophy that is in earnest. For if anything in the world is worth wishing for—so well worth
wishing for that even the ignorant and dull herd in its
more reflective moments would prize it more than silver
and gold—it is that a ray of light should fall on the obscurity of our being, and that we should gain some explanation of our mysterious existence, in which nothing
is clear but its misery and its vanity. But even if this

is in itself attainable, it is made impossible by imposed and compulsory solutions.

We shall now subject to a general consideration the different ways of satisfying this strong metaphysical need.

By *metaphysics* I understand all knowledge that pretends to transcend the possibility of experience, thus to transcend nature or the given phenomenal appearance of things, in order to give an explanation of that by which, in some sense or other, this experience or nature is conditioned; or, to speak in popular language, of that which is behind nature, and makes it possible. But the great original diversity in the power of understanding, besides the cultivation of it, which demands much leisure, makes so great a difference between men, that as soon as a people has emerged from the state of savages, no *one* metaphysic can serve for them all. Therefore among civilised nations we find throughout two different kinds of metaphysics, which are distinguished by the fact that the one has its evidence *in itself,* the other *outside itself.* Since the metaphysical systems of the first kind require reflection, culture, and leisure for the recognition of their evidence, they can be accessible only to a very small number of men; and, moreover, they can only arise and maintain their existence in the case of advanced civilisation. On the other hand, the systems of the second kind exclusively are for the great majority of men who are not capable of thinking, but only of believing, and who are not accessible to reasons, but only to authority. These systems may therefore be called metaphysics of the people, after the analogy of poetry of the people, and also wisdom of the people, by which is understood proverbs. These systems, however, are known under the name of religions, and are found among all nations, not excepting even the most savage. Their evidence

is, as has been said, external, and as such is called
revelation, which is authenticated by signs and miracles. Their arguments are principally threats of eternal,
and indeed also temporal evils, directed against un-
believers, and even against mere doubters. As *ultima
ratio theologorum* (last argument of theologians), we
find among many nations the stake or things similar to
it. If they seek a different authentication, or if they
make use of other arguments, they already make the
transition into the systems of the first kind, and may
degenerate into a mixture of the two, which brings more
danger than advantage, for their invaluable prerogative
of being imparted to *children* gives them the surest
guarantee of the permanent possession of the mind, for
thereby their dogmas grow into a kind of second inborn
intellect, like the twig upon the grafted tree; while, on
the other hand, the systems of the first kind only appeal to grown-up people, and in them always find a system of the second kind already in possession of their
convictions. Both kinds of metaphysics, whose difference
may be briefly expressed by the words reasoned conviction and faith, have this in common, that every one of
their particular systems stands in a hostile relation to
all the others of its kind. Between those of the first
kind war is waged only with word and pen; between
those of the second with fire and sword as well. Several
of the latter owe their propagation in part to this last
kind of polemic, and all have by degrees divided the
earth between them, and indeed with such decided authority that the peoples of the earth are distinguished
and separated more according to them than according
to nationality or government. They alone *reign,* each
in its own province. The systems of the first kind, on
the contrary, are at the most *tolerated,* and even this
only because, on acount of the small number of their ad-

herents, they are for the most part not considered worth
the trouble of combating with fire and sword—although,
where it seemed necessary, these also have been employed against them with effect; besides, they occur only
in a sporadic form. Yet in general they have only been
endured in a tamed and subjugated condition, for the
system of the second kind which prevailed in the country
ordered them to conform their teaching more or less
closely to its own. Sometimes it not only subjugated
them, but even employed their services and used them
as a support, which is however a dangerous experiment.
For these systems of the first kind, since they are deprived of power, believe they may advance themselves
by craft, and never entirely lay aside a secret ill-will
which at times comes unexpectedly into prominence and
inflicts injuries which are hard to heal. For they are
further made the more dangerous by the fact that all
the real sciences, not even excepting the most innocent,
are their secret allies against the systems of the second
kind, and without themselves being openly at war with
the latter, suddenly and unexpectedly do great mischief
in their province. Besides, the attempt which is aimed
at by the enlistment referred to of the services of the
systems of the first kind by the second—the attempt
to add an inner authentication to a system whose original
authentication was external, is in its nature perilous;
for, if it were capable of such an authentication, it
would never have required an external one. And in general it is always a hazardous thing to attempt to place
a new foundation under a finished structure. Moreover,
how should a religion require the suffrage of a philosophy? It has everything upon its side—revelation, tradition, miracles, prophecies, the protection of the government, the highest rank, as is due to the truth, the
consent and reverence of all, a thousand temples in

which it is proclaimed and practised, bands of sworn priests, and, what is more than all, the invaluable privilege of being allowed to imprint its doctrines on the mind at the tender age of childhood, whereby they became almost like innate ideas. With such wealth of means at its disposal, still to desire the assent of poor philosophers it must be more covetous, or to care about their contradiction it must be more fearful, than seems to be compatible with a good conscience.

To the distinction established above between metaphysics of the first and of the second kind, we have yet to add the following:—A system of the first kind, thus a philosophy, makes the claim, and has therefore the obligation, in everything that it says, *sensu stricto et proprio,* to be true, for it appeals to thought and conviction. A religion, on the other hand, being intended for the innumerable multitude who, since they are incapable of examination and thought, would never comprehend the profoundest and most difficult truths *sensu proprio,* has only the obligation to be true *sensu allegorico.* Truth cannot appear naked before the people. A symptom of this *allegorical* nature of religions is the *mysteries* which are to be found perhaps in them all, certain dogmas which cannot even be distinctly thought, not to speak of being literally true. Indeed, perhaps it might be asserted that some absolute contradictions, some actual absurdities, are an essential ingredient in a complete religion, for these are just the stamp of its allegorical nature, and the only adequate means of making the ordinary mind and the uncultured understanding *feel* what would be incomprehensible to it, that religion has ultimately to do with quite a different order of things, with an order of *things in themselves,* in the presence of which the laws of this phenomenal world, in conformity with which it must speak, vanish; and that therefore not only the contradictory but also the comprehensible dogmas are really only allegories and accommodations to the human power of comprehension. It seems to me that it was in this spirit that Augustine and even Luther adhered to the mysteries of Christianity in opposition to Pelagianism, which sought to reduce everything to the dull level of comprehensibility. From this point of view it is also conceivable how Tertullian could say in all seriousness: "It is credible, because foolish; certain, because impossible." This *allegorical* nature of religions makes them independent of the proofs which are incumbent on philosophy, and in general withdraws them from investigation. Instead of this they require faith, that is, a voluntary admission that such is the state of the case. Since, then, faith guides action, and the allegory is always so framed that, as regards the practical, it leads precisely to that which the truth *sensu proprio* would also lead to, religion is justified in promising to those who believe eternal salvation. Thus we see that in the main, and for the great majority, who cannot apply themselves to thought, religions very well supply the place of metaphysics in general, the need of which man feels to be imperative. They do this partly in a practical interest, as the guiding star of their action, the unfurled standard of integrity and virtue, as Kant admirably expresses it; partly as the indispensable comfort in the heavy sorrows of life, in which capacity they fully supply the place of an objectively true metaphysic, because they lift man above himself and his existence in time, as well perhaps as such a metaphysic ever could. In this their great value and indeed necessity shows itself very clearly. On the other hand, the only stumbling-stone is this, that religions never dare to confess their allegorical nature, but have to assert that they are true *sensu proprio*. They thereby encroach on the province of metaphysics proper, and call forth the antagonism of the latter, which has therefore expressed itself at all times when it was not chained up. The controversy which is so perseveringly carried on in our own day between supernaturalists and rationalists also rests on the failure to recognise the allegorical nature of all religion. Both wish to have Christianity true *sensu proprio;* in this sense the former wish to maintain it without deduction, as it were with skin and hair; and thus they have a hard stand to make against the knowledge and general culture of the age. The latter wish to explain away all that is properly Christian; whereupon they retain something which is neither *sensu proprio* nor *sensu allegorico* true, but rather a mere platitude, little better than Judaism, or at the most a shallow Pelagianism, and, what is worst, an abject optimism, absolutely foreign to Christianity proper. Moreover, the attempt to found a religion upon reason removes it into the other class of metaphysics, that which has its authentication *in itself,* thus to the foreign ground of the philosophical systems, and into the conflict which these wage against each other in their own arena, and consequently exposes it to the light fire of scepticism and the heavy artillery of the "Critique of Pure Reason;" but for it to venture there would be clear presumption.

It would be most beneficial to both kinds of metaphysics that each of them should remain clearly separated from the other and confine itself to its own province, that it may there be able to develop its nature fully. Instead of which, through the whole Christian era, the endeavour has been to bring about a fusion of the two, for the dogmas and conceptions of the one have been carried over into the other, whereby both are spoiled. This has taken place in the most open manner in our own day in that strange hermaphrodite or centaur, the so-called philosophy of religion, which, as a kind of gnosis, endeavours to interpret the given religion, and to explain what is true *sensu allegorico* through something which is true *sensu proprio.* But for this we would have to know and possess the truth *sensu proprio* already; and in that case such an interpretation would be superfluous. For to seek first to find metaphysics, *i. e.,* the truth *sensu proprio,* merely out of religion by explanation and interpretation would be a doubtful and dangerous undertaking, to which one would only make up one's mind if it were proved that truth, like iron and other base metals, could only be found in a mixed, not in a pure form, and therefore one could only obtain it by reduction from the mixed ore.

Religions are necessary for the people, and an inestimable benefit to them. But if they oppose themselves to the progress of mankind in the knowledge of the truth, they must with the utmost possible forbearance be set aside. And to require that a great mind—a Shakespeare; a Goethe—should make the dogmas of any religion implicitly his conviction is to require that a giant should put on the shoe of a dwarf.

Religions, being calculated with reference to the power of comprehension of the great mass of men, can only have indirect, not immediate truth. To require of them the latter is as if one wished to read the letters set up in the form-chase, instead of their impression. The value of a religion will accordingly depend upon the greater or less content of truth which it contains under the veil of allegory, and then upon the greater or less distinctness with which it becomes visible through this veil, thus upon the transparency of the latter. It almost seems that, as the oldest languages are the most perfect, so also are the oldest religions. If I were to take the results of my philosophy as the standard of truth, I would be obliged to concede to Buddhism the pre-eminence over the rest. In any case it must be a satisfaction to me to see my teaching in such close agreement with a religion which the majority of men upon the earth hold as their own; for it numbers far more adherents than any other. This agreement, however, must be the more satisfactory to me because in my philosophising I have certainly not been under its influence. For up till 1818, when my work appeared, there were very few, exceedingly incomplete and scanty, accounts of Buddhism to be found in Europe, which were almost entirely limited to a few essays in the earlier volumes of "Asiatic Researches," and were principally concerned with the Buddhism of the Burmese. Only since then has fuller information about this religion gradually reached us, chiefly through the profound and instructive essays of the meritorious member of the St. Petersburg Academy, J. J. Schmidt, in the proceedings of his Academy, and then little by little through several English and French scholars, so that I was able to give a fairly numerous list of the best works on this religion in my work, "On the Will in Nature," under the heading *Sinologie*. Unfortunately Csoma Körösi, that persevering Hungarian, who, in order to study the language and sacred writings of Buddhism, spent many years in Tibet, and for the most part in Buddhist monasteries, was carried off by death just as he was beginning to work out for us the results of his researches. I cannot, however, deny the pleasure with which I read, in his provisional accounts, several passages cited directly from the Kahgyur itself; for example, the following conversation of the dying Buddha with Brahma, who is doing him homage: "There is a description of their conversation on the subject of creation,—by whom was the world made? Shakya asks several questions of Brahma,—whether was it he who made or produced such and such things, and endowed or blessed them with such and such virtues or properties,—whether was it he who caused the several revolutions in the destruction and regeneration of the world. He denies that he had ever done anything to that effect. At last he himself asks Shakya how the world was made,—by whom? Here are attributed all changes in the world to the moral works of the animal beings, and it is stated that in the world all is illusion, there is no reality in the things; all is empty. Brahma, being instructed in his doctrine, becomes his follower" (Asiatic Researches, vol. xx, p. 434).

I cannot place, as is always done, the fundamental difference of all religions in the questions whether they are monotheistic, polytheistic, pantheistic, or atheistic, but only in the question whether they are optimistic or pessimistic, that is, whether they present the existence of the world as justified by itself, and therefore praise and value it, or regard it as something that can only be conceived as the consequence of our guilt, and therefore properly ought not to. be, because they recognise that pain and death cannot lie in the eternal, original, and immutable order of things, in that which in every respect ought to be. The power by virtue of which Christianity was able to overcome first Judaism, and then the heathenism of Greece and Rome, lies solely in its pessimism, in the confession that our state is both exceedingly wretched and sinful, while Judaism and heathenism were optimistic. That truth, profoundly and painfully felt by all, penetrated, and bore in its train the need of redemption.

I turn to a general consideration of the other kind of metaphysics, that which has its authentication in itself, and is called *philosophy*. I remind the reader of its origin, mentioned above, in a *wonder* concerning the world

and our own existence, inasmuch as these press upon the
intellect as a riddle, the solution of which therefore occupies mankind without intermission. Here, then, I wish
first of all to draw attention to the fact that this could
not be the case if, in Spinoza's sense, which in our own
day has so often been brought forward again under
modern forms and expositions as pantheism, the world
were an *"absolute substance,"* and therefore an *absolutely necessary existence.* For this means that it exists with so great a necessity that beside it every other
necessity comprehensible to our understanding as such
must appear as an accident. It would then be something
which comprehended in itself not only all actual but
also all possible existence, so that, as Spinoza indeed
declares, its possibility and its actuality would be absolutely one. Its non-being would therefore be impossibility itself; thus it would be something the non-being
or other-being of which must be completely inconceivable, and which could therefore just as little be thought
away as, for example, space or time. And since, further,
we ourselves would be parts, modes, attributes, or accidents of such an absolute substance, which would be
the only thing that, in any sense, could ever or anywhere exist, our and its existence, together with its
properties, would necessarily be very far from presenting itself to us as remarkable, problematical, and indeed as an unfathomable and ever-disquieting riddle,
but, on the contrary, would be far more self-evident
than that two and two make four. For we would necessarily be incapable of thinking anything else than that
the world is, and is, as it is; and therefore we would
necessarily be as little conscious of its existence *as such,*
i. e., as a problem for reflection, as we are of the incredibly fast motion of our planet.

All this, however, is absolutely not the case. Only to

the brutes, who are without thought, does the world and
existence appear as a matter of course; to man, on the
contrary, it is a problem, of which even the most unedu-
cated and narrow-minded becomes vividly conscious in
certain brighter moments, but which enters more distinctly and more permanently into the consciousness of
each one of us the clearer and more enlightened that
consciousness is, and the more material for thought it
has acquired through culture, which all ultimately rises,
in minds that are naturally adapted for philosophising,
to Plato's *wonder* which comprehends in its whole magnitude that problem which unceasingly occupies the
nobler portion of mankind in every age and in every
land, and gives it no rest. In fact, the pendulum which
keeps in motion the clock of metaphysics, that never
runs down, is the consciousness that the non-existence
of this world is just as possible as its existence. Thus,
then, the Spinozistic view of it as an absolutely necessary existence, that is, as something that absolutely and
in every sense ought to and must be, is a false one.
Even simple Theism, since in its cosmological proof it
tacitly starts by inferring the previous non-existence
of the world from its existence, thereby assumes beforehand that the world is something contingent. Nay,
what is more, we very soon apprehend the world
as something the non-existence of which is not only
conceivable, but indeed preferable to its existence.
Therefore our wonder at it easily passes into a
brooding over the *fatality* which could yet call forth
its existence, and by virtue of which such stupendous
power as is demanded for the production and maintenance of such a world could be directed so much against
its own interest. The philosophical astonishment is therefore at bottom perplexed and melancholy; philosophy,
like the overture to "Don Juan," commences with a minor

chord. It follows from this that it can neither be Spinozism nor optimist. The more special nature, which has just been indicated, of the astonishment which leads us to philosophise clearly springs from the sight of the *suffering and the wickedness* in the world, which, even if they were in the most just proportion to each other, and also were far outweighed by good, are yet something which absolutely and in general ought not to be. But since now nothing can come out of nothing, these also must have their germ in the origin or in the kernel of the world itself. It is hard for us to assume this if we look at the magnitude, the order and completeness, of the physical world, for it seems to us that what had the power to produce such a world must have been able to avoid the suffering and the wickedness. That assumption (the truest expression of which is Ormuzd and Ahrimines), it is easy to conceive, is hardest of all for Theism. Therefore the freedom of the will was primarily invented to account for wickedness. But this is only a concealed way of making something out of nothing, for it assumes an effect that proceeded from no being. Then it was sought to get rid of evil by attributing it to matter, or to unavoidable necessity, whereby the devil, who is really the right expedient, was unwillingly set aside. To evil also belongs *death;* but wickedness is only the throwing of the existing evil from oneself on to another. Thus, as was said above, it is wickedness, evil, and death that qualify and intensify the philosophical astonishment. Not merely that the world exists, but still more that it is such a wretched world, is the itching point of metaphysics, the problem which awakens in mankind an unrest that cannot be quieted by scepticism nor yet by criticism.

We find *physics* also (in the widest sense of the word) occupied with the explanation of the phenomena in the world. But it lies in the very nature of its explanations themselves that they cannot be sufficient. Physics cannot stand on its own feet, but requires a metaphysic to lean upon, whatever airs it may give itself towards the latter. For it explains the phenomena by something still more unknown than they are themselves; by laws of nature, resting upon forces of nature, to which the power of life also belongs. Certainly the whole present condition of all things in the world, or in nature, must necessarily be explicable from purely physical causes. But such an explanation—supposing one actually succeeded so far as to be able to give it—must always just as necessarily be tainted with two imperfections (as it were with two sores, or like Achilles with the vulnerable heel, or the devil with the horse's hoof), on account of which everything so explained really remains still unexplained. First with this imperfection, that the *beginning* of every explanatory chain of causes and effects, *i. e.*, of connected changes, can absolutely *never* be reached, but, just like the limits of the world in space and time, unceasingly recedes *in infinito*. Secondly with this, that the whole of the efficient causes out of which everything is explained constantly rest upon something which is completely inexplicable, the original *qualities* of things and the *natural forces* which play a prominent part among them, by virtue of which they produce a specific kind of effect, *e.g.*, weight, hardness, impulsive force, elasticity, warmth, electricity, chemical forces, &c., and which now remain in every explanation which is given, like an unknown quantity, which absolutely cannot be eliminated, in an otherwise perfectly solved algebraical equation. Accordingly there is no fragment of clay, however little worth, that is not entirely composed of inexplicable qualities. Thus these two inevitable defects in every purely physical, *i. e.*, causal, explanation show that such an explanation can only be *relative*, and that its whole method and nature cannot be the only one, the ultimate and thus the sufficient one, *i. e.*, cannot be the method of explanation that can ever lead to the satisfactory solution of the difficult riddle of things, and to the true understanding of the world and existence; but that the physical explanation in general and as such requires further a *metaphysical* explanation, which affords us the key to all its assumptions, but just on this account must necessarily follow quite a different path. The first step to this is that one should bring to distinct consciousness and firmly retain the difference of the two, hence the difference between *physics* and *metaphysics*. It rests in general on the Kantian distinction between *phenomenon* and *thing in itself*. Just because Kant held the latter to be absolutely unknowable, there was, according to him, no *metaphysics*, but merely immanent knowledge, *i. e., physics*, which throughout can speak only of phenomena, and also a critique of the reason which strives after metaphysics. Here, however, in order to show the true point of connection between my philosophy and that of Kant, I shall anticipate the second book, and give prominence to the fact that Kant, in his beautiful exposition of the compatibility of freedom and necessity (Critique of Pure Reason, first edition, p. 532–554; and Critique of Practical Reason, p. 224–231 of Rosenkranz's edition), shows how one and the same action may in one aspect be perfectly explicable as necessarily arising from the character of the man, the influence to which he has been subject in the course of his life, and the motives which are now present to him, but yet in another aspect must be regarded as the work of his free will; and in the same sense he says, § 53 of the "Prolegomena": "Certainly natural necessity will belong to every connection of cause and effect in the world of sense; yet, on the other hand,

freedom will be conceded to that cause which is not itself a phenomenon (though indeed it is the ground of
phenomena), thus nature and freedom may without contradiction be attributed to the same thing, but in a different reference—in the one case as a phenomenon, in
the other case as a thing in itself." What, then, Kant
teaches of the phenomenon of man and his action my
teaching extends to *all* phenomena in nature, in that it
makes the *will* as a thing in itself their foundation. This
proceeding is justified first of all by the fact that it must
not be assumed that man is specifically *toto genere* radically different from the other beings and things in nature, but rather that he is different only in degree. I
turn back from this premature digression to our consideration of the inadequacy of physics to afford us the ultimate explanation of things. I say, then, everything certainly is physical, but yet nothing is explicable physically. As for the motion of the projected bullet, so also
for the thinking of the brain, a physical explanation
must ultimately be in itself possible, which would make
the latter just as comprehensible as in the former. But
even the former, which we imagine we understand so perfectly, is at bottom as obscure to us as the latter; for
what the inner nature of expansion in space may be—
of impenetrability, mobility, hardness, elasticity, and
gravity remains, after all physical explanations, a mystery, just as much as thought. But because in the case of
thought the inexplicable appears most immediately, a
spring was at once made here from physics to metaphysics, and a substance of quite a different kind from
all corporeal substances was hypostatised—a soul was
set up in the brain. But if one had not been so dull as
only to be capable of being struck by the most remarkable of phenomena, one would have had to explain digestion by a soul in the stomach, vegetation by a soul in the
plant, affinity by a soul in the reagents, nay, the falling

of a stone by a soul in the stone. For the quality of every unorganised body is just as mysterious as the life in the living body. In the same way, therefore, the physical explanation strikes everywhere upon what is metaphysical, by which it is annihilated, *i. e.,* it ceases to be explanation. Strictly speaking, it may be asserted that no natural science really achieves anything more than what is also achieved by Botany: the bringing together of similars, classification. A physical system which asserted that its explanations of things—in the particular from causes, and in general from forces—were really sufficient, and thus exhausted the nature of the world, would be the true *Naturalism.* From Leucippus, Democritus, and Epicurus down to the *Système de la Nature,* and further, to Delamark, Cabanis, and to the materialism that has again been warmed up in the last few years, we can trace the persistent attempt to set up a *system of physics without metaphysics,* that is, a system which would make the phenomenon the thing in itself. But all their explanations seek to conceal from the explainers themselves and from others that they simply assume the principal matter without more ado. They endeavour to show that all phenomena, even those of mind, are physical. And they are right; only they do not see that all that is physical is in another aspect also metaphysical. But, without Kant, this is indeed difficult to see, for it presupposes the distinction of the phenomenon from the thing in itself. Yet without this Aristotle, much as he was inclined to empiricism, and far as he was removed from the Platonic hyperphysics, kept himself free from this limited point of view. Such an *absolute system of physics* as is described above, which leaves room for no *metaphysics,* would make the *Natura naturata* into the *Natura naturans;* it would be physics established on the throne of metaphysics, yet it would comport itself in this high position almost like Holberg's theatrical would-be politician who was made burgomaster. Indeed behind the reproach of atheism, in itself absurd, and for the most part malicious, there lies, as its inner meaning and truth, which gives it strength, the obscure conception of such an absolute system of physics without metaphysics. Certainly such a system would necessarily be destructive of ethics; and while Theism has falsely been held to be inseparable from morality, this is really true only of *metaphysics in general, i. e.,* of the knowledge that the order of nature is not the only and absolute order of things. Therefore we may set up this as the necessary *Credo* of all just and good men: "I believe in metaphysics." In this respect it is important and necessary that one should convince oneself of the untenable nature of an *absolute system of physics,* all the more as this, the true *naturalism,* is a point of view which of its own accord and ever anew presses itself upon a man, and can only be done away with through profound speculation. In this respect, however, all kinds of systems and faiths, so far and so long as they are accepted, certainly serve as a substitute for such speculation. But that a fundamentally false view presses itself upon man of its own accord, and must first be skilfully removed, is explicable from the fact that the intellect is not originally intended to instruct us concerning the nature of things, but only to show us their relations, with reference to our will; it is, as we shall find in the second book, only the medium of motives. Now, that the world schematises itself in the intellect in a manner which exhibits quite a different order of things from the absolutely true one, because it shows us, not their kernel, but only their outer shell, happens accidentally, and cannot be used as a reproach to the intellect; all the less as it nevertheless finds in itself the means of rectifying this error, in that it arrives at the distinction between the phenomenal appearance and the inner being of things, which distinction existed in sub-

stance at all times, only for the most part was very imperfectly brought to consciousness, and therefore was
inadequately expressed, indeed often appeared in strange
clothing. The Christian mystics, when they call it the
light of nature, declare the intellect to be inadequate to
the comprehension of the true nature of things. It is, as
it were, a mere surface force, like electricity, and does
not penetrate to the inner being.

With naturalism, then, or the purely physical way of
looking at things, we shall never attain our end; it is
like a sum that never comes out. Causal series without
beginning or end, fundamental forces which are inscrutable, endless space, beginningless time, infinite, divisibil-
ity of matter, and all this further conditioned by a knowing brain, in which alone it exists just like a dream, and
without which it vanishes—constitute the labyrinth in
which naturalism leads us ceaselessly round. The height
to which in our time the natural sciences have risen in
this respect entirely throws into the shade all previous
centuries, and is a summit which mankind reaches for the
first time. But however great are the advances which
physics (understood in the wide sense of the ancients)
may make, not the smallest step towards *metaphysics* is
thereby taken, just as a plane can never obtain cubical
content by being indefinitely extended. For all such advances will only perfect our knowledge of the *phenomenon;* while *metaphysics* strives to pass beyond the
phenomenal appearance itself, to that which so appears.
And if indeed it had the assistance of an entire and
complete experience, it would, as regards the main point,
be in no way advantaged by it. Nay, even if one wan-
dered through all the planets and fixed stars, one would
thereby have made no step in *metaphysics*. It is rather
the case that the greatest advances of physics will make
the need of metaphysics ever more felt; for it is just the
corrected, extended, and more thorough knowledge of na-

ture which, on the one hand, always undermines and ultimately overthrows the metaphysical assumptions which
till then have prevailed, but, on the other hand, presents
the problem of metaphysics itself more distinctly, more
correctly, and more fully, and separates it more clearly
from all that is merely physical; moreover, the more perfectly and accurately known nature of the particular
thing more pressingly demands the explanation of the
whole and the general, which, the more correctly, thoroughly, and completely it is known empirically, only presents itself as the more mysterious. Certainly the individual, simple investigator of nature, in a special branch
of physics, does not at once become clearly conscious of
all this; he rather sleeps contentedly by the side of his
chosen maid, in the house of Odysseus, banishing all
thoughts of Penelope (cf. ch. 12 at the end). Hence we
see at the present day the *husk of nature* investigated in
its minutest details, the intestines of intestinal worms
and the vermin of vermin known to a nicety. But if some
one comes, as, for example, I do, and speaks of the *kernel
of nature,* they will not listen; they even think it has
nothing to do with the matter, and go on sifting their
husks. One finds oneself tempted to call that over-micro-
scopical and micrological investigator of nature the cot-
quean of nature. But those persons who believe that cru-
cibles and retorts are the true and only source of all wisdom are in their own way just as perverse as were formerly their antipodes the Scholastics. As the latter, absolutely confined to their abstract conceptions, used these
as their weapons, neither knowing nor investigating anything outside them, so the former, absolutely confined
to their empiricism, allow nothing to be true except what
their eyes behold, and believe they can thus arrive at
the ultimate ground of things, not discerning that between the phenomenon and that which manifests itself
in it, the thing in itself, there is a deep gulf, a radical

difference, which can only be cleared up by the knowledge and accurate delimitation of the subjective element of the phenomenon, and the insight that the ultimate and most important conclusions concerning the nature of things can only be drawn from self-consciousness; yet without all this one cannot advance a step beyond what is directly given to the senses, thus can get no further than to the problem. Yet, on the other hand, it is to be observed that the most perfect possible knowledge of nature is the corrected *statement of the problem* of metaphysics. Therefore no one ought to venture upon this without having first acquired a knowledge of all the branches of natural science, which, though general, shall be thorough, clear, and connected. For the problem must precede its solution. Then, however, the investigator must turn his glance inward; for the intellectual and ethical phenomena are more important than the physical, in the same proportion as, for example, animal magnetism is a far more important phenomenon than mineral magnetism. The last fundamental secret man carries within himself, and this is accessible to him in the most immediate manner; therefore it is only here that he can hope to find the key to the riddle of the world and gain a clue to the nature of all things. The special province of metaphysics thus certainly lies in what has been called mental philosophy.

> "The ranks of living creatures thou dost lead
> Before me, teaching me to know my brothers
> In air and water and the silent wood:
>
> .   .   .   .
>
> Then to the cave secure thou leadest me,
> Then show'st me mine own self, and in my breast
> The deep, mysterious miracles unfold."[1]

[1] [Bayard Taylor's translation of Faust, vol. i, 180. Trs.]

Finally, then, as regards the *source or the foundation* of metaphysical knowledge, I have already declared myself above to be opposed to the assumption, which is even repeated by Kant, that it must lie *in mere conceptions.* In no knowledge can conceptions be what is first; for they are always derived from some perception. What has led, however, to that assumption is probably the example of mathematics. Mathematics can leave perception altogether, and, as is especially the case in algebra, trigonometry, and analysis, can operate with purely abstract conceptions, nay, with conceptions which are represented only by signs instead of words, and can yet arrive at a perfectly certain result, which is still so remote that any one who adhered to the firm ground of perception could not arrive at it. But the possibility of this depends, as Kant has clearly shown, on the fact that the conceptions of mathematics are derived from the most certain and definite of all perceptions, from the *a priori* and yet intuitively known relations of quantity, and can therefore be constantly realised again and controlled by these, either arithmetically, by performing the calculations which are merely indicated by those signs, or geometrically, by means of what Kant calls the construction of the conceptions. This advantage, on the other hand, is not possessed by the conceptions out of which it was believed metaphysics could be built up; such, for example, as essence, being, substance, perfection, necessity, reality, finite, infinite, absolute, ground, &c. For such conceptions are by no means original, as fallen from heaven, or innate; but they also, like all conceptions, are derived from perceptions; and as, unlike the conceptions of mathematics, they do not contain the mere form of perception, but more, empirical perceptions must lie at their foundation. Thus nothing can be drawn from them which the empirical perceptions did not also contain, that is, nothing which was not a matter of experience, and which, since these conceptions are very wide abstractions, we would receive with much greater certainty at first hand from experience. For from conceptions nothing more can ever be drawn than the perceptions from which they are derived contain. If we desire pure conceptions, *i. e.,* such as have no empirical source, the only ones that can be produced are those which concern space and time, *i. e.,* the merely formal part of perception, consequently only the mathematical conceptions, or at most also the conception of causality, which indeed does not originate in experience, but yet only comes into consciousness by means of it (first in sense-perception); therefore experience indeed is only possible by means of it; but it also is only valid in the sphere of experience, on which account Kant has shown that it only serves to communicate the connection of experience, and not to transcend it; that thus it admits only of physical application, not of metaphysical. Certainly only its *a priori* origin can give apodictic certainty to any knowledge; but this limits it to the mere *form* of experience in general, for it shows that it is conditioned by the subjective nature of the intellect. Such knowledge, then, far from taking us beyond experience, gives only one *part* of experience itself, the *formal* part, which belongs to it throughout, and therefore is universal, consequently mere form without content. Since now metaphysics can least of all be confined to this, it must have also *empirical* sources of knowledge; therefore that preconceived idea of a metaphysic to be found purely *a priori* is necessarily vain. It is really a *petitio principii* of Kant's, which he expresses most distinctly in § 1 of the Prolegomena, that metaphysics must not draw its fundamental conceptions and principles from experience. In this it is assumed beforehand that only what we knew *before* all experience can extend beyond all possible experience. Supported by this, Kant then comes and shows that all such knowledge is nothing more than the form of the intellect for the purpose of experience, and consequently can never lead beyond experience, from which he then rightly deduces the impossibility of all metaphysics. But does it not rather seem utterly perverse that in order to discover the secret of experience, *i. e.*, of the world which alone lies before us, we should look quite away from it, ignore its content, and take and use for its material only the empty forms of which we are conscious *a priori?* Is it not rather in keeping with the matter that *the science of experience in general,* and as such, should also be drawn from experience? Its problem itself is given it empirically; why should not the solution of it call in the assistance of experience? Is it not senseless that he who speaks of the nature of things should not look at things themselves, but should confine himself to certain abstract conceptions? The task of metaphysics is certainly not the observation of particular experiences, but yet it is the correct explanation of experience as a whole. Its foundation must therefore, at any rate, be of an empirical nature. Indeed the *a priori* nature of a part of human knowledge will be apprehended by it as a given *fact,* from which it will infer the subjective origin of the same. Only because the consciousness of its *a priori* nature accompanies it is it called by Kant *transcendental* as distinguished from *transcendent,* which signifies "passing beyond all possibility of experience," and has its opposite in *immanent, i. e.*, remaining within the limits of experience. I gladly recall the original meaning of this expression introduced by Kant, with which, as also with that of the Categories, and many others, the apes of philosophy carry on their game at the present day. Now, besides this, the source of the knowledge of metaphysics is not *outer* experience alone, but also *inner*. Indeed, what is most peculiar to it, that by which the decisive step which alone can solve the great question becomes possible for it, consists, as I have fully and thoroughly proved in "On the Will in Nature," under the heading, "Physical Astronomy," in this, that at the right place it combines outer experience with inner, and uses the latter as a key to the former.

The origin of metaphysics in empirical sources of knowledge, which is here set forth, and which cannot fairly be denied, deprives it certainly of that kind of apodictic certainty which is only possible through knowledge *a priori*. This remains the possession of logic and mathematics—sciences, however, which really only teach what every one knows already, though not distinctly. At most the primary elements of natural science may also be deduced from knowledge *a priori*. By this confession metaphysics only surrenders an ancient claim, which, according to what has been said above, rested upon misunderstanding, and against which the great diversity and changeableness of metaphysical systems, and also the constantly accompanying scepticism, in every age has testified. Yet against the possibility of metaphysics in general this changeableness cannot be urged, for the same thing affects just as much all branches of natural science, chemistry, physics, geology, zoology, &c., and even history has not remained exempt from it. But when once, as far as the limits of human intellect allow, a true system of metaphysics shall have been found, the unchangeableness of a science which is known *a priori* will yet belong to it; for its foundation can only be *experience in general*, and not the particular and special experiences by which, on the other hand, the natural sciences are constantly modified and new material is always being provided for history. For experience as a whole and in general will never change its character for a new one.

The next question is: How can a science drawn from experience pass beyond it and so merit the name of metaphysics? It cannot do so perhaps in the same way as we find a fourth number from three proportionate ones, or a triangle from two sides and an angle. This was the way of the pre-Kantian dogmatism, which, according to certain laws known to us *a priori*, sought to reason from the given to the not given, from the consequent to the reason, thus from experience to that which could not possibly be given in any experience. Kant proved the impossibility of a metaphysic upon this path, in that he showed that although these laws were not drawn from experience, they were only valid for experience. He therefore rightly taught that in such a way we cannot transcend the possibility of all experience. But there are other paths to metaphysics. The whole of experience is like a cryptograph, and philosophy the deciphering of it, the correctness of which is proved by the connection appearing everywhere. If this whole is only profoundly enough comprehended, and the inner experience is connected with the outer, it must be capable of being *interpreted, explained* from itself. Since Kant has irrefutably proved to us that experience in general proceeds from two elements, the forms of knowledge and the inner nature of things, and that these two may be distinguished in experience from each other, as that of which we are conscious *a priori* and that which is added *a posteriori*, it is possible, at least in general, to say, what in the given experience, which is primarily merely phenomenal, belongs to the *form* of this phenomenon, conditioned by the intellect, and what, after deducting this, remains over for the *thing in itself*. And although no one can discern the thing in itself through the veil of the forms of perception, on the other hand every one carries it in himself, indeed is it himself; therefore in self-consciousness it must be in some way accessible to him, even though only conditionally. Thus the bridge by which metaphysics passes beyond experience is nothing else than that analysis of experience into phenomenon and thing in itself in which I have placed Kant's greatest merit. For it contains the proof of a kernel of the phenomenon different from the phenomenon itself. This can indeed never be entirely separated from the phenomenon and regarded in itself as an *ens extramundanum,* but is always known only in its relations to and connections with the phenomenon itself. But the interpretation and explanation of the latter, in relation to the former, which is its inner kernel, is capable of affording us information with regard to it which does not otherwise come into consciousness. In this sense, then, metaphysics goes beyond the phenomenon, *i. e.,* nature, to that which is concealed in or behind it, always regarding it, however, merely as that which manifests itself in the phenomenon, not as independent of all phenomenal appearance; it therefore remains immanent, and does not become transcendent. For it never disengages itself entirely from experience, but remains merely its interpretation and explanation, since it never speaks of the thing in itself otherwise than in its relation to the phenomenon. This at least is the sense in which I, with reference throughout to the limitations of human knowledge proved by Kant, have attempted to solve the problem of metaphysics. Therefore his Prolegomena to future metaphysics will be valid and suitable for mine also. Accordingly it never really goes beyond experience, but only discloses the true understanding of the world which lies before it in experience. It is neither, according to the definition of metaphysics which even Kant repeats, a science of mere conceptions, nor is it a system of deductions from *a priori* principles, the uselessness of which for the *end* of metaphysics has been shown by

Kant. But it is rational knowledge, drawn from perception of the external actual world and the information
which the most intimate fact of self-consciousness affords us concerning it, deposited in distinct conceptions.
It is accordingly the science of experience; but its subject and its source is not particular experiences, but the
totality of all experience. I completely accept Kant's
doctrine that the world of experience is merely phenomenal, and that the *a priori* knowledge is valid only in relation to phenomena; but I add that just as phenomenal
appearance, it is the manifestation of that which appears,
and with him I call this the thing in itself. This must
therefore express its nature and character in the world
of experience, and consequently it must be possible to
interpret these from this world, and indeed from the matter, not the mere form, of experience. Accordingly philosophy is nothing but the correct and universal understanding of experience itself, the true exposition of its
meaning and content. To this the metaphysical, *i. e.,* that
which is merely clothed in the phenomenon and veiled
in its forms, is that which is related to it as thought to
words.

Such a deciphering of the world with reference to that
which manifests itself in it must receive its confirmation
from itself, through the agreement with each other in
which it places the very diverse phenomena of the world,
and which without it we do not perceive. If we find a
document the alphabet of which is unknown, we endeavour to make it out until we hit upon an hypothesis as
to the significance of the letters in accordance with
which they make up comprehensible words and connected
sentences. Then, however, there remains no doubt as to
the correctness of the deciphering, because it is not possible that the agreement and connection in which all the
letters of that writing are placed by this explanation is

merely accidental, and that by attributing quite a different value to the letters we could also recognise words and sentences in this arrangement of them. In the same way the deciphering of the world must completely prove itself from itself. It must throw equal light upon all the phenomena of the world, and also bring the most heterogeneous into agreement, so that the contradiction between those which are most in contrast may be abolished. This proof from itself is the mark of genuineness. For every false deciphering, even if it is suitable for some phenomena, will conflict all the more glaringly with the rest. So, for example, the optimism of Leibnitz conflicts with the palpable misery of existence; the doctrine of Spinoza, that the world is the only possible and absolutely necessary substance, is incompatible with our wonder at its existence and nature; the Wolfian doctrine, that man obtains his existence and essence from a will foreign to himself, is contradicted by our moral responsibility for the actions which proceed with strict necessity from these, in conflict with the motives; the oft-repeated doctrine of the progressive development of man to an ever higher perfection, or in general of any kind of becoming by means of the process of the world, is opposed to the *a priori* knowledge that at any point of time an infinite time has already run its course, and consequently all that is supposed to come with time would necessarily have already existed; and in this way an interminable list might be given of the contradictions of dogmatic assumptions with the given reality of things. On the other hand, I must deny that any doctrine of my philosophy could fairly be added to such a list, because each of them has been thought out in the presence of the perceived reality, and none of them has its root in abstract conceptions alone. There is yet in it a fundamental thought which is applied to all the phenomena of the world as their key;

but it proves itself to be the right alphabet at the application of which all words and sentences have sense and
significance. The discovered answer to a riddle shows
itself to be the right one by the fact that all that is said
in the riddle is suitable to it. In the same way my doctrine introduces agreement and connection into the confusion of the contrasting phenomena of this world, and
solves the innumerable contradictions which, when regarded from any other point of view, it presents. Therefore, so far, it is like a sum that comes out right, yet by
no means in the sense that it leaves no problem over to
solve, no possible question unanswered. To assert anything of that sort would be a presumptuous denial of the
limits of human knowledge in general. Whatever torch
we may kindle, and whatever space it may light, our
horizon will always remain bounded by profound night.
For the ultimate solution of the riddle of the world must
necessarily be concerned with the things in themselves,
no longer with the phenomena. But all our forms of
knowledge are adapted to the phenomena alone; therefore we must comprehend everything through coexistence, succession, and causal relations. These forms, however, have meaning and significance only with reference
to the phenomenon; the things in themselves and their
possible relations cannot be apprehended by means of
those forms. Therefore the actual, positive solution of
the riddle of the world must be something that human
intellect is absolutely incapable of grasping and thinking; so that if a being of a higher kind were to come and
take all pains to impart it to us, we would be absolutely
incapable of understanding anything of his expositions.
Those, therefore, who profess to know the ultimate, *i. e.*,
the first ground of things, thus a primordial being, an
absolute, or whatever else they choose to call it, together
with the process, the reasons, motives, or whatever it
may be, in consequence of which the world arises from

it, or springs, or falls, or is produced, set in existence, "discharged," and ushered forth, are playing tricks, are vain boasters, when indeed they are not charlatans.

I regard it as a great excellence of my philosophy that all its truths have been found independently of each other, by contemplation of the real world; but their unity and agreement, about which I had been unconcerned, has always afterwards appeared of itself. Hence also it is rich, and has wide-spreading roots in the ground of perceptible reality, from which all nourishment of abstract truths springs; and hence, again, it is not wearisome—a quality which, to judge from the philosophical writings of the last fifty years, one might regard as essential to philosophy. If, on the other hand, all the doctrines of a philosophy are merely deduced the one out of the other, and ultimately indeed all out of one first principle, it must be poor and meagre, and consequently wearisome, for nothing can follow from a proposition except what it really already says itself. Moreover, in this case everything depends upon the correctness of *one* proposition, and by a single mistake in the deduction the truth of the whole would be endangered. Still less security is given by the systems which start from an intellectual intuition, *i. e.,* a kind of ecstasy or clairvoyance. All knowledge so obtained must be rejected as subjective, individual, and consequently problematical. Even if it actually existed it would not be communicable, for only the normal knowledge of the brain is communicable; if it is abstract, through conceptions and words; if purely perceptible or concrete, through works of art.

If, as so often happens, metaphysics is reproached with having made so little progress, it ought also to be considered that no other science has grown up like it under constant oppression, none has been so hampered and hindered from without as it has always been by the religion of every land, which, everywhere in possession of a monopoly of metaphysical knowledge, regards metaphysics as a weed growing beside it, as an unlicensed worker, as a horde of gipsies, and as a rule tolerates it only under the condition that it accommodates itself to serve and follow it. For where has there ever been true freedom of thought? It has been vaunted sufficiently; but whenever it wishes to go further than perhaps to differ about the subordinate dogmas of the religion of the country, a holy shudder seizes the prophets of tolerance, and they say: "Not a step further!" What progress of metaphysics was possible under such oppression? Nay, this constraint which the privileged metaphysics exercises is not confined to the *communication* of thoughts, but extends to *thinking* itself, for its dogmas are so firmly imprinted in the tender, plastic, trustful, and thoughtless age of childhood, with studied solemnity and serious airs, that from that time forward they grow with the brain, and almost assume the nature of innate thoughts, which some philosophers have therefore really held them to be, and still more have pretended to do so. Yet nothing can so firmly resist the comprehension of even the *problem* of metaphysics as a previous solution of it intruded upon and early implanted in the mind. For the necessary starting-point for all genuine philosophy is the deep feeling of the Socratic: "This one thing I know, that I know nothing." The ancients were in this respect in a better position than we are, for their national religions certainly limited somewhat the imparting of thoughts; but they did not interfere with the freedom of thought itself, because they were not formally and solemnly impressed upon children, and in general were not taken so seriously. Therefore in metaphysics the ancients are still our teachers.

Whenever metaphysics is reproached with its small progress, and with not having yet reached its goal in spite of such sustained efforts, one ought further to consider that in the meanwhile it has constantly performed the invaluable service of limiting the boundless claims of the privileged metaphysics, and yet at the same time combatting naturalism and materialism proper, which are called forth by it as an inevitable reaction. Consider to what a pitch the arrogance of the priesthood of every religion would rise if the belief in their doctrines was as firm and blind as they really wish. Look back also at the wars, disturbances, rebellions, and revolutions in Europe from the eighth to the eighteenth century; how few will be found that have not had as their essence, or their pretext, some controversy about beliefs, thus a metaphysical problem, which became the occasion of exciting nations against each other. Yet is that whole thousand years a continual slaughter, now on the battlefield, now on the scaffold, now in the streets, in metaphysical interests! I wish I had an authentic list of all crimes which Christianity has really prevented, and all good deeds it has really performed, that I might be able to place them in the other scale of the balance.

Lastly, as regards the *obligations* of metaphysics, it has only one; for it is one which endures no other beside it—the obligation to be *true*. If one would impose other obligations upon it besides this, such as to be spiritualistic, optimistic, monotheistic, or even only to be moral, one cannot know beforehand whether this would not interfere with the fulfilment of that first obligation, without which all its other achievements must clearly be worthless. A given philosophy has accordingly no other standard of its value than that of truth. For the rest, philosophy is essentially *world-wisdom:* its problem is the world. It has to do with this alone, and leaves the gods in peace—expects, however, in return, to be left in peace by them.

CHAPTER XVIII[1]

ON THE POSSIBILITY OF KNOWING THE THING IN ITSELF

IN 1836 I already published, under the title "On the Will in Nature" (second ed., 1854; third ed., 1867), the most essential supplement to this book, which contains the most peculiar and important step in my philosophy, the transition from the phenomenon to the thing in itself, which Kant gave up as impossible. It would be a great mistake to regard the foreign conclusions with which I have there connected my expositions as the real material and subject of that work, which, though small as regards its extent, is of weighty import. These conclusions are rather the mere occasion starting from which I have there expounded that fundamental truth of my philosophy with so much greater clearness than anywhere else, and brought it down to the empirical knowledge of nature. And indeed this is done most exhaustively and stringently under the heading "Physical Astronomy"; so that I dare not hope ever to find a more correct or accurate expression of that core of my philosophy than is given there. Whoever desires to know my philosophy thoroughly and to test it seriously must therefore give attention before everything to that section. Thus, in general, all that is said in that little work would form the chief content of these supplements, if it had not to be excluded on account of having preceded them; but, on the other hand, I here take for granted that it is known, for otherwise the very best would be wanting.

I wish now first of all to make a few preliminary ob-

[1] This chapter is connected with § 18 of the first volume.

servations from a general point of view as to the sense in which we can speak of a knowledge of the thing in itself and of its necessary limitation.

What is *knowledge?* It is primarily and essentially *idea?* What is *idea?* A very complicated *physiological* process in the brain of an animal, the result of which is the consciousness of a *picture* there. Clearly the relation between such a picture and something entirely different from the animal in whose brain it exists can only be a very indirect one. This is perhaps the simplest and most comprehensible way of disclosing the *deep gulf between the ideal and the real.* This belongs to the things of which, like the motion of the earth, we are not directly conscious; therefore the ancients did not observe it, just as they did not observe the motion of the earth. Once pointed out, on the other hand, first by Descartes, it has ever since given philosophers no rest. But after Kant had at last proved in the most thorough manner the complete diversity of the ideal and the real, it was an attempt, as bold as it was absurd, yet perfectly correctly calculated with reference to the philosophical public in Germany, and consequently crowned with brilliant results, to try to assert the *absolute identity* of the two by dogmatic utterances, on the strength of a pretended intellectual intuition. In truth, on the contrary, a subjective and an objective existence, a being for self and a being for others, a consciousness of one's own self, and a consciousness of other things, is given us directly, and the two are given in such a fundamentally different manner that no other difference can compare with this. About himself every one knows directly, about all others only very indirectly. This is the fact and the problem.

Whether, on the other hand, through further processes in the interior of a brain, general conceptions (*Univer-*

salia) are abstracted from the perceptible ideas or images that have arisen within it, for the assistance of further combinations, whereby knowledge becomes *rational*, and is now called *thinking*—this is here no longer the essential question, but is of subordinate significance. For all such *conceptions* receive their content only from the perceptible idea, which is therefore *primary knowledge*, and has consequently alone to be taken account of in an investigation of the relation between the ideal and the real. It therefore shows entire ignorance of the problem, or at least it is very inept, to wish to define that relation as that between *being* and *thinking*. Thinking has primarily only a relation to *perceiving*, but *perception* has a relation to the *real being* of what is perceived, and this last is the great problem with which we are here concerned. Empirical being, on the other hand, as it lies before us, is nothing else than simply being given in perception; but the relation of the latter to *thinking* is no riddle, for the conceptions, thus the immediate materials of thought, are obviously *abstracted* from perception, which no reasonable man can doubt. It may be said in passing that one can see how important the choice of expressions in philosophy is from the fact that that inept expression condemned above, and the misunderstanding which arose from it, became the foundation of the whole Hegelian pseudo-philosophy, which has occupied the German public for twenty-five years.

If, however, it should be said: "The perception is itself the knowledge of the thing in itself: for it is the effect of that which is outside of us, and as this *acts*, so it *is*: its action is just its being;" to this we reply: (1.) that the law of causality, as has been sufficiently proved, is of subjective origin, as well as the sensation from which the perception arises; (2.) that at any rate time and space, in which the object presents itself, are of subjective origin; (3.) that if the being of the object consists simply in its action, this means that it consists merely in the changes which it brings about in others; therefore itself and in itself it is nothing at all. Only of *matter* is it true, that its being consists in its action, that it is through and through only causality, thus is itself causality objectively regarded; hence, however, it is also nothing in itself, but as an ingredient in the perceived object, is a mere abstraction, which for itself alone can be given in no experience. It will be fully considered later on in a chapter of its own. But the perceived object must be something *in itself,* and not merely something *for others.* For otherwise it would be altogether merely idea, and we would have an absolute idealism, which would ultimately become theoretical egoism, with which all reality disappears and the world becomes a mere subjective phantasm. If, however, without further question, we stop altogether at the *world as idea,* then certainly it is all one whether I explain objects as ideas in my head or as phenomena exhibiting themselves in time and space; for time and space themselves exist only in my head. In this sense, then, an identity of the ideal and the real might always be affirmed; only, after Kant, this would not be saying anything new. Besides this, however, the nature of things and of the phenomenal world would clearly not be thereby exhausted; but with it we would always remain still upon the ideal side. The *real* side must be something *toto genere* different from *the world as idea,* it must be that which things are *in themselves;* and it is this entire diversity between the ideal and the real which Kant has proved in the most thorough manner.

Locke had denied to the senses the knowledge of things as they are in themselves; but Kant denied this also to the perceiving *understanding,* under which name

I here comprehend what he calls the *pure* sensibility, and, as it is given *a priori,* the law of causality which brings about the empirical perception. Not only are both right, but we can also see quite directly that a contradiction lies in the assertion that a thing is known as it is in and for itself, *i. e.,* outside of knowledge. For all knowing is, as we have said, essentially a perceiving of ideas; but my perception of ideas, just because it is mine, can never be identical with the inner nature of the thing outside of me. The being in and for itself, of everything, must necessarily be *subjective;* in the idea of another, however, it exists just as necessarily as *objective* —a difference which can never be fully reconciled. For by it the whole nature of its existence is fundamentally changed; as objective it presupposes a foreign subject, as whose idea it exists, and, moreover, as Kant has shown, has entered forms which are foreign to its own nature, just because they belong to that foreign subject, whose knowledge is only possible by means of them. If I, absorbed in this reflection, perceive, let us say lifeless bodies, of easily surveyed magnitude and regular, comprehensible form, and now attempt to conceive this spatial existence, in its three dimensions, as their being in itself, consequently as the existence which to the things is subjective, the impossibility of the thing is at once apparent to me, for I can never think those objective forms as the being which to the things is subjective, rather I become directly conscious that what I there perceive is only a picture produced in my brain, and existing only for me as the knowing subject, which cannot constitute the ultimate, and therefore subjective, being in and for itself of even these lifeless bodies. But, on the other hand, I must not assume that even these lifeless bodies exist only in my idea, but, since they have inscrutable qualities, and, by virtue of these, activity, I

must concede to them a *being in itself* of some kind.
But this very inscrutableness of the properties, while,
on the one hand, it certainly points to something which
exists independently of our knowledge, gives also, on the
other hand, the empirical proof that our knowledge, because it consists simply in *framing ideas* by means of
subjective forms, affords us always mere *phenomena,*
not the true being of things. This is the explanation of
the fact that in all that we know there remains hidden
from us a certain something, as quite inscrutable, and we
are obliged to confess that we cannot thoroughly understand even the commonest and simplest phenomena. For
it is not merely the highest productions of nature, living creatures, or the *complicated* phenomena of the unorganised world that remain inscrutable to us, but even
every rock-crystal, every iron-pyrite, by reason of its
crystallographical, optical, chemical, and electrical properties, is to the searching consideration and investigation
an abyss of incomprehensibilities and mysteries. This
could not be the case if we knew things as they are in
themselves; for then at least the simpler phenomena,
the path to whose qualities was not barred for us by
ignorance, would necessarily be thoroughly comprehensible to us, and their whole being and nature would
be able to pass over into our knowledge. Thus it lies not
in the defectiveness of our acquaintance with things, but
in the nature of knowledge itself. For if our perception,
and consequently the whole empirical comprehension of
the things that present themselves to us, is already essentially and in the main determined by our faculty of
knowledge, and conditioned by its forms and functions,
it cannot but be that things exhibit themselves in a manner which is quite different from their own inner nature,
and therefore appear as in a mask, which allows us
merely to assume what is concealed beneath it, but

never to know it; hence, then, it gleams through as an inscrutable mystery, and never can the nature of anything entire and without reserve pass over into knowledge; but much less can any real thing be construed *a priori,* like a mathematical problem. Thus the empirical inscrutableness of all natural things is a proof *a posteriori* of the ideality and merely phenomenal-actuality of their empirical existence.

According to all this, upon the path of *objective knowledge,* hence starting from the *idea,* one will never get beyond the idea, *i. e.,* the phenomenon. One will thus remain at the outside of things, and will never be able to penetrate to their inner nature and investigate what they are in themselves, *i. e.,* for themselves. So far I agree with Kant. But, as the counterpart of this truth, I have given prominence to this other truth, that we are not merely the *knowing subject,* but, in another aspect, we ourselves also belong to the inner nature that is to be known, *we ourselves are the thing in itself;* that therefore a *way from within* stands open for us to that inner nature belonging to things themselves, to which we cannot penetrate *from without,* as it were a subterranean passage, a secret alliance, which, as if by treachery, places us at once within the fortress which it was impossible to take by assault from without. The thing in itself can, as such, only come into conscousness quite directly, in this way, that *it is itself conscious of itself:* to wish to know it objectively is to desire something contradictory. Everything objective is idea, therefore appearance, mere phenomenon of the brain.

Kant's chief result may in substance be thus concisely stated: "All conceptions which have not at their foundation a perception in space and time (sensuous intuition), that is to say then, which have not been drawn from such a preception, are absolutely empty, *i. e.,* give no knowledge. But since now perception can afford us only *phenomena,* not things in themselves, we have also absolutely no knowledge of things in themselves." I grant this of everything, with the single exception of the knowledge which each of us has of his own *willing:* this is neither a perception (for all perception is spatial) nor is it empty; rather it is more real than any other. Further, it is not *a priori,* like merely formal knowledge, but entirely *a posteriori;* hence also we cannot anticipate it in the particular case, but are hereby often convicted of error concerning ourselves. In fact, our *willing* is the one opportunity which we have of understanding from within any event which exhibits itself without, consequently the one thing which is known to us *immediately,* and not, like all the rest merely given in the idea. Here, then, lies the datum which alone is able to become the key to everything else, or, as I have said, the single narrow door to the truth. Accordingly we must learn to understand nature from ourselves, not conversely ourselves from nature. What is known to us immediately must give us the explanation of what we only know indirectly, not conversely. Do we perhaps understand the rolling of a ball when it has received an impulse more thoroughly than our movement when we feel a motive? Many may imagine so, but I say it is the reverse. Yet we shall attain to the knowledge that what is essential in both the occurrences just mentioned is identical; although identical in the same way as the lowest audible note of harmony is the same as the note of the same name ten octaves higher.

Meanwhile it should be carefully observed, and I have always kept it in mind, that even the inward experience which we have of our own will by no means affords us an exhaustive and adequate knowledge of the thing in itself. This would be the case if it were entirely an immediate experience; but it is effected in this way: the will, with and by means of the corporisation, provides itself also with an intellect (for the sake of its relations to the external world), and through this now knows itself as will in self-consciousness (the necessary counterpart of the external world); this knowledge therefore of the thing in itself is not fully adequate. First of all, it is bound to the form of the idea, it is apprehension, and as such falls asunder into subject and object. For even in self-consciousness the I is not absolutely simple, but consists of a knower, the intellect, and a known, the will. The former is not known, and the latter does not know, though both unite in the consciousness of an I. But just on this account that I is not thoroughly *intimate* with itself, as it were transparent, but is opaque, and therefore remains a riddle to itself, thus even in inner knowledge there also exists a difference between the true being of its object and the apprehension of it in the knowing subject. Yet inner knowledge is free from two forms which belong to outer knowledge, the form of *space* and the form of *causality,* which is the means of effecting all sense-perception. On the other hand, there still remains the form of *time,* and that of being known and knowing in general. Accordingly in this inner knowledge the thing in itself has indeed in great measure thrown off its veil, but still does not yet appear quite naked. In consequence of the form of time which still adheres to it, every one knows his will only in its successive *acts,* and not as a whole, in and for itself: therefore no one knows his character *a priori,* but only learns it through experience and always incompletely. But yet the apprehension, in which we know the affections and acts of our own will, is far more immediate than any other. It is the point at which the thing in itself most directly enters the phenomenon and is most closely examined by the knowing subject; therefore the event thus intimately known is alone fitted to become the interpreter of all others.

For in every emergence of an act of will from the obscure depths of our inner being into the knowing consciousness a direct transition occurs of the thing in itself, which lies outside time, into the phenomenal world. Accordingly the act of will is indeed only the closest and most distinct *manifestation* of the thing in itself; yet it follows from this that if all other manifestations or phenomena could be known by us as directly and inwardly, we would be obliged to assert them to be that which the will is in us. Thus in this sense I teach that the inner nature of everything is *will,* and I call will the thing in itself. Kant's doctrine of the unknowableness of the thing in itself is hereby modified to this extent, that the thing in itself is only not absolutely and from the very foundation knowable, that yet by far the most immediate of its phenomena, which by this immediateness is *toto genere* distinguished from all the rest, represents it for us; and accordingly we have to refer the whole world of phenomena to that one in which the thing in itself appears in the very thinnest of veils, and only still remains phenomenon in so far as my intellect, which alone is capable of knowledge, remains ever distinguished from me as the willing subject, and moreover does not even in *inner* perfection put off the form of knowledge of *time.*

Accordingly, even after this last and furthest step, the question may still be raised, what that will, which exhibits itself in the world and as the world, ultimately and absolutely is in itself? *i. e.,* what it is, regarded altogether apart from the fact that it exhibits itself as will, or in general *appears, i. e.,* in general is *known.* This question can never be answered: because, as we

have said, becoming known is itself the contradictory
of being in itself, and everything that is known is as
such only phenomenal. But the possibility of this question
shows that the thing in itself, which we know most
directly in the will, may have, entirely outside all possible
phenomenal appearance, ways of existing, determinations,
qualities, which are absolutely unknowable
and incomprehensible to us, and which remain as
the nature of the thing in itself, when, as is explained
in the fourth book, it has voluntarily abrogated itself
as *will*, and has therefore retired altogether from the
phenomenon, and for our knowledge, *i. e.*, as regards the
world of phenomena, has passed into empty nothingness.
If the will were simply and absolutely the thing in itself
this nothing would also be *absolute*, instead of which
it expressly presents itself to us there as only *relative*.

I now proceed to supplement with a few considerations
pertinent to the subject the exposition given both
in our second book and in the work "On the Will in
Nature," of the doctrine that what makes itself known
to us in the most immediate knowledge as will is
also that which objectifies itself at different grades in
all the phenomena of this world; and I shall begin by
citing a number of psychological facts which prove that
first of all in our own consciousness the will always appears
as primary and fundamental, and throughout asserts
its superiority to the intellect, which, on the other
hand, always presents itself as secondary, subordinate
and conditioned. This proof is the more necessary as
all philosophers before me, from the first to the last,
place the true being or the kernel of man in the *knowing*
consciousness, and accordingly have conceived and explained
the I, or, in the case of many of them, its transcendental
hypostasis called soul, as primarily and essentially
knowing, nay, *thinking*, and only in consequence

THE WORLD AS WILL AND IDEA   331

of this, secondarily and derivatively, as *willing*. This ancient and universal radical error, must before everything be set aside, and instead of it the true state of the case must be brought to perfectly distinct consciousness. Since, however, this is done here for the first time, after thousands of years of philosophising, some fulness of statement will be appropriate. The remarkable phenomenon, that in this most essential point all philosophers have erred, nay, have exactly reversed the truth, might, especially in the case of those of the Christian era, be partly explicable from the fact that they all had the intention of presenting man as distinguished as widely as possible from the brutes, yet at the same time obscurely felt that the difference between them lies in the intellect, not in the will; whence there arose unconsciously within them an inclination to make the intellect the essential and principal thing, and even to explain volition as a mere function of the intellect. Hence also the conception of a soul is not only inadmissible, because it is a transcendent hypostasis, as is proved by the "Critique of Pure Reason," but it becomes the source of irremediable errors, because in its "simple substance" it establishes beforehand an indivisible unity of knowledge and will, the separation of which is just the path to the truth. That conception must therefore appear no more in philosophy, but may be left to German doctors and physiologists, who, after they have laid aside scalpel and spattle, amuse themselves by philosophising with the conceptions they received when they were confirmed. They might certainly try their luck in England. The French physiologists and zootomists have (till lately) kept themselves free from that reproach.

The first consequence of their common fundamental error, which is very inconvenient to all these philosophers, is this: since in death the knowing consciousness obviously perishes, they must either allow death to be the annihilation of the man, to which our inner being is opposed, or they must have recourse to the assumption of a continued existence of the knowing consciousness, which requires a strong faith, for his own experience has sufficiently proved to every one the thorough and complete dependence of the knowing consciousness upon the brain, and one can just as easily believe in digestion without a stomach as in a knowing consciousness without a brain. My philosophy alone leads out of this dilemma, for it for the first time places the true being of man not in the consciousness but in the will, which is not essentially bound up with consciousness, but is related to consciousness, *i. e.*, to knowledge, as substance to accident, as something illuminated to the light, as the string to the resounding-board, and which enters consciousness from within as the corporeal world does from without. Now we can comprehend the indestructibleness of this our real kernel and true being, in spite of the evident ceasing of consciousness in death, and the corresponding non-existence of it before birth. For the intellect is as perishable as the brain, whose product or rather whose action it is. But the brain, like the whole organism, is the product or phenomenon, in short, the subordinate of the will, which alone is imperishable.

CHAPTER XLIV

THE METAPHYSICS OF THE LOVE OF THE SEXES

"Ye wise men, highly, deeply learned,
Who think it out and know,
How, when, and where do all things pair?
Why do they kiss and love?
Ye men of lofty wisdom, say
What happened to me then;
Search out and tell me where, how, when,
And why it happened thus."
                                        —BÜRGER.

WE are accustomed to see poets principally occupied
with describing the love of the sexes. This is as a rule
the chief theme of all dramatic works, tragical as well
as comical, romantic as well as classical, Indian as well
as European. Not less is it the material of by far the
largest part of lyrical and also of epic poetry, especially if we class with the latter the enormous piles of
romances which for centuries every year has produced
in all the civilised countries of Europe as regularly as
the fruits of the earth. As regards their main contents,
all these works are nothing else than many-sided brief
or lengthy descriptions of the passion we are speaking of.
Moreover, the most successful pictures of it—such, for
example, as Romeo and Juliet, *La Nouvelle Hélöise*,
and *Werther*—have gained immortal fame. Yet, when
Rochefoucauld imagines that it is the same with passionate love as with ghosts, of which every one speaks,
but which no one has seen; and Lichtenberg also in his
essay, "On the Might of Love," disputes and denies the
reality and naturalness of that passion, they are greatly
in error. For it is impossible that something which is

foreign and contrary to human nature, thus a mere imaginary caricature, could be unweariedly represented by poetic genius in all ages, and received by mankind with unaltered interest; for nothing that is artistically beautiful can be without truth:—

"Rien n'est beau que le vrai; le vrai seul est aimable."
—BOILEAU.

Certainly, however, it is also confirmed by experience, although not by the experience of every day, that that which as a rule only appears as a strong yet still controlable inclination may rise under certain circumstances to a passion which exceeds all others in vehemence, and which then sets aside all considerations, overcomes all obstacles with incredible strength and perseverance, so that for its satisfaction life is risked without hesitation, nay, if that satisfaction is still withheld, is given as the price of it. Werthers and Jacopo Ortis exist not only in romance, but every year can show at least half a dozen of them in Europe; for their sorrows find no other chroniclers than the writers of official registers or the reporters of the newspapers. Yet the readers of the police news in English and French journals will attest the correctness of my assertion. Still greater, however, is the number of those whom the same passion brings to the madhouse. Finally, every year can show cases of the double suicide of a pair of lovers who are opposed by outward circumstances. In such cases, however, it is inexplicable to me how those who, certain of mutual love, expect to find the supremest bliss in the enjoyment of this, do not withdraw themselves from all connections by taking the extremest steps, and endure all hardships, rather than give up with life a pleasure which is greater than any other they can conceive. As regards the lower grades of that passion, and the mere approaches to it, every one has them daily before his eyes, and, as long as he is not old, for the most part also in his heart.

So then, after what has here been called to mind, no one can doubt either the reality or the importance of the matter; and therefore, instead of wondering that a philosophy should also for once make its own this constant theme of all poets, one ought rather to be surprised that a thing which plays throughout so important a part in human life has hitherto practically been disregarded by philosophers altogether, and lies before us as raw material. The one who has most concerned himself with it is Plato, especially in the "Symposium" and the "Phædrus." Accordingly I have no predecessors either to make use of or to refute. The subject has pressed itself upon me objectively, and has entered of its own accord into the connection of my consideration of the world. Moreover, least of all can I hope for approbation from those who are themselves under the power of this passion, and who accordingly seek to express the excess of their feeling in the sublimest and most ethereal images. To them my view will appear too physical, too material, however metaphysical and even transcendent it may be at bottom. Meanwhile let them reflect that if the object which to-day inspires them to write madrigals and sonnets had been born eighteen years earlier it would scarcely have won a glance from them.

For all love, however ethereally it may bear itself, is rooted in the sexual impulse alone, nay, it absolutely is only a more definitely determined, specialised, and indeed in the strictest sense individualised sexual impulse. If now, keeping this in view, one considers the important part which the sexual impulse in all its degrees and nuances plays not only on the stage and in novels, but also in the real world, where, next to the love of life, it shows itself the strongest and most powerful of motives, constantly lays claim to half the powers and thoughts of the younger portion of mankind, is the ultimate goal of almost all human effort, exerts an adverse influence on the most important events, interrupts the most serious occupations every hour, sometimes embarrasses for a while even the greatest minds, does not hesitate to intrude with its trash interfering with the negotiations of statesmen and the investigations of men of learning, knows how to slip its love letters and locks of hair even into ministerial portfolios and philosophical manuscripts, and no less devises daily the most entangled and the worst actions, destroys the most valuable relationships, breaks the firmest bonds, demands the sacrifice sometimes of life or health, sometimes of wealth, rank, and happiness, nay, robs those who are otherwise honest of all conscience, makes those who have hitherto been faithful, traitors; accordingly, on the whole, appears as a malevolent demon that strives to pervert, confuse, and overthrow everything;—then one will be forced to cry, Wherefore all this noise? Wherefore the straining and storming, the anxiety and want? It is merely a question of every Hans finding his Grethe. Why should such a trifle play so important a part, and constantly introduce disturbance and confusion into the well-regulated life of man? But to the earnest investigator the spirit of truth gradually reveals the answer. It is no trifle that is in question here; on the contrary, the importance of the matter is quite proportionate to the seriousness and ardour of the effort. The ultimate end of all love affairs, whether they are played in sock or cothurnus, is really more important than all other ends of human life, and is therefore quite worthy of the profound seriousness with which every one pursues it. That which is decided by it is nothing less than *the composition of the next generation*. The *dramatis personæ* who shall appear when we are withdrawn are here determined, both as regards their existence and their nature, by these frivolous love affairs. As the being of these future persons is absolutely conditioned by our sexual impulse generally, so their nature, is determined by the individual selection in its satisfaction, *i. e.,* by sexual love, and is in every respect irrevocably fixed by this. This is the key of the problem: we shall arrive at a more accurate knowledge of it in its application if we go through the degrees of love, from the passing inclination to the vehement passion, when we shall also recognise that the difference of these grades arises from the degree of the individualisation of the choice.

The collective love affairs of the present generation taken together are accordingly, of the whole human race, the serious *meditation on the composition of the future generation*. This high importance of the matter, in which it is not a question of individual weal or woe, as in all other matters, but of the existence and special nature of the human race in future times, and therefore the will of the individual appears at a higher power as the will of the species;—this it is on which the pathetic and sublime elements in affairs of love depend, which for thousands of years poets have never wearied of representing in innumerable examples; because no theme can equal in interest this one, which stands to all others which only concern the welfare of individuals as the solid body to the surface, because it concerns the weal and woe of the species. Just on this account, then, is it so difficult to impart interest to a drama without the element of love, and, on the other hand, this theme is never worn out even by daily use.

That which presents itself in the individual consciousness as sexual impulse in general, without being directed
towards a definite individual of the other sex, is in itself, and apart from the phenomenon, simply the will to
live. But what appears in consciousness as a sexual impulse directed to a definite individual is in itself the
will to live as a definitely determined individual. Now
in this case the sexual impulse, although in itself a subjective need, knows how to assume very skilfully the
mask of an objective admiration, and thus to deceive our
consciousness; for nature requires this stratagem to attain its ends. But yet that in every case of falling in
love, however objective and sublime this admiration may
appear, what alone is looked to is the production of an
individual of a definite nature is primarily confirmed by
the fact that the essential matter is not the reciprocation
of love, but possession, *i. e.*, the physical enjoyment. The
certainty of the former can therefore by no means console us for the want of the latter; on the contrary, in
such a situation many a man has shot himself. On the
other hand, persons who are deeply in love, and can obtain no return of it, are contented with possession, *i. e.*,
with the physical enjoyment. This is proved by all forced
marriages, and also by the frequent purchase of the favour
of a woman, in spite of her dislike, by large presents or
other sacrifices, nay, even by cases of rape. That this
particular child shall be begotten is, although unknown
to the parties concerned, the true end of the whole love
story; the manner in which it is attained is a secondary
consideration. Now, however loudly persons of lofty and
sentimental soul, and especially those who are in love,
may cry out here about the gross realism of my view,
they are yet in error. For is not the definite determination of the individualities of the next generation a much
higher and more worthy end than those exuberant feel-

ings and supersensible soap bubbles of theirs? Nay, among earthly aims, can there be one which is greater or more important? It alone corresponds to the profoundness with which passionate love is felt, to the seriousness with which it appears, and the importance which it attributes even to the trifling details of its sphere and occasion. Only so far as this end is assumed as the true one do the difficulties encountered, the infinite exertions and annoyances made and endured for the attainment of the loved object, appear proportionate to the matter. For it is the future generation, in its whole individual determinateness, that presses into existence by means of those efforts and toils. Nay, it is itself already active in that careful, definite, and arbitrary choice for the satisfaction of the sexual impulse which we call love. The growing inclination of two lovers is really already the will to live of the new individual which they can and desire to produce; nay, even in the meeting of their longing glances its new life breaks out, and announces itself as a future individuality harmoniously and well composed. They feel the longing for an actual union and fusing together into a single being, in order to live on only as this; and this longing receives its fulfilment in the child which is produced by them, as that in which the qualities transmitted by them both, fused and united in one being, live on. Conversely, the mutual, decided and persistent aversion between a man and a maid is a sign that what they could produce would only be a badly organised, in itself inharmonious and unhappy being.

But, finally, what draws two individuals of different sex exclusively to each other with such power is the will to live, which exhibits itself in the whole species, and which here anticipates in the individual which these two can produce an objectification of its nature answer-

ing to its aims. This individual will have the will, or
character, from the father, the intellect from the mother,
and the corporisation from both; yet, for the most part,
the figure will take more after the father, the size after
the mother,—according to the law which comes out in
the breeding of hybrids among the brutes, and principally depends upon the fact that the size of the fœtus
must conform to the size of the uterus. Just as inexplicable as the quite special individuality of any man, which
is exclusively peculiar to him, is also the quite special
and individual passion of two lovers; indeed at bottom
the two are one and the same: the former is explicit
what the latter was implicit. The moment at which the
parents begin to love each other—to fancy each other,
as the very happy English expression has it—is really
to be regarded as the first appearance of a new individual, and, as has been said, in the meeting and fixing of
their longing glances there appears the first germ of the
new being, which certainly, like all germs, is generally
crushed out. This new individual is to a certain extent a
new (Platonic) Idea; and now, as all Ideas strive with
the greatest vehemence to enter the phenomenal world,
eagerly seizing for this end upon the matter which the
law of causality divides among them all, so also does this
particular Idea of a human individuality strive with the
greatest eagerness and vehemence towards its realisation
in the phenomenon. This eagerness and vehemence is
just the passion of the two future parents for each other.
It has innumerable degrees, the two extremes of which
may at any rate be described as the earthly and heavenly
Aphrodite; in its nature, however, it is everywhere the
same. On the other hand, it will be in degree so much
the more powerful the more *individualised* it is; that is,
the more the loved individual is exclusively suited, by
virtue of all his or her parts and qualities, to satisfy the

desire of the lover and the need established by his or her own individuality. What is really in question here will become clear in the further course of our exposition. Primarily and essentially the inclination of love is directed to health, strength, and beauty, consequently also to youth; because the will first of all seeks to exhibit the specific character of the human species as the basis of all individuality: ordinary amorousness does not go much further. To these, then, more special claims link themselves on, which we shall investigate in detail further on, and with which, when they see satisfaction before them, the passion increases. But the highest degrees of this passion spring from that suitableness of two individualities to each other on account of which the will, *i. e.,* the character, of the father and the intellect of the mother, in their connection, make up precisely that individual towards which the will to live in general which exhibits itself in the whole species feels a longing proportionate to this its magnitude, and which therefore exceeds the measure of a mortal heart, and the motives of which, in the same way, lie beyond the sphere of the individual intellect. This is thus the soul of a true and great passion. Now the more perfect is the mutual adaptation of two individuals to each other in each of the many respects which have further to be considered, the stronger will be their mutual passion. Since there do not exist two individuals exactly alike, there must be for each particular man a particular woman—always with reference to what is to be produced—who corresponds most perfectly. A really passionate love is as rare as the accident of these two meeting. Since, however, the possibility of such a love is present in every one, the representations of it in the works of the poets are comprehensible to us. Just because the passion of love really turns about that which is to be produced, and its qualities, and because its kernel lies here, a friendship without any admixture of sexual love can exist between two young and good-looking persons of different sex, on account of the agreement of their disposition, character, and mental tendencies; nay, as regards sexual love there may even be a certain aversion between them. The reason of this is to be sought in the fact that a child produced by them would have physical or mental qualities which were inharmonious; in short, its existence and nature would not answer the ends of the will to live as it exhibits itself in the species. On the other hand, in the case of difference of disposition, character, and mental tendency, and the dislike, nay, enmity, proceeding from this, sexual love may yet arise and exist; when it then blinds us to all that; and if it here leads to marriage it will be a very unhappy one.

Let us now set about the more thorough investigation of the matter. Egoism is so deeply rooted a quality of all individuals in general, that in order to arouse the activity of an individual being egoistical ends are the only ones upon which we can count with certainty. Certainly the species has an earlier, closer, and greater claim upon the individual than the perishable individuality itself. Yet when the individual has to act, and even make sacrifices for the continuance and quality of the species, the importance of the matter cannot be made so comprehensible to his intellect, which is calculated merely with regard to individual ends, as to have its proportionate effect. Therefore in such a case nature can only attain its ends by implanting a certain illusion in the individual, on account of which that which is only a good for the species appears to him as a good for himself, so that when he serves the species he imagines he is serving himself; in which process a mere chimera, which vanishes immediately afterwards, floats before him, and takes the place of a real thing as a motive. This illusion is instinct. In the great majority of cases this is to be regarded as the sense of the species, which presents what is of benefit to *it* to the will. Since, however, the will has here become individual, it must be so deluded that it apprehends through the sense of the individual what the sense of the species presents to it, thus imagines it is following individual ends while in truth it is pursuing ends which are merely general (taking this word in its strictest sense). The external phenomenon of instinct we can best observe in the brutes where its rôle is most important; but it is in ourselves alone that we arrive at a knowledge of its internal process, as of everything internal. Now it is certainly supposed that man has almost no instinct; at any rate only this, that the new-born babe seeks for and seizes the breast of its mother. But, in fact, we have a very definite, distinct, and complicated instinct, that of the selection of another individual for the satisfaction of the sexual impulse, a selection which is so fine, so serious, and so arbitrary. With this satisfaction in itself, *i. e.*, so far as it is a sensual pleasure resting upon a pressing want of the individual, the beauty or ugliness of the other individual has nothing to do. Thus the regard for this which is yet pursued with such ardour, together with the careful selection which springs from it, is evidently connected, not with the chooser himself—although he imagines it is so—but with the true end, that which is to be produced, which is to receive the type of the species as purely and correctly as possible. Through a thousand physical accidents and moral aberrations there arise a great variety of deteriorations of the human form; yet its true type, in all its parts, is always again established: and this takes place under the guidance of the sense of beauty, which always directs the sexual impulse, and without which this sinks to the level of a disgusting necessity. Accordingly,

in the first place, every one will decidedly prefer and
eagerly desire the most beautiful individuals, *i. e.*, those
in whom the character of the species is most purely impressed; but, secondly, each one will specially regard as
beautiful in another individual those perfections which
he himself lacks, nay, even those imperfections which
are the opposite of his own. Hence, for example, little
men love big women, fair persons like dark, &c., &c. The
delusive ecstasy which seizes a man at the sight of a
woman whose beauty is suited to him, and pictures to
him a union with her as the highest good, is just the *sense
of the species*, which, recognising the distinctly expressed
stamp of the same, desires to perpetuate it with this individual. Upon this decided inclination to beauty depends
the maintenance of the type of the species: hence it acts
with such great power. We shall examine specially further on the considerations which it follows. Thus what
guides man here is really an instinct which is directed
to doing the best for the species, while the man himself
imagines that he only seeks the heightening of his own
pleasure. In fact, we have in this an instructive lesson
concerning the inner nature of all instinct, which, as
here, almost always sets the individual in motion for
the good of the species. For clearly the pains with which
an insect seeks out a particular flower, or fruit, or dung,
or flesh, or, as in the case of the ichneumonidæ, the larva
of another insect, in order to deposit its eggs there only,
and to attain this end shrinks neither from trouble nor
danger, is thoroughly analogous to the pains with which
for his sexual satisfaction a man carefully chooses a woman with definite qualities which appeal to him individually, and strives so eagerly after her that in order to
attain this end he often sacrifices his own happiness in
life, contrary to all reason, by a foolish marriage, by
love affairs which cost him wealth, honour, and life, even

by crimes such as adultery or rape, all merely in order to serve the species in the most efficient way, although at the cost of the individual, in accordance with the will of nature which is everywhere sovereign. Instinct, in fact, is always an act which seems to be in accordance with the conception of an end, and yet is entirely without such a conception. Nature implants it wherever the acting individual is incapable of understanding the end, or would be unwilling to pursue it. Therefore, as a rule, it is given only to the brutes, and indeed especially to the lowest of them which have least understanding; but almost only in the case we are here considering it is also given to man, who certainly could understand the end, but would not pursue it with the necessary ardour, that is, even at the expense of his individual welfare. Thus here, as in the case of all instinct, the truth assumes the form of an illusion, in order to act upon the will. It is a voluptuous illusion which leads the man to believe he will find a greater pleasure in the arms of a woman whose beauty appeals to him than in those of any other; or which indeed, exclusively directed to a single individual, firmly convinces him that the possession of her will ensure him excessive happiness. Therefore he imagines he is taking trouble and making sacrifices for his own pleasure, while he does so merely for the maintenance of the regular type of the species, or else a quite special individuality, which can only come from these parents, is to attain to existence. The character of instinct is here so perfectly present, thus an action which seems to be in accordance with the conception of an end, and yet is entirely without such a conception, that he who is drawn by that illusion often abhors the end which alone guides it, procreation, and would like to hinder it; thus it is in the case of almost all illicit love affairs. In accordance with the character of the matter which has been explained, every lover will experience a marvellous disillusion after the pleasure he has at last attained, and will wonder that what was so longingly desired accomplishes nothing more than every other sexual satisfaction; so that he does not see himself much benefited by it. That wish was related to all his other wishes as the species is related to the individual, thus as the infinite to the finite. The satisfaction, on the other hand, is really only for the benefit of the species, and thus does not come within the consciousness of the individual, who, inspired by the will of the species, here served an end with every kind of sacrifice, which was not his own end at all. Hence, then, every lover, after the ultimate consummation of the great work, finds himself cheated; for the illusion has vanished by means of which the individual was here the dupe of the species.

But all this reflects light on the instincts and mechanical tendencies of the brutes. They also are, without doubt, involved in a kind of illusion, which deceives them with the prospect of their own pleasure, while they work so laboriously and with so much self-denial for the species, the bird builds its nest, the insect seeks the only suitable place for its eggs, or even hunts for prey which, unsuited for its own enjoyment, must be laid beside the eggs as food for the future larvæ, the bees, the wasps, the ants apply themselves to their skilful dwellings and highly complicated economy. They are all guided with certainty by an illusion, which conceals the service of the species under the mask of an egotistical end. This is probably the only way to comprehend the inner or subjective process that lies at the foundation of the manifestations of instinct. Outwardly, however, or objectively, we find in those creatures which are to a large extent governed by instinct, especially in insects, a preponderance of the ganglion system, i. e., the *subjective* nervous system, over the objective or cerebral system; from which we must conclude that they are moved, not so much by objective, proper apprehension as by subjective ideas exciting desire, which arise from the influence of the ganglion system upon the brain, and accordingly by a kind of illusion; and this will be the *physiological* process in the case of all instinct. For the sake of illustration I will mention as another example of instinct in the human species, although a weak one, the capricious appetite of women who are pregnant. It seems to arise from the fact that the nourishment of the embryo sometimes requires a special or definite modification of the blood which flows to it, upon which the food which produces such a modification at once presents itself to the pregnant woman as an object of ardent longing, thus here also an illusion arises. Accordingly woman has one instinct more than man; and the ganglion system is also much more developed in the woman.

Now that an instinct entirely directed to that which is to be produced lies at the foundation of all sexual love will receive complete confirmation from the fuller analysis of it, which we cannot therefore avoid. First of all we have to remark here that by nature man is inclined to inconstancy in love, woman to constancy. The love of the man sinks perceptibly from the moment it has obtained satisfaction; almost every other woman charms him more than the one he already possesses; he longs for variety. The love of the woman, on the other hand, increases just from that moment. This is a consequence of the aim of nature which is directed to the maintenance, and therefore to the greatest possible increase, of the species. The man can easily beget over a hundred children a year; the woman, on the contrary, with however many men, can yet only bring one child a year into the world (leaving twin births out of account). Therefore the man always looks about after other women; the woman, again, sticks firmly to the one man; for nature moves her, instinctively and without reflection, to retain the nourisher and protector of the future offspring. Accordingly faithfulness in marriage is with the man artificial, with the woman it is natural, and thus adultery on the part of the woman is much less pardonable than on the part of the man, both objectively on account of the consequences and also subjectively on account of its unnaturalness.

But in order to be thorough and gain full conviction that the pleasure in the other sex, however objective it may seem to us, is yet merely disguised instinct, *i. e.,* sense of the species, which strives to maintain its type, we must investigate more fully the considerations which guide us in this pleasure, and enter into the details of this, rarely as these details which will have to be mentioned here may have figured in a philosophical work before. These considerations divide themselves into those which directly concern the type of the species, *i. e.,* beauty, those which are concerned with physical qualities, and lastly, those which are merely relative, which arise from the requisite correction or neutralisation of the one-sided qualities and abnormities of the two individuals by each other. We shall go through them one by one.

The first consideration which guides our choice and inclination is age. Youth without beauty has still always attraction; beauty without youth has none. Clearly the unconscious end which guides us here is the possibility of reproduction in general: therefore every individual loses attraction for the opposite sex in proportion as he or she is removed from the fittest period for begetting or conceiving. The second consideration is that of health. Acute diseases only temporarily disturb us, chronic diseases or cachexia repel us, because they are transmitted to the child. The third consideration is the skeleton, because it is the basis of the type of the species. Next to age and disease nothing repels us so much as a deformed figure; even the most beautiful face cannot atone for it; on the contrary, even the ugliest face when accompanied by a straight figure is unquestionably preferred. Further, we feel every disproportion of the skeleton most strongly; for example, a stunted, dumpy, short-boned figure, and many such; also a halting gait, where it is not the result of an extraneous accident. On the other hand, a strikingly beautiful figure can make up for all defects: it enchants us. Here also comes in the great value which all attach to the smallness of the feet: it depends upon the fact that they are an essential characteristic of the species, for no animal has the tarsus and the metatarsus taken together so small as man, which accords with his upright walk; he is a plantigrade. Accordingly Jesus Sirach also says (xxvi. 23, according to the revised translation by Kraus): "A woman with a straight figure and beautiful feet is like columns of gold in sockets of silver." The teeth also are important; because they are essential for nourishment and quite specially hereditary. The fourth consideration is a certain fulness of flesh; thus a predominance of the vegetative function, of plasticity; because this promises abundant nourishment for the fœtus; hence great leanness repels us in a striking degree. A full female bosom exerts an exceptional charm upon the male sex; because, standing in direct connection with the female functions of propagation, it promises abundant nourishment to the newborn child. On the other hand, excessively fat women excite our disgust: the cause is that this indicates atrophy of the uterus, thus barrenness; which is not known by the head, but by instinct. The last consideration of all is the beauty of the face. Here also before everything else the bones are considered; therefore we look principally for a beautiful nose, and a short turned-up nose spoils everything. A slight inclination of the nose downwards or upwards has decided the happiness in life of innumerable maidens, and rightly so, for it concerns the type of the species. A small mouth, by means of small maxillæ, is very essential as specifically characteristic of the human countenance, as distinguished from the muzzle of the brutes. A receding or, as it were, cut-away chin is especially disagreeable, because a prominent chin is an exclusive characteristic of our species. Finally comes the regard for beautiful eyes and forehead; it is connected with the psychical qualities, especially the intellectual which are inherited from the mother.

The unconscious considerations which, on the other hand, the inclination of women follows naturally cannot be so exactly assigned. In general the following may be asserted: They give the preference to the age from thirty to thirty-five years, especially over that of youths who yet really present the height of human beauty. The reason is that they are not guided by taste but by instinct, which recognises in the age named the acme of reproductive power. In general they look less to beauty, especially of the face. It is as if they took it upon themselves alone to impart this to the child. They are principally won by the strength of the man, and the courage which is connected with this; for these promise the production of stronger children, and also a brave protector for them. Every physical defect of the man, every divergence from the type, may with regard to the child be removed by the woman in reproduction, through the fact that she herself is blameless in these respects, or even exceeds in the opposite direction. Only those qualities of the man have to be excepted which are peculiar to his sex, and which therefore the mother cannot give to the child: such are the manly structure of the skeleton, broad shoulders, slender hips, straight bones, muscular power, courage, beard, &c. Hence it arises that women often love ugly men, but never an unmanly man, because they cannot neutralise his defects.

The second class of the considerations which lie at the foundation of sexual love are those which regard psychical qualities. Here we shall find that the woman is throughout attracted by the qualities of the heart or character in the man, as those which are inherited from the father. The woman is won especially by firmness of will, decision, and courage, and perhaps also by honesty and good-heartedness. On the other hand, intellectual gifts exercise no direct and instinctive power over her, just because they are not inherited from the father. Want of understanding does a man no harm with women; indeed extraordinary mental endowment, or even genius, might sooner influence them unfavourably as an abnormity. Hence one often sees an ugly, stupid, and coarse fellow get the better of a cultured, able, and amiable man with women. Also marriages from love are sometimes consummated between natures which are mentally very different: for example, the man is rough, powerful, and stupid; the woman tenderly sensitive, delicately thoughtful, cultured, æsthetic, &c.; or the man is a genius and learned, the woman a goose.

The reason is, that here quite other considerations than the intellectual predominate,—those of instinct. In marriage what is looked to is not intellectual entertainment, but the production of children: it is a bond of the heart, not of the head. It is a vain and absurd pretence when women assert that they have fallen in love with the mind of a man, or else it is the over-straining of a degenerate nature. Men, on the other hand, are not determined in their instinctive love by the qualities of character of the woman; hence so many Socrateses have found their Xantippes; for example, Shakespeare, Albrecht Dürer, Byron, &c. The intellectual qualities, however, certainly influence here, because they are inherited from the mother. Yet their influence is easily outweighed by that of physical beauty, which acts directly, as concerning a more essential point. However, it happens, either from the feeling or the experience of that influence, that mothers have their daughters taught the fine arts, languages, and so forth in order to make them attractive to men, whereby they wish to assist the intellect by artificial means, just as, in case of need, they assist the hips and the bosom. Observe that here we are speaking throughout only of that entirely immediate instinctive attraction from which alone love properly so called grows. That a woman of culture and understanding prizes understanding and intellect in a man, that a man from rational reflection should test and have regard to the character of his bride, has nothing to do with the matter with which we are dealing here. Such things lie at the bottom of a rational choice in marriage, but not of the passionate love, which is our theme.

Hitherto I have only taken account of the *absolute* considerations, *i. e.,* those which hold good for every one: I come now to the *relative* considerations, which are individual, because in their case what is looked to is the rectification of the type of the species, which is already defectively presented, the correction of the divergences from it which the chooser's own person already bears in itself, and thus the return to the pure presentation of the type. Here, then, each one loves what he lacks. Starting from the individual constitution, and directed to the individual constitution, the choice which rests upon such relative considerations is much more definite, de-

cided, and exclusive than that which proceeds merely
from the absolute considerations; therefore the source
of really passionate love will lie, as a rule, in these relative considerations, and only that of the ordinary and
slighter inclination in the absolute considerations. Accordingly it is not generally precisely correct and perfect beauties that kindle great passions. For such a truly
passionate inclination to arise something is required
which can only be expressed by a chemical metaphor:
two persons must neutralise each other, like acid and
alkali, to a neutral salt. The essential conditions demanded for this are the following. First: all sex is one-
sided. This one-sidedness is more distinctly expressed in
one individual than in another; therefore in every individual it can be better supplemented and neutralised
by one than by another individual of the opposite sex,
for each one requires a one-sidedness which is the opposite of his own to complete the type of humanity in
the new individual that is to be produced, the constitution of which is always the goal toward which all tends.
Accordingly, the neutralisation of two individualities by
each other, of which we are speaking, demands that the
definite degree of *his* manhood shall exactly correspond to the definite degree of *her* womanhood; so that
the one-sidedness of each exactly annuls that of the
other. Accordingly, the most manly man will seek the most
womanly woman, and *vice versâ*, and in the same way
every individual will seek another corresponding to him
or her in degree of sex. Now how far the required relation exits between two individuals is instinctively felt
by them, and, together with the other relative considerations, lies at the foundation of the higher degrees of
love. While, therefore, the lovers speak pathetically of
the harmony of their souls, the heart of the matter is for
the most part the agreement or suitableness pointed out

here with reference to the being which is to be produced and its perfection, and which is also clearly of much more importance than the harmony of their souls, which often, not long after the marriage, resolves itself into a howling discord. Now, here come in the further relative considerations, which depend upon the fact that every one endeavours to neutralise by means of the other his weaknesses, defects, and deviations from the type, so that they will not perpetuate themselves, or even develop into complete abnormalities in the child which is to be produced. The weaker a man is as regards muscular power the more will he seek for strong women; and the woman on her side will do the same. But since now a less degree of muscular power is natural and regular in the woman, women as a rule will give the preference to strong men. Further, the size is an important consideration. Little men have a decided inclination for big women, and *vice versâ;* and indeed in a little man the preference for big women will be so much the more passionate if he himself was begotten by a big father, and only remains little through the influence of his mother; because he has inherited from his father the vascular system and its energy, which was able to supply a large body with blood. If, on the other hand, his father and grandfather were both little, that inclination will make itself less felt. At the foundation of the aversion of a big woman to big men lies the intention of nature to avoid too big a race, if with the strength which *this* woman could impart to them they would be too weak to live long. If, however, such a woman selects a big husband, perhaps for the sake of being more presentable in society, then, as a rule, her offspring will have to atone for her folly. Further, the consideration as to the complexion is very decided. Blondes prefer dark persons, or brunettes; but the latter seldom prefer the former. The

reason is, that fair hair and blue eyes are in themselves
a variation from the type, almost an abnormity, analogous to white mice, or at least to grey horses. In no part
of the world, not even in the vicinity of the pole, are
they indigenous, except in Europe, and are clearly of
Scandinavian origin. I may here express my opinion in
passing that the white colour of the skin is not natural
to man, but that by nature he has a black or brown skin,
like our forefathers the Hindus; that consequently a
white man has never originally sprung from the womb
of nature, and that thus there is no such thing as a
white race, much as this is talked of, but every white
man is a faded or bleached one. Forced into the strange
world, where he only exists like an exotic plant, and like
this requires in winter the hothouse, in the course of
thousands of years man became white. The gipsies, an
Indian race which immigrated only about four centuries
ago, show the transition from the complexion of the
Hindu to our own. Therefore in sexual love nature
strives to return to dark hair and brown eyes as the
primitive type; but the white colour of the skin has become a second nature, though not so that the brown of
the Hindu repels us. Finally, each one also seeks in the
particular parts of the body the corrective of his own
defects and aberrations, and does so the more decidedly
the more important the part is. Therefore snub-nosed
individuals have an inexpressible liking for hook-noses,
parrot-faces; and it is the same with regard to all other
parts. Men with excessively slim, long bodies and limbs
can find beauty in a body which is even beyond measure stumpy and short. The considerations with regard
to temperament act in an analogous manner. Each will
prefer the temperament opposed to his own; yet only in
proportion as his one is decided. Whoever is himself in
some respect very perfect does not indeed seek and love

imperfection in this respect, but is yet more easily reconciled to it than others; because he himself insures the children against great imperfection of this part. For example, whoever is himself very white will not object to a yellow complexion; but whoever has the latter will find dazzling whiteness divinely beautiful. The rare case in which a man falls in love with a decidedly ugly woman occurs when, besides the exact harmony of the degree of sex explained above, the whole of her abnormities are precisely the opposite, and thus the corrective, of his. The love is then wont to reach a high degree.

The profound seriousness with which we consider and ponder each bodily part of the woman, and she on her part does the same, the critical scrupulosity with which we inspect a woman who begins to please us, the capriciousness of our choice, the keen attention with which the bridegroom observes his betrothed, his carefulness not to be deceived in any part, and the great value which he attaches to every excess or defect in the essential parts, all this is quite in keeping with the importance of the end. For the new being to be produced will have to bear through its whole life a similar part. For example, if the woman is only a little crooked, this may easily impart to her son a hump, and so in all the rest. Consciousness of all this certainly does not exist. On the contrary, every one imagines that he makes that careful selection in the interest of his own pleasure (which at bottom cannot be interested in it at all); but he makes it precisely as, under the presupposition of his own corporisation, is most in keeping with the interest of the species, to maintain the type of which as pure as possible is the secret task. The individual acts here, without knowing it, by order of something higher than itself, the species; hence the importance which it attaches to things which may and indeed must be, indifferent to itself as such. There is something quite peculiar in the profound unconscious seriousness with which two young persons of opposite sex who see each other for the first time regard each other, in the searching and penetrating glance they cast at one another, in the careful review which all the features and parts of their respective persons have to endure. This investigating and examining is the *meditation of the genius of the species* on the individual which is possible through these two and the combination of its qualities. According to the result of this meditation is the degree of their pleasure in each other and their yearning for each other. This yearning, even after it has attained a considerable degree, may be suddenly extinguished again by the discovery of something that had previously remained unobserved. In this way, then, the genius of the species meditates concerning the coming race in all who are capable of reproduction. The nature of this race is the great work with which Cupid is occupied, unceasingly active, speculating, and pondering. In comparison with the importance of his great affair, which concerns the species and all coming races, the affairs of individuals in their whole ephemeral totality are very trifling; therefore he is always ready to sacrifice these regardlessly. For he is related to them as an immortal to mortals, and his interests to theirs as infinite to finite. Thus, in the consciousness of managing affairs of a higher kind than all those which only concern individual weal or woe, he carries them on sublimely, undisturbed in the midst of the tumult of war, or in the bustle of business life, or during the raging of a plague, and pursues them even into the seclusion of the cloister.

We have seen in the above that the intensity of love increases with its individualisation, because we have shown that the physical qualities of two individuals can be such that, for the purpose of restoring as far as possible the type of the species, the one is quite specially and perfectly the completion or supplement of the other, which therefore desires it exclusively. Already in this case a considerable passion arises, which at once gains a nobler and more sublime appearance from the fact that it is directed to an individual object, and to it alone; thus, as it were, arises at the special order of the species. For the opposite reason, the mere sexual impulse is ignoble, because without individualisation it is directed to all, and strives to maintain the species only as regards quantity, with little respect to quality. But the individualising, and with it the intensity of the love, can reach so high a degree that without its satisfaction all the good things in the world, and even life itself, lose their value. It is then a wish which attains a vehemence that no other wish ever reaches, and therefore makes one ready for any sacrifice, and in case its fulfilment remains unalterably denied, may lead to madness or suicide. At the foundation of such an excessive passion there must lie, besides the considerations we have shown above, still others which we have not thus before our eyes. We must therefore assume that here not only the corporisation, but the *will* of the man and the *intellect* of the woman are specially suitable to each other, in consequence of which a perfectly definite individual can be produced by them alone, whose existence the genius of the species has here in view, for reasons which are inaccessible to us, since they lie in the nature of the thing in itself. Or, to speak more exactly, the will to live desires here to objectify itself in a perfectly definite individual, which can only be produced by this father with this mother. This metaphysical desire of the will in itself has primarily no other sphere of action in the series of existences than the hearts of the future parents, which accordingly are seized with this ardent longing, and now imagine themselves to desire on their own account what really for the present has only a purely metaphysical end, *i. e.*, an end which lies outside the series of actually existing things. Thus it is the ardent longing to enter existence of the future individual which has first become possible here, a longing which proceeds from the primary source of all being, and exhibits itself in the phenomenal world as the lofty passion of the future parents for each other, paying little regard to all that is outside itself; in fact, as an unparalleled illusion, on account of which such a lover would give up all the good things of this world to enjoy the possession of this woman, who yet can really give him nothing more than any other. That yet it is just this possession that is kept in view here is seen from the fact that even this lofty passion, like all others, is extinguished in its enjoyment—to the great astonishment of those who are possessed by it. It also becomes extinct when, through the woman turning out barren (which, according to Hufeland, may arise from nineteen accidental constitutional defects), the real metaphysical end is frustrated; just as daily happens in millions of germs trampled under foot, in which yet the same metaphysical life principle strives for existence; for which there is no other consolation than that an infinity of space, time, and matter, and consequently inexhaustible opportunity for return, stands open to the will to live.

The longing of love, which the poets of all ages are unceasingly occupied with expressing in innumerable forms, and do not exhaust the subject, nay, cannot do it justice, this longing, which attaches the idea of endless happiness to the possession of a particular woman, and unutterable pain to the thought that this possession cannot be attained,—this longing and this pain cannot obtain their material from the wants of an ephemeral individual; but they are the sighs of the spirit of the species, which sees here, to be won or lost, a means for the attainment of its ends which cannot be replaced, and therefore groans deeply. The species alone has infinite life, and therefore is capable of infinite desires, infinite satisfaction, and infinite pain. But these are here imprisoned in the narrow breast of a mortal. No wonder, then, if such a breast seems like to burst, and can find no expression for the intimations of infinite rapture or infinite misery with which it is filled. This, then, affords the materials for all erotic poetry of a sublime kind, which accordingly rises into transcendent metaphors, soaring above all that is earthly. This is the theme of Petrarch, the material for the St. Preuxs, Werthers, and Jacopo Ortis, who apart from it could not be understood nor explained. For that infinite esteem for the loved one cannot rest upon some spiritual excellences, or in general upon any objective, real qualities of hers; for one thing, because she is often not sufficiently well known to the lover, as was the case with Petrarch. The spirit of the species alone can see at one glance what *worth* she has for *it*, for its ends. And great passions also arise, as a rule, at the first glance:

"Who ever loved that loved not at first sight?"
—SHAKESPEARE, "As You Like It," iii, 5.

Here, honour, which hitherto outweighed every interest, is beaten out of the field as soon as sexual love, *i. e.*, the interest of the species, comes into play, and sees before it a decided advantage; for this is infinitely superior to every interest of mere individuals, however important it may be. Therefore to this alone honour, duty, and fidelity yield after they have withstood every other temptation, including the threat of death. In the same way we find in private life that conscientiousness is in no point so rare as in this: it is here sometimes set aside even by persons who are otherwise honest and just, and adultery is recklessly committed when passionate love, *i. e.*, the interest of the species, has mastered them. It even seems as if in this they believed themselves to be conscious of a higher right than the interests of individuals can ever confer; just because they act in the interest of the species. Whoever is inclined to be incensed at this should be referred to the remarkable indulgence which the Saviour shows in the Gospel to the woman taken in adultery, in that He also assumes the same guilt in the case of all present. From this point of view the greater part of the "Decameron" appears as mere mocking and jeering of the genius of the species at the rights and interests of individuals which it tramples under foot. Differences of rank and all similar circumstances, when they oppose the union of passionate lovers, are set aside with the same ease and treated as nothing by the genius of the species, which, pursuing its ends that concern innumerable generations, blows off as spray such human laws and scruples. From the same deep-lying grounds, when the ends of passionate love are concerned, every danger is willingly encountered, and those who are otherwise timorous here become courageous. In plays and novels also we see, with ready sympathy, the young persons who are fighting the battle of their love, *i. e.*, the interest of the species, gain the victory over their elders, who are thinking only of the welfare of the individuals. For the efforts of the lovers appear to us as much more important, sublime, and therefore right, than anything that can be opposed to them, as the species is more important than the individual. Accordingly the fundamental theme of almost all comedies is the appearance of the genius of the species with its aims, which are opposed to the personal interest of the individuals presented, and therefore threaten to undermine their happiness. As a rule it attains its end, which, as in accordance with poetical justice, satisfies the spectator, because he feels that the aims of the species are much to be preferred to those of the individual. Therefore at the conclusion he leaves the victorious lovers quite confidently, because he shares with them the illusion that they have founded their own happiness, while they have rather sacrificed it to the choice of the species, against the will and foresight of their elders. It has been attempted in single, abnormal comedies to reverse the matter and bring about the happiness of the individuals at the cost of the aims of the species; but then the spectator feels the pain which the genius of the species suffers, and is not consoled by the advantages which are thereby assured to the individuals. As examples of this kind two very well-known little pieces occur to me: "*La reine de 16 ans*," and "*Le marriage de raison.*" In tragedies containing love affairs, since the aims of the species are frustrated, the lovers who were its tools, generally perish also; for example, in "Romeo and Juliet," "Tancred," "Don Carlos," "Wallenstein," "The Bride of Messina," and many others.

The love of a man often affords comical, and sometimes also tragical phenomena; both because, taken possession of by the spirit of the species, he is now ruled by this, and no longer belongs to himself; his conduct thereby becomes unsuited to the individual. That which in the higher grades of love imparts such a tinge of poetry and sublimeness to his thoughts, which gives them even a transcendental and hyperphysical tendency, on account of which he seems to lose sight altogether of his real, very physical aim, is at bottom this, that he is now inspired by the spirit of the species whose affairs are infinitely more important than all those which concern mere individuals, in order to found under the special directions of this spirit the whole existence of an indefinitely

long posterity with this individual and exactly determined nature, which it can receive only from him as
father and the woman he loves as mother, and which
otherwise could never, *as such*, attain to existence, while
the objectification of the will to live expressly demands
this existence. It is the feeling that he is acting in affairs
of such transcendent importance which raises the lover
so high above everything earthly, nay, even above himself, and gives such a hyperphysical clothing to his very
physical desires, that love becomes a poetical episode
even in the life of the most prosaic man; in which last
case the matter sometimes assumes a comical aspect.
That mandate of the will which objectifies itself in the
species exhibits itself in the consciousness of the lover
under the mask of the anticipation of an infinite blessedness which is to be found for him in the union with this
female individual. Now, in the highest grades of love
this chimera becomes so radiant that if it cannot be attained life itself loses all charm, and now appears so
joyless, hollow, and insupportable that the disgust at it
even overcomes the fear of death, so that it is then sometimes voluntarily cut short. The will of such a man has
been caught in the vortex of the will of the species, or
this has obtained such a great predominance over the individual will that if such a man cannot be effective in the
first capacity, he disdains to be so in the last. The individual is here too weak a vessel to be capable of enduring the infinite longing of the will of the species concentrated upon a definite object. In this case, therefore, the
issue is suicide, sometimes the double suicide of the two
lovers; unless, to save life, nature allows madness to in-
tervene, which then covers with its veil the consciousness
of that hopeless state. No year passes without proving
the reality of what has been expounded by several cases
of all these kinds.

Not only, however, has the unsatisfied passion of love sometimes a tragic issue, but the satisfied passion also leads oftener to unhappiness than to happiness. For its demands often conflict so much with the personal welfare of him who is concerned that they undermine it, because they are incompatible with his other circumstances, and disturb the plan of life built upon them. Nay, not only with external circumstances is love often in contradiction, but even with the lover's own individuality, for it flings itself upon persons who, apart from the sexual relation, would be hateful, contemptible, and even abhorrent to the lover. But so much more powerful is the will of the species than that of the individual that the lover shuts his eyes to all those qualities which are repellent to him, overlooks all, ignores all, and blinds himself for ever to the object of his passion—so entirely is he blinded by that illusion, which vanishes as soon as the will of the species is satisfied, and leaves behind a detested companion for life. Only from this can it be explained that we often see very reasonable and excellent men bound to termagants and she-devils, and cannot conceive how they could have made such a choice. On this account the ancients represented love as blind. Indeed, a lover may even know distinctly and feel bitterly the faults of temperament and character of his bride, which promise him a miserable life, and yet not be frightened away:—

> "I ask not, I care not,
>   If guilt's in thy heart,
> I know that I love thee
>   Whatever thou art."

For ultimately he seeks not his own things, but those of a third person, who has yet to come into being, although he is involved in the illusion that what he seeks is his own affair. But it is just this not seeking of one's own

things which is everywhere the stamp of greatness, that
gives to passionate love also a touch of sublimity, and
makes it a worthy subject of poetry. Finally, sexual love
is compatible even with the extremest hatred towards its
object: therefore Plato has compared it to the love of the
wolf for the sheep. This case appears when a passionate
lover, in spite of all efforts and entreaties, cannot obtain
a favourable hearing on any condition:—

> "I love and hate her."
> —SHAKESPEARE, *Cymb.*, iii., 5.

The hatred of the loved one which then is kindled sometimes goes so far that the lover murders her, and then
himself. One or two examples of this generally happen
every year; they will be found in the newspapers. Therefore Goethe's lines are quite correct:—

> "By all despised love! By hellish element!
> Would that I knew a worse, that I might swear by!"

It is really no hyperbole if a lover describes the coldness
of his beloved and the delight of her vanity, which feeds
on his sufferings, as cruelty; for he is under the influence
of an impulse which, akin to the instinct of insects, compels him, in spite of all grounds of reason, to pursue his
end unconditionally, and to undervalue everything else:
he cannot give it up. Not one but many a Petrarch has
there been who was compelled to drag through life the
unsatisfied ardour of love, like a fetter, an iron weight at
his foot, and breathe his sighs in lonely woods; but only
in the one Petrarch dwelt also the gift of poetry; so that
Goethe's beautiful lines hold good of him:—

> "And when in misery the man was dumb
> A god gave me the power to tell my sorrow."

In fact, the genius of the species wages war throughout with the guardian geniuses of individuals, is their pursuer and enemy, always ready relentlessly to destroy personal happiness in order to carry out its ends; nay, the welfare of whole nations has sometimes been sacrificed to its humours. An example of this is given us by Shakespeare in "Henry VI.," pt. iii., act 3, sc. 2 and 3. All this depends upon the fact that the species, as that in which the root of our being lies, has a closer and earlier right to us than the individual; hence its affairs take precedence. From the feeling of this the ancients personified the genius of the species in Cupid, a malevolent, cruel, and therefore ill-reputed god, in spite of his childish appearance; a capricious, despotic demon, but yet lord of gods and men. A deadly shot, blindness, and wings are his attributes. The latter signify inconstancy; and this appears, as a rule, only with the disillusion which is the consequence of satisfaction.

Because the passion depended upon an illusion, which represented that which has only value for the species as valuable for the individual, the deception must vanish after the attainment of the end of the species. The spirit of the species which took possession of the individual sets it free again. Forsaken by this spirit, the individual falls back into its original limitation and narrowness, and sees with wonder that after such a high, heroic, and infinite effort nothing has resulted for its pleasure but what every sexual gratification affords. Contrary to expectation, it finds itself no happier than before. It observes that it has been the dupe of the will of the species. Therefore, as a rule, a Theseus who has been made happy will forsake his Ariadne. If Petrarch's passion had been satisfied, his song would have been silenced from that time forth, like that of the bird as soon as the eggs are laid.

Marriages from love are made in the interest of the species, not of the individuals. Certainly the persons concerned imagine they are advancing their own happiness; but their real end is one which is foreign to themselves, for it lies in the production of an individual which is only possible through them. Brought together by this aim, they ought henceforth to try to get on together as well as possible. But very often the pair brought together by that instinctive illusion, which is the essence of passionate love, will, in other respects, be of very different natures. This comes to light when the illusion vanishes, as it necessarily must. Accordingly love marriages, as a rule, turn out unhappy; for through them the coming generation is cared for at the expense of the present. *"Quien se casa por amores, ha de vivir con dolores"* (Who marries from love must live in sorrow), says the Spanish proverb. The opposite is the case with marriages contracted for purposes of convenience, generally in accordance with the choice of the parents. The considerations prevailing here, of whatever kind they may be, are at least real, and cannot vanish of themselves. Through them, however, the happiness of the present generation is certainly cared for, to the disadvantage of the coming generation, and notwithstanding this it remains problematical. The man who in his marriage looks to money more than to the satisfaction of his inclination lives more in the individual than in the species; which is directly opposed to the truth; hence it appears unnatural, and excites a certain contempt. A girl who, against the advice of her parents, rejects the offer of a rich and not yet old man, in order, setting aside all considerations of convenience, to choose according to her instinctive inclination alone, sacrifices her individual welfare to the species. But just on this account one cannot withhold from her a certain approbation; for she has preferred what is of most importance, and has acted in the spirit of nature (more exactly, of the species), while the parents advised in the spirit of individual egoism. In accordance with all this, it appears as if in making a marriage either the individual or the interests of the species must come off a loser. And this is generally the case; for that convenience and passionate love should go hand in hand is the rarest of lucky accidents. The physical, moral, or intellectual deficiency of the nature of most men may to some extent have its ground in the fact that marriages are ordinarily entered into not from pure choice and inclination, but from all kinds of external considerations, and on account of accidental circumstances. If, however, besides convenience, inclination is also to a certain extent regarded, this is, as it were, an agreement with the genius of the species. Happy marriages are well known to be rare; just because it lies in the nature of marriage that its chief end is not the present but the coming generation. However, let me add, for the consolation of tender, loving natures, that sometimes passionate sexual love associates itself with a feeling of an entirely different origin—real friendship based upon agreement of disposition, which yet for the most part only appears when sexual love proper is extinguished in its satisfaction. This friendship will then generally spring from the fact that the supplementing and corresponding physical, moral, and intellectual qualities of the two individuals, from which sexual love arose, with reference to the child to be produced, are, with reference also to the individuals themselves, related to each other in a supplementary manner as opposite qualities of temperament and mental gifts, and thereby form the basis of a harmony of disposition.

The whole metaphysics of love here dealt with stands in close connection with my metaphysics in general, and the light which it throws upon this may be summed up as follows:

We have seen that the careful selection for the satisfaction of the sexual impulse, a selection which rises through innumerable degrees up to that of passionate love, depends upon the highly serious interest which man takes in the special personal constitution of the next generation. Now this exceedingly remarkable interest confirms two truths which have been set forth in the preceding chapters. (1) The indestructibility of the true nature of man, which lives on in that coming generation. For that interest which is so lively and eager, and does not spring from reflection and intention, but from the inmost characteristics and tendencies of our nature, could not be so indelibly present and exercise such great power over man if he were absolutely perishable, and were merely followed in time by a race actually and entirely different from him. (2) That his true nature lies more in the species than in the individual. For that interest in the special nature of the species, which is the root of all love, from the passing inclination to the serious passion, is for every one really the highest concern, the success or failure of which touches him most sensibly; therefore it is called *par excellence* the affair of the heart. Moreover, when this interest has expressed itself strongly and decidedly, everything which merely concerns one's own person is postponed and necessarily sacrificed to it. Through this, then, man shows that the species lies closer to him than the individual, and he lives more immediately in the former than in the latter. Why does the lover hang with complete abandonment on the eyes of his chosen one, and is ready to make every sacrifice for her? Because it is his immortal part that longs after her; while it is only his mortal part that desires everything else. That vehement or intense longing directed to a particular

woman is accordingly an immediate pledge of the indestructibility of the kernel of our being, and of its continued existence in the species. But to regard this continued existence as something trifling and insufficient is
an error which arises from the fact that under the conception of the continued life of the species one thinks
nothing more than the future existence of beings similar
to us, but in no regard identical with us; and this again
because, starting from knowledge directed towards without, one takes into consideration only the external form
of the species as we apprehend it in perception, and not
its inner nature. But it is just this inner nature which
lies at the foundation of our own consciousness as its
kernel, and hence indeed is more immediate than this itself, and, as thing in itself, free from the principle of
individuation, is really the same and identical in all individuals, whether they exist together or after each other.
Now this is the will to live, thus just that which desires
life and continuance so vehemently. This accordingly is
spared and unaffected by death. It can attain to no better
state than its present one; and consequently for it, with
life, the constant suffering and striving of the individuals
is certain. To free it from this is reserved for the denial
of the will to live, as the means by which the individual
will breaks away from the stem of the species, and surrenders that existence in it. We lack conceptions for that
which it now is; indeed all data for such conceptions are
wanting. We can only describe it as that which is free to
be will to live or not. Buddhism denotes the latter case
by the word Nirvana. It is the point which remains for
ever unattainable to all human knowledge, just as such.

If now, from the standpoint of this last consideration,
we contemplate the turmoil of life, we behold all occupied
with its want and misery, straining all their powers to
satisfy its infinite needs and to ward off its multifarious

sorrows, yet without daring to hope anything else than simply the preservation of this tormented existence for a short span of time. In between, however, in the midst of the tumult, we see the glances of two lovers meet longingly: yet why so secretly, fearfully, and stealthily? Because these lovers are the traitors who seek to perpetuate the whole want and drudgery, which would otherwise speedily reach an end; this they wish to frustrate, as others like them have frustrated it before.

CHAPTER L

EPIPHILOSOPHY

AT the conclusion of my exposition a few reflections concerning my philosophy itself may find their place. My
philosophy does not pretend to explain the existence of
the world in its ultimate grounds: it rather sticks to the
facts of external and internal experience as they are accessible to every one, and shows the true and deepest
connection of them without really going beyond them to
any extra-mundane things and their relations to the
world. It therefore arrives at no conclusions as to what
lies beyond all possible experience, but affords merely an
exposition of what is given in the external world and in
self-consciousness, thus contents itself with comprehending the nature of the world in its inner connection with
itself. It is consequently *immanent,* in the Kantian sense
of the word. But just on this account it leaves many questions untouched; for example, why what is proved as
a fact is as it is and not otherwise, &c. All such questions,
however, or rather the answers to them, are really transcendent, *i. e.,* they cannot be thought by the forms and
functions of our intellect, do not enter into these; it is
therefore related to them as our sensibility is related to
the possible properties of bodies for which we have no
senses. After all my explanations one may still ask, for
example, whence has sprung this will that is free to assert itself, the manifestation of which is the world, or to
deny itself, the manifestation of which we do not know.
What is the fatality lying beyond all experience which
has placed it in the very doubtful dilemma of either appearing as a world in which suffering and death reign,

or else denying its very being?—or again, what can have prevailed upon it to forsake the infinitely preferable peace of blessed nothingness? An individual will, one may add, can only turn to its own destruction through error in the choice, thus through the fault of knowledge; but the will in itself, before all manifestation, consequently still without knowledge, how could it go astray and fall into the ruin of its present condition? Whence in general is the great discord that permeates this world? It may, further, be asked how deep into the true being of the world the roots of individuality go; to which it may certainly be answered: they go as deep as the assertion of the will to live; where the denial of the will appears they cease, for they have arisen with the assertion. But one might indeed even put the question, "What would I be if I were not will to live?" and more of the same kind. To all such questions we would first have to reply that the expression of the most universal and general form of our intellect is the *principle of sufficient reason;* but that just on this account that principle finds application only to the phenomenon, not to the being in itself of things. Yet all whence and why depend upon that principle alone. As a result of the Kantian philosophy it is no longer an *æterna veritas,* but merely the form, *i. e.,* the function, of our intellect, which is essentially cerebral, and originally a mere tool in the service of the will, which it therefore presupposes together with all its objectifications. But our whole knowing and conceiving is bound to its forms; accordingly we must conceive everything in time, consequently as a before and after, then as cause and effect, and also as above and below, whole and part, &c., and cannot by any means escape from this sphere in which all possibility of our knowledge lies. Now these forms are utterly unsuited to the problems raised here, nor are they fit or able to comprehend their solution even if it were given. Therefore with our intellect, this mere tool of the will, we are everywhere striking upon insoluble problems, as against the walls of our prison. But, besides this, it may at least be assumed as probable that not only *for us* is knowledge of all that has been asked about impossible, but no such knowledge is possible in general, thus never and in no way; that these relations are not only relatively but absolutely insusceptible of investigation; that not only does no one know them, but that they are in themselves unknowable, because they do not enter into the form of knowledge in general. For knowableness in general, with its most essential, and therefore constantly necessary form of subject and object, belongs merely to the phenomenal appearance, not to the being in itself of things. Where knowledge, and consequently idea, is, there is also only phenomenon, and we stand there already in the province of the phenomenal; nay, knowledge in general is known to us only as a phenomenon of brain, and we are not only unjustified in conceiving it otherwise, but also incapable of doing so. What the world is as world may be understood: it is phenomenal manifestation; and we can know that which manifests itself in it, directly from ourselves, by means of a thorough analysis of self-consciousness. Then, however, by means of this key to the nature of the world, the whole phenomenal manifestation can be deciphered, as I believe I have succeeded in doing. But if we leave the world in order to answer the questions indicated above, we have also left the whole sphere in which, not only connection according to reason and consequent, but even knowledge itself is possible. The nature of things before or beyond the world, and consequently beyond the will, is open to no investigation; because knowledge in general is itself only a phenomenon, and therefore exists only in the world as the world exists only in it. The inner being in itself of things is nothing that knows, no intellect, but an unconscious; knowledge is only added as an accident, a means of assistance to the phenomenon of that inner being, and can therefore apprehend that being itself only in proportion to its own nature, which is designed with reference to quite different ends (those of the individual will), consequently very imperfectly. Here lies the reason why a perfect understanding of the existence, nature, and origin of the world, extending to its ultimate ground and satisfying all demands, is impossible. So much as to the limits of my philosophy, and indeed of all philosophy.

The "One and All," *i. e.*, that the inner nature in all things is absolutely one and the same, my age had already grasped and understood, after the Eleatics, Scotus Erigena, Giordano Bruno, and Spinoza had thoroughly taught, and Schelling had revived this doctrine. But *what* this one is, and how it is able to exhibit itself as the many, is a problem the solution of which is first found in my philosophy. Certainly from the most ancient times man had been called the microcosm. I have reversed the proposition, and shown the world as the macranthropos: because will and idea exhaust its nature as they do that of man. But it is clearly more correct to learn to understand the world from man than man from the world; for one has to explain what is indirectly given, thus external perception from what is directly given, thus self-consciousness—not conversely.

With the Pantheists, then, I have certainly that "One and All" in common, but not the "All God"; because I do not go beyond experience (taken in its widest sense), and still less do I put myself in contradiction with the data which lie before me. Scotus Erigena, quite consistently with the spirit of Pantheism, explains every phenomenon as a theophany; but then this conception must also be applied to the most terrible and abominable phenomena. Fine theophanies! What further distinguishes me from Pantheism is principally the following: (1) That their "God" is an x, an unknown quantity; the will, on the other hand, is of all possible things the one that is known to us most exactly, the only thing given immediately, and therefore exclusively fitted for the explanation of the rest. For what is unknown must always be explained by what is better known; not conversely. (2) That their "God" manifests himself to unfold his glory, or, indeed, to let himself be admired. Apart from the vanity here attributed to him, they are placed in the position of being obliged to sophisticate away the colossal evil of the world; but the world remains in glaring and terrible contradiction with that imagined excellence. With me, on the contrary, the *will* arrives through its objectification however this may occur, at self-knowledge, whereby its abolition, conversion, salvation becomes possible. And accordingly, with me alone ethics has a sure foundation and is completely worked out in agreement with the sublime and profound religions, Brahmanism, Buddhism, and Christianity, not merely with Judaism and Mohammedanism. The metaphysic of the beautiful also is first fully cleared up as a result of my fundamental truth, and no longer requires to take refuge behind empty words. With me alone is the evil of the world honestly confessed in its whole magnitude: this is rendered possible by the fact that the answer to the question as to its origin coincides with the answer to the question as to the origin of the world. On the other hand, in all other systems, since they are all optimistic, the question as to the origin of evil is the incurable disease, ever breaking out anew, with which they are affected, and in consequence of which they struggle along with palliatives and quack remedies. (3) That I start from experience and the natural self-consciousness given to every one, and lead to

the will as that which alone is metaphysical; thus I adopt
the ascending, analytical method. The Pantheists, again,
adopt the opposite method, the descending or synthetical.
They start from their "God," which they beg or take by
force, although sometimes under the name substance, or
absolute, and this unknown is then supposed to explain
everything that is better known. (4) That with me the
world does not fill the whole possibility of all being, but
in this there still remains much room for that which we
denote only negatively as the denial of the will to live.
Pantheism, on the other hand, is essentially optimism:
but if the world is what is best, then the matter may rest
there. (5) That to the Pantheists the perceptible world,
thus the world of idea, is just the intentional manifestation of the God indwelling in it, which contains no real
explanation of its appearance, but rather requires to be
explained itself. With me, on the other hand, the world
as idea appears merely *per accidens,* because the intellect, with its external perception, is primarily only the
medium of motives for the more perfect phenomena of
will, which gradually rises to that objectivity of perceptibility, in which the world exists. In this sense its origin,
as an object of perception, is really accounted for, and
not, as with the Pantheists, by means of untenable fictions.

Since, in consequence of the Kantian criticism of all
speculative theology, the philosophers of Germany almost all threw themselves back upon Spinoza, so that the
whole series of futile attempts known by the name of
the post-Kantian philosophy are simply Spinozism taste-
lessly dressed up, veiled in all kinds of unintelligible language, and otherwise distorted, I wish, now that I have
explained the relation of my philosophy to Pantheism in
general, to point out its relation to Spinozism in particular. It stands, then, to Spinozism as the New Testament

stands to the Old. What the Old Testament has in common with the New is the same God-Creator. Analogous to this, the world exists, with me as with Spinoza, by its inner power and through itself. But with Spinoza his eternal substance, the inner nature of the world, which he himself calls God, is also, as regards its moral character and worth, Jehovah, the God-Creator, who applauds His own creation, and finds that all is very good. Spinoza has deprived Him of nothing but personality. Thus, according to him also, the world and all in it is wholly excellent and as it ought to be; he is even to rejoice in his life as long as it lasts; entirely in accordance with Ecclesiastes ix, 7–10. In short, it is optimism: therefore its ethical side is weak, as in the Old Testament; nay, it is even false, and in part revolting. With me, on the other hand, the will, or the inner nature of the world, is by no means Jehovah, it is rather, as it were, the crucified Saviour, or the crucified thief, according as it resolves. Therefore my ethical teaching agrees with that of Christianity, completely and in its highest tendencies, and not less with that of Brahmanism and Buddhism. Spinoza could not get rid of the Jews. His contempt for the brutes, which, as mere things for our use, he also declares to be without rights, is thoroughly Jewish, and, in union with Pantheism, is at the same time absurd and detestable (*Eth.*, iv., appendix, c. 27). With all this Spinoza remains a very great man. But in order to estimate his work correctly we must keep in view his relation to Descartes. The latter had sharply divided nature into mind and matter, *i. e.*, thinking and extended substance, and had also placed God and the world in complete opposition to each other; Spinoza also, so long as he was a Cartesian, taught all that in his *"Cogitatis Metaphysics,"* c. 12, i. I., 1665. Only in his later years did he see the fundamental falseness of that double dualism; and accordingly his own philosophy principally consists of the indirect abolition of these two antitheses. Yet partly to avoid injuring his teacher, partly in order to be less offensive, he gave it a positive appearance by means of a strictly dogmatic form, although its content is chiefly negative. His identification of the world with God has also this negative significance alone. For to call the world God is not to explain it: it remains a riddle under the one name as under the other. But these two negative truths had value for their age, as for every age in which there still are conscious or unconscious Cartesians. He makes the mistake, common to all philosophers before Locke, of starting from conceptions, without having previously investigated their origin, such, for example, as substance, cause, &c., and in such a method of procedure these conceptions then receive a much too extensive validity. Those who in the most recent times refused to acknowledge the Neo-Spinozism which had appeared, for example, Jacobi, were principally deterred from doing so by the bugbear of fatalism. By this is to be understood every doctrine which refers the existence of the world, together with the critical position of mankind in it, to any absolute necessity, *i. e.*, to a necessity that cannot be further explained. Those who feared fatalism, again, believed that all that was of importance was to deduce the world from the free act of will of a being existing outside it; as if it were antecedently certain which of the two was more correct, or even better merely in relation to us. What is, however, especially assumed here is the *there is no third*, and accordingly hitherto every philosophy has represented one or the other. I am the first to depart from this; for I have actually established the *Third:* the act of will from which the world arises is our own. It is free; for the principle of sufficient reason, from which alone all necessity derives its significance, is merely the form of its phenomenon. Just on this account this phenomenon, if it once exists, is absolutely necessary in its course; in consequence of this alone we can recognise in it the nature of the act of will, and accordingly *eventualiter* will otherwise.

ON THE WILL IN NATURE

COMPARATIVE ANATOMY

Now, from my proposition: that the Will is what Kant calls the "thing in itself" or the ultimate substratum of every phenomenon, I had however not only deduced that the will is the agent in all inner, unconscious functions of the body, but also that the organism itself is nothing but the will which has entered the region of representation, the will itself, perceived in the cognitive form of Space. I had accordingly said that, just as each single momentary act of willing presents itself at once directly and infallibly in the outer perception of the body as one of its actions, so also must the collective volition of each animal, the totality of its efforts, be faithfully portrayed in its whole body, in the constitution of its organism; and that the means supplied by its organisation for attaining the aims of its will must as a whole exactly correspond to those aims—in short, that the same relation must exist between the whole character of its volition and the shape and nature of its body, as between each single act of its will and the single bodily action which carries it out. Even this too has recently been recognised as a fact, and accordingly been confirmed *à posteriori,* by thoughtful zootomists and physiologists from their own point of view and independently of my doctrine: their judgments on this point make Nature testify even here to the truth of my theory.

In Pander and d'Alton's admirable illustrated work[1] we find: "Just as all that is characteristic in the formation of bones springs from the *character* of the animals, so does that character, on the other hand, develop out of their *tendencies and desires.* These *tendencies and de-*

[1] Pander and d'Alton, "Ueber die Skelette der Raubthiere," 1822, p. 7.

sires of animals, which are *so vividly expressed* in their whole organisation and of which that organisation only appears to be the medium, cannot be explained by special primary forces, since we can only deduce their inner reason from the general life of Nature." By this last turn the author shows indeed that he has arrived at the point where, like all other investigators of Nature, he is brought to a standstill by the metaphysical; but he also shows, that up to this point beyond which Nature eludes investigation, *tendencies and desires* (*i. e.*, will) were the utmost thing knowable. The shortest expression for his last conclusion about animals would be "As they will, so they are."

The learned and thoughtful Burdach,[1] when treating of the ultimate reason of the genesis of the embryo in his great work on Physiology, bears witness no less explicitly to the truth of my view. I must not, unfortunately, conceal the fact that in a weak moment, misled Heaven knows by what or how, this otherwise excellent man brings in just here a few sentences taken from that utterly worthless, tyrannically imposed pseudo-philosophy, about 'thought' being what is primary (it is just what is last and most conditioned of all) yet 'no representation' (that is to say, a wooden iron). Immediately after however, under the returning influence of his own better self, he proclaims the real truth: "The brain curves itself outwards to the retina, because the central part of the embryo *desires* to take in the impressions of the activity of the world; the mucous membrane of the intestinal canal develops into the lung, because the organic body *desires* to enter into relation with the elementary substances of the universe; organs of generation spring from the vascular system, because the individual only lives in the species, and because the life which has commenced in the

1 Burdach, "Physiologie," vol. 2, § 474.

individual desires to multiply." In fact, every organ must be looked upon as the expression of a universal manifestation of the will, *i. e.,* of one made once for all, of a fixed longing, of an act of volition proceeding, not from the individual, but from the species. Every animal form is a longing of the will to live which is roused by circumstances; for instance, the will is seized with a longing to live on trees, to hang on their branches, to devour their leaves, without contention with other animals and without ever touching the ground: this longing presents itself throughout endless time in the form (or Platonic Idea) of the sloth. It can hardly walk at all, being only adapted for climbing; helpless on the ground, it is agile on trees and looks itself like a moss-clad bough in order to escape the notice of its pursuers. But now let us consider the matter from a somewhat more methodical and less poetical point of view.

The manifest adaptation of each animal for its mode of life and outward means of subsistence, even down to the smallest detail, together with the exceeding perfection of its organisation, form abundant material for teleological contemplation, which has always been a favourite occupation of the human mind, and which, extended even to inanimate Nature, has become the argument of the Physico-theological Proof. The universal fitness for their ends, the obviously intentional design in all the parts of the organism of the lower animals without exception, proclaim too distinctly for it ever to have been seriously questioned, that here no forces of Nature acting by chance and without plan have been at work, but a will. Now, that a will should act otherwise than under the guidance of knowledge was inconceivable, according to empirical science and views. For, up to my time, as has been shown in the last chapter, *will* and *intellect* had been regarded as absolutely inseparable, nay, the will was looked upon as a mere operation of the intellect, that presumptive basis of all that is spiritual. Accordingly wherever the will acted, knowledge must have been its guide; consequently it must have been its guide here also. But the meditation of knowledge, which, as such, is exclusively directed towards the outside, brings with it, that a will acting by means of it, can only act outwardly, that is, only from *one* being upon *another*. Therefore the will, of which unmistakable traces had been found, was not sought for where these were discovered, but was removed to the outside, and the animal became the product of a will foreign to it, guided by knowledge, which must have been very clear knowledge indeed, nay, the deeply excogitated conception of a purpose; and this purpose must have preceded the animal's existence, and, together with the will, whose product the animal is, have lain outside that animal. According to this, the animal would have existed in representation before existing in reality. This is the basis of the train of thought on which the Physico-theological Proof is founded. But this proof is no mere scholastic sophism, like the Ontological Proof: nor does it contain an untiring natural opponent within itself, like the Cosmological Proof, in that very same law of causality to which it owes its existence. On the contrary, it is, in reality, for the educated, what the Keraunological Proof is for the vulgar, and its plausibility is so great, so potent, that the most eminent and at the same time least prejudiced minds have been deeply entangled in it. Voltaire, for instance, who, after all sorts of other doubts, always comes back to it, sees no possibility of getting over it and even places its evidence almost on a level with that of a mathematical demonstration. Even Priestley too declares it to be irrefutable.[1] Hume's reflection and acumen alone

[1] Priestley, "Disqu. on Matter and Spirit," sect. 16, p. 188.

COMPARATIVE ANATOMY   387

stood the test, even in this case; in his "Dialogues on Natural Religion,"[1] which are so well worth reading, this true precursor of Kant calls attention to the fact, that there is no resemblance at all between the works of Nature and those of an Art which proceeds according to a design. Now it is precisely where he cuts asunder the *nervus probandi* of this extremely insidious proof, as well as that of the two others—in his Critique of Judgment and in his Critique of Pure Reason—that Kant's merit shines most brilliantly. Kant has earned for himself great merit by it; for nothing stands so much in the way of a correct insight into Nature and into the essence of things as this view, by which they are looked upon as having been made according to a preconceived plan. Therefore, if a Duke of Bridgewater offers a prize of high value for the confirmation and perpetuation of such fundamental errors, let it be our task, following in the footsteps of Hume and Kant, to work undauntedly at their destruction, without any other reward than truth. Truth deserves respect: not what is opposed to it. Nevertheless here, as elsewhere, Kant has confined himself to negation; but a negation only takes full effect when it has been completed by a correct affirmation, this alone giving entire satisfaction and in itself dislodging and superseding error. First of all therefore we say: the world is not made with the help of knowledge, consequently also not from the outside, but from the inside; and next we endeavour to point out the *punctum saliens*[2] of the world-egg. The physico-theological thought, that Nature must have been regulated and fashioned by an intellect, however well it may suit the untutored mind, is nevertheless fundamentally wrong. For the intellect is only known to us in animal nature, consequently as an

[1] Part 7, and in other places.
[2] The point at which the life-spark is kindled. [Tr.]

absolutely secondary and subordinate principle in the world, a product of the latest origin; it can never therefore have been the condition of the existence of that world. Now the will on the contrary, being that which fills every thing and manifests itself immediately in each —thus showing each thing to be its phenomenon—appears everywhere as that which is primary. It is just for this reason, that the explanation of all teleological facts is to be found in the will of the being itself in which they are observed.

Besides, the Physico-theological Proof may be simply invalidated by the empirical observation, that works produced by animal instinct, such as the spider's web, the bee's honeycomb and its cells, the white ant's constructions, &c., &c., are throughout constituted as if they were the result of an intentional conception, of a wide-reaching providence and of rational deliberation; whereas they are evidently the work of a blind impulse, *i. e.*, of a will not guided by knowledge. From this it follows, that the conclusion from such and such a nature to such and such a mode of coming into being, has not the same certainty as the conclusion from a consequent to its reason, which is in all cases a sure one.

Now, if we enter more closely into the above-mentioned fitness of every animal's organisation for its mode of life and means of subsistence, the question that first presents itself is, whether that mode of life has been adapted to the organisation, or *vice versâ*. At first sight, the former assumption would seem to be the more correct one; since, in Time, the organisation precedes the mode of life, and the animal is thought to have adopted the mode of existence for which its structure was best suited, making the best use of the organs it found within itself: thus, for instance, we think that the bird flies because it has wings, and that the ox butts because it has horns; not conversely. Only this assumption does not explain how, collectively, the quite different parts of an animal's organism so exactly correspond to its way of life: how no organ interferes with another, each rather assisting the others and none remaining unemployed; also that no subordinate organ would be better suited to another mode of existence, while the life which the animal really leads is determined by the principal organs alone, but, on the contrary, each part of the animal not only corresponds to every other part, but also to its mode of life: its claws, for instance, are invariably adapted for seizing the prey which its teeth are suited to tear and break, and its intestinal canal to digest: its limbs are constructed to convey it where that prey is to be found, and no organ ever remains unemployed. The ant-bear, for instance, is not only armed with long claws on its fore-feet, in order to break into the nests of the white ant, but also with a prolonged cylindrical muzzle, in order to penetrate into them, with a small mouth and a long, threadlike tongue, covered with a glutinous slime, which it inserts into the white ants' nests and then withdraws covered with the insects that adhere to it: on the other hand it has no teeth, because it does not want them. Who can fail to see that the ant-bear's form stands in the same relation to the white ants, as an act of the will to its motive? The contradiction between the powerful fore-feet and long, strong, curved claws of the ant-bear and its complete lack of teeth, is at the same time so extraordinary, that if the earth ever undergoes a fresh transformation, the newly arising race of rational beings will find it an insoluble enigma, if white ants are unknown to them. The necks of birds, as of quadrupeds, are generally as long as their legs, to enable them to reach down to the ground where they pick up their food; but those of aquatic birds are often a good deal longer, because they have to fetch up their nourishment from under the water while swimming. Moor-fowl have exceedingly long legs, to enable them to wade without drowning or wetting their bodies, and a correspondingly long neck and beak, this last being more or less strong, according to the things (reptiles, fishes or worms) which have to be crushed; and the intestines of these animals are invariably adapted likewise to this end. On the other hand, moor-fowl are provided neither with talons, like birds of prey, nor with web-feet, like ducks: for the law of parsimony admits of no superfluous organ. Now, it is precisely this very law, added to the circumstance, that no organ required for its mode of life is ever wanting in any animal, and that all, even the most heterogeneous, harmonize together and are, as it were, calculated for a quite specially determined way of life, for the element in which the prey dwells, for the pursuit, the overcoming, the crushing and digesting of that prey,—all this, we say, proves, that the animal's structure has been determined by the mode of life by which the animal desired to find its sustenance, and not *vice versâ*. It also proves, that the result is exactly the same as if a knowledge of that mode of life and of its outward conditions had preceded the structure, and as if therefore each animal had chosen its equipment before it assumed a body; just as a sportsman before starting chooses his whole equipment, gun, powder, shot, pouch, hunting-knife and dress, according to the game he intends chasing. The latter does not take aim at the wild boar because he happens to have a rifle: he took the rifle with him and not a fowling-piece, because he intended to hunt the wild boar; and the ox does not butt because it happens to have horns: it has horns because it intends to butt. Now, to render this proof complete, we have the additional circumstance, that in many animals, during the time they are growing, the effort of the will to which a limb is destined to minister, manifests itself before the existence of the limb itself, its employment thus anticipating its existence. Young he-goats, rams, calves, for instance, butt with their bare polls before they have any horns; the young boar tries to gore on either side, before its tusks are fully developed which would respond to the intended effect, while on the other hand, it neglects to use the smaller teeth it already has in its mouth and with which it might really bite. Thus its mode of defending itself does not adapt itself to the existing weapons, but *vice versâ*. This had already been noticed by Galenus and by Lucretius before him. All these circumstances give us complete certainty, that the will does not, as a supplementary thing proceeding from the intellect, employ those instruments which it may happen to find, or use the parts because just they and no others chance to be there; but that what is primary and original, is the endeavour to live in this particular way, to contend in this manner, an endeavour which manifests itself not only in the employment, but even in the existence of the weapon: so much so indeed, that the use of the weapon frequently precedes its existence, thus denoting that it is the weapon which arises out of the existence of the endeavour, not, conversely, the desire to use it out of the existence of the weapon. From which it follows, that the structure of each animal is adapted to its will.

This truth forces itself upon thoughtful zoologists and zootomists with such cogency, that unless their mind is at the same time purified by a deeper philosophy, it may lead them into strange errors. Now this actually happened to a very eminent zoologist, the immortal De Lamarck, who has acquired everlasting fame by his discovery of the classification of animals in *vertebrata* and *non-vertebrata,* so admirable in depth of view. For he

quite seriously maintains and tries to prove[1] at length,
that the shape of each animal species, the weapons peculiar to it, and its organs of every sort destined for
outward use, were by no means present at the origin of
that species, but have on the contrary *come into being*
gradually *in the course of time* and through continued
generation, in consequence of the exertions of the animal's will, evoked by the nature of its position and surroundings, through its own repeated efforts and the
habits to which these gave rise. Aquatic birds and mam-
malia that swim, he says, have only become web-footed
through stretching their toes asunder in swimming;
moor-fowl acquired their long legs and necks by wading;
horned cattle only gradually acquired horns because as
they had no proper teeth for combatting, they fought
with their heads, and this combative propensity in course
of time produced horns or antlers; the snail was originally, like other *mollusca,* without feelers; but out of the
desire to feel the objects lying before it, these gradually
arose; the whole feline species acquired claws only in
course of time, from their desire to tear the flesh of their
prey, and the moveable coverings of those claws, from
the necessity of protecting them in walking without
being prevented from using them when they wished; the
giraffe, in the barren, grassless African deserts, being
reduced for its food to the leaves of lofty trees, stretched
out its neck and forelegs until at last it acquired its sin-
gular shape, with a height in front of twenty feet, and
thus De Lamarck goes on describing a multitude of animal species as arising according to the same principle, in
doing which he overlooks the obvious objection which
may be made, that long before the organs necessary for
its preservation could have been produced by means of

[1] De Lamarck, "Philosophie Zoologique," vol. i., c. 7, and
"Histoire Naturelle des Animaux sans Vertèbres," vol. i. In-
trod. pp. 180–212.

such endeavours as these through countless generations, the whole species must have died out from the want of them. To such a degree may we be blinded by a hypothesis which has once laid hold of us! Nevertheless in this instance the hypothesis arose out of a very correct and profound view of Nature: it is an error of genius, which in spite of all the absurdity it contains, still does honour to its originator. The true part of it belongs to De Lamarck, as an investigator of Nature; he saw rightly that the primary element which has determined the animal's organisation, is the will of that animal itself. The false part must be laid to the account of the backward state of Metaphysics in France, where the views of Locke and of his feeble follower, Condillac, in fact still hold their ground and therefore bodies are held to be things in themselves, Time and Space qualities of things in themselves; and where the great doctrine of the Ideal nature of Space and of Time and of all that is represented in them, which has been so extremely fertile in its results, has not yet penetrated. De Lamarck therefore could not conceive his construction of living beings otherwise than in Time, through succession. Errors of this sort, as well as the gross, absurd, atomic theory of the French and the edifying physico-theological considerations of the English, have been banished for ever from Germany by Kant's profound influence. So salutary was the effect produced by this great mind, even upon a nation capable of subsequently forsaking him to run after charlatanism and empty bombast. But the thought could never enter into De Lamarck's head, that the animal's will, as a thing in itself, might lie outside Time, and in this sense be prior to the animal itself. Therefore he assumes the animal to have first been without any clearly defined organs, but also without any clearly defined tendencies, and to have been equipped only with perception. Through this it learns to know the circumstances in which it has to live and from that knowledge arises its desires, *i. e.,* its will, from which again spring its organs or definite embodiment; this last indeed with the help of generation and therefore in boundless Time. If De Lamarck had had the courage to carry out his theory fully, he ought to have assumed a primary animal which, to be consistent, must have originally had neither shape nor organs, and then proceeded to transform itself according to climate and local conditions into myriads of animal shapes of all sorts, from the gnat to the elephant.——But this primary animal is in truth the *will to live;* as such however, it is metaphysical, not physical. Most certainly the shape and organisation of each animal species has been determined by its own will according to the circumstances in which it wished to live; not however as a thing physical in Time, but on the contrary as a thing metaphysical outside Time. The will did not proceed from the intellect, nor did the intellect exist, together with the animal, before the will made its appearance as a mere accident, a secondary, or rather tertiary, thing. It is on the contrary the will which is the *prius,* the thing in itself: its phenomenon (mere representation in the cognitive intellect and its forms of Space and Time) is the animal, fully equipped with all its organs which represent the will to live in those particular circumstances. Among these organs is the intellect also—knowledge itself—which, like the rest of those organs, is exactly adapted to the mode of life of each animal; whereas, according to De Lamarck, it is the will which arises out of knowledge. Behold the countless varieties of animal shapes; how entirely is each of them the mere image of its volition, the evident expression of the strivings of the will which constitute its character! Their difference in shape is only the portrait of their difference in character. Ferocious animals, destined for combat and rapine, appear armed with formidable teeth and claws and strong muscles; their sight is adapted for great distances, especially when they have to mark their prey from a dizzy height, as is the case with eagles and condors. Timid animals, whose will it is to seek their safety in flight instead of contest, present themselves with light, nimble legs and sharp hearing in lieu of all weapons; a circumstance which has even necessitated a striking prolongation of the outer ear in the most timid of them all, the hare. The interior corresponds to the exterior: carnivorous animals have short intestines; herbivorous animals long ones, suited to a protracted assimilation. Vigorous respiration and rapid circulation of the blood, represented by appropriate organs, always accompany great muscular strength and irritability as their necessary conditions, and nowhere is contradiction possible. Each particular striving of the will presents itself in a particular modification of shape. The abode of the prey therefore has determined the shape of its pursuer: if that prey takes refuge in regions difficult of access, in remote hiding places, in night or darkness, the pursuer assumes the form best suited to those circumstances, and no shape is rejected as too grotesque by the will to live, in order to attain its ends. The cross-bill presents itself with this abnormal form of its organ of nutrition, in order to be able to extract the seeds out of the scales of the fir-cone. Moor-fowls appear equipped with extra long legs, extra long necks and extra long beaks, in short, the strangest shapes, in order to seek out reptiles in their marshes. Then we have the ant-bear with its body four feet long, its short legs, its strong claws, and its long, narrow, toothless muzzle provided with a threadlike, glutinous tongue for the purpose of digging out the white ants from their nests. The pelican goes fishing with a huge pouch under its beak in which to pack its fish, when caught. In order to surprise their prey while asleep in the night, owls fly out provided with enormous pupils which enable them to see in the dark, and with very soft feathers to make their flight noiseless and thus permit them to fall unawares upon their sleeping prey without awakening it by their movements. *Silurus, gymnotus* and *torpedo* bring a complete electric apparatus into the world with them, in order to stun their prey before they can reach it; and also as a defence against *their own* pursuers. For wherever anything living breathed, there immediately came another to devour it, and every animal is in a way designed and calculated throughout, down to the minutest detail, for the purpose of destroying some other animal. Ichneumons, for instance, among insects, lay their eggs in the bodies of certain caterpillars and similar *larvæ,* in which they bore holes with their stings, in order to ensure nourishment for their future brood. Now those kinds which feed on *larvæ* that crawl about freely, have short stings not more than about one-third of an inch long, whereas *pimpla manifestator,* which feeds upon *chelostoma maxillosa,* whose *larvæ* lie hidden in old trees at great depth and are not accessible to it, has a sting two inches long; and the sting of the *ichneumon strobillæ* which lays its egg in *larvæ* dwelling in fir-cones, is nearly as long. With these stings they penetrate to the *larva* in which they bore a hole and deposit one egg, whose product subsequently devours this *larva.* Just as clearly does the will to escape their enemies manifest itself in the defensive equipment of animals that are the objects of pursuit. Hedgehogs and porcupines raise up a forest of spears; armadillos, scaly ant-eaters and tortoises appear cased from head to foot in armour which

is inaccessible to tooth, beak or claw; and so it is, on a
smaller scale, with the whole class of *crustacea.* Others
again seek protection by deceiving their pursuers rather
than by resisting them physically: thus the sepia has
provided itself with materials for surrounding itself
with a dark cloud on the approach of danger. The sloth
is deceptively like its moss-clad bough, and the frog its
leaf; and many insects resemble their dwelling-places.
The negro's louse is black; so, to be sure, is our flea also;
but the latter, in providing itself with an extremely powerful apparatus for making irregular jumps to a considerable distance, trusted to these for protection.—We can
however make the anticipation in all these arrangements
more intelligible to ourselves by the same anticipation
which shows itself in the mechanical instincts of animals. Neither the young spider nor the ant-lion know the
prey for which they lay traps, when they do it for the
first time. And it is the same when they are on the defensive. According to Latreille, the insect *bombex* kills
the *parnope* with its sting, although it neither eats it
nor is attacked by it, simply because the *parnope* will
lay its eggs in the *bombex's* nest, and by doing this will
interfere with the development of its eggs; yet it does
not know this. Anticipations of this kind once more confirm the ideal nature of Time, which indeed always becomes manifest as soon as the will as thing in itself is in
question. Not only with respect to the points here mentioned, but to many others besides, the mechanical instincts and physiological functions of animals serve to
explain each other mutually, because the will without
knowledge is the agent in both.

As the will has equipped itself with every organ and
every weapon, offensive as well as defensive, so has it
likewise provided itself in every animal shape with an
intellect, as a means of preservation for the individual

and the species. Accordingly the intellect, being exclusively destined to serve the will, always exactly corresponds to it. Beasts of prey stood in greater need of intellect, and in fact have more intelligence, than herbivorous animals. The elephant certainly forms an exception, and so does even the horse to a certain extent; but the admirable intelligence of the elephant was necessary on account of the length of its life (200 years) and of the scantiness of its progeny, which obliged it to provide for a longer and surer preservation of the individual: and this moreover in countries teeming with the most rapacious, the strongest and the nimblest beasts of prey. The horse too has a longer life and a scantier progeny than the ruminants, and as it has neither horns, tusks, trunk, nor indeed any weapon save perhaps its hoofs, it needed greater intelligence and swiftness in order to elude pursuit. Monkeys needed their extraordinary intelligence, partly because of the length of their life, which even in the moderate-sized animal extends to fifty years; partly also because of their scanty progeny, which is limited to one at a time, but especially because of their *hands,* which, to be properly used, required the direction of an understanding. For monkeys depend upon their hands, not only for their defence by means of outer weapons such as sticks and stones, but also for their nourishment, this last necessitating a variety of artificial means and a social and artificial system of rapine in general, the passing from hand to hand of stolen fruit, the placing of sentinels, &c., &c. Add to this, that it is especially in their youth, before they have attained their full muscular development, that this intelligence is most prominent. In the *pongo* or ourang-outang for instance, the brain plays a far more important part and the understanding is much greater during its youth than at its maturity, when the muscular powers having attained full development, they take the place of the proportionately declining intellect. This holds good of all sorts of monkeys, so that here therefore the intellect acts for a time vicariously for the yet undeveloped muscular strength. We find this process discussed at length in the *"Résumé des Observations de Fr. Cuvier sur l'instinct et l'intelligence des animaux,"* par Flourens (1841), from which I have quoted the whole passage referring to this question in the second volume of my chief work, at the end of the thirty-first chapter, and this is my only reason for not repeating it here. On the whole, intelligence gradually increases from the rodents to the ruminants, from the ruminants to the pachyderms, and from these again to the beasts of prey and finally to the *quadrumana,* and anatomy shows a gradual development of the brain in similar order which corresponds to this result of external observation. (According to Flourens and Fr. Cuvier.) Among the reptiles, serpents are the most intelligent, for they may even be trained; this is so, because they are beasts of prey and propagate more slowly than the rest—especially the venomous ones. And here also, as with the physical weapons, we find the will everywhere as the *prius;* its equipment, the intellect, as the *posterius.* Beasts of prey do not hunt, nor do foxes thieve, because they have more intelligence; on the contrary, they have more intelligence, just as they have stronger teeth and claws too, because they wished to live by hunting and thieving. The fox even made up at once for his inferiority in muscular power and strength of teeth by the extraordinary subtility of his understanding. Our thesis is singularly illustrated by the case of the bird *dodo* or *dronte* (*didus ineptus*) on the island of Mauritius, whose species, it is well known, has died out, and which, as its Latin name denotes, was exceedingly stupid, and this explains its disappearance; so that here it seems indeed as if Nature had for once gone too far in her law of parsimony and thereby in a sense brought forth an abortion in the species, as she so often does in the individual, which was unable to subsist, precisely because it was an abortion. If, on this occasion, anyone were to raise the question as to whether Nature ought not to have provided insects with at least sufficient intelligence to prevent them from flying into the flame of a candle, our answer would be: most certainly; only she did not know that men would make candles and light them, and "nature does nothing in vain." Insect intelligence is therefore only insufficient where the surroundings are artificial.

Everywhere indeed intelligence depends in the first instance upon the cerebral system, and this stands in a necessary relation to the rest of the organism; therefore cold-blooded animals are greatly inferior to warm-blooded ones, and invertebrate animals to *vertebrata.* But the organism is precisely nothing but the will become visible, to which, as that which is absolutely *prius,* everything constantly refers. The needs and aims of that will give in each phenomenon the rule for the means to be employed, and these means must harmonize with one another. Plants have no self-consciousness because they have no power of locomotion; for of what use would self-consciousness be to them unless it enabled them to seek what was salutary and flee what was noxious to them? And conversely, of what use could power of locomotion be to them, as they have no self-consciousness with which to guide it. The inseparable duality of Sensibility and Irritability does not yet appear therefore in the plant; they continue slumbering in the reproductive force which is their fundament, and in which alone the will here objectifies itself. The sun-flower, and every other plant, wills for light; but as yet their movement towards light is not separate from their apprehension of it, and both coincide with their growth.—Human understanding, which is so superior to that of all other beings, and is assisted by Reason (the faculty for non-perceptible representations, *i. e.,* for conceptions; reflection, thinking faculty), is nevertheless only just proportionate, partly to Man's requirements, which greatly surpass those of animals and multiply to infinity; partly to his entire lack of all natural weapons and covering, and to his relatively weaker muscular strength, which is greatly inferior to that of monkeys of his own size; lastly also, to the slowness with which his race multiplies and the length of his childhood and life, which demand secure preservation of the individual. All these great requirements had to be satisfied by means of intellectual powers, which, for this reason, predominate in him. But we find the intellect secondary and subordinate everywhere, and destined exclusively to serve the purposes of the will. As a rule too, it always remains true to its destiny and subservient to the will. How nevertheless, it frees itself in particular instances from this bondage through an abnormal preponderance of cerebral life, whereby purely objective cognition becomes possible which may be enhanced to genius, I have shown at length in the æsthetic part of my chief work.

Now, after all these reflections upon the precise agreement between the will and the organisation of each animal, if we inspect a well-arranged osteological collection from this point of view, it will certainly seem to us as if we saw one and the same being (De Lamarck's primary animal, or, more properly, *the will to live*) changing its shape according to circumstances, and thus producing all this multiplicity of forms out of the same number and arrangement of its bones, by prolonging and curtailing, strengthening and weakening them. This number and arrangement of the bones, which Geoffroy de St. Hilaire called the anatomical element, continues, as he has thoroughly shown, in all essential points unchanged: it is a constant magnitude, something which is absolutely given beforehand, irrevocably fixed by an unfathomable necessity—an immutability which I should compare with the permanence of matter in all physical and chemical changes: but to this I shall soon return. Conjointly with this immutability of the anatomical element, we have the greatest susceptibility to modification, the greatest plasticity and flexibility of these same bones with reference to size, shape and adaptation to different purposes, all which we see determined by the will with primary strength and freedom according to the aims prescribed to it by external circumstances: it makes out of these materials whatever its necessity for the time being requires. If it desires to climb about in trees, it catches at the boughs at once with four hands, while it stretches the *ulva* and *radius* to an excessive length and immediately prolongs the *os coccygis* to a curly tail, a yard long, in order to hang by it to the boughs and swing itself from one branch to another. If, on the other hand, it desires to crawl in the mud as a crocodile, to swim as a seal, or to burrow as a mole, these same arm-bones are shortened till they are no longer recognisable; in the last case the *metacarpus* and *phalanges* are enlarged to disproportionately large shovel-paws, to the prejudice of the other bones. But if it wishes to fly through the air as a bat, not only are the *os humeri, radius* and *alnus* prolonged in an incredible manner, but the usually small and subordinate *carpus, metacarpus* and *phalanges digitorum* expand to an immense length, as in St. Anthony's vision, outmeasuring the length of the animal's body, in order to spread out the wing-membrane. If, in order to browse upon the tops of very tall African trees, it has, as a giraffe, placed itself upon extraordinarily high fore-legs, the same seven *vertebræ* of the neck, which never vary as to number and which, in the mole, were con-tracted so as to be no longer recognisable, are now pro-longed to such a degree, that here, as everywhere else, the neck acquires the same length as the fore-legs, in order to enable the head to reach down to drinking-water. But where, as is the case when it appears as the elephant, a long neck could not have borne the weight of the enormous, unwieldy head—a weight increased more-over by tusks a yard long—the neck remains short, as an exception, and a trunk is let down as an expedient, to lift up food and draw water from below and also to reach up to the tops of trees. In accordance with these transformations, we see in all of them the skull, the re-ceptacle containing the understanding, at the same time proportionately expand, develop, curve itself, as the mode of procuring nourishment becomes more or less dif-ficult and requires more or less intelligence; and the dif-ferent degrees of the understanding manifest themselves clearly to the practised eye in the curves of the skull.

Now, in all this, that *anatomical element* we have men-tioned above as fixed and invariable, certainly remains in so far an enigma, as it does not come within the teleo-logical explanation, which only begins after the assump-tion of that element; since the intended organ might in many cases have been rendered equally suitable for its purpose even with a different number and disposition of bones. It is easy to understand, for instance, why the human skull should be formed out of eight bones: that is, to enable them to be drawn together by the fontanels during birth; but we do not see why a chicken which breaks through its egg-shell should necessarily have the same number of skull-bones. We must therefore assume this anatomical element to be based, partly on the unity and identity of the will to live in general, partly on the circumstance, that the archetypal forms of animals have proceeded one from the other, wherefore the fundamental type of the whole race was preserved.

No other explanation or assumption enables us nearly as well to understand either the complete suitableness to purpose and to the external conditions of existence I have here shown in the skeleton, or the admirable harmony and fitness of internal mechanism in the structure of each animal, as the truth I have elsewhere firmly established: that the body of an animal is precisely nothing but the *will itself* of that animal brought to cerebral perception as representation—through the forms of Space, Time and Causality—in other words, the mere visibility, objectivity of the Will. For, if this is once pre-supposed, everything in and belonging to that body must conspire towards the final end: the life of this animal. Nothing superfluous, nothing deficient, nothing inappropriate, nothing insufficient or incomplete of its kind, can therefore be found in it; on the contrary, all that is required must be there, and just in the proportion needed, never more. For here artist, work and materials are one and the same. Each organism is therefore a consummate master-piece of exceeding perfection. Here the will did not first cherish the intention, first recognise the end and then adapt the means to it and conquer the material; its willing was rather immediately the aim and immediately the attainment of that aim; no foreign appliances needing to be overcome were wanted—willing, doing and attaining were here one and the same. Thus the organism presents itself as a miracle which admits of no comparison with any work of human artifice wrought by the lamplight of knowledge.

Our admiration for the consummate perfection and fitness for their ends in all the works of Nature is at the bottom based upon our viewing them in the same light as we do our own works. In these, in the first place, the will to do the work and the work are two different things; then again two other things lie between these two: firstly, the medium of representation, which, taken by itself, is foreign to the will, through which the will must pass before it realizes itself here; and secondly the material foreign to the will here at work, on which a form foreign to it has to be forced, which it resists, because the material already belongs to another will, that is to say, to its own nature, its *forma substantialis*, the (Platonic) idea, expressed by it: therefore this material has first to be overcome, and however deeply the artificial form may have penetrated, will always continue inwardly resisting. It is quite a different thing with Nature's works, which are not, like our own, indirect, but on the contrary, direct manifestations of the will. Here the will acts in its primordial nature, that is, unconsciously. No mediating representation here separates the will and the work: they are one. And even the material is one with them: for matter is the mere visibility of the will. Therefore here we find Matter completely permeated by Form; or, better still, they are of quite the same origin, only existing mutually one for the other; and in so far they are one. That we separate them in works of Nature as well as in works of Art, is a mere abstraction. Pure Matter, absolutely without Form or quality, which we think as the material of a product of Nature, is merely an *ens rationis* and cannot enter into any experience; whereas the material of a work of Art is empirical Matter, consequently already has a Form. The [distinctive] character of Nature's products is the identity of form and substance; that of products of Art the diversity of these two. It is because Matter is the mere visibility of Form in Nature's products, that, even empirically, we see Form appear as a mere production of Matter, bursting forth from its inside in crystallisation, in vegetable and animal spontaneous generation, which last can not be doubted, at any rate in the *epizoa*.—For this reason we may even assume that nowhere, either on any planet or satellite, will Matter come to a state of endless repose, but rather that its inherent forces (*i. e.*, the will, whose mere visibility it is) will always put an end again to the repose which has commenced, always awaking again from their sleep, to resume their activity as mechanical, physical, chemical, organic forces; since at all times they only wait for the opportunity to do so.

But if we want to understand Nature's proceeding, we must not try to do it by comparing her works with our own. The real essence of every animal form, is an act of the will outside representation, consequently outside its forms of Space and Time also; which act, just on that account, knows neither sequence nor juxtaposition, but has, on the contrary, the most indivisible unity. But when our cerebral perception comprehends that form, and still more when its inside is dissected by the anatomical knife, then that which originally and in itself was foreign to knowledge and its laws, is brought under the light of knowledge; but then also, it has to present itself in conformity with the laws and forms of knowledge. The original unity and indivisibility of that act of the will, of that truly metaphysical being, then appears divided into parts lying side by side and functions following one upon another, which all nevertheless present themselves as connected together in closest relationship one to another for mutual help and support, as means and ends one to the other. The understanding, in thus apprehending these things, now perceives the original unity re-establishing itself out of a multiplicity which its own form of knowledge had first brought about, and in-

voluntarily taking for granted that its own way of perceiving this is the way in which this animal form comes
into being, it is now struck with admiration for the profound wisdom with which those parts are arranged, those
functions combined. This is the meaning of Kant's great
doctrine, that Teleology is brought into Nature by our
own understanding, which accordingly wonders at a miracle of its own creation. If I may use a trivial simile to
elucidate so sublime a matter, this astonishment very
much resembles that of our understanding when it dis-
covers that all multiples of 9, when their single figures
are added together, give as their product either the number 9 or one whose single figures again make 9; yet it is
that very understanding itself which has prepared for itself this surprise in the decimal system. According to the
Physico-theological argument, the actual existence of the
world has been preceded by its existence in an intellect:
if the world is designed for an end, it must have existed
as representation before it came into being. Now I say,
on the contrary, in Kant's sense: if the world is to be
representation, it must present itself as designed for an
end; and this only takes place in an intellect.

It undoubtedly follows from my doctrine, that every
being is its own work. Nature, which is incapable of
falsehood and is as *naïve* as genius, asserts the same
thing downright; since each being merely kindles the
spark of life at another exactly similar being, and then
makes itself before our eyes, taking the materials for this
from outside, form and movement from its own self: this
process we call growth and development. Thus, even empirically, each being stands before us as its own work.
But Nature's language is not understood because it is
too simple.

PHYSICAL ASTRONOMY

No part of my doctrine could I have less hoped to see corroborated by empirical science than that, in which the fundamental truth, that Kant's thing in itself is the Will, is applied by me even to inorganic Nature, and in which I show the active principle in all fundamental forces of Nature to be absolutely identical with what is known to us within ourselves as the Will.——It has therefore been particularly gratifying to me to have found that an eminent empiricist, yielding to the force of truth, had gone so far as to express this paradox in the exposition of his scientific doctrine. I allude to Sir John Herschel and to his "Treatise on Astronomy," the first edition of which appeared in 1833, and a second enlarged one in 1849, under the title "Outlines of Astronomy." Herschel,——who, as an astronomer, was acquainted with gravity, not only in the one-sided and really coarse part which it acts on earth, but also in the nobler one performed by it in universal Space, where the celestial bodies play with each other, betray mutual inclination, exchange as it were amorous glances, yet never allow themselves to come into rude contact, and thus continue dancing their dignified minuet to the music of the spheres, while they keep at a respectful distance from one another—when he comes to the statement of the law of gravitation in the seventh chapter, expresses himself as follows:——

"All bodies with which we are acquainted, when raised into the air and quietly abandoned, descend to the earth's surface in lines perpendicular to it. They are therefore urged thereto by a force or effort, the direct or indirect result of a consciousness and a will existing somewhere, though beyond our power to trace, which force we term *gravity*."

The immediate manifestation of gravity is more evident in each part of liquid, than of solid, matter, owing to the perfect freedom of motion of the parts among each other. In order therefore to penetrate into this *aperçu*, which is the true source of Herschel's assertion, let us look attentively at a torrent dashing headlong over rocks and ask ourselves whether so determined an impetus, so boisterous a vehemence, can arise without an exertion of strength, and whether an exertion of strength is conceivable without will. And so it is precisely in every case in which we become aware of anything moving spontaneously, of any primary, uncommunicated force: we are constrained to think its inermost essence as will.—This much at any rate is certain, that Herschel, like all the empiricists in so many different branches of science whose evidence I have quoted above, had arrived here at the limit where nothing more is left behind the Physical but the Metaphysical; that this had brought him to a standstill, and that he, as well as the rest of them, was unable to find anything beyond that limit, but the *will*.

Herschel moreover, like most of these empiricists, is here still hampered by the opinion that will is inseparable from consciousness. As I have expatiated enough above upon this fallacy, and its correction through my doctrine, it is needless for me to enter into it here again.

The attempt has repeatedly been made, since the beginning of this century, to ascribe *vitality* to the inorganic world. Quite wrongly: for living and inorganic are convertible conceptions, and with death the organic ceases to be organic. But no limit in the whole of Nature is so sharply drawn as the line which separates the organic from the inorganic: that is to say, the line between the region in which Form is the essential and permanent,

Matter the accidental and changing,—and the region in which this relation is entirely reversed. This is no vacillating boundary like that perhaps between animals and plants, between solid and liquid, between gas and steam: to endeavour to destroy it therefore, is intentionally to bring confusion into our ideas. On the other hand, I am the first who has asserted that a *will* must be attributed to all that is lifeless and inorganic. For, with me, the will is not, as has hitherto been assumed, an accident of cognition and therefore of life; but life itself is manifestation of will. Knowledge, on the contrary, is really an accident of life, and life of Matter. But Matter itself is only the perceptibility of the phenomena of the will. Therefore we are compelled to recognise *volition* in every effort or tendency which proceeds from the nature of a material body, and properly speaking constitutes that nature, or manifests itself as phenomenon by means of that nature; and there can consequently be no Matter without manifestation of will. The lowest and on that account most universal manifestation of will is *gravity*, wherefore it has been called a primary and essential property of Matter.

The usual view of Nature assumes *two* fundamentally different principles of motion, therefore it supposes that the movement of a body may have *two different origins: i. e.,* that it proceeds either from the inside, in which case it is attributed to the *will;* or from the outside, and then it is occasioned by *causes.* This principle is generally taken for granted as a matter of course and only occasionally brought explicitly into prominence.

Now here however I must say, in opposition to this principle, however great may be its antiquity and universality, that there are *not* two origins of movement differing fundamentally from one another; that movement does *not* proceed either from inside, when it is ascribed to the will, or from outside, when it is brought about by causes; but that both things are inseparable and take place simultaneously with every movement made by a body. For movement which is admitted to arise from the *will*, always presupposes a *cause* also: this cause, in beings that have knowledge, is a *motive;* but without it, even in these beings, movement is impossible. On the other hand, the movement of a body which is admitted to have been brought about by an outward *cause*, is nevertheless in itself a manifestation of the *will* of that body which has only been evoked by that cause. Accordingly there is only one, uniform, universal and exceptionless principle of all movement, whose inner condition is *will* and whose outer occasion is *cause*, which latter may also take the form of a *stimulus* or of a *motive*, according to the nature of the thing moved.

All that is known to us of things in a merely empirical or *à posteriori* way, is in itself *will;* whereas, so far as they can be determined *à priori*, things belong exclusively to *representation*, to mere phenomenon. Natural phenomena therefore become proportionately less easy to comprehend, the more distinctly the will manifests itself in them, *i. e.*, the higher they stand on the scale of beings; whereas, they become more and more comprehensible the smaller the amount of their empirical content, because they remain more and more within the sphere of mere representation, the forms of which, known to us *à priori*, are the principle of comprehensibility. Accordingly, it is only so long as we limit ourselves to this sphere—that is to say, only when we have before us mere representation, mere form without empirical content— that our comprehension is complete and thorough: that is, in the *à priori* sciences, Arithmetic, Geometry, Phoronomy, and Logic. Here everything is in the highest degree comprehensible; our insight is quite clear and satisfactory: it leaves nothing to be desired, since we are even unable to conceive that anything could be otherwise than it is. This comes from our having here exclusively to do with the forms of our own intellect. Thus the more we are able to comprehend in a relation, the more it consists of mere phenomenon and the less it has to do with the thing in itself. Applied Mathematics, Mechanics, Hydraulics, &c., &c., deal with the lowest degrees of objectification of the will, in which the largest part still remains within the sphere of mere representation; nevertheless even here there is already an empirical element which stands in the way of entire comprehension, which makes the transparency less complete, and in which the inexplicable shows itself. For the same reason, only few departments of Physics and of Chemistry continue to admit of a mathematical treatment; whereas higher up in the scale of beings this has to be entirely done away with, precisely because of the preponderance of content over form in these phenomena. This content is will, the *à posteriori*, the thing in itself, the free, the causeless. Under the heading "Physiology of Plants," I have shown how—in beings that live and have knowledge—motive and act of will, representation and volition, separate and detach themselves more and more distinctly one from the other, the higher we ascend in the scale of being. Now, in inorganic Nature also, the cause separates itself from the effect in just the same proportion, and the purely empirical—which is precisely phenomenon of the will—detaches itself more and more prominently; but, just with this, comprehensibility diminishes. This point merits fuller investigation, and I request my readers to give their whole and undivided attention to what I am about to say, as it is calculated to place the leading thought of my doctrine in the strongest possible light, both as to comprehensibility and cogency. But this is all I can do;

for it is beyond my power to induce my contemporaries to prefer thoughts to verbiage; I can only console myself for not being the man of the age.

On the lowest step of the scale of Nature, cause and effect are quite homogeneous and quite equivalent. Here therefore we have perfect comprehension of the causal connection: for instance, the cause of the movement of one ball propelled by impact, is the movement of another, which loses just as much movement as the first one receives. Here causality is in the highest degree intelligible. What notwithstanding still remains mysterious, is restricted to the possibility of the passage of movement —of a thing incorporeal—from one body to another. The receptivity of bodies in this mode is so slight, that the effect to be produced has to pass over completely from its cause. The same holds good of all purely mechanical influences; and if they are not all just as instantaneously understood, it is either because they are hidden from us by accessory circumstances, or because we are confused by the complicated connection of many causes and effects. In itself, mechanical causality is everywhere equally, that is, in the highest degree, comprehensible; because cause and effect do not differ here as to *quality*, and because where they differ as to *quantity*, as in the lever, mere Space and Time relations suffice to make the thing clear. But as soon as weights come also into play, a second mysterious element supervenes, *gravity:* and, where elastic bodies are concerned, *elasticity* also.—Things change as soon as we begin to ascend in the scale of phenomena. Heat, considered as cause, and expansion, liquefaction, volatilization or crystallization, as effects, are not homogeneous; therefore their causal connection is not intelligible. The comprehensibility of causality has diminished: what a lower degree of heat caused to liquefy, a higher degree makes evaporate: that which crystallizes with less heat, melts when the heat is augmented. Warmth softens wax and hardens clay; light whitens wax and blackens chloride of silver. And, to go still further, when two salts are seen to decompose each other mutually and to form two new ones, elective affinity presents itself to us as an impenetrable mystery, and the properties of the two new bodies are not a combination of the properties of their separate elements. Nevertheless we are still able to follow the process and to indicate the elements out of which the new bodies are formed; we can even separate what has been united and restore the original quantities. Thus noticeable heterogeneousness and incommensurability between cause and effect have here made their appearance: causality has become more mysterious. And this becomes still more apparent when we compare the effects of electricity or of the Voltaic pile with their causes, $i.\ e.$, with the friction of glass, or the piling and oxidation of the plates. Here all similarity between cause and effect at once vanishes; causality becomes shrouded in a thick veil, which men like Davy, Faraday and Ampère have strenuously endeavoured to lift. The only thing now discernible through that veil, are the laws ruling its mode of action, which may be brought into a schema such as $+$ E $-$ E, communication, distribution, shock, ignition, analysis, charging, isolation, discharging, electric current, &c., &c., to this schema we are able to reduce and even to direct the effect; but of the process itself we know nothing: that remains an x. Here therefore cause and effect are completely heterogeneous, their connection is unintelligible, and we see bodies show great susceptibility to causal influences, the nature of which remains a secret for us. Moreover in proportion as we mount higher in the scale, the effect seems to contain more, the cause less. When we reach organic Nature therefore, in which the phenomenon of life presents itself, this is the case in a far higher degree still. If, as is done in China, we fill a pit with decaying wood, cover it with leaves from the same tree as the wood, and pour a solution of sulphur repeatedly over it, an abundant crop of edible mushrooms will spring up. A world of rapidly moving *infusoria* will arise from a little hay well watered. What a difference lies here between effect and cause! How much more does the former seem to contain than the latter! When we compare the seed, sometimes centuries, nay even thousands of years old, with the tree, or the soil with the specifically and strikingly different juices of innumerable plants—some healthy, some poisonous, some again nutritious—which spring from the same earth, upon which the same sun shines and the same rain falls, all resemblance ceases, and with it all comprehensibility for us. For here causality already appears in increased potency: that is, as stimulus and as susceptibility for stimulus. The schema of cause and effect alone has remained; we know that this is cause, that effect; but we know nothing whatever of the nature and disposition of causality. Between cause and effect there is not only no qualitative resemblance, but no quantitative relation: the relatively greater importance of the effect as compared with its cause increases more and more; the effect of the stimulus too does not augment in proportion with the enhancement of that stimulus; in fact just the contrary often takes place. Finally, when we come to the sphere of beings which have knowledge, there is no longer any sort of resemblance or relation between the action performed and the object which, as representation, evokes it. Animals, however, as they are restricted to *perceptible* representations, still need the *presence* of the object acting as a motive, which action is then immediate and infallible (if we leave training, *i. e.*, habit enforced by fear, out of the question). For animals are unable to carry about with them conceptions that might render them independent of present impressions, enable them to reflect, and qualify them for deliberate action. Man can do this. Therefore when at last we come to rational beings, the motive is even no longer a present, perceptible, actually existing, real thing, but a mere conception having its present existence only in the brain of the person who acts, but which is extracted from many multifarious perceptions, from the experience of former years, or has been handed down in words. Here the separation between cause and effect is so wide, the effect has grown so much stronger as compared with the cause, that the vulgar mind no longer perceives the existence of a cause at all, and the acts of the will appear to it to be unconditioned, causeless: that is to say, free. This is just why, when we reflect upon them from outside, the movements of our own body present themselves as if they took place without cause, or to speak more properly, by a miracle. Experience and reflection alone teach us that these movements, like all others, are only possible as the effects of causes, here called motives, and that, on this ascending scale, it is only as to material reality that the cause has failed to keep pace with the effect; whereas it has kept pace with it as to dynamical reality, energy.—At this degree of the scale therefore— the highest in Nature—causality has become less intelligible to us than ever. Nothing but the bare schema, taken in a quite general sense, now remains, and the ripest reflection is needed to recognise its applicability and the necessity that schema brings with it everywhere.

In the Grotto of Pausilippo, darkness continues to augment as we advance towards the interior; but when once we have passed the middle, day-light again appears at the other end and shows us the way; so also in this case: just at the point where the outwardly directed light of the understanding with its form of causality, gradually yielding to increasing darkness, had been reduced to a feeble, flickering glimmer, behold! we are met by a totally different light proceeding from quite another quarter, from our own inner self, through the chance circumstance, that we, the judges, happen here to be the very objects that are to be judged. The growing difficulty of the comprehension of the causal nexus, at first so clear, had now become so great for perception and for the understanding—the agent in it—that, in animal actions, the very existence of that nexus seemed almost doubtful and those actions appeared to be a sort of miracle. But, just at this point, the observer receives from his own inner self the direct information that the agent in them is the will—that very will, which he knows better and more intimately than anything that external perception can ever supply. This knowledge alone must be the philosopher's key to an insight into the heart of all those processes in unconscious Nature, concerning which causal explanation—although, here, to be sure, more satisfactory than in the processes last considered, and the clearer, the farther those processes were removed from these—nevertheless had still left an unknown x, and could never quite illumine the inside of the process, even in a body propelled by impact or attracted by gravity. This x had continued expanding till finally, on the highest degree of the scale, it had wholly repelled causal explanation. But then, just when the power of causal explanation had been reduced to a minimum, that x revealed itself as *the will*—reminding us of Mephistopheles when, yielding to Faust's learned exorcisms, he steps forth out of the huge grown poodle whose kernel he was. In consequence of the considerations I have here set forth at length, we can surely hardly avoid recognising *the identity of this x*, even on the lowest degrees of the scale, where it was but faintly perceptible; then higher up, where it extended its obscurity more and more; and finally on the highest degrees, where it cast a shadow upon all things—till, at the very top, it reveals itself to our consciousness in our own phenomenal being, as *the will*. The two primarily different sources of our knowledge, that is to say the inward and the outward source, have to be connected together at this point by reflection. It is quite exclusively out of this connection that our comprehension of Nature, and of our own selves arises; but then the inner side of Nature is disclosed to our intellect, which by itself alone can never reach further than to the mere outside; and the mystery which philosophy has so long tried to solve, lies open before us. For then indeed we clearly see what the Real and the Ideal (the thing in itself and the phenomenon) properly are; and this settles the principal question which has engaged the attention of philosophers since Descartes: that is to say, the question as to the relation between these two, whose complete diversity Kant had shown most thoroughly and with unexampled depth, yet whose absolute identity was immediately afterwards proclaimed by humbugs on the credit of intellectual intuition. But if we decline to avail ourselves of this insight, which is really the one strait gate to truth, we can never acquire comprehension of the intrinsic essence of Nature, to which absolutely no other road leads; for then indeed we fall into an irremovable error. Then, as I have already said, we maintain the view, that motion has two radically different primary principles with a solid partition-wall between them: *i. e.*, movement by means of causes, and movement by means of the will. The first of these must then remain for ever incomprehensible as to its innermost essence, because, after all its explanations, there is still left that unknown x which contains the more, the higher the object under consideration stands in the scale of beings; while the second, movement by the will, presents itself as entirely disconnected from the principle of causality; as without reason; as freedom in individual actions: in other words, as completely opposed to Nature and utterly unexplainable. On the other hand, if the above-mentioned union of our external and internal knowledge has once been accomplished at the point where both meet, we then recognise two identities in spite of all accidental differences. That is to say, we recognize the identity of causality with itself on every degree of the scale of beings, and the identity of the x, which at first was unknown (*i. e.,* of physical forces and vital phenomena), with the will which is within us. We recognize, I say, firstly the essential identity of causality under the various forms it is forced to assume on the different degrees of the scale, as it may manifest itself, now as a mechanical, chemical, or physical cause, now as a stimulus, and again as a perceptible or an abstract motive: we know it to be one and the same, not only when a propelling body loses as much movement as it imparts by impact, but also when in the combats of thought against thought, the victorious one, as the more powerful motive, sets Man in motion, a motion which follows with no less necessity than that of the ball which is struck. Where we ourselves are the things set in motion, where therefore the kernel of the process is well and intimately known to us, instead of allowing ourselves to be dazzled and confused by this light and thereby losing sight of the causal connection as it lies before us everywhere else in the whole of Nature; instead of shutting out this insight for ever, we now apply the new knowledge we have acquired from within as a key to the knowledge of things outside us, and then we recognise the second identity, that of our will with the hitherto mysterious x that remains over after all causal explanation as an insoluble residue. Consequently

we then say: even in cases in which the effect is brought
about by the most palpable cause, the mysterious x in
the process, the real innermost core of it, the true agent,
the *in-itself* of all phenomena—which, after all, is only
given us as representation and according to the forms
and laws of representation—is essentially one and the
same with what is known to us immediately and intimately as *the will* in the actions of our own body, which
body is likewise given us as intuition and representation.
—This is (say what you will) the basis of true philosophy, and if the present age does not see this, many
following ages will.—Thus, just as, on the one hand,
the essence of causality, which appears most clearly
only on the lowest degree of the objectification of the
will, is recognised by us again at every ascending step,
even at the highest; so also, on the other hand, is the
essence of the will recognised by us at every descending
step in that ladder, even at the lowest, although this
knowledge is only immediately acquired at the very
highest. The old error asserts, that where there is will,
there is no causality; and that where there is causality,
there is no will. But we say: everywhere where there is
causality, there is will; and no will acts without causality. The *punctum controversiæ* therefore, is, whether
will and causality can and must subsist together in one
and the same process at the same time. What makes the
knowledge, that this is indeed the case, so difficult, is the
circumstance, that we know causality and will in two
fundamentally different ways: causality entirely from
outside, quite indirectly, quite through the understanding; will entirely from inside, quite directly; and that
accordingly the clearer the knowledge of the one in
each given instance, the less clear is the knowledge of
the other. Therefore we recognise the essence of the will
least readily, where causality is most intelligible; and,

where the will is most unmistakably evident, causality becomes so obscured, that the vulgar mind could venture to deny its existence altogether.—Now, as Kant has taught us, causality is nothing but the form of the understanding itself, knowable *à priori:* that is, the essence of *representation,* as such, which is one side of the world; the other side is *will:* which is the thing in itself. That relative increase and decrease of clearness in inverse proportion of causality and of the will, that mutual advancing and receding of both, depends consequently upon the fact, that the more a thing is given us as mere phenomenon, *i. e.,* as representation, the more clearly does the *à priori* form of representation, *i. e.,* causality, manifest itself: this is the case in inanimate Nature; conversely, the more immediate our knowledge of the will, the more does the form of representation recede into the background: this is the case with ourselves. That is: the nearer one side of the world approaches to us, the more do we lose sight of the other.

PARERGA AND PARALIPOMENA
SELECTIONS

ON EDUCATION

THE human intellect is said to be so constituted that *general ideas* arise by abstraction from *particular observations*, and therefore come after them in point of time. If this is what actually occurs, as happens in the case of a man who has to depend solely upon his own experience for what he learns,—who has no teacher and no book,—such a man knows quite well which of his particular observations belong to and are represented by each of his general ideas. He has a perfect acquaintance with both sides of his experience, and accordingly he treats everything that comes in his way from a right standpoint. This might be called the *natural* method of education.

Contrarily, the *artificial* method is to hear what other people say, to learn and to read, and so to get your head crammed full of general ideas before you have any sort of extended acquaintance with the world as it is, and as you may see it for yourself. You will be told that the particular observations which go to make these general ideas will come to you later on in the course of experience; but until that time arrives you apply your general ideas wrongly, you judge men and things from a wrong standpoint, you see them in a wrong light, and treat them in a wrong way. So it is that education perverts the mind.

This explains why it so frequently happens that, after a long course of learning and reading, we enter upon the world in our youth, partly with an artless ignorance of things, partly with wrong notions about them; so that our demeanour savours at one moment of a nervous

425

anxiety, at another of a mistaken confidence. The reason
of this is simply that our head is full of general ideas
which we are now trying to turn to some use, but which
we hardly ever apply rightly. This is the result of acting
in direct opposition to the natural development of the
mind by obtaining general ideas first, and particular
observations last: it is putting the cart before the horse.
Instead of developing the child's own faculties of dis-
cernment, and teaching it to judge and think for itself,
the teacher uses all his energies to stuff its head full of
the ready-made thoughts of other people. The mistaken
views of life, which spring from a false application of
general ideas, have afterwards to be corrected by long
years of experience; and it is seldom that they are
wholly corrected. This is why so few men of learning
are possessed of common-sense, such as is often to be met
with in people who have had no instruction at all.

To acquire a knowledge of the world might be defined as the aim of all education; and it follows from
what I have said that special stress should be laid upon
beginning to acquire this knowledge *at the right end*.
As I have shown, this means, in the main, that the particular observation of a thing shall precede the general
idea of it; further, that narrow and circumscribed ideas
shall come before ideas of a wide range. It means, therefore, that the whole system of education shall follow in the
steps that must have been taken by the ideas themselves
in the course of their formation. But whenever any of
these steps are skipped or left out the instruction is defective, and the ideas obtained are false; and finally a
distorted view of the world arises, peculiar to the individual himself—a view such as almost everyone entertains for some time, and most men for as long as they
live. No one can look into his own mind without seeing
that it was only after reaching a very mature age, and

in some cases when he least expected it, that he came
to a right understanding or a clear view of many matters in his life that, after all, were not very difficult or
complicated. Up till then they were points in his knowledge of the world which were still obscure, due to his
having skipped some particular lesson in those early
days of his education, whatever it may have been like—
whether artificial and conventional, or of that natural
kind which is based upon individual experience.

It follows that an attempt should be made to find out
the strictly natural course of knowledge, so that education may proceed methodically by keeping to it; and
that children may become acquainted with the ways of
the world without getting wrong ideas into their heads,
which very often cannot be got out again. If this plan
were adopted, special care would have to be taken to
prevent children from using words without clearly
understanding their meaning and application. The fatal
tendency to be satisfied with words instead of trying to
understand things—to learn phrases by heart, so that
they may prove a refuge in time of need, exists, as a
rule, even in children; and the tendency lasts on into
manhood, making the knowledge of many learned persons to consist in mere verbiage.

However, the main endeavour must always be to let
particular observations precede general ideas, and not
vice versâ, as is usually and unfortunately the case; as
though a child should come feet foremost into the world,
or a verse be begun by writing down the rhyme! The
ordinary method is to imprint ideas and opinions, in the
strict sense of the word, *prejudices,* on the mind of the
child, before it has had any but a very few particular
observations. It is thus that he afterwards comes to view
the world and gather experience through the medium
of those ready-made ideas, rather than to let his ideas

be formed for him out of his own experience of life, as they ought to be.

A man sees a great many things when he looks at the world for himself, and he sees them from many sides; but this method of learning is not nearly so short or so quick as the method which employs abstract ideas and makes hasty generalisations about everything. Experience, therefore, will be a long time in correcting preconceived ideas, or perhaps never bring its task to an end; for, wherever a man finds that the aspect of things seems to contradict the general ideas he has formed, he will begin by rejecting the evidence it offers as partial and one-sided; nay, he will shut his eyes to it altogether and deny that it stands in any contradiction at all with his preconceived notions, in order that he may thus preserve them uninjured. So it is that many a man carries about a burden of wrong notions all his life long— crotchets, whims, fancies, prejudices, which at last become fixed ideas. The fact is that he has never tried to form his fundamental ideas for himself out of his own experience of life, his own way of looking at the world, because he has taken over his ideas ready-made from other people; and this it is that makes him—as it makes how many others!—so shallow and superficial.

Instead of that method of instruction care should be taken to educate children on the natural lines. No idea should ever be established in a child's mind otherwise than by what the child can see for itself, or at any rate it should be verified by the same means; and the result of this would be that the child's ideas, if few, would be well-grounded and accurate. It would learn how to measure things by its own standard rather than by another's; and so it would escape a thousand strange fancies and prejudices, and not need to have them eradicated by the lessons it will subsequently be taught in the school of life. The child would, in this way, have its mind once for all habituated to clear views and thorough-going knowledge: it would use its own judgment and take an unbiased estimate of things.

And, in general, children should not form their notions of what life is like from the copy before they have learned it from the original, to whatever aspect of it their attention may be directed. Instead, therefore, of hastening to place *books,* and books alone, in their hands, let them be made acquainted, step by step, with *things*—with the actual circumstances of human life. And above all let care be taken to bring them to a clear and objective view of the world as it is, to educate them always to derive their ideas directly from real life, and to shape them in conformity with it—not to fetch them from other sources, such as books, fairy tales, or what people say, and then apply them ready-made to real life. For this will mean that their heads are full of wrong notions, and that they will either see things in a false light or try in vain to *remodel the world* to suit their views, and so enter upon false paths; and that, too, whether they are only constructing theories of life or engaged in the actual business of it. It is incredible how much harm is done when the seeds of wrong notions are laid in the mind in those early years, later on to bear a crop of prejudice; for the subsequent lessons which are learned from real life in the world have to be devoted mainly to their extirpation. *To unlearn the evil* was the answer which, according to Diogenes Laertius,[1] Antisthenes gave, when he was asked what branch of knowledge was most necessary; and we can see what he meant.

No child under the age of fifteen should receive instruction in subjects which may possibly be the vehicle

[1] vi. 7.

of serious error, such as philosophy, religion, or any
other branch of knowledge where it is necessary to take
large views; because wrong notions imbibed early can
seldom be rooted out, and of all the intellectual faculties, judgment is the last to arrive at maturity. The child
should give its attention either to subjects where no
error is possible at all, such as mathematics, or to those
in which there is no particular danger in making a mistake, such as languages, natural science, history, and
so on. And in general, the branches of knowledge which
are to be studied at any period of life should be such as
the mind is equal to at that period and can perfectly
understand. Childhood and youth form the time for collecting materials, for getting a special and thorough
knowledge of individual and particular things. In those
years it is too early to form views on a large scale; and
ultimate explanations must be put off to a later date.
The faculty of judgment, which cannot come into play
without mature experience, should be left to itself; and
care should be taken not to anticipate its action by in-
culcating prejudice, which will paralyse it for ever.

On the other hand, the memory should be specially
taxed in youth, since it is then that it is strongest and
most tenacious. But in choosing the things that should
be committed to memory the utmost care and fore-
thought must be exercised; as lessons well learnt in
youth are never forgotten. This precious soil must therefore be cultivated so as to bear as much fruit as possible. If you think how deeply rooted in your memory
are those persons whom you knew in the first twelve
years of your life, how indelible the impression made
upon you by the events of those years, how clear your
recollection of most of the things that happened to you
then, most of what was told or taught you, it will seem
a natural thing to take the susceptibility and tenacity of
the mind at that period as the groundwork of education.

This may be done by a strict observance of method, and a systematic regulation of the impressions which the mind is to receive.

But the years of youth allotted to man are short, and memory is, in general, bound within narrow limits; still more so the memory of any one individual. Since this is the case, it is all-important to fill the memory with what is essential and material in any branch of knowledge, to the exclusion of everything else. The decision as to what is essential and material should rest with the master-minds in every department of thought; their choice should be made after the most mature deliberation, and the outcome of it fixed and determined. Such a choice would have to proceed by sifting the things which it is necessary and important for a man to know in general, and then necessary and important for him to know in any particular business or calling. Knowledge of the first kind would have to be classified, after an encyclopædic fashion, in graduated courses, adapted to the degree of general culture which a man may be expected to have in the circumstances in which he is placed; beginning with a course limited to the necessary requirements of primary education, and extending upwards to the subjects treated of in all the branches of philosophical thought. The regulation of the second kind of knowledge would be left to those who had shown genuine mastery in the several departments into which it is divided; and the whole system would provide an elaborate rule or canon for intellectual education, which would, of course, have to be revised every ten years. Some such arrangement as this would employ the youthful power of the memory to best advantage, and supply excellent working material to the faculty of judgment, when it made its appearance later on.

A man's knowledge may be said to be mature, in other words, to have reached the most complete state

of perfection to which he, as an individual, is capable
of bringing it, when an exact correspondence is established between the whole of his abstract ideas and the
things he has actually perceived for himself. This will
mean that each of his abstract ideas rests, directly or
indirectly, upon a basis of observation, which alone en-
dows it with any real value; and also that he is able to
place every observation he makes under the right abstract
idea which belongs to it. Maturity is the work of experience alone; and therefore it requires time. The knowledge we derive from our own observation is usually distinct from that which we acquire through the medium of
abstract ideas; the one coming to us in the natural way,
the other by what people tell us, and the course of instruction we receive, whether it is good or bad. The result is that in youth there is generally very little agreement or correspondence between our abstract ideas,
which are merely phrases fixed in the mind, and that
real knowledge which we have obtained by our own
observation. It is only later on that a gradual approach
takes place between these two kinds of knowledge, accompanied by a mutual correction of error; and knowledge is not mature until this coalition is accomplished.
This maturity or perfection of knowledge is something
quite independent of another kind of perfection, which
may be of a high or a low order—the perfection, I mean,
to which a man may bring his own individual faculties;
which is measured, not by any correspondence between
the two kinds of knowledge, but by the degree of intensity which each kind attains.

For the practical man the most needful thing is to
acquire an accurate and profound knowledge of *the
ways of the world*. But this, though the most needful,
is also the most wearisome of all studies, as a man may
reach a great age without coming to the end of his task;

whereas, in the domain of the sciences, he masters the more important facts when he is still young. In acquiring that knowledge of the world, it is while he is a novice, namely, in boyhood and in youth, that the first and hardest lessons are put before him; but it often happens that even in later years there is still a great deal to be learned.

The study is difficult enough in itself; but the difficulty is doubled by *novels,* which represent a state of things in life and the world such as, in fact, does not exist. Youth is credulous, and accepts these views of life, which then become part and parcel of the mind; so that, instead of a merely negative condition of ignorance, you have positive error—a whole tissue of false notions to start with; and at a later date these actually spoil the schooling of experience, and put a wrong construction on the lessons it teaches. If, before this, the youth had no light at all to guide him, he is now misled by a will-o'-the-wisp; still more often is this the case with a girl. They have both had a false view of things foisted on to them by reading novels; and expectations have been aroused which can never be fulfilled. This generally exercises a baneful influence on their whole life. In this respect those whose youth has allowed them no time or opportunity for reading novels —those who work with their hands and the like—are in a position of decided advantage. There are a few novels to which this reproach cannot be addressed—nay, which have an effect the contrary of bad. First and foremost, to give an example, *Gil Blas,* and the other works of Le Sage (or rather their Spanish originals); further, *The Vicar of Wakefield,* and, to some extent, Sir Walter Scott's novels. *Don Quixote* may be regarded as a satirical exhibition of the error to which I am referring.

ON WOMEN

SCHILLER's poem in honour of women, *Würde der Frauen,* is the result of much careful thought, and it appeals to the reader by its antithetic style and its use of contrast; but as an expression of the true praise which should be accorded to them, it is, I think, inferior to these few words of Jouy's: *Without women the beginning of our life would be helpless; the middle, devoid of pleasure; and the end, of consolation.* The same thing is more feelingly expressed by Byron in *Sardanapalus:*—

> *The very first*
> *Of human life must spring from women's breast,*
> *Your first small words are taught you from her lips,*
> *Your first tears quench'd by her, and your last sighs*
> *Too often breathed out in a woman's hearing,*
> *When men have shrunk from the ignoble care*
> *Of watching the last hour of him who led them.*
>
> (Act I. Scene 2.)

These two passages indicate the right standpoint for the appreciation of women.

You need only look at the way in which she is formed to see that woman is not meant to undergo great labour, whether of the mind or of the body. She pays the debt of life not by what she does but by what she suffers; by the pains of childbearing and care for the child, and by submission to her husband, to whom she should be a patient and cheering companion. The keenest sorrows and joys are not for her, nor is she called upon to display a great deal of strength. The current of her life should be more gentle, peaceful and trivial than man's, without being essentially happier or unhappier.

Women are directly fitted for acting as the nurses and teachers of our early childhood by the fact that they are themselves childish, frivolous and short-sighted; in a word, they are big children all their life long—a kind of intermediate stage between the child and the full-grown man, who is man in the strict sense of the word. See how a girl will fondle a child for days together, dance with it and sing to it; and then think what a man, with the best will in the world, could do if he were put in her place.

With young girls Nature seems to have had in view what, in the language of the drama, is called *a coup de théâtre*. For a few years she dowers them with a wealth of beauty and is lavish in her gift of charm, at the expense of the rest of their life, in order that during those years they may capture the fantasy of some man to such a degree that he is hurried into undertaking the honourable care of them, in some form or other, as long as they live—a step for which there would not appear to be any sufficient warranty if reason only directed his thoughts. Accordingly Nature has equipped woman, as she does all her creatures, with the weapons and implements requisite for the safeguarding of her existence, and for just as long as it is necessary for her to have them. Here, as elsewhere, Nature proceeds with her usual economy; for just as the female ant, after fecundation, loses her wings, which are then superfluous, nay, actually a danger to the business of breeding; so, after giving birth to one or two children, a woman generally loses her beauty; probably, indeed, for similar reasons.

And so we find that young girls, in their hearts, look upon domestic affairs or work of any kind as of secondary importance, if not actually as a mere jest. The only business that really claims their earnest attention is love, making conquests, and everything connected with this—dress, dancing, and so on.

The nobler and more perfect a thing is, the later and slower it is in arriving at maturity. A man reaches the maturity of his reasoning powers and mental faculties hardly before the age of twenty-eight; a woman, at eighteen. And then, too, in the case of woman, it is only reason of a sort—very niggard in its dimensions. That is why women remain children their whole life long; never seeing anything but what is quite close to them, cleaving to the present moment, taking appearance for reality, and preferring trifles to matters of the first importance. For it is by virtue of his reasoning faculty that man does not live in the present only, like the brute, but looks about him and considers the past and the future; and this is the origin of prudence, as well as of that care and anxiety which so many people exhibit. Both the advantages and the disadvantages which this involves, are shared in by the woman to a smaller extent because of her weaker power of reasoning. She may, in fact, be described as intellectually shortsighted, because, while she has an intuitive understanding of what lies quite close to her, her field of vision is narrow and does not reach to what is remote: so that things which are absent or past or to come have much less effect upon women than upon men. This is the reason why women are more often inclined to be extravagant, and sometimes carry their inclination to a length that borders upon madness. In their hearts woman think that it is men's business to earn money and theirs to spend it—if possible during their husband's life, but, at any rate, after his death. The very fact that their husband hands them over his earnings for purposes of houskeeping strengthens them in this belief.

However many disadvantages all this may involve, there is at least this to be said in its favour: that the woman lives more in the present than the man, and that, if the present is at all tolerable, she enjoys it more eagerly. This is the source of that cheerfulness which is peculiar to woman, fitting her to amuse man in his hours of recreation, and, in case of need, to console him when he is borne down by the weight of his cares.

It is by no means a bad plan to consult women in matters of difficulty, as the Germans used to do in ancient times; for their way of looking at things is quite different from ours, chiefly in the fact that they like to take the shortest way to their goal, and, in general, manage to fix their eyes upon what lies before them; while we, as a rule, see far beyond it, just because it is in front of our noses. In cases like this, we need to be brought back to the right standpoint, so as to recover the near and simple view.

Then, again, women are decidedly more sober in their judgment than we are, so that they do not see more in things than is really there; whilst, if our passions are aroused, we are apt to see things in an exaggerated way, or imagine what does not exist.

The weakness of their reasoning faculty also explains why it is that women show more sympathy for the unfortunate than men do, and so treat them with more kindness and interest; and why it is that, on the contrary, they are inferior to men in point of justice, and less honourable and conscientious. For it is just because their reasoning power is weak that present circumstances have such a hold over them, and those concrete things which lie directly before their eyes exercise a power which is seldom counteracted to any extent by abstract principles of thought, by fixed rules of conduct, firm resolutions, or, in general, by consideration for the past and the future, or regard for what is absent and remote. Accordingly, they possess the first and main elements that go to make a virtuous character, but they are deficient in those secondary qualities which are often a necessary instrument in the formation of it.

Hence it will be found that the fundamental fault of the female character is that it has *no sense of justice*. This is mainly due to the fact, already mentioned, that women are defective in the powers of reasoning and deliberation; but it is also traceable to the position which Nature has assigned to them as the weaker sex. They are dependent, not upon strength, but upon craft; and hence their instinctive capacity for cunning, and their ineradicable tendency to say what is not true. For as lions are provided with claws and teeth, and elephants and boars with tusks, bulls with horns, and the cuttle fish with its cloud of inky fluid, so Nature has equipped woman, for her defence and protection, with the arts of dissimulation; and all the power which Nature has conferred upon man in the shape of physical strength and reason has been bestowed upon women in this form. Hence dissimulation is innate in woman, and almost as much a quality of the stupid as of the clever. It is as natural for them to make use of it on every occasion as it is for those animals to employ their means of defence when they are attacked; they have a feeling that in doing so they are only within their rights. Therefore a woman who is perfectly truthful and not given to dissimulation is perhaps an impossibility, and for this very reason they are so quick at seeing through dissimulation in others that it is not a wise thing to attempt it with them. But this fundamental defect which I have stated, with all that it entails, gives rise to falsity, faithlessness, treachery, ingratitude, and so on. Perjury in a court of justice is more often committed by women than

by men. It may, indeed, be generally questioned whether
women ought to be sworn at all. From time to time one
finds repeated cases everywhere of ladies, who want
for nothing, taking things from shop-counters when no
one is looking and making off with them.

Nature has appointed that the propagation of the
species shall be the business of men who are young,
strong and handsome; so that the race may not degenerate. This is the firm will and purpose of Nature in
regard to the species, and it finds its expression in the
passions of women. There is no law that is older or more
powerful than this. Woe, then, to the man who sets up
claims and interests that will conflict with it; whatever
he may say and do, they will be unmercifully crushed at
the first serious encounter. For the innate rule that governs women's conduct, though it is secret and unformu-
lated, nay, unconscious in its working, is this: *We are
justified in deceiving those who think they have acquired rights over the species by paying little attention
to the individual, that is, to us. The constitution and,
therefore, the welfare of the species have been placed in
our hands and committed to our care, through the control we obtain over the next generation, which proceeds
from us; let us discharge our duties conscientiously.*
But women have no abstract knowledge of this leading
principle; they are conscious of it only as a concrete
fact; and they have no other method of giving expression to it than the way in which they act when the
opportunity arrives. And then their conscience does
not trouble them so much as we fancy; for in the
darkest recesses of their heart they are aware that, in
committing a breach of their duty towards the individual, they have all the better fulfilled their duty towards
the species, which is infinitely greater.

And since women exist in the main solely for the

propagation of the species, and are not destined for anything else, they live, as a rule, more for the species than for the individual, and in their hearts take the affairs of the species more seriously than those of the individual. This gives their whole life and being a certain levity; the general bent of their character is in a direction fundamentally different from that of man; and it is this which produces that discord in married life which is so frequent, and almost the normal state.

The natural feeling between men is mere indifference, but between women it is actual enmity. The reason of this is that trade-jealousy which, in the case of men, does not go beyond the confines of their own particular pursuit but with women embraces the whole sex; since they have only one kind of business. Even when they meet in the street women look at one another like Guelphs and Ghibellines. And it is a patent fact that when two women make first acquaintance with each other they behave with more constraint and dissimulation than two men would show in a like case; and hence it is that an exchange of compliments between two women is a much more ridiculous proceeding than between two men. Further, whilst a man will, as a general rule, always preserve a certain amount of consideration and humanity in speaking to others, even to those who are in a very inferior position, it is intolerable to see how proudly and disdainfully a fine lady will generally behave towards one who is in a lower social rank (I do not mean a woman who is in her service), whenever she speaks to her. The reason of this may be that, with women, differences of rank are much more precarious than with us; because, while a hundred considerations carry weight in our case, in theirs there is only one, namely, with which man they have found favour; as also that they stand in much nearer relations with one another than men do, in consequence of the one-sided nature of their calling. This makes them endeavour to lay stress upon differences of rank.

It is only the man whose intellect is clouded by his sexual impulses that could give the name of *the fair sex* to that undersized, narrow-shouldered, broad-hipped, and short-legged race: for the whole beauty of the sex is bound up with this impulse. Instead of calling them beautiful, there would be more warrant for describing women as the unæsthetic sex. Neither for music, nor for poetry, nor for fine art, have they really and truly any sense or susceptibility; it is a mere mockery if they make a pretence of it in order to assist their endeavour to please. Hence, as a result of this, they are incapable of taking a *purely objective interest* in anything; and the reason of it seems to me to be as follows. A man tries to acquire *direct* mastery over things, either by understanding them or by forcing them to do his will. But a woman is always and everywhere reduced to obtaining this mastery *indirectly,* namely through a man; and whatever direct mastery she may have is entirely confined to him. And so it lies in woman's nature to look upon everything only as a means for conquering man; and if she takes an interest in anything else it is simulated—a mere roundabout way of gaining her ends by coquetry and feigning what she does not feel. Hence even Rousseau declared: *Women have, in general, no love of any art; they have no proper knowledge of any; and they have no genius.*[1]

No one who sees at all below the surface can have failed to remark the same thing. You need only observe the kind of attention women bestow upon a concert, an opera, or a play—the childish simplicity, for example, with which they keep on chattering during the finest

[1] Lettre à d'Alembert. Note xx.

passages in the greatest masterpieces. If it is true that the Greeks excluded women from their theatres, they were quite right in what they did; at any rate you would have been able to hear what was said upon the stage. In our day, besides, or in lieu of saying, *Let a woman keep silence in the church,* it would be much to the point to say, *Let a woman keep silence in the theatre.* This might, perhaps, be put up in big letters on the curtain.

And you cannot expect anything else of women if you consider that the most distinguished intellects among the whole sex have never managed to produce a single achievement in the fine arts that is really great, genuine, and original; or given to the world any work of permanent value in any sphere. This is most strikingly shown in regard to painting, where mastery of technique is at least as much within their power as within ours—and hence they are diligent in cultivating it; but still, they have not a single great painting to boast of, just because they are deficient in that objectivity of mind which is so directly indispensable in painting. They never get beyond a subjective point of view. It is quite in keeping with this that ordinary women have no real susceptibility for art at all; for Nature proceeds in strict sequence—*non facit saltum.* The case is not altered by particular and partial exceptions; taken as a whole, women are, and remain, thorough-going philistines, and quite incurable. Hence, with that absurd arrangement which allows them to share the rank and title of their husbands, they are a constant stimulus to his ignoble ambitions. And, further, it is just because they are philistines that modern society, where they take the lead and set the tone, is in such a bad way. Napoleon's saying—that *women have no rank*—should be adopted as the right standpoint in determining their position in society; and as regards their other qualities Chamfort makes the very true remark: *They are made to trade with our own weaknesses and our follies, but not with our reason. The sympathies that exist between them and men are skin-deep only, and do not touch the mind or the feelings or the character.* They form the *sexus sequior*—the second sex, inferior in every respect to the first; their infirmities should be treated with consideration; but to show them great reverence is extremely ridiculous, and lowers us in their eyes. When Nature made two divisions of the human race, she did not draw the line exactly through the middle. These divisions are polar and opposed to each other, it is true; but the difference between them is not qualitative merely, it is also quantitative.

This is just the view which the ancients took of woman, and the view which people in the East take now; and their judgment as to her proper position is much more correct than ours, with our old French notions of gallantry and our preposterous system of reverence—that highest product of Teutonico-Christian stupidity. These notions have served only to make women more arrogant and overbearing; so that one is occasionally reminded of the holy apes in Benares, who in the consciousness of their sanctity and inviolable position think they can do exactly as they please.

But in the West the woman, and especially the *lady,* finds herself in a false position; for woman, rightly called by the ancients *sexus sequior,* is by no means fit to be the object of our honour and veneration, or to hold her head higher than man and be on equal terms with him. The consequences of this false position are sufficiently obvious. Accordingly it would be a very desirable thing if this Number Two of the human race were in Europe also relegated to her natural place, and an end put to that lady-nuisance, which not only moves all

Asia to laughter but would have been ridiculed by Greece and Rome as well. It is impossible to calculate the good effects which such a change would bring about in our social, civil and political arrangements. There would be no necessity for the Salic law: it would be a superfluous truism. In Europe the *lady,* strictly so-called, is a being who should not exist at all; she should be either a housewife or a girl who hopes to become one; and she should be brought up, not to be arrogant, but to be thrifty and submissive. It is just because there are such people as *ladies* in Europe that the women of the lower classes, that is to say, the great majority of the sex, are much more unhappy than they are in the East. And even Lord Byron says: *Thought of the state of women under the ancient Greeks—convenient enough. Present state, a remnant of the barbarism of the chivalric and the feudal ages—artificial and unnatural. They ought to mind home—and be well fed and clothed—but not mixed in society. Well educated, too, in religion—but to read neither poetry nor politics— nothing but books of piety and cookery. Music— drawing—dancing—also a little gardening and ploughing now and then. I have seen them mending the roads in Epirus with good success. Why not, as well as hay-making and milking?*

The laws of marriage prevailing in Europe consider the woman as the equivalent of the man—start, that is to say, from a wrong position. In our part of the world where monogamy is the rule, to marry means to halve one's rights and double one's duties. Now when the laws gave women equal rights with man, they ought to have also endowed her with a masculine intellect. But the fact is that, just in proportion as the honours and privileges which the laws accord to women exceed the amount which Nature gives, there is a diminution in the number of women who really participate in these privileges; and all the remainder are deprived of their natural rights by just so much as is given to the others over and above their share. For the institution of monogamy, and the laws of marriage which it entails, bestow upon the woman an unnatural position of privilege, by considering her throughout as the full equivalent of the man, which is by no means the case; and seeing this men who are shrewd and prudent very often scruple to make so great a sacrifice and to acquiesce in so unfair an arrangement.

Moreover, the bestowal of unnatural rights upon women has imposed upon them unnatural duties, and nevertheless a breach of these duties makes them unhappy. Let me explain. A man may often think that his social or financial position will suffer if he marries, unless he makes some brilliant alliance. His desire will then be to win a woman of his own choice under conditions other than those of marriage, such as will secure her position and that of the children. However fair, reasonable, fit and proper these conditions may be, if the woman consents by foregoing that undue amount of privilege which marriage alone can bestow, she to some extent loses her honour, because marriage is the basis of civic society; and she will lead an unhappy life, since human nature is so constituted that we pay an attention to the opinion of other people which is out of all proportionate to its value. On the other hand, if she does not consent, she runs the risk either of having to be given in marriage to a man whom she does not like, or of being landed high and dry as an old maid; for the period during which she has a chance of being settled for life is very short. And in view of this aspect of the institution of monogamy, Thomasius' profoundly learned treatise *On Concubinage* is well worth reading; for it shows that, amongst all nations and in all ages, down to the Lutheran Reformation, concubinage was permitted; nay, that it was an institution which was to a certain extent actually recognised by law, and attended with no dishonour. It was only the Lutheran Reformation that degraded it from this position. It was seen to be a further justification for the marriage of the clergy; and then, after that, the Catholic Church did not dare to remain behindhand in the matter.

The first love of a mother for her child is, with the lower animals as with men, of a purely *instinctive* character, and so it ceases when the child is no longer in a physically helpless condition. After that, the first love should give way to one that is based on habit and reason; but this often fails to make its appearance, especially where the mother did not love the father. The love of a father for his child is of a different order, and more likely to last; because it has its foundation in the fact that in the child he recognises his own inner self; that is to say, his love for it is metaphysical in its origin.

In almost all nations, whether of the ancient or the modern world, even amongst the Hottentots, property is inherited by the male descendants alone; it is only in Europe that a departure has taken place; but not amongst the nobility, however. That the property which has cost men long years of toil and effort, and been won with so much difficulty, should afterwards come into the hands of women, who then, in their lack of reason, squander it in a short time, or otherwise fool it away, is a grievance and a wrong, as serious as it is common, which should be prevented by limiting the right of women to inherit. In my opinion the best arrangement would be that by which women, whether widows or daughters, should never receive anything beyond the interest for life on property secured by mortgage, and in no case the property itself, or the capital, except where all male descendants fail. The people who make money are men, not women; and it follows from this that women are neither justified in having unconditional possession of it, nor fit persons to be entrusted with its administration. When wealth, in any true sense of the word, that is to say, funds, houses or land, is to go to them as an inheritance, they should never be allowed the free disposition of it. In their case a guardian should always be appointed; and hence they should never be given the free control of their own children, wherever it can be avoided. The vanity of women, even though it should not prove to be greater than that of men, has this much danger in it that it takes an entirely material direction. They are vain, I mean, of their personal beauty, and then of finery, show and magnificence. That is just why they are so much in their element in society. It is this, too, which makes them so inclined to be extravagant, all the more as their reasoning power is low. But with men vanity often takes the direction of non-material advantages, such as intellect, learning, courage.

That woman is by nature meant to obey may be seen by the fact that every woman who is placed in the unnatural position of complete independence, immediately attaches herself to some man, by whom she allows herself to be guided and ruled. It is because she needs a lord and master. If she is young, it will be a lover; if she is old, a priest.